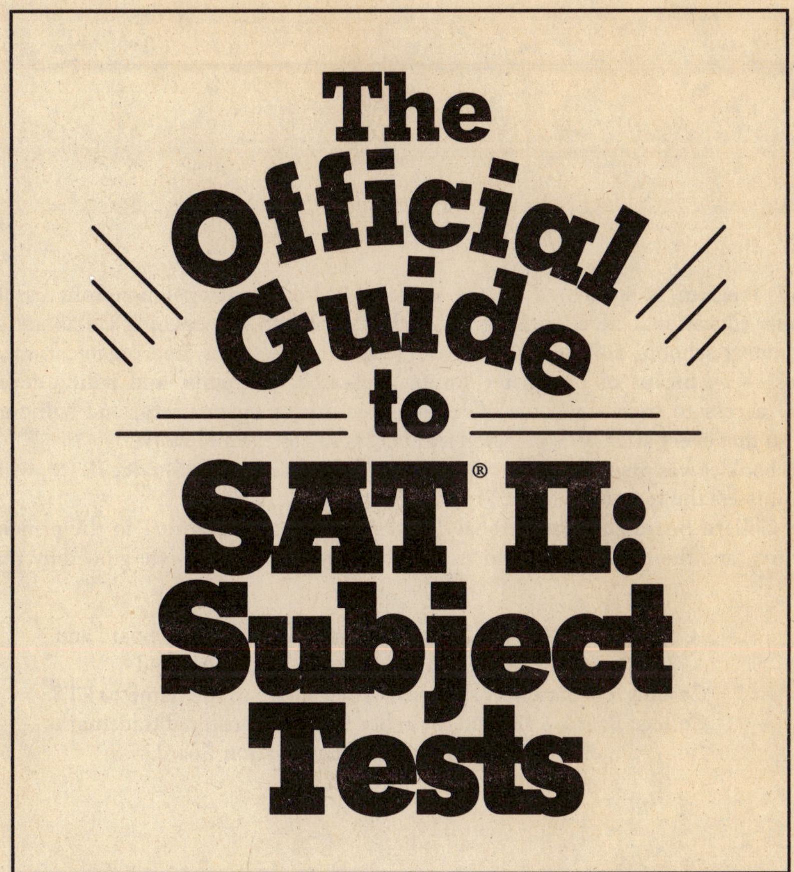

A revision of *The College Board Achievement Tests*

Featuring the new Writing Test,
full-length practice tests, and descriptions of the
new Foreign Language Tests with Listening

The SAT Program is sponsored by the College Board, a national nonprofit association that champions educational excellence for all students through the ongoing collaboration of nearly 2,900 member schools, colleges, universities, education systems, and organizations. The Board promotes — by means of responsive forums, research, programs, and policy development — universal access to high standards of learning, equity of opportunity, and sufficient financial support so that every student is prepared for success in college and work.

This booklet was prepared and produced by Educational Testing Service (ETS), which develops and administers the tests of the SAT Program for the College Board.

The College Board and Educational Testing Service are dedicated to the principle of equal opportunity, and their programs, services, and employment policies are guided by that principle.

Library of Congress Catalog Card Number 94-070821

Cover design by Terrence M. Fehr

Printed in U.S.A.

9 8 7 6 5 4 3 2 1

Contents

Introduction

The College Board has made this book available to help students and teachers become better acquainted with the SAT II: Subject Tests. In this book you will find:

- descriptions of the tests;
- discussions of the types of questions used in the tests;
- advice on how to prepare for the tests;
- a recently administered, full-length edition of nine of the tests;
- answers to the test questions;
- instructions on how to score the nine tests; and
- sample mini tests for the language tests.

This book contains information about the SAT II: Subject Tests as of 1994. Although these tests are not expected to change in major ways during the next few years, there are occasionally minor modifications in content coverage, types of questions, or the schedule and level of offerings.

The most up-to-date descriptions of each year's test offerings are found in the booklet *Taking the SAT II: Subject Tests,* which is free to every student who registers to take a Subject Test. Copies are available at high school guidance offices or by writing or calling the College Board SAT Program at 609/771-7600.

By making these tests and the accompanying information available, the College Board hopes that students and teachers will have a better understanding of what the Subject Tests are intended to measure, the kinds of questions they contain, how they are scored, and how colleges use the scores.

About the Tests

SAT II: Subject Tests is the new name for the tests formerly known as the College Board Achievement Tests. Like the Achievement Tests, the Subject Tests measure your knowledge or skills in a particular subject and your ability to apply that knowledge. The tests fall into five general subject areas:

- English
  Writing, Literature
- History and Social Studies
  American History and Social Studies, World History
- Mathematics
  Mathematics Level I, Mathematics Level 1C (Calculator), Mathematics Level IIC (Calculator)
- Sciences
  Biology, Chemistry, Physics
- Foreign Languages
  Chinese with Listening, French, French with Listening, German, German with Listening, Modern Hebrew, Italian, Japanese with Listening, Latin, Spanish, Spanish with Listening

All the Subject Tests take one hour of testing time and consist entirely of multiple-choice questions, with the exception of the Writing Test, which consists of a 20-minute essay and 40 minutes of multiple-choice questions.

In addition to a new name, some significant changes to the tests themselves were introduced in 1993-94. Among them are the following (all of which are reflected in the test descriptions and the practice questions found in this book).

- The new SAT II: Writing Test, introduced in May 1994, replaces the English Composition Test with Essay and the all-multiple-choice English Composition Test. When you take the Writing Test, you can also order the new Writing Sample Copy Service and receive three copies of your scored essay to send to colleges.
- The Mathematics Level IIC Test (with calculator) replaces the Mathematics Level II Test beginning May 1994. Math IIC tests the same skills but requires the use of a calculator capable of performing scientific functions.
- The Mathematics Level IC Test (with calculator) will be offered for the first time in June 1995. For further information, please refer to the 1994-95 edition of *Taking the SAT II.*
- A fifth foreign language Subject Test with Listening — Chinese with Listening — was introduced in April 1994. Note that the foreign language Subject Tests with Listening are not offered at test centers or on national test dates. They may be taken only at participating high schools and require separate registration using a different form. Contact your school counselor for additional information about any of these tests.
- A new name — World History — better reflects the current content of the test previously known as European History and World Cultures.
- One type of question on the Chemistry Test has a new format that requires students to complete a special new section of their answer sheet.

How the Tests Are Used

Some colleges require SAT II: Subject Test scores for admission. Because academic achievement is generally a good predictor of future performance, scores on the Subject Tests can help assess how well prepared you are for different programs of college study. The scores are particularly appropriate for use in admissions because they are independent of specific textbooks, grading procedures, and methods of instruction. This independence allows comparison of students whose course preparation and backgrounds vary. Used in combination with your high school record, results of tests such as the SAT, teacher recommendations, and other background information, Subject Test scores provide a reliable measure of your academic achievement.

Many institutions use the Subject Tests for placement and guidance. At some colleges the scores from these tests are used to place new students in particular freshman courses. At others, advisers use the scores in guidance discussions with students to help them select courses. Some colleges also use scores from the language Subject Tests for course placement.

Planning to Take the Tests

Before you decide which Subject Tests to take, make a tentative list of all the colleges to which you've been thinking of applying. You can find out from their catalogs or a directory of colleges what their Subject Test requirements are. Some will specify which tests you must take; others will allow you to choose. (Remember that some colleges may still refer to "Subject Tests" as "Achievement Tests" in their admission materials. Don't worry; these are different names for the same thing.)

This list of colleges and their admission requirements will also be useful as you plan your high school course schedule. You may want to consider adjusting your schedule in light of the colleges' requirements. For example, you may decide to take another year of a foreign language if you learn that a college you want to attend requires or recommends a foreign language Subject Test for admission, or that the college might exempt you from a freshman requirement if you do well.

A good source of information about colleges' requirements concerning Subject Tests is *The College Handbook*, published by the College Board. The final word on requirements, however, should always be the catalogs and other publications of the institutions to which you are applying.

Many colleges that don't require Subject Tests will nevertheless look at these results, if you make them available, to help them learn more about your academic background as they are making admission and placement decisions.

When to Take the Tests

You'll probably do best on a Subject Test if you take it as close as possible to completing a course (or courses) in the subject, while the material is still fresh in your mind. If you decide to take a Subject Test in a subject you haven't studied recently, you should review the course content material thoroughly and methodically over several weeks' time. Last-minute cramming is not likely to be of much use.

Colleges that use Subject Test results as part of their admission process often require that you take the tests no later than December or January of your senior year. (While many colleges will accept November scores for early decision, some may require earlier scores.) If the colleges in which you're interested use Subject Test results only to help with placement decisions, you might be able to test as late as May or June of your senior year.

For More Information about Taking the Tests

The *Registration Bulletin* for the SAT and Subject Tests contains a Registration Form and all the information you'll need to register for the tests and to have your scores reported to the colleges of your choice. In order to avoid late fees, your Registration Form must be post-

SAT II: Subject Test — Schedule

Test Name	Test Date[1]						
	May 7, 1994	June 4, 1994	Nov. 5, 1994	Dec. 3, 1994	Jan. 28, 1995	May 6, 1995	June 3, 1995
Writing[2]	•	•	•	•	•	•	•
Literature	•	•	•	•	•	•	•
American History & Social Studies	•	•	•	•	•	•	•
World History		•		•			•
Math Level I	•	•	•	•	•	•	•
Math Level 1C (Calculator)							•
Math Level IIC (Calculator)	•	•	•	•	•	•	•
Biology	•	•	•	•	•	•	•
Chemistry	•	•	•	•	•	•	•
Physics	•	•	•	•	•	•	•
French (reading only)	•	•		•	•	•	•
German (reading only)		•					•
Modern Hebrew		•					•
Italian				•			
Latin		•		•			•
Spanish (reading only)	•	•		•	•	•	•

[1] Sunday test administrations are available the day after each scheduled Saturday test date for students who cannot test on Saturday because of religious convictions.

[2] The Writing Test must always be taken during the first hour of testing.

Chinese, French, German, Japanese, and Spanish with Listening

Chinese with Listening will be offered for the first time on April 26, 1994, and only at participating high schools. Foreign language Subject Tests with Listening in Chinese, French, German, Japanese, and Spanish will be offered in November 1994 only at participating high schools. You must contact your school if you are interested in taking any of these tests.

marked by the regular registration deadline. Registration by telephone is also available. (To register for the foreign language tests with listening, you will need a special registration form and instructions. See your counselor or language teacher.)

A supply of the *Bulletin* is sent to all high schools each year. High school students should be able to pick up a copy at their school guidance or counseling office. If you're not currently in high school, you can get a copy at a local high school or by writing or calling the College Board SAT Program.

College Board SAT Program
P.O. Box 6200
Princeton, N.J. 08541-6200

609/771-7600

Score Choice: A New Option

Score Choice is an option that allows you to review your Subject Test scores and decide whether you want them to become part of your cumulative score record. By selecting Score Choice when you register for the tests, you are placing a hold on your scores until you have had a chance to review your performance on the tests you took on that particular day. Once you have reviewed your scores, you can release any or all of them at any time into your cumulative score record. Once released, however, those particular scores may not be withheld again. For more information, see the current *Registration Bulletin*.

Preregistration

When you register, you'll be asked to indicate which specific Subject Tests you plan to take on the test date you select. You may take one, two, or three tests on any given test date; your testing fee will vary accordingly. Your selections at the time of registration are not binding; you may change your mind on the day of the test and select from any of the Subject Tests offered on that day. For more information, see the current *Registration Bulletin*.

How to Prepare for the Tests

Know What to Expect

The best way to prepare for the tests is to familiarize yourself with their organization, the types of questions that will appear on them, and what will be expected of you on the test day. To make sure you are prepared for the test, you should do the following.

- Review *Taking the SAT II* and this book. They will help you understand how each test is organized.
- Study the sample questions for the test you plan to take. They will give you a good idea of the kinds of questions that appear on the tests. The more familiar you are with the sample questions, the more comfortable you'll feel when you see the questions in your test book on the day of the tests.
- Study and understand the test directions. The directions for answering the questions in this booklet are like those in the test book. If you study the directions now, you will spend less time reading and figuring them out on the test day and will have more time for answering the questions.

Test-Taking Tips

Here are some specific test-taking tips that will help when you actually take the tests.

- Within each group of questions of the same type, the easier questions are usually at the beginning of the group and the more difficult ones at the end. Test questions that contain a reading passage or a diagram followed by several questions are an exception. Such questions are ordered according to the logic and organization of the preceding material.
- If you're working on a group of questions and find that the questions are getting too difficult, quickly read through the rest of the questions in that group and answer only those you think you know. Then go on to the next group of questions in that section. (Again, this advice does not necessarily apply to the questions immediately following a reading passage or a diagram. In that case, a difficult question might be followed by an easier one.)
- You get just as much credit for correctly answering easy questions as you do for correctly answering hard ones. So answer all the questions that seem easy before you spend time on those that seem difficult.

- You get one point for each question you answer correctly. You lose a fraction of a point for each question you answer incorrectly. You neither gain nor lose credit for questions you omit. For information on how the essay portion of the Writing Test is scored, see the section on the Writing Test.
- You can omit questions. Many students who do well omit some. You can return to the ones you've omitted within that test if you finish before time is up.
- You can guess. If you know that one or more answer choices for a question are wrong, then it's generally to your advantage to guess from the remaining choices. But, because of the way the tests are scored, random guessing with no knowledge of any of the choices is unlikely to increase your score.
- Use the test book for scratch work and to mark questions you omitted so you can go back to them if you have time. You will not receive credit for any responses written in the book. You must mark your responses to test questions on the separate answer sheet.
- Do not make extra marks on the answer sheet. If the scoring machine reads what looks like two answers for one question, it will consider the question unanswered. So it's in your best interest to keep your answer sheet free of stray marks.
- If you erase all responses to an individual Subject Test, this will be considered a request for cancellation, and scores from *all* Subject Tests taken on that date will be canceled.
- Any three-choice question for which you mark the fourth or fifth answer ovals (D or E), or any four-choice question for which you mark the fifth answer oval (E), will be treated as an omitted question. You will not receive credit for that response.
- Mark only one answer for each question. To be certain that your answer will be read by the scoring machine, make sure your mark is dark and completely fills the oval, as shown in the first example below.

CORRECT	WRONG	WRONG
Ⓐ Ⓑ ● Ⓓ Ⓔ	Ⓐ Ⓑ ✓ Ⓓ Ⓔ	Ⓐ Ⓑ ✗ Ⓓ Ⓔ
WRONG	**WRONG**	**WRONG**
Ⓐ Ⓑ Ⓒ Ⓓ Ⓔ	Ⓐ Ⓑ Ⓒ Ⓓ Ⓔ	Ⓐ Ⓑ ⦿ Ⓓ Ⓔ

The Day Before the Tests

Learn as much as you can about the tests well before you plan to take them. Then, on the day before the tests, it might help if you do the following.

- Review the sample questions, explanations, and test directions in this book or in *Taking the SAT II*. Hours of intense study the night before probably will not help your performance on the tests and may even make you more anxious. A short review of the information you studied earlier probably will make you feel more comfortable and better prepared.
- Get together your testing materials and put them in a place that will be convenient for you in the morning. Use this checklist:
  - ✔ Admission ticket
  - ✔ Acceptable identification (you won't be admitted to the test center without it. See the *Registration Bulletin* for specific examples)
  - ✔ Two No. 2 (soft-lead) pencils with erasers
  - ✔ A scientific or graphing calculator for the Mathematics Level IC and Level IIC Tests only

  > The use of a calculator is prohibited on all Subject Tests except Mathematics Level IC and Mathematics Level IIC.

  - ✔ Directions to the test center, if you need them
  - ✔ All the materials you will need to register as a standby, if you have not preregistered (see the *Registration Bulletin*)
- Spend the evening relaxing. You'll accomplish little by worrying about the tests. Read a book, watch TV, or do anything else you find relaxing.

After the Tests

About five weeks after you take Subject Tests you will receive your Score Report, which will include your scores, your percentile ranks, and interpretive information. Some scores may take longer to report because of such problems as late receipt of answer sheets or inconsistent identification information. In any case, you should receive your score report no more than 10 weeks after the test.

The College Board Subject Test Development Committees, 1993–94

American History and Social Studies
Marion W. Roydhouse, Philadelphia College of Textiles and Science, *Chair*
Archibald T. Bryant, Evanston Township High School, Evanston, Illinois
John R. Chavez, Southern Methodist University
Jack D. Marietta, University of Arizona
Louisa B. Moffitt, Marist School, Atlanta, Georgia

Biology
Randy Landgren, Middlebury College, *Chair*
J. José Bonner, Indiana University
Karen Fujii, American High School, Fremont, California
Henry Horn, Princeton University
Navalene Thurstone, Oak Ridge High School, Conroe, Texas

Chinese
Richard Chi, University of Utah, *Chair*
Kathy Chen, The High School of Commerce, Springfield, Massachusetts
Rong Rong Le, Mamaroneck High School, Mamaroneck, New York
Lisa Crooks Lin, Akron Public Schools, Akron, Ohio
Kenneth Luk, California State University at Sacramento
Toa-chung (Ted) Yao, Mount Holyoke College

Chemistry
Philip H. Reiger, Brown University, *Chair*
Mary Ann C. Goddard, Tenafly High School, Tenafly, New Jersey
Mary C. Johnson, Detroit Country Day School, Birmingham, Michigan
Martin Vala, University of Florida
Edward D. Walton, California State Polytechnic University

French
Nicole S. Desrosiers, Lenox Memorial High School, Lenox, Massachusetts, *Chair*
Anthony A. Ciccone, University of Wisconsin-Milwaukee
Matuku Ngame, University of Vermont
Jean Marie Schultz, University of California at Berkeley
Françoise von Mayer, Garrison Forrest School, Owings Mills, Maryland

German
Sieglinde Lug, University of Denver, *Chair*
George Koenig, SUNY College at Oswego
Irmgard S. Langacker, Strath Haven High School, Wallingford, Pennsylvania
Nicholas T. Lasoff, Buckingham Browne and Nichols School, Cambridge, Massachusetts
David Price, University of Texas at Austin

Modern Hebrew
Adina Ofek, Jewish Theological Seminary of America, *Chair*
Athalia Brison, Shulamith High School for Girls, Brooklyn, New York
Joseph Cohen, North Central High School, Indianapolis, Indiana
Ilea S. Goldberg, Highland Park High School, Highland Park, Illinois
Yona Sabar, University of California at Los Angeles

Italian
Meme Amosso Irwin, Johns Hopkins University, *Chair*
Paola Blelloch, Trenton State College
Susan Mancini, St. Francis de Sales High School, Columbus, Ohio
Joseph Perricone, Fordham University
Maria Roos, Miami Coral Park Senior High School, Miami, Florida

Japanese
Akiko Hirota, California State University at Northridge, *Chair*
Hiroshi Nara, University of Pittsburgh
Mari Noda, Ohio State University
Michael Rubin, New York City Public Schools, New York, New York
Hitomi Tamura, West Linn High School, Oregon
Yasuko Wada, Charles Wright Academy, Tacoma, Washington

Latin
Jill Crooker, Pittsford Mendon High School, Pittsford, New York, *Chair*
Donald H. Hoffman, St. Ignatius College Prep, Chicago, Illinois
J.C. Douglas Marshall, St. Paul's School, Concord, New Hampshire
Thomas F. Scanlon, University of California at Riverside
Salle Ann Schueter-Gill, Radford University

Literature
Ellen Greenblatt, University High School, San Francisco, California, *Chair*
Oliver Arnold, Princeton University
Sandra Govan, University of North Carolina, Charlotte
Jamieson Spencer, Mary Institute & St. Louis Country Day School, St. Louis, Missouri
Gordon Taylor, University of Tulsa

Mathematics
John A. Dossey, Illinois State University, *Chair*
Helen L. Compton, North Carolina School of Science and Mathematics, Durham, North Carolina
William S. Hadley, Pittsburgh Public Schools, Pittsburgh, Pennsylvania
Anne Papakonstantinou, Houston Independent School District, Houston, Texas
Anthony Peressini, University of Illinois at Urbana-Champaign
Alba G. Thompson, San Diego State University

Physics
Nuria Rodriguez, Santa Monica College, *Chair*
Robert B. Clark, Texas A & M University
Hugh Haskell, North Carolina School of Science and Mathematics, Durham, North Carolina
Martha Takats, Ursinus College
Joseph Wesney, Greenwich High School, Greenwich, Connecticut

Spanish
María Elena Villalba, Miami Palmetto Senior High School, Miami, Florida, *Chair*
Miriam Grodberg, Wellesley High School, Wellesley, Massachusetts
William Little, California Polytechnic State University
Samuel Saldívar, United States Military Academy
Fernando Soldevilla, Hawken School, Gates Mill, Ohio

World History
Peter von Sivers, University of Utah, *Chair*
John Brackett, University of Cincinnati
Michelle Forman, Middlebury Union High School, Middlebury, Vermont
Harriett Lillich, UMS-Wright Preparatory School, Mobile, Alabama
Jiu-Hwa L. Upshur, Eastern Michigan University

Writing
Jane C. Mallison, Trinity School, New York, New York, *Chair*
Mark Angney, Concord-Carlisle Regional High School, Concord, Massachusetts
Bradford Gioia, The Darlington School, Rome, Georgia
Joyce M. Jarrett, Hampton University
John F. Sena, Ohio State University
Joan D. Vinson, Arlington Heights High School, Fort Worth, Texas
Agnes Yamada, California State University

The SAT II: Writing Subject Test

The SAT II: Writing Subject Test is offered five times a year during all national administrations of SAT II: Subject Tests. One hour long, the Writing Test replaces the English Composition Test (ECT) and the Test of Standard Written English (TSWE).

Consisting of 60 multiple-choice questions and a 20-minute writing sample, the Writing Test measures the ability to express ideas effectively in standard written English, to recognize faults in usage and structure, and to use language with sensitivity to meaning. The Writing Test differs from the other Subject Tests in that it measures skills you have developed over many years. These skills are gained through extensive experience with language, especially written language.

The multiple-choice questions in the test do not ask you to define or to use grammatical terms, nor do they test spelling or capitalization. In some questions, punctuation marks such as the semicolon are important in arriving at the correct answer, but these questions primarily test the structure in which the punctuation appears.

The following chart illustrates common writing problems covered by questions in the Writing Test. In the chart, each kind of problem is accompanied by a sentence illustrating that problem. These sentences are *not* examples of questions in the test.

Common Writing Problems Covered by the SAT II: Writing Subject Test

Writing Problems	Illustrative Sentences
Being consistent	
Sequence of tenses	After he broke his arm, he is home for two weeks.
Shift of pronoun	If one is tense, they should try to relax.
Parallelism	She skis, plays tennis, and flying hang gliders.
Noun agreement	Ann and Sarah want to be a pilot.
Pronoun reference	Several people wanted the job, and he or she filled out the required applications.
Subject-verb agreement	There is eight people on the shore.
Expressing ideas logically	
Coordination and subordination	Nancy has a rash, and she is probably allergic to something.
Logical comparison	Harry grew more vegetables than his neighbor's garden.
Modification and word order	Barking loudly, the tree had the dog's leash wrapped around it.
Being clear and precise	
Ambiguous and vague pronouns	In the newspaper they say that few people voted.
Diction	He circumvented the globe on his trip.
Wordiness	There are many problems in the contemporary world in which we live.
Improper modification	If your car is parked here while not eating in the restaurant, it will be towed away.
Following conventions	
Pronoun case	He sat between you and I at the stadium.
Idiom	Natalie had a different opinion towards her.
Comparison of modifiers	Of the sixteen executives, Meg makes more money.
Sentence fragment	Fred having to go home early.
Double negative	Manuel has scarcely no free time.

Some sentences require students to recognize that there is no error.

Multiple-Choice Questions

Three types of multiple-choice questions are currently used in the SAT II: Writing Subject Test. The directions that follow are identical to those in the test. For the multiple-choice questions, you must choose the best response from the five choices offered.

Identifying Sentence Errors

The first type of question tests your ability to detect an error in underlined portions of a sentence.

Test Directions and Sample Question with Explanation

Directions: The following sentences test your knowledge of grammar, usage, diction (choice of words), and idiom.

Some sentences are correct.

No sentence contains more than one error.

You will find that the error, if there is one, is underlined and lettered. Elements of the sentence that are not underlined will not be changed. In choosing answers, follow the requirements of standard written English.

If there is an error, select the one underlined part that must be changed to make the sentence correct, and fill in the corresponding oval on your answer sheet.

If there is no error, fill in oval E.

EXAMPLE:	SAMPLE ANSWER
The other delegates and (A) him (B) immediately (C) accepted the resolution drafted by the (D) neutral states. No error (E)	Ⓐ ● Ⓒ Ⓓ Ⓔ

As you can see from the example, this type of question consists of a sentence in which four short portions are underlined and lettered A, B, C, and D, followed by a fifth underline, "No error," lettered E. Sometimes the underlined portion of the sentence is only a single word, as in (B) and (C) above. In other cases, a group of words or a phrase is underlined, as in (A) and (D).

For each question, you must decide whether one of the underlined portions must be changed to make the sentence acceptable in standard written English. In the example above, (B) must be changed because the pronoun "him" is incorrect. Therefore, the answer to the example is (B). Changes could be made in the other underlined portions of the example sentence, but none of them is necessary to make the sentence acceptable.

In some sentences of this type you could imagine changing parts of the sentence that are not underlined. However, you should focus only on changing the underlined words.

Notice that if none of the underlined portions needs to be changed, the correct answer is (E). By choosing (E) as the answer, you are indicating that the sentence is correct as written.

Sample Questions with Explanation

1. **Many travelers claim having seen (A) the Abominable Snowman, but (B) no one has proved that such a creature (C) actually (D) exists. No error (E)**

The answer is (A). In the context of this sentence, the verb "claim" requires the expression "to have seen"; "claim having seen" is not idiomatic in standard written English and is therefore not acceptable. The word "but" at (B) provides a link between the two major parts of the sentence and appropriately suggests a contrast between the ideas they present. The expression at (C), "such a creature," and the adverb "actually" at (D) are acceptable although other expressions and adverbs could be substituted.

2. **The commission investigating (A) the accident at the laboratory was less interested in why the experiment was conducted than in (B) whether they were (C) conducted properly. (D) No error (E)**

Looking carefully at the underlined portions of the sentence, you should recognize that the error is in choice (C). The pronoun "they" is plural, and it is therefore the incorrect pronoun to use to refer to "the experiment," which is singular. In (A), "investigating" is correctly used to describe the activities of the commission. In (B), "than in" correctly introduces the second part of the comparison that begins with "less interested in." In (D), "properly" is correct as an adverb modifying the verb immediately before it.

3. Some genetic research has become highly controversial because the results of the studies suggest that people may eventually be able to manipulate the development of the human race. No error

(Underlined portions: A = "Some"; B = "has become"; C = "highly"; D = "may eventually be able"; E = "No error")

The correct response to this question is (E). Each part of the sentence conforms to the requirements of standard written English; no error in grammar, usage, or idiom is present in the sentence.

Improving Sentences

The second type of multiple-choice question tests your ability to identify an error in a sentence and to select the best revision of an unacceptable portion of the sentence (or of the entire sentence). The best revision of an unacceptable part of the sentence will eliminate the original problem and introduce no others.

Test Directions and Sample Question with Explanation

Directions: The following sentences test correctness and effectiveness of expression. In choosing answers, follow the requirements of standard written English; that is, pay attention to grammar, choice of words, sentence construction, and punctuation.

In each of the following sentences, part of the sentence or the entire sentence is underlined. Beneath each sentence you will find five ways of phrasing the underlined part. Choice (A) repeats the original; the other four are different.

Choose the answer that best expresses the meaning of the original sentence. If you think the original is better than any of the alternatives, choose it; otherwise choose one of the others. Your choice should produce the most effective sentence — clear and precise, without awkwardness or ambiguity.

EXAMPLE: **SAMPLE ANSWER**

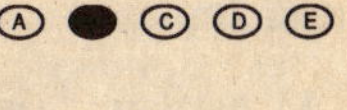

Laura Ingalls Wilder published her first book and she was sixty-five years old then.

(A) and she was sixty-five years old then
(B) when she was sixty-five
(C) being age sixty-five years old
(D) upon the reaching of sixty-five years
(E) at the time when she was sixty-five

The example above is a sentence in which the connection between the two major ideas is weak. The use of "and" to join the two clauses suggests that the ideas are of equal importance in the sentence, but the wording and the ideas in the clauses themselves suggest that the first idea should actually be the major point of the sentence and that the second should be secondary to it. Versions (B), (C), (D), and (E) all begin with more appropriate connecting words, but (B) is the only one in which the second idea of the sentence is clearly, concisely, and idiomatically expressed. Therefore, (B) is the correct choice.

Sample Questions with Explanation

4. After placing the meatballs in a pan, the cook sautéed them until they were brown and then let them simmer in the sauce.

(A) and then let them simmer
(B) then they were simmered
(C) and then simmering it
(D) then letting them simmer
(E) and then the simmering was done

You should have read the original sentence quickly, noting that the portions not underlined will remain the same in all versions of the sentence. The original sentence and choice (A) may have seemed plausible, but you should have gone on to the other versions before making a final decision. In the (B) version, the unexpected shift from the "cook" as the subject to "they" (the meatballs) is awkward and somewhat confusing. The (C) version uses "simmering" where "simmered" is needed to parallel "sautéed." Furthermore, the pronoun "it" does not seem to refer back to anything named earlier in the sentence. In the (D) version, the use of "letting" rather than "let" again disrupts the parallel with "sautéed." The (E) version is wordy and, like the (B) version, involves a shift in which a passive construction replaces a more appropriate active one and in which the action is described without reference to the person responsible for it. Therefore, the best version of the sentence in this case is the original one, and the correct choice is (A).

5. **The Dutch had been trading with Asia since the sixteenth century, their ships have visited Persia and Japan.**

   (A) **century, their ships have visited**
   (B) **century, while their ships had visited**
   (C) **century, but their ships had been visiting**
   (D) **century, when their ships visited**
   (E) **century, where their ships were visiting**

The original sentence presents two problems. First, two independent statements are joined by a comma, with no indication of the relationship between them. Second, the tense of the verb "have visited" is not consistent with the tense of "had been trading" earlier in the sentence. The (B) version may appear to be acceptable, but the relationship between the ideas in the sentence is not the one implied by "while," and the use of "while" makes the sentence illogical. Similarly, the (C) version appears plausible, but the contrast implied by "but" is not appropriate to the relationship between the two parts of the sentence. The (D) version corrects both of the problems presented in the original sentence and is more logical than either (B) or (C). Notice that the tense of "visited" is consistent with the earlier verb "had been trading." The sentence suggests that Dutch ships had traveled to Persia and Japan in the sixteenth century and that such travel was part of a process of Dutch trade with Asia that continued until some later unspecified time. Version (E) resembles (D) except that "where" is substituted for "when" and "were visiting" for "visited." Since the connection with century is clearly one of time rather than place, the use of "where" is not appropriate. Furthermore, the use of "were visiting" would imply emphasis on visits occurring over a period of time. Such emphasis is not called for because the purpose in this part of the sentence is to describe the point at which the Dutch began trading with Asia. Therefore, (D) expresses most effectively the ideas in the two parts of the sentence as well as the relationship between them. The correct choice is (D).

Improving Paragraphs

The third type of question asks you to revise sentences in the context of a student draft of an essay. You will be presented with an essay and then asked questions about ways to revise parts of it. Each question will ask you to revise particular parts of the essay in a way that is most appropriate to the rest of the essay. The revisions required in these questions are similar to those you make in your own writing to eliminate errors and to achieve clarity.

Test Directions and Sample Questions with Explanation

Directions: Each of the following passages is an early draft of a student essay. Some parts of the passages need to be rewritten.

Read each passage and answer the questions that follow. Some questions are about particular sentences or parts of sentences and ask you to make decisions about sentence structure, word choice, and usage. Other questions refer to parts of the essay or the entire essay and ask you to consider organization, development, and appropriateness of language. Choose the answer that most effectively expresses the meaning and follows the requirements of standard written English. After you have chosen your answer, fill in the corresponding oval on your answer sheet.

Questions 6-9 are based on the following essay, which is a response to an assignment to write about an economic issue facing the United States today.

(1) Recently a group of workers from a clothing factory in my hometown picketed peacefully in front of a department store. (2) They carried signs, and passing shoppers were urged by them to buy products that were made in the United States. (3) A newspaper article suggested that they were wrong. (4) It pointed out that nearly all stores now sell goods that are not made in this country. (5) However, I would argue that the demonstrators are right, consumers should think about the effect they can have on industries here in the United States.

(6) Consumers have the right to buy whatever they want. (7) They should consider the effects of their choices. (8) In the last several years, hundreds of thousands of workers in United States industries have lost their jobs. (9) They represent billions of dollars of lost wages and taxes. (10) Consumers should know that consumer goods that are not made in the United States contribute to the loss of jobs in many different American industries and businesses. (11) Buying goods made in the United States means investing in our future. (12) Without government subsidies, our industries only have the American consumer to help them compete in the world market and therefore guarantee jobs for hundreds of thousands of workers in the United States.

6. **In context, which is the best version of the underlined portion of sentence 2 (reproduced below)?**

They carried signs, and passing shoppers were urged by them to buy products that were made in the United States.

(A) (As it is now)
(B) They carry signs and urge passing shoppers
(C) Carrying signs and urging passing shoppers, the workers asked them
(D) The workers carried signs that urged the passing shoppers
(E) These signs urged passing shoppers

In answering this question, choice (A) requires that you first determine if there is any error to be corrected in the underlined part of the sentence. You should recognize that the underlined phrase does not clearly and logically express an idea. The pronoun "them" could refer to either "signs" or "workers." Also, the underlined phrase presents an unnecessary shift from the active voice ("They carried signs") to the passive voice ("passing shoppers were urged by them"). Among the other answer choices, the best revision is choice (D), which makes it clear that the workers' signs are urging the shoppers. Choice (B) contains an error in tense. The verb "carry" should be in the past tense to be consistent with the tense used elsewhere in the paragraph. Choice (C) awkwardly separates "carrying signs" from "the workers." Although choice (E) is grammatically correct, it is incorrect in the context of the passage because the phrase "These signs" does not refer to anything that is mentioned in the part of the passage that precedes sentence 2.

7. **In context, which is the best way to revise and combine the underlined portions of sentences 3 and 4 (reproduced below)?**

A newspaper article suggested that they were wrong. It pointed out that nearly all stores now sell goods that are not made in this country.

(A) A newspaper article suggested that the demonstrators were wrong, pointing out
(B) They were wrong, a newspaper article suggested, it pointed out that
(C) Suggesting that they are wrong, in a newspaper article it says
(D) The newspaper article suggests that the shoppers were wrong,
(E) In the newspaper article was the suggestion that they were wrong and

This question asks you to connect two related ideas. Choice (A) is the correct answer. Choice (B) incorrectly and awkwardly connects two clauses with a comma. In choices (C) and (E), the pronoun "they" is ambiguous and could refer to either "workers" or "shoppers." Choice (C) also has a structural problem. The opening phrase, "Suggesting that they are wrong," should be immediately followed by the phrase "a newspaper article" that it modifies. Choice (D) may be grammatically correct, but the use of the definite article "The" and the present-tense verb "suggests" in choice (D) is inappropriate in the context of the passage.

8. **Which of the following best replaces the word "They" in sentence 9?**

(A) The consumers
(B) These lost jobs
(C) The industries
(D) Those arguments
(E) The United States

Examined outside of the context of the sentence, sentence 9 appears to be grammatically correct. Within the context of the sentence, however, it begins with a pronoun that has no clear antecedent. Sentence 9 would be much clearer if revised so that the reader knows specifically what "represents billions of dollars." The answer to this question is choice (B).

9. **Which sentence would be most appropriate to follow sentence 12?**

(A) I see now that the demonstrators were right.
(B) Consumers have rights, too.
(C) In conclusion, we have no one else to blame.
(D) The next time you go shopping, think of the workers and their families in your community.
(E) We, the American consumers, must find out how to invest in our industries.

This question asks you to select the sentence that would, in effect, be the best concluding sentence for the passage; it therefore requires that you consider the development and organization of the entire passage. The correct answer is choice (D). Choice (D) fits the development of ideas in the second paragraph. It logically follows sentence 12, which explains why the consumer must help industries, and the main idea of the second paragraph, which is an appeal to consumers to "consider the effects of their choices." Choice (D) also effectively restates the passage's main argument as expressed in sentence 5, namely, that "consumers should think about the effect they can have on industries here in the United States." Choices (A), (B), (C), and (E) do not fit the logic, development, and organization of the passage. Choice (A) would be out of place at the end of the second paragraph since sentence 5 has already stated that the "demonstrators are right." Choice (B) contradicts the argument made in the second paragraph and the passage's main focus on the appeal to consumers to help out workers and the industries in which they work. Choice (C) would not follow sentence 12 because there is nothing in the passage that would lead to the conclusion that "we have no one else to blame." Choice (E) would be inappropriate because the very focus of the passage is how consumers can invest in domestic industries by choosing to buy their products.

The Writing Sample

All administrations of the SAT II: Writing Subject Test include 40 minutes of multiple-choice questions and 20 minutes of writing on an assigned topic. The topic does not require specialized knowledge of any particular academic discipline but gives students an opportunity to use a broad range of knowledge and experiences in support of their discussions.

The impromptu essays are scored by readers who are experienced high school and college teachers. The readers have reasonable expectations of the quality of writing done by students at the end of high school or the beginning of college. Each essay is scored twice on a 6-point scale, with 6 as the highest score and 1 as the lowest. The total score is the sum of the two readers' scores and is weighted to equal one-third of the total SAT II: Writing Subject Test score. Any essay whose readers' scores are more than two points apart is read by a third reader to resolve the discrepancy in scores.

Responses written in only 20 minutes to an assigned topic are not expected to be polished compositions. Readers judge the quality of a response in terms of the total impression it creates; they take into account such aspects of writing as organization, choice of words, sentence structure, and punctuation as well as appropriateness of examples, logical presentation, and development of ideas.

Reproduced below are: the test directions and topic used in the field trials of the SAT II: Writing Subject Test, some actual student essays, and the Guide for Scoring Student Responses to the SAT II: Writing Subject Test. The errors in the essays are those of the students. The directions are identical to those that were given in the field test.

Test Directions and Topic

You have 20 minutes to write an essay on the topic assigned below. DO NOT WRITE ON ANOTHER TOPIC. AN ESSAY ON ANOTHER TOPIC IS NOT ACCEPTABLE.

The essay is assigned to give you an opportunity to show how well you can write. You should, therefore, take care to express your thoughts on the topic clearly and effectively. How well you write is much more important than how much you write, but to cover the topic adequately you may want to write more than one paragraph. Be specific.

Your essay must be written on the lines provided on your answer sheet. You will receive no other paper on which to write. You will find that you have enough space if you write on every line, avoid wide margins, and keep your handwriting to a reasonable size.

Consider carefully the following quotation and the assignment below it. Then plan and write your essay as directed.

"Any advance involves some loss."

Assignment: Choose a specific example from personal experience, current events, or from your reading in history, literature, or other subjects and use this example as the basis for an essay in which you agree or disagree with the statement above. Be sure to be specific.

WHEN THE SUPERVISOR ANNOUNCES THAT TWENTY MINUTES HAVE PASSED, YOU MUST STOP WRITING THE ESSAY AND GO ON TO PART B IF YOU HAVE NOT ALREADY DONE SO. IF YOU FINISH YOUR ESSAY BEFORE THIS ANNOUNCEMENT, GO ON TO PART B AT ONCE.

YOU MAY MAKE NOTES ON THIS PAGE BUT YOU MUST WRITE YOUR ESSAY ON THE ANSWER SHEET.

Guide for Scoring Student Responses to the SAT II: Writing Subject Test

General Directions for Scoring: Scores given to papers range from 6 down to 1. Readers should reward what has been done well. Scores should reflect the range in excellence in the papers that have been written on the topic. The range finders and sample papers will provide examples of responses at the various score levels and will guide your understanding of both the diversity and limits of the range at each score level.

Because each topic places unique demands on student writers, readers should score papers primarily in reference to the standards that emerge from the sample papers. There are, however, some broad categories that define the range of scores no matter what topic has been administered and no matter how broad or narrow the range of skills of those responding. These categories are listed below. Readers' interpretation of terms such as "competence," "effectively," and "well developed" in the descriptions below should be significantly influenced by the sample papers on the topic being scored.

SCORE OF 6

A paper in this category demonstrates *clear and consistent competence* though it may have occasional errors. Such a paper

— effectively and insightfully addresses the writing task
— is well organized and fully developed, using clearly appropriate examples to support ideas
— displays consistent facility in the use of language, demonstrating variety in sentence structure and range of vocabulary

SCORE OF 5

A paper in this category demonstrates *reasonably consistent competence* though it will have occasional errors or lapses in quality. Such a paper

— effectively addresses the writing task
— is generally well organized and adequately developed, using appropriate examples to support ideas
— displays facility in the use of language, demonstrating some syntactic variety and range of vocabulary

SCORE OF 4

A paper in this category demonstrates *adequate competence* with occasional errors and lapses in quality. Such a paper

— addresses the writing task
— is organized and somewhat developed, using examples to support ideas
— displays adequate but inconsistent facility in the use of language, presenting some errors in grammar or diction
— presents minimal sentence variety

SCORE OF 3

A paper in this category demonstrates *developing competence.* Such a paper may contain one or more of the following weaknesses:

— inadequate organization or development
— inappropriate or insufficient details to support ideas
— an accumulation of errors in grammar, diction, or sentence structure

SCORE OF 2

A paper in this category demonstrates *some incompetence.* Such a paper is flawed by one or more of the following weaknesses:

— poor organization
— thin development
— little or inappropriate detail to support ideas
— frequent errors in grammar, diction, and sentence structure

SCORE OF 1

A paper in this category demonstrates *incompetence.* Such a paper is seriously flawed by one or more of the following weaknesses:

— very poor organization
— very thin development
— usage and syntactical errors so severe that meaning is somewhat obscured

Essays that appear to be off topic or that pose unusual challenges in handwriting or other areas should be given to the Table Leader.

Actual Student Samples

Writing Samples with a Total Score of 12 (Each reader gave the Sample a score of 6.)

Although essays in this category may differ in approach, style, and opinion, and have slight differences in quality, they all demonstrate the clear and consistent competence specified in the scoring guide. They are characterized by good organization, good command of the language, pertinent support for the ideas being developed, and an interesting presentation. These essays are not perfect, nor are they expected to be, for each is only a first draft written in the 20 minutes allotted.

The following two essays are representative of Writing Samples given a total score of 12.

— 1 —

Since the beginning of time, men have sought out ways to make life easier. When the first human discovered and used fire for a means of protection, he started civilization on an upward climb on a downhill road.

All through history, the discovery of one great good has brought about the discovery of some great evil. When atomic power was used to operate machines and create weapons, very few people realized it's deadly capabilities. After Hiroshima was bombed during WWII, their was great rejoicing for the allies because it signified an end to a war, but for the Japanese it signified a horror that will always be remembered. The bomb and the lingering radiation destroyed acres of land and wildlife along with thousands of people who one day may have discovered a cure for diseases or famine. When the bomb was dropped, the war ended and many possibilities also ended.

The same thing holds true with refrigerator coolants and the ozone. When the coolants were first marketed, they were considered a great step forward for man. It was now much easier to store foods which only years before would have had to be used immeadiately. But with the use of these coolants, there came a high price. During manufacturing and use of the coolants, the ozone layer was slowly eaten away. By the year 2050, there will be no ozone and people will be forced to wear protective clotheing just to go outside.

It appears that no matter what we use to advance ourselves, we continnually bring about the loss of something needed to survive. Hopefully in the future, man and nature will be able to advance together.

— 2 —

In almost all areas of science, the advancement of a technology will cause a subsequent loss. Highly touted discoveries and new methods in any field will usually include a loss that offsets the advance. One of the recent scientific discoveries is the use of atomic power as a source of energy.

During the Manhattan Project of the later half of this century, scientists at Los Alamos national laboratories in New Mexico discovered the immense power created by splitting atoms. Within the next decade, this source of power was highly regarded, and plants were soon built to utilize it in the production of energy. Soon, however, questions were raised about the safety of the new discovery.

Scientists and people involved in the new atomic movement were aware of the power they held. Never before had man held the power to create energy on such a vast scale. Soon enough, however, people realized that this discovery had its drawbacks. Any leakage of the materials used in the new methods were very detrimental to all forms of life. In the second half of the last decade, humans became aware of the serious consequences of this technology. The leakage at Chernobyl in the USSR caused widespread contamination, from Europe to the Midwest of the United States.

The discovery of the power that could be generated by splitting atoms is only one of the many technological advances we have witnessed in this century. Although there benefits might be obvious very quickly, we should not ignore the losses that might occur as a result of the new discovery.

Writing Samples with a Total Score of 10 (Each reader gave the Sample a score of 5.)

Essays in this category demonstrate the reasonably consistent competence described in the scoring guide. They present pertinent examples and a developed argument. These essays, however, do contain lapses that keep them out of the top category These lapses range from an awkward sentence or two to a failure to maintain a consistent tone. Still, whatever the flaw, it does not detract from the overall impression that the writing is well done.

The following two essays are representative of Writing Samples given a total score of 10.

— 1 —

Advancement is a common term used at school and in the business world today. Like many competitive students in the world, I was given the opportunity to advance to a higher level of math during my middle school years which involved a significant loss in my social life.

At the beginning of my sixth grade year, I was advanced to the seventh grade pre-algebra class. My parents approved of this action and I was very excited. However, I struggled with an inner conflict for quite a period of time. By advancing to a higher level, I was leaving my friends behind. Due to jealousy and other factors, my friends began to ridicule and exclude me. I wanted to remain in the higher math level where I would actually be challenged on a daily basis due to the difficulty of the material. Yet, I did not want to be excluded by my friends. I struggled with this conflict for approximately two weeks. During that period of time, I was alone. Everyone deserted me.

Now if I think about the situation, I'm glad I decided to remain in the higher math class. Although I lost my old friends, I was able to conclude that if they were my true friends, they would not have left me. Instead, they should have supported me.

Although this advancement involved a loss of friends, at that time, my education was of top priority in my life. Perhaps if I was faced with this same conflict today, I believe I would once again sacrifice my friendships for the advancement in my education.

— 2 —

The quotation, "Any advance involves some loss" is true in regards to my own personal experiences. Throughout my life, I have found when I advance in one area, I will fall back in another area. One specific incident that I remember occurred in my eleventh grade year of high school.

Ever since I was in elementary school, I studied dance. My favorite part of the day was going to dance class, and I always dreamed of how magnificent it would be to someday be a part of a professional dance company. However, as I entered high school, I started losing interest in dancing. I was introduced to a whole new world of activities. Thus, I started taking an interest in drama and sports, so I joined the diving team in eleventh grade, and auditioned for the school musical. I was able to participate in the musical as a dancer, choreographer, and an actor, but I had diving practices as well, so I had to put my dance classes aside temporarily. I enjoyed diving and performing in the musical immensely, but at the same time I missed studying dance.

During my senior year I had the same schedule as I did the year before, and I had to stop dancing again. Although I regret putting my dancing career aside, I enjoyed acting and diving tremendously. Because of the amount of satisfaction I received from diving and acting, my loss of dancing was not as difficult to bear, and I feel I made the wisest decisions.

Writing Samples with a Total Score of 8 (Each reader gave the Sample a score of 4.)

As the scoring guide describes, essays in this category demonstrate adequate competence and only occasional errors and lapses in quality. Although the papers show that the writers have some command of the skills needed for good writing, they contain the kinds of flaws that keep them out of the top ranges.

The following two essays are representative of Writing Samples given a total score of 8.

— 1 —

In the year 1981, NASA launched the Space Shuttle Columbia which propelled the U.S. space program forward. Many years of research and effort went into developing and getting the shuttle program off the ground. Shuttle missions went on with great success in the years following. However, a few years ago, the Space Shuttle Challenger was launched with a crew of seven that included a civilian teacher. This launch ended in tradgedy. All members of the Challenger crew were lost. This loss touched the lives of every man, woman, and child in this country and around the world.

After this tradgedy advancements and improvements were done to the safety and design specifications of the shuttles. Also, more precautions were taken prior to each launch. These new proceudres eventually led to the launch of the next successful shuttle.

It was a shame that those brave men and woman lost their lives. Many good things came out of it as well. Not only is the space program rejuvenated, it is better and safer than ever before. This just exemplifies the statement "Any advance involves some loss."

— 2 —

Gustave Flaubert gives an excellent example of losses through advancement in his novel Madame Bovary. *Emma's entire lifestyle is based upon making romantic advances. These advances are the foundation of her downfall. Her first, and most important, advance comes when she marries Charles. She thinks that her marriage to Charles will reflect the romantic liasons that occur in the books that she reads. Unfortunately, Emma is only satisfied with her new life for a short period of time. What she thought would be an advance in her life ends up disappointing her.*

She feels as if she has been let down by Charles and her marriage. Emma then decides to seek other methods of fulfilling her desires. She has affairs with Leon and Rodolph and she convinces Charles that they should move to Tostes. In the beginning of her affairs and when she moves, Emma feels that she is advancing in terms of self-fulfillment. After she moves, she finds that Tostes is like her former home and her affairs turn out to be negative ones. She thought in the beginning of her affairs that they would give her great pleasure. Emma's hopes to advance her personal life lead to her self-destruction and her eventual death. The losses Emma suffers when the advances she though would change her being do not meet her expectations. She is so distraught she turns to suicide.

Writing Samples with a Total Score of 6 (Each reader gave the Sample a score of 3.)

Essays in this category demonstrate developing competence. Although they show that the writers have a fairly good grasp of sentence structure and the ability to organize their ideas, these papers usually have such problems as limited development, inconsistent logic, or accumulated errors in grammar and diction.

The following two essays are representative of Writing Samples given a total score of 6.

— 1 —

As you go forward in life, your bound to have a loss in something you want also. That something may be time spent with your friends, or time spent with your parents. The advance, if it is that important is going to be worth the loss It is like a professional sports athlete. That athlete wanted to advance in life, and he chose sports. He gave up party time, family time, and some of his time. He did all this to better himself, to get advanced in his chosen career. The advance that he gets is money, and the satisfaction that he is one of the very few who get to the professional level. So, in a sense, what I'm trying to say is anything that you do will involve a loss in something else that you like to do.

We as a nation have had to advance with the rest of the world. Today that advancement has had a great deal of losses. First, we are putting people out of jobs. And second, which I think is the most important of the losses is, that the advancements are way too expensive to keep doing, day in and day out. It is because of the expensiveness of these advances that

— 2 —

I disagree with the statement. Not all advance involves some loss. You may advance and not lose anything at all. Other cases, you may lose, so it all depends on what you are doing.

In the fourth grade, I was the winner from my grade and school in the spelling bee. I went on to compete with several other students from other schools. When it was my turn, I got nervous and spelled the word wrong, therefore I lost.

My brother, on the other hand, was also in the spelling bee. He was in the sixth grade. He went all the way and spelled every word right. He won.

When I was younger, I played soccer. Our team was so good that we were undefeated for the season. We were the number one team in our league. We got a couple of trophies and awards for it.

Then, I was also on a baseball team. We were so bad. I don't think that we won even one gam.

Writing Samples with a Total Score of 4 (Each reader gave the Sample a score of 2.)

The scoring guide describes essays in this category as demonstrating some incompetence. They are generally not well developed, and they are usually flawed by such problems as poor organization, inappropriate detail, or frequent errors in grammar, diction, or sentence structure.

The following two essays are representative of Writing Samples given a total score of 4.

— 1 —

There is truth in this statement, it complis with the law in science, for every action their is an opposite reaction. Sometimes the loss it not aparent in the begining. Life is always like this the good and the bad. For me it is my job. I have wanted a job for a long time, to be able to have my own money. But because of my job I couldn't play softball and my homework has suffered. Even though there is a loss it does not mean you should not enjoy the advances. I enjoy my money very much and spend it on what I want an now I make sure I make time for homework. I think it is very rare that their is not a loss with all advances. Another example of this is when people come into money, either the person with the money changes or the people around the person changes. No matter who changes their is most likely to be a loss of friends.

— 2 —

In my opion any advance involves some loss. Whenever you try to get ahead you always lose something in the process. Wether it is time, money, or someone close to you.

I remember my 9th grade year in high school. I was an honor student until I was moved to more advanced classes. Befor I was moved I only had about a half hour of homework. Know I had over an hour every night. This is were I lose time. I also had to quit my job because I needed ore time to study for quizes and Tests this is were I lost money. Therefor I could not go out so I lost a lot of my friends.

So you see any advance involves some loss. Even if it is an advance to better yourself.

Writing Samples with a Total Score of 2 (Each reader gave the Sample a score of 1.)

Essays in this category are the poorest of those being scored. They are seriously flawed, and the scoring guide describes them as demonstrating incompetence. Weaknesses evident in these papers include very poor organization, very thin development, and errors in grammar that may obscure the meaning intended.

The following two essays are representative of Writing Samples given a total score of 2.

— 1 —

I think that all or most advances have losts. For example: If you were to start a company. You would have to pay money first to start the business and then gain from that business. Another example is that if you were a worker and you wanted to move up to a higher rank. You would have to loss some time off and work a little harder. You wouldn't have all the rest of the rest of the time to relax and have fun. You would have to give that time up to gain or move up. This is why when you want to advance you have to loss something on the way. Even if the advance is small you still loss something. I agree with this statement. It doesn't really matter how you advance or move up. You always have to lose something

— 2 —

My composition that I am writing is in regard to the title "Any Advance involve some loss". I agree with this statement because of personal experience and current events. In the news the situation with the war went well however many people died. The advance definitely involved loss. Personally I feel that all good things have a flaw or minor setback. For these reasons I agree with the statement.

SAT II:

Writing Subject Test

The test that follows is representative of a typical SAT II: Writing Subject Test. It has already been administered. So that you may have an idea of what the national test administration will be like, try to take the test in this book under conditions as close as possible to those of the nationally administered test. It will probably help if you do the following.

- Set aside an hour for the test when you will not be interrupted, so that you can complete all of it in one sitting.
- Sit at a desk with no other papers or books. You can't take a dictionary, other books, or notes into the test room.
- Have a kitchen timer or clock in front of you for timing yourself.
- Tear out an answer sheet from the back of this book and fill it in just as you would on the day of the test. You can use one answer sheet for as many as three Subject Tests.
- Read the instructions that precede the test. When you take the test, you will be asked to read them before you begin answering questions.
- After you finish the test, read the sections on "How to Score the SAT II: Writing Subject Test" and "Reviewing Your Test Performance," which follow the test.

FORM 30NP3-WPS

WRITING TEST

The top portion of the section of the answer sheet that you will use in taking the Writing test must be filled in exactly as shown in the illustration below. Note carefully that you have to do all of the following on your answer sheet.

1. Print WRITING on the line under the words "Subject (print)."

2. In the shaded box labeled "Test Code" fill in four ovals:

   —Fill in oval 1 in the row labeled V.

   —Fill in oval 6 in the row labeled W.

   —Fill in oval 3 in the row labeled X.

   —Fill in oval C in the row labeled Y.

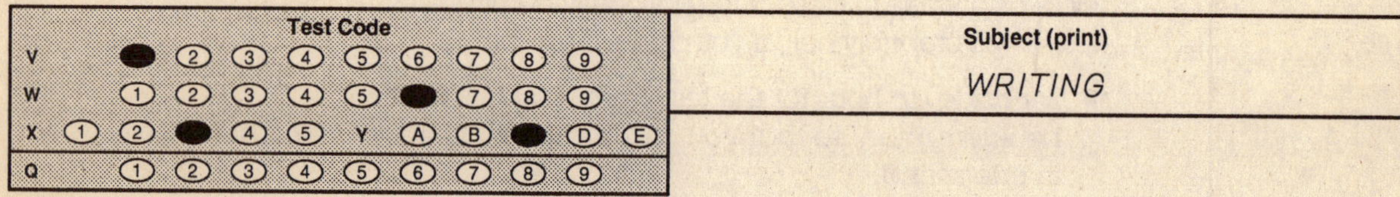

You are to leave blank the nine ovals in the row labeled Q.

When the supervisor gives the signal, turn the page and begin the Writing test. There are 100 numbered ovals on the answer sheet and 58 questions in the Writing test. Therefore, use only ovals 1 to 58 for recording your answers.*

*The SAT II: Writing Subject Test normally has 60 multiple-choice questions. In the 1992 field test, however, there were only 58.

PART A	Time—20 minutes 1 Question	ESSAY

You have 20 minutes to write an essay on the topic assigned below. DO NOT WRITE ON ANOTHER TOPIC. AN ESSAY ON ANOTHER TOPIC IS NOT ACCEPTABLE.

The essay is assigned to give you an opportunity to show how well you can write. You should, therefore, take care to express your thoughts on the topic clearly and effectively. How well you write is much more important than how much you write, but to cover the topic adequately you may want to write more than one paragraph. Be specific.

Your essay must be written on the lines provided on your answer sheet. You will receive no other paper on which to write. You will find that you have enough space if you write on every line, avoid wide margins, and keep your handwriting to a reasonable size.

Consider carefully the following quotation and the assignment below it. Then plan and write your essay as directed.

"Any advance involves some loss."

Assignment: Choose a specific example from personal experience, current events, or from your reading in history, literature, or other subjects and use this example as the basis for an essay in which you agree or disagree with the statement above. Be sure to be specific.

WHEN THE SUPERVISOR ANNOUNCES THAT 20 MINUTES HAVE PASSED, YOU MUST STOP WRITING THE ESSAY AND GO ON TO PART B. IF YOU FINISH YOUR ESSAY BEFORE THIS ANNOUNCEMENT, YOU MAY GO ON TO PART B.

YOU MAY MAKE NOTES ON THIS PAGE AND ON THE OPPOSITE PAGE BUT YOU MUST WRITE YOUR ESSAY ON THE ANSWER SHEET.

You may use this page to make notes as you plan your essay. Remember, however, that your essay MUST be written on the lined pages of the separate answer sheet.

PART B	Time—40 minutes 58 Questions	For each question in this part, select the best answer from among the choices given and fill in the corresponding oval on the answer sheet.

Directions: The following sentences test your knowledge of grammar, usage, diction (choice of words), and idiom.

Some sentences are correct.
No sentence contains more than one error.

You will find that the error, if there is one, is underlined and lettered. Elements of the sentence that are not underlined will not be changed. In choosing answers, follow the requirements of standard written English.

If there is an error, select the one underlined part that must be changed to make the sentence correct and fill in the corresponding oval on your answer sheet.

If there is no error, fill in oval E.

EXAMPLE:

The other (A) delegates and him (B) immediately (C) accepted the resolution drafted by (D) the neutral states. No error (E)

SAMPLE ANSWER

1. Alexis has discovered (A) that she can express her creativity more freely through (B) her sketches (C) and not in (D) her photography. No error (E)

2. Although (A) a lottery may seem a relatively easy (B) way for a state to increase (C) revenues, they (D) may encourage some individuals to gamble excessively. No error (E)

3. Charles Dickens' novel *Great Expectations* focuses on (A) the character Pip, who as a young adult has scarcely no (B) understanding of (C) his own (D) origins. No error (E)

4. At the 1984 Olympic Games, John Moffet and Pablo Morales, who (A) were (B) swimmers on the United States team, set (C) world records. (D) No error (E)

5. Reaching (A) lengths of twelve inches, banana slugs are (B) the much larger (C) of the slug species that inhabit (D) North America. No error (E)

6. Although science offers the hope of preventing (A) serious genetic diseases, there is (B) difficult ethical questions raised by (C) the possibility of (D) altering human heredity. No error (E)

7. Many of the delegates which (A) were attending the convention found the daily meeting schedule so hectic (B) that they (C) were exhausted by early afternoon. (D) No error (E)

GO ON TO THE NEXT PAGE

8. Researchers in Scotland have set up telescopes,
A
hydrophones, and video cameras around Loch
Ness, hoping that it will document the existence of
B C D
the famous monster. No error
E

9. Advanced training in a foreign language is intellectually
A B
satisfying and is likely to be helpful in such fields as
C D
education and international business. No error
E

10. A brilliant pianist, Art Tatum brought together the
A
distinctly different techniques of jazz and classical
B
music as effortlessly than any jazz musician
C
ever has. No error
D E

11. A newly formed organization of homeowners and
businesspeople have met with the transportation
A
department to voice its concerns about plans for
B C D
a shopping mall in the community. No error
E

12. Though she was one of the few women of her time
to gain international prominence, Clara Barton
A
would not have described herself as a proponent of
B C D
women's rights. No error
E

13. In his report Mr. Liu stated that the competing
A B
contractor's maintenance agreement was not so
C
detailed as the current contractor. No error
D E

14. The labor leaders called a meeting to propose a new
A B
plan after union members had rejected several other
C
possible solutions toward the dispute. No error
D E

15. Voters justified their apathy by saying that they
A B
had no viable choice because the candidates
C
were indifferent from one another. No error
D E

16. More and more women are enrolling in programs
A
to train as a pilot of both propeller and jet
B C D
aircraft. No error
E

17. Devotees of classic films might well say
A
that introducing color into such famous black-and-
B C
white films as *Casablanca* is as unnecessary as
D
floodlighting a natural waterfall. No error
E

18. Princeton University officials first broke with a tradi-
A
tion of awarding honorary degrees only to men when
B C
they awarded it to author Willa Cather. No error
D E

19. The condition known as laryngitis usually causes
A
the vocal cords and surrounding tissue to swell,
thus preventing the cords to move freely. No error
B C D E

20. Photographs of genetic molecules have revealed
how close the images of DNA resemble the theoret-
A
ical model that scientists have used for so long.
B C D
No error
E

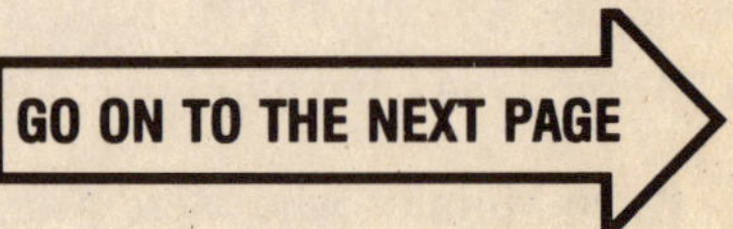

Directions: The following sentences test correctness and effectiveness of expression. In choosing answers, follow the requirements of standard written English; that is, pay attention to grammar, choice of words, sentence construction, and punctuation.

In each of the following sentences, part of the sentence or the entire sentence is underlined. Beneath each sentence you will find five ways of phrasing the underlined part. Choice A repeats the original; the other four are different.

Choose the answer that best expresses the meaning of the original sentence. If you think the original is better than any of the alternatives, choose it; otherwise choose one of the others. Your choice should produce the most effective sentence—clear and precise, without awkwardness or ambiguity.

EXAMPLE:

Laura Ingalls Wilder published her first book and she was sixty-five years old then.

(A) and she was sixty-five years old then
(B) when she was sixty-five
(C) being age sixty-five years old
(D) upon the reaching of sixty-five years
(E) at the time when she was sixty-five

SAMPLE ANSWER

21. The complex trajectories of the knuckleball providing one of baseball's greatest challenges to physicists.

(A) The complex trajectories of the knuckleball providing
(B) The knuckleball with its complex trajectories having provided
(C) Providing that the complex trajectories of the knuckleball is
(D) It is the complex trajectories of the knuckleball providing
(E) The complex trajectories of the knuckleball provide

22. In 1827 *Freedom's Journal* was the first Black American newspaper in the United States, it was published in New York City.

(A) In 1827 *Freedom's Journal* was the first Black American newspaper in the United States, it was published in New York City.
(B) In 1827 the first Black American newspaper in the United States, *Freedom's Journal*, was published in New York City.
(C) In New York City in 1827 *Freedom's Journal*, the first Black American newspaper in the United States, was published there.
(D) With publication in New York City in 1827, it was the first Black American newspaper in the United States, *Freedom's Journal*.
(E) The first Black American newspaper published in the United States was when there was *Freedom's Journal* in New York City in 1827.

23. Home computers themselves are becoming less expensive, but video display terminals, printers, and links to other computers cause the total financial cost to rise up greatly.

(A) cause the total financial cost to rise up greatly
(B) greatly increase the total cost
(C) highly inflate the cost totals
(D) drive up the expense totally
(E) totally add to the expense

24. Arguably the most distinctive regional cuisine in the United States, the South is noted for such specialties as Brunswick stew and hush puppies.

(A) the South is noted for such specialties as
(B) the South has such specialties of note as
(C) the South includes among its noteworthy specialties
(D) southern cooking includes such noteworthy specialties as
(E) southern cooking is including such specialties of note as

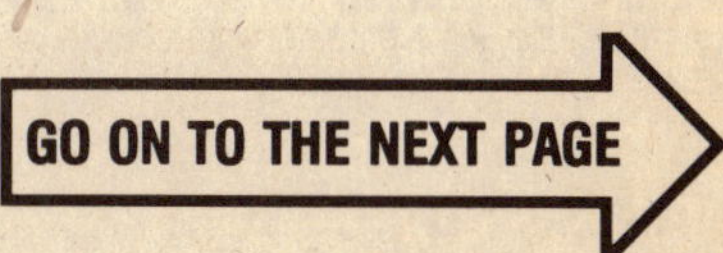

25. When I.M. Pei designed a hotel in Beijing, traditional Chinese architectural forms were evoked, but it was not directly imitated by him.

(A) traditional Chinese architectural forms were evoked, but it was not directly imitated by him
(B) traditional Chinese architectural forms were evoked, but he did not imitate it directly
(C) traditional Chinese architectural forms were evoked by him and not directly imitated
(D) he evoked traditional Chinese architectural forms, but they had not been directly imitated
(E) he evoked, but did not directly imitate, traditional Chinese architectural forms

26. Originally, cultured milk products were popular not so much for their nutritional value or flavor but for their being resistant to spoilage.

(A) but for their being resistant to spoilage
(B) the reason being their resistance to spoilage
(C) the reason was their being resistant to spoilage
(D) but for their being spoilage-resistant
(E) as for their resistance to spoilage

27. Morgan had the complete support of her party, this partisan approval enabled her to win the mayoral election easily.

(A) this
(B) therefore
(C) and this
(D) of which
(E) that

28. In neighborhoods throughout the United States, one can encounter hundreds of different rope-jumping games, each with its own rules.

(A) each with its own rules
(B) each having their own rules
(C) when they each have their own rules
(D) which has its own rules
(E) they each have rules of their own

29. In ancient Rome officials called censors were employed to monitor the morals and conduct of citizens as well as taking the census.

(A) as well as taking the census
(B) and they also took the census
(C) as well as to take the census
(D) the census also being taken by them
(E) together with taking the census

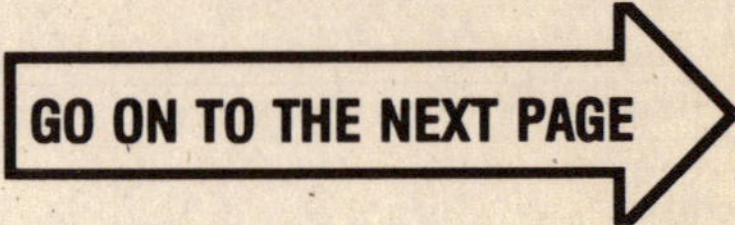
GO ON TO THE NEXT PAGE

30. Vietnamese Americans are active in the city's cultural life; this includes the contributions of a weekly newspaper and a program on FM radio.

(A) life; this includes the contributions of
(B) life, which includes contributions of
(C) life, whose contributions include
(D) life; their contributions include
(E) life; its contribution includes

31. In their zeal to make beachfront living widely available, developers have overbuilt, thereby they endanger fragile coastlines.

(A) overbuilt, thereby they endanger fragile coastlines
(B) overbuilt they endanger fragile coastlines as a result
(C) overbuilt and thereby have endangered fragile coastlines
(D) overbuilt; fragile coastlines endangered thereby
(E) overbuilt, the fragile coastlines are endangered by this

32. Eating food that has a high concentration of fat causes essentially the same reaction in the stomach than if you eat too fast.

(A) than if you eat
(B) than to eat
(C) as if one eats
(D) as eating
(E) as it does when eating

33. In 1982 Zimbabwe celebrated its second anniversary, honoring at the same time those who died in the struggle for independence.

(A) honoring at the same time those who died in the struggle for independence
(B) and those who died in the struggle for independence were those who were honored
(C) those who died in the struggle for independence were honored at the same time
(D) for the honoring of those who died in the struggle for independence
(E) and with this was the honoring of those who died in the struggle for independence

34. Participants in the executive leadership workshop expect a program of outstanding speakers and gaining information about new approaches to management.

(A) and gaining information
(B) as well as information
(C) as well as being informed
(D) and also being informed
(E) in addition they expect to gain information

35. The students' fieldwork in the state forest proved more exciting and more dangerous than any of them had anticipated, having to be rescued by helicopter during a fire.

(A) anticipated, having to be
(B) anticipated; when they had to be
(C) anticipated: they had to be
(D) anticipated: among which was their being
(E) anticipated and so they had been

36. During the summer months, several thousand people a day visit the park, which is known for its waterfalls and rock formations.

(A) During the summer months, several thousand people a day visit the park, which is known for its waterfalls and rock formations.
(B) Known for its waterfalls and rock formations, several thousand people a day visit the park during the summer months.
(C) Several thousand people a day visit the park during the summer months known for its waterfalls and rock formations.
(D) Several thousand people had visited the park a day, which is known for its waterfalls and rock formations during the summer months.
(E) During the summer months, knowing its waterfalls and rock formations, several thousand people a day visit the park.

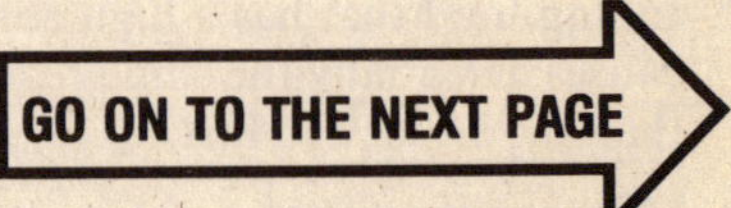

Directions: The following passages are early drafts of student essays. Some parts of the passages need to be rewritten.

Read the passages and answer the questions that follow. Some questions are about particular sentences or parts of sentences and ask you to make decisions about sentence structure, word choice, and usage. Other questions refer to the entire essay or parts of the essay and ask you to consider organization, development, and appropriateness of language. Choose the answer that most effectively expresses the meaning and follows the requirements of standard written English. After you have chosen your answer, fill in the corresponding oval on your answer sheet.

Questions 37-42 are based on the following passage.

(1) I used to be convinced that people didn't actually win radio contests; I thought that the excited winners I heard were only actors. (2) Sure, people could win T-shirts. (3) They couldn't win anything of real value.

(4) I've always loved sports. (5) My friends fall asleep to the music of U2. (6) I listen to "Sports Night with Dave Sims." (7) His show is hardly usual fare for a teen-aged girl. (8) One night I heard Dave Sims announce this sports trivia contest with cash prizes of two thousand dollars. (9) I jump at the chance to combine my talk-show knowledge with everything my father had taught me about sports in my almost sixteen years. (10) I sent in my self-addressed stamped envelope. (11) I forgot about the whole matter. (12) Then the questionnaire appeared in my mailbox ten days later. (13) Its arrival gave me a rude surprise. (14) Instead of sitting down and whipping through it, I trudged to libraries and spent hours digging for answers to such obscure questions as "Which NHL goalie holds the record for most career shutouts?"

(15) Finally, after days of double-checking answers, I mailed off my answer sheet, certain I would hear no more about the matter. (16) Certain, until two weeks later, I ripped open the envelope with the NBC peacock and read "Congratulations . . . " (17) I was a winner, a winner of more than a T-shirt.

37. Which of the following is the best way to revise the underlined portions of sentences 2 and 3 (reproduced below) so that the two sentences are combined into one?

    Sure, people could win T-shirts. They couldn't win anything of real value.

    (A) T-shirts, and they couldn't win
    (B) T-shirts, but they couldn't win
    (C) T-shirts, but not being able to win
    (D) T-shirts, so they do win
    (E) T-shirts, while there was no winning

38. Which of the following sentences, if added after sentence 3, would best link the first paragraph with the rest of the essay?

    (A) I have held this opinion about contests for a long time.
    (B) The prizes offered did not inspire me to enter the contests.
    (C) However, I recently changed my opinion about these contests.
    (D) Usually the questions on these contests are really easy to answer.
    (E) Sometimes my friends try to convince me to enter such contests.

39. To vary the pattern of short, apparently unrelated sentences in the second paragraph, which of the following would be the best way to combine sentences 5 and 6 (reproduced below)?

My friends fall asleep to the music of U2. I listen to "Sports Night with Dave Sims."

(A) While my friends fall asleep to the music of U2, "Sports Night with Dave Sims" is what my listening is.
(B) In contrast to my friends falling asleep to the music of U2, I will be listening to "Sports Night with Dave Sims."
(C) My friends were falling asleep to the music of U2, I was listening to "Sports Night with Dave Sims."
(D) My friends fall asleep to the music of U2 and I am not the same because I listen to "Sports Night with Dave Sims."
(E) Unlike my friends, who fall asleep to the music of U2, I listen to "Sports Night with Dave Sims."

40. In the context of the second paragraph, which of the following is the best version of the underlined portion of sentence 9 (reproduced below)?

<u>I jump at the chance to combine</u> my talk-show knowledge with everything my father had taught me about sports in my almost sixteen years.

(A) (As it is now)
(B) I jumped at the chance to combine
(C) Having jumped at the chance to combine
(D) Jumping at the chance and combining
(E) Jumping at the chance by combining

41. Which of the following is the best way to revise and combine sentences 10 and 11 (reproduced below)?

I sent in my self-addressed stamped envelope. I forgot about the whole matter.

(A) Having sent in my self-addressed stamped envelope, the whole matter was forgotten.
(B) After sending in my self-addressed stamped envelope, the matter was wholly forgotten.
(C) After my self-addressed stamped envelope was sent in, it was then that I forgot the whole matter.
(D) After sending in my self-addressed stamped envelope, I forgot about the whole matter.
(E) Forgetting about the whole matter after sending in my self-addressed stamped envelope.

42. All of the following strategies are used by the writer of the passage EXCEPT

(A) selecting specific examples
(B) telling a story to develop a point
(C) criticizing those whose opinions differ from hers
(D) building suspense with references to the passage of time
(E) disproving the assumption stated in the first sentence of the passage

Questions 43-48. The following passage was written in response to an assignment to write a letter to the editor of a local newspaper.

(1) Our community needs more parks and play areas. (2) Living in a world where concrete surrounds us, it is important that we create places that are green and natural so that children can run and play.

(3) It is possible to do much with little expense to the city. (4) An abandoned lot can become a big patch of green grass ideal for running games. (5) And buying expensive playground equipment and strange pieces of modern art for children to climb on is unnecessary. (6) Children will climb on anything if one lets them. (7) A large concrete pipe or an old truck with its wheels and doors removed makes an imaginative plaything. (8) Simply remove any part that may be breakable or unsafe, then paint them with bright colors. (9) Bury the truck or pipe a foot or two deep so that it is stable. (10) Great opportunities for fun! (11) Children can play for hours, crawling through a secret tunnel or navigating to a distant planet. (12) Neighborhood committees could contribute other discards.

(13) We should do these things because children need oases in this concrete desert we live in. (14) This may take time, but if people get together and they would have contributed both ideas and labor, much can be completed successfully.

43. Which of the following is the best way to revise the underlined portion of sentence 2 (reproduced below)?

 Living in a world where concrete surrounds us, it is important that we create places that are green and natural so that children can run and play.

 (A) Living in a world in which concrete surrounds us, the important thing is to
 (B) Surrounded by a world of concrete, we need to
 (C) Surrounding us with a world of concrete, we need to
 (D) Being surrounded by a world of concrete, it is important to
 (E) We live in a world where concrete surrounds us, it is important that we

44. Which of the following would be the best replacement for "*And*" at the beginning of sentence 5 (reproduced below)?

 And buying expensive playground equipment and strange pieces of modern art for children to climb on is unnecessary.

 (A) Despite this,
 (B) Instead,
 (C) Furthermore,
 (D) Nevertheless,
 (E) Excepting this,

45. In context, which version of the underlined portion of sentence 8 (reproduced below) is the clearest?

 Simply remove any part that may be breakable or unsafe, then paint them with bright colors.

 (A) (as it is now)
 (B) then paint these things
 (C) then paint it
 (D) it should be painted
 (E) then paint the equipment

GO ON TO THE NEXT PAGE

46. The writer of the passage could best improve sentence 12 by

(A) acknowledging drawbacks to suggestions
(B) providing specific examples
(C) including personal opinions
(D) discussing other community problems
(E) defining the idea of a neighborhood

47. The phrase "*do these things*" in sentence 13 can best be made more specific if rewritten as

(A) accomplish our intentions
(B) help these children
(C) consider other options
(D) build these play areas
(E) have new ideas

48. Which of the following versions of the underlined portion of sentence 14 (reproduced below) is best?

This may take time, but if people get together and they would have contributed both ideas and labor, much can be completed successfully.

(A) (as it is now)
(B) and if people get together and they contribute
(C) but if people will get together and they will also contribute
(D) but if people get together and contribute
(E) however, if people get together, also contributing

GO ON TO THE NEXT PAGE

Note: These directions are exactly the same as the directions already given. They are repeated for easy reference as you work with the sentences that follow.

Directions: The following sentences test your knowledge of grammar, usage, diction (choice of words), and idiom.

Some sentences are correct.
No sentence contains more than one error.

You will find that the error, if there is one, is underlined and lettered. Elements of the sentence that are not underlined will not be changed. In choosing answers, follow the requirements of standard written English.

If there is an error, select the one underlined part that must be changed to make the sentence correct and fill in the corresponding oval on your answer sheet.

If there is no error, fill in answer oval E.

EXAMPLE:

The other (A) delegates and him (B) immediately (C) accepted the resolution drafted by (D) the neutral states. No error (E)

SAMPLE ANSWER

49. It was expected, however, that researchers will continue (A) their (B) work to find ways to lessen (C) the undesirable effects of (D) the Africanized honeybee. No error (E)

50. Galaxies, far from being (A) randomly (B) scattered throughout the universe, appear (C) to be distributed (D) in bubble-shaped patterns. No error (E)

51. In the nineteenth century, careers in business and law were (A) prestigious, but it (B) did not require (C) practitioners to hold (D) college degrees. No error (E)

52. Now that Michiko finished (A) the research, she feels reasonably confident (B) about writing (C) her paper on the rise of (D) the progressive movement in the United States. No error (E)

53. In a democracy the voters are supposed (A) to decide which of (B) the candidates is (C) most capable to be (D) the officeholder. No error (E)

54. Changes in the balance of trade seem (A) remote from (B) everyday concerns, but they can drastically (C) affect how you and I (D) spend our money. No error (E)

55. According to (A) many economists, neither inflation nor (B) unemployment are (C) the foremost cause of increases in (D) personal bankruptcies. No error (E)

56. Insomniacs have often established so firm a pattern
A B
of sleeplessness that the very act of lying down can
C
make them more alert. No error
D E

57. Chess players find that playing against a computer is
helpful to improve their skills, even though no chess-
A B C
playing computer has yet won a championship.
D
No error
E

58. Since the novels of Elizabeth Phelps are less well
A
known today than many of her contemporaries, one
B C
is surprised to learn that she was once a best-selling
D
author. No error
E

END OF TEST

IF YOU FINISH BEFORE TIME IS CALLED, YOU MAY CHECK YOUR WORK ON EITHER PART OF THIS TEST.

How to Score the SAT II: Writing Subject Test

When you take the SAT II: Writing Subject Test, you will receive an overall composite score as well as two subscores: one for the multiple-choice section and one for the Writing Sample section. The multiple-choice and Writing Sample scores are reported on the College Board's 20-80 scale. However, the composite score, which is the most significant of the scores reported to the colleges you specify, is in the form of the College Board's 200-800 scale. In order for you to calculate your own scores on the SAT II: Writing Subject Test reproduced in this book, we have organized the following flow chart.

The Multiple-Choice Scoring Process

The multiple-choice section of the SAT II: Writing Subject Test is scored by computer. The resulting raw multiple-choice score includes one point for each correct answer but no points for missing or multiply marked answers; a quarter point is deducted for each wrong answer. You can calculate your raw score on the multiple-choice section of the SAT II: Writing Subject Test yourself. Just follow the steps given in Table MC.1.

Your score: ______

Your raw multiple-choice score must now be converted to a scaled multiple-choice score. You can do this by referring to Table MC.3. Locate the score you calculated by following the directions in Table MC.1 and read across to the corresponding Scaled Score. This score, you might observe, is what the College Board reports on its 20-80 scale.

Your score: ______

The Writing Sample Scoring Process

The Writing Sample is scored on a 6-point scale. Two readers score each Sample, however, so each Sample's total raw score can range from 0 to 12. When you score your own Writing Sample, you should double the score you give yourself in order to simulate a real-life situation. Better yet, ask one or two persons other than yourself to score your essay for you.

Your score: ______

Total raw scores for the Writing Sample are converted to scaled scores, and Table WS.1 gives the scaled Writing Sample subscores corresponding with each raw score. Thus, for example, a raw score of 2 converts to a scaled score of 23; a raw score of 6 converts to a scaled score of 37; and so on. This scaled subscore, you might observe, is the College Board's 20-80 scale.

Your score: ______

In order to calculate your composite score, you must first combine the multiple-choice score with a *weighted* Writing Sample score. The weighting makes the Writing Sample constitute only one-third of the combined score. To perform this calculation, follow the steps given in Table CS.1.*

Your score: ______

The final step is to convert your raw composite score to the College Board's 200-800 scale. This can be done by referring to Table CS.2.

YOUR SCORE: ______

While following this chart should be relatively straightforward, you may find it difficult to obtain a score for your Writing Sample. You can minimize this problem by calculating a range of scores: since each weighted Writing Sample score is worth about 3 points, your range would be calculated by subtracting and adding 6 points to the value found in Step 2 of Table CS.1.

---

* For those of you who are curious about how the calculation works, the weighting is done in standard deviation units, a measure of score variability, with the standard deviation of the weighted Writing Sample subscore set equal to one-half the standard deviation of the multiple-choice subscore. This weighting reflects the amount of time spent on the two sections of the test — 40 minutes on the multiple-choice questions and 20 minutes on the Writing Sample. Thus, for example, if your raw multiple-choice score is 45, your range of raw composite scores could start at 45 — no essay response — and peak at 81 — an essay score of 12. Still assuming that your raw multiple-choice subscore is 45, this procedure would produce scaled scores that range from 420 to 690, depending on your essay performance.

TABLE MC.1
FINDING YOUR RAW MULTIPLE-CHOICE SCORE

Step 1:	Table MC.2 lists the correct answers for all the multiple-choice questions on the SAT II: Writing Subject Test that is reproduced in this book. It also serves as a worksheet for you to calculate your raw multiple-choice score. • Compare your answers with those given in the table. • Put a check in the column marked "Right" if your answer is correct. • Put a check in the column marked "Wrong" if your answer is incorrect. • Leave both columns blank if you omitted the question.
Step 2:	Count the number of right answers and enter the total here: .... ________
Step 3:	Count the number of wrong answers and enter the total here: .... ________
Step 4:	Divide the number of wrong answers by 4 and enter the result here: .... ________
Step 5:	Subtract the result obtained in Step 4 from the total you obtained in Step 2. Enter the result here: .... ________
Step 6:	Round the number obtained in Step 5 to the nearest whole number. Enter the result here: .... ________

The number you obtained in Step 6 is your raw multiple-choice score.

TABLE MC.2

Answers and Worksheet for the Multiple-Choice Questions on the SAT II: Writing Subject 1992 Field Test*

Question Number	Correct Answer	Right	Wrong	Percentage of Students Answering the Question Correctly**	Question Number	Correct Answer	Right	Wrong	Percentage of Students Answering the Question Correctly**
1	D			70	31	C			87
2	D			77	32	D			59
3	B			74	33	A			67
4	E			85	34	B			74
5	C			87	35	C			41
6	B			84	36	A			61
7	A			80	37	B			97
8	C			78	38	C			87
9	E			86	39	E			94
10	C			82	40	B			86
11	A			55	41	D			88
12	E			79	42	C			79
13	D			51	43	B			51
14	D			44	44	C			82
15	D			56	45	E			51
16	C			61	46	B			82
17	E			43	47	D			72
18	D			57	48	D			81
19	C			26	49	A			56
20	A			44	50	E			70
21	E			91	51	B			81
22	B			93	52	A			51
23	B			92	53	D			38
24	D			44	54	E			62
25	E			68	55	C			42
26	E			49	56	E			42
27	C			52	57	A			38
28	A			63	58	B			31
29	C			55					
30	D			51					

*The SAT II: Writing Subject Test has 60 multiple-choice questions. In the 1992 field test, however, there were only 58.

**The column labeled "Percentage of Students Answering the Question Correctly" gives the proportion of the 4,400 students who took the 1992 field test who answered a particular question correctly. Thus, for example, 31% of the field test candidates answered question number 58 correctly. Generally, you may thus deduce that a typical SAT II student has a 31% percent chance of answering question number 58 correctly.

TABLE MC.3

Multiple-Choice Raw and Scaled Scores

Raw Score	Scaled Score	Raw Score	Scaled Score
58	79	22	40
57	77	21	39
56	74	20	39
55	73	19	38
54	71	18	37
53	70	17	37
52	69	16	36
51	67	15	35
50	65	14	35
49	64	13	34
48	62	12	33
47	61	11	32
46	60	10	32
45	59	9	31
44	58	8	30
43	57	7	29
42	56	6	28
41	56	5	27
40	55	4	26
39	54	3	25
38	53	2	24
37	52	1	23
36	51	0	22
35	50	−1	21
34	49	−2	20
33	49	−3	20
32	48	−4	20
31	47	−5	20
30	46	−6	20
29	45	−7	20
28	45	−8	20
27	44	−9	20
26	43	−10	20
25	42	−11	20
24	42	−12	20
23	41		

TABLE WS.1

Conversion Table: Raw and Scaled Writing Sample Scores

Raw Writing Sample Score*	Scaled Writing Sample Score
12	71
11	65
10	60
9	54
8	48
7	42
6	37
5	33
4	30
3	26
2	23
0	20

*The raw scores given here are the sum of the scores given by two readers. When calculating your own Writing Sample score, you should double it before using this chart.

TABLE CS.1 PROCEDURE FOR FINDING THE RAW COMPOSITE SCORE	
Step 1:	Enter your unrounded raw multiple-choice score from Step 5 (of table MC.1) here: ...... ________
Step 2:	Multiply your Writing Sample raw score by 3.* Enter the product here: .... ________
Step 3:	Add the two scores found in Steps 1 and 2, round them to the nearest whole number, and enter the sum here: .... ________
This number is your raw composite score.	

* The number 3 works well except for very high raw scores. For very high raw scores, it is better to use 3.021.

TABLE CS.2

Table for Converting Raw Composite Scores to Scaled Composite Scores

Raw Score	Scaled Score	Raw Score	Scaled Score
94	800	47	430
93	800	46	430
92	790	45	420
91	780	44	420
90	770	43	410
89	760	42	410
88	750	41	400
87	730	40	390
86	730	39	390
85	720	38	380
84	710	37	380
83	700	36	370
82	700	35	370
81	690	34	360
80	680	33	360
79	670	32	350
78	660	31	350
77	650	30	340
76	640	29	340
75	630	28	330
74	620	27	330
73	610	26	320
72	610	25	320
71	600	24	310
70	590	23	300
69	580	22	300
68	570	21	290
67	570	20	290
66	560	19	280
65	550	18	280
64	550	17	270
63	540	16	260
62	530	15	260
61	520	14	250
60	520	13	240
59	510	12	240
58	500	11	230
57	500	10	220
56	490	9	220
55	490	8	210
54	480	7	200
53	470	6	200
52	470	5	200
51	460	4	200
50	450	3	200
49	450	2	200
48	440	1	200
		0	200
		– 1 through – 14	200

Reviewing Your Test Performance

After you have scored your test, you should take some time to consider the following points in relation to your performance on the test.

- *Did you run out of time before you reached the end of the test?*

  If you did, you may want to consider pacing yourself better. For example, you may have spent too much time working on one or two difficult questions. A better approach might have been to continue the test and return to those questions after you had attempted to answer the remaining questions on the test.

- *Did you take a long time reading the directions for the test?*

  The directions in this test are the same as or very similar to those in the SAT II: Writing Subject Tests now being administered. You will save time when you take the test if you become thoroughly familiar with them in advance.

- *How did you handle questions you were unsure of?*

  If you were able to eliminate one or more of the answer choices and you guessed from the remaining choices, then your approach probably worked to your advantage. On the other hand, omitting questions about which you have some knowledge or guessing answers haphazardly would probably be a mistake.

- *How difficult were the questions for you compared with other students who took the test?*

  By referring to Table MC.2, you can find out how difficult these questions were for the group of students who took this test in 1992. The right-hand column in the table tells you what percentage of this group answered each question correctly. A question that was answered correctly by almost everyone in the group is obviously an easy question. Question 22, for example, was answered correctly by 93 percent of the students in the sample. On the other hand, question 19 was answered correctly by only 26 percent.

  It is important to remember that these percentages are based on only one particular group of students; had this edition of the test been given to other groups of students at the time, the percentages would probably have been different.

The SAT II: Literature Subject Test

The SAT II: Literature Subject Test is designed to measure how well you have learned to read literature. It consists of approximately 60 multiple-choice questions based on six to eight reading selections, about half of which are poetry and half prose. The selections are complete short poems or excerpts from various works including longer poems, stories, novels, nonfiction writing, and drama. There is no prescribed or suggested reading list. You are not expected to have read or studied any of the particular poems or passages that appear on the test. Many of the questions require a high level of verbal ability, including reading comprehension and general sensitivity to language, but the test focuses on those interpretive skills necessary to read poetry and prose from different periods and cultures.

The questions on the test are based on selections from works written in English from the Renaissance to the present (see the chart to the right). Only works originally written in English are included. Each selection is followed by a set of questions. A set could contain as many as 12 or as few as 4 questions. Normally, several questions in each set ask about meaning, including effect and argument or theme, and about form: structure, genre, and method of organization (how one part develops from or differs from another). Where appropriate, the questions may consider the narrative voice (the characterization of the speaker, the possible distinction between the speaker and the author, the speaker's attitude) and the tone. If a character is represented, several questions may ask about the distinguishing traits of the character and the techniques by which the character is presented and the traits revealed. Still other questions may consider the characteristic use of language in the selection (imagery, figures of speech, diction). Questions also ask about the meanings of specific words, phrases, and lines in the context of the passage or poem. Some of these questions concern denotation and syntax, but most concern connotations and implications established by the particular language of the selection.

The best way to prepare for the test is close, critical reading in both English and American literature from a variety of historical periods and literary genres. This reading can be concentrated in a one-year course or spread out over several courses. In general, the greater the breadth and depth of your literary study, the better prepared you will be. The test seeks to measure your skill in reading literature, not your knowledge of the literary background of a period, the life of an author, or the critical opinions about a particular work. Extensive knowledge of literary terminology is not essential, but a good working knowledge of basic terminology ("speaker," "tone," "image," "irony," "alliteration," "stanza," etc.) is expected.

Basis for Questions on the Literature Test

	Approximate Percentage of Test*
Source of Questions	
English Literature	40-50
American Literature	40-50
Other Literature Written in English	0-10
Chronology	
Renaissance and 17th Century	30
18th and 19th Centuries	30
20th Century	40
Genre	
Poetry	45-50
Prose	45-50
Drama and Other	0-1C

*The distribution of passages may vary in different editions of the test. The chart above indicates typical or average content.

The Literature Subject Test included in this book contains 60 questions based on seven selections — a James Thurber fable, William Drummond's "This world a hunting is . . .," Gwendolyn Brooks's "Kitchenette Building," Erza Pound's "The Garden," Tobias Smollett's *The Adventures of Peregrine Pickle*, Nathaniel Hawthorne's *The Marble Faun*, and John Cheever's *The Wapshot Chronicle*. As frequently happens when tests are composed of lengthy sets of questions based on relatively few selections, the distribution of passages in a particular test differs somewhat from the typical or average content — the one summarized in the chart above. The test in this book, for example, contains more passages from American and twentieth-century literature than average, and none from plays.

Questions Used in the Test

All of the questions on the Literature Subject Test are five-choice completion questions, the type of question with which you are probably most familiar. This type of completion question can be posed as a complete statement ("Which of the following best describes the style of the passage?") or as an incomplete statement ("The style of the passage is best described as"). Each question on the Literature Subject Test can be categorized as one of three types — the regular multiple-choice question, the NOT or EXCEPT question, or the Roman numeral question. Most questions on the test are regular multiple-choice questions that ask you to select the best of the responses offered ("The tone of the poem is best described as") or to evaluate the relevance of the five responses offered, all of which may be at least partly true, and to select the one that is *most precise* or *most suitable* ("In the context of the passage, which of the following statements about character X is most accurate?"). In the NOT or EXCEPT question, you are given four appropriate choices and *one inappropriate* choice and must select the choice that is LEAST applicable to the situation described by the question ("All of the following statements about the diction of this poem are true EXCEPT").

The Roman numeral question is used occasionally to allow for the possibility of combinations of correct statements about a selection. In literary-analysis questions, it is sometimes desirable to phrase questions in a way that acknowledges that words or images have multiple meanings; such questions are meant to test your awareness of the richness and complexity of a poem or passage. In multiple-choice questions of this type, several statements labeled by Roman numerals are printed below the question. The statements are followed by five lettered choices, each of which consists of some combination of the Roman numerals that label the statements. You are asked to select the choice that gives the statement or the combination of statements that best answers the question. For this kind of question, you must evaluate each statement independently of the others in order to select the most appropriate combination. The answer to a question such as "Which of the following statements about the title of the poem is (are) true?" might be expressed by a choice such as "I, II, and IV only."

All of the questions on the Literature Subject Test are grouped into sets based on poems or prose passages. The number of questions in a set is related to the length and complexity of the passage or poem; a set usually consists of five to ten questions. The questions in a set approach the passage or poem in a logical sequence, but each question is designed to be independent of the others; that is, you do not have to answer one question correctly in order to answer subsequent questions correctly. The questions refer to the passage, not to the other questions. A set of questions often begins by asking about the setting or the speaker's situation, then about specific parts of the passage or poem, and concludes by asking about theme, tone, or structure.

Sample Questions

The James Merrill poem below and many of the questions that follow it are fairly easy; however, some of the other passages and questions used in the Literature Subject Test are likely to be more difficult.

James Merrill is a contemporary American poet; therefore, according to the Basis for Questions chart on the preceding page, all of the questions on this poem would be classified as American Literature, Twentieth Century, Poetry.

The directions used in the test book precede the poem.

Directions: This test consists of selections from literary works and questions on their content, form, and style. After reading each passage or poem, choose the best answer to each question and fill in the corresponding oval on the answer sheet.

Note: Pay particular attention to the requirement of questions that contain the words NOT, LEAST, or EXCEPT.

Questions 1-6. Read the following poem carefully before you choose your answers.

Kite Poem

"One is reminded of a certain person,"
Continued the parson, settling back in his chair
With a glass of port, "who sought to emulate
The sport of birds (it was something of a chore)
By climbing up on a kite. They found his coat
Two counties away; the man himself was missing."

His daughters tittered: it was meant to be a lesson
To them — they had been caught kissing, or some such nonsense,
The night before, under the crescent moon.
So, finishing his pheasant, their father began
This thirty-minute discourse ending with
A story improbable from the start. He paused for breath,

Having shown but a few of the dangers. However, the wind
Blew out the candles and the moon wrought changes
Which the daughters felt along their stockings. Then,
Thus persuaded, they fled to their young men
Waiting in the sweet night by the raspberry bed,
And kissed and kissed, as though to escape on a kite.

1. The attitude of the parson (line 2) toward the "certain person" (lines 1-6) is one of

(A) admiration
(B) anxiety
(C) disdain
(D) curiosity
(E) grief

Choice (C) is the correct response to this question. In order to warn his daughters of the danger of imprudent behavior, the parson uses the tale of the person who climbed up on a kite. It is unlikely, given this purpose, that he would feel either "admiration," "anxiety," "curiosity," or "grief" for the man, and nothing in the poem suggests that the parson had any of these feelings. His attitude is one of disdain for a person whose behavior he regards as foolish.

2. **The descriptive detail "settling back in his chair/ With a glass of port" (lines 2-3) underscores the parson's**

   (A) authority
   (B) complacency
   (C) hypocrisy
   (D) gentleness
   (E) indecisiveness

The poem suggests that the parson is a rather rigid, formal man given to lengthy moralizing. It can be inferred from the context that complacency is one element of his character; (B) is the correct response. There is no evidence in the poem that the parson is either hypocritical, gentle, or indecisive. Out of context, the quotation from the poem might be interpreted as behavior associated with someone in a position of authority. In context, however, the parson is more notable for his lack of authority — his daughters titter when he lectures and ignore his advice.

3. **The chief reason the parson's daughters "tittered" (line 7) is that they**

   (A) were embarrassed to have been caught kissing
   (B) knew where the missing man in their father's story was
   (C) wanted to flatter their father
   (D) did not take their father's lecture seriously
   (E) took cruel pleasure in the kite flyer's disaster

The most plausible explanation of why the daughters "tittered" is (D) — they did not take their father's lecture seriously. This view is supported by the daughters' actions — as soon as their father paused for breath, they did what his "thirty-minute discourse" warned them not to do. There is no indication in the poem that (B) or (E) is true, and if the daughters had wanted to flatter their father, as (C) claims, they certainly would not have tittered during his serious lecture. If (A) were true, it is unlikely that the daughters would have "fled to their young men" so quickly the second time.

4. **The speaker's tone suggests that the reader should regard the parson's "thirty-minute discourse" (line 11) as**

   (A) scholarly and enlightening
   (B) serious and important
   (C) entertaining and amusing
   (D) verbose and pedantic
   (E) grisly and morbid

The speaker's tone suggests that the reader should regard the parson's "thirty-minute discourse" as "verbose and pedantic," choice (D). The parson is presented as one who speaks at length, telling "improbable" stories and taking 30 minutes to show "but a few of the dangers" he wanted to warn his daughters about. He uses lengthy phrases such as "emulate/The sport of birds" when a simple verb such as "fly" would have sufficed. The parson might well have intended his discourse to seem "scholarly and enlightening," choice (A), and "serious and important," choice (B), but neither the daughters nor the speaker suggests that the parson succeeded, and the reader has no reason to assess the effectiveness of the discourse differently from the speaker and the daughters. The reader may be entertained and amused by the speaker's account of the discourse, but that response is not the same as being amused by the discourse itself, as (C) states. Choice (E) is implausible.

5. **The daughters are "persuaded" (line 16) by**

   (A) their own fear of danger
   (B) the fate of the kite flyer
   (C) their own natural impulses
   (D) the parson's authority
   (E) respect for their father

The daughters are "persuaded" by their own natural impulses," choice (C). According to the poem, "the moon wrought changes/Which the daughters felt along their stockings" (lines 14-15). These natural impulses were, ironically, more persuasive than the long discourse delivered by their father in an attempt to dissuade them. The daughters, like the kite flyer, are attracted to the possibility of "escape on a kite" (line 18) and are not deterred by solemn and tedious warnings of danger.

6. **All of the following are elements of opposition in the development of the poem EXCEPT**

   (A) indoors . . outdoors
   (B) talking . . kissing
   (C) caution . . adventure
   (D) work . . play
   (E) settling back . . flying

Choice (D) is the only opposition that is not evident in the poem. Actions such as "climbing up on a kite" and "kissing . . . under the crescent moon" might be regarded as forms of play, but the poem really does not offer any contrasting examples of work. (A), (B), (C), and (E) illustrate the contrasting actions and attitudes of the parson on the one hand and the daughters and/or the kite flyer on the other.

SAT II:

Literature Subject Test

The test that follows is representative of a typical SAT II: Literature Subject Test. It has already been administered. So that you may have an idea of what the national test administration will be like, try to take the test in this book under conditions as close as possible to those of the nationally administered test. It will probably help if you do the following.

- Set aside an hour for the test when you will not be interrupted, so that you can complete all of it in one sitting.
- Sit at a desk with no other papers or books. You can't take a dictionary, other books, or notes into the test room.
- Have a kitchen timer or clock in front of you for timing yourself.
- Tear out an answer sheet from the back of this book and fill it in just as you would on the day of the test. You can use one answer sheet for as many as three Subject Tests.
- Read the instructions that precede the test. When you take the test, you will be asked to read them before you begin answering questions.
- After you finish the test, read the sections on "How to Score the SAT II: Literature Subject Test" and "Reviewing Your Test Performance," which follow the test.

FORM 3EAC

LITERATURE TEST

The top portion of the section of the answer sheet that you will use in taking the Literature test must be filled in exactly as shown in the illustration below. Note carefully that you have to do all of the following on your answer sheet.

1. Print LITERATURE on the line under the words "Subject (print)."

2. In the shaded box labeled "Test Code" fill in four ovals:

   —Fill in oval 3 in the row labeled V.

   —Fill in oval 1 in the row labeled W.

   —Fill in oval 1 in the row labeled X.

   —Fill in oval D in the row labeled Y.

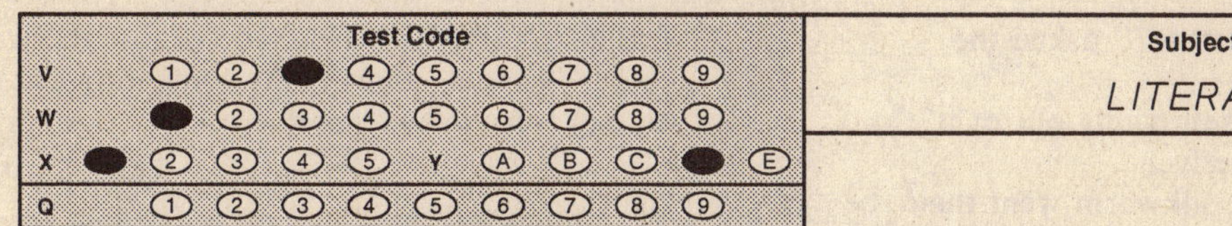

3. Please answer the two questions below by filling in the appropriate ovals in the row labeled Q on the answer sheet. The information you provide is for statistical purposes only and will not affect your score on the test.

Answer both questions on the basis of the authors and works read in your English classes in grade 10 to the present.

Question I

How many semesters of English courses that were predominantly devoted to the study of literature have you taken from grade 10 to the present? (If you are studying literature in the current semester, count the current semester as a full semester.) Fill in only one oval of ovals 1-3.

- One semester or less —Fill in oval 1.
- Two semesters —Fill in oval 2.
- Three semesters or more —Fill in oval 3.

Question II

Of the following, which content areas made up a significant part (at least 10 percent) of the literature you read in your English classes in grades 10-12 ? Fill in as many ovals as apply.

- British and/or North American writers writing before 1800 —Fill in oval 4.
- European writers in translation —Fill in oval 5.
- Black American writers —Fill in oval 6.
- Ethnic American writers (Hispanic American, Asian American, American Indian, etc.) —Fill in oval 7.
- Latin American writers in translation —Fill in oval 8.
- Writers from Africa or India writing in English —Fill in oval 9.

When the supervisor gives the signal, turn the page and begin the Literature test. There are 100 numbered ovals on the answer sheet and 60 questions in the Literature test. Therefore, use only ovals 1 to 60 for recording your answers.

LITERATURE TEST

Directions: This test consists of selections from literary works and questions on their content, form, and style. After reading each passage or poem, choose the best answer to each question and fill in the corresponding oval on the answer sheet.

Note: Pay particular attention to the requirement of questions that contain the words NOT, LEAST, or EXCEPT.

Questions 1-6. Read the following fable carefully before you choose your answers.

A weaver watched in wide-eyed wonder a silkworm spinning its cocoon in a white mulberry tree.

"Where do you get that stuff?" asked the admiring weaver.

"Do you want to make something out of it?" inquired the silkworm, eagerly.

Then the weaver and the silkworm went their separate ways, for each thought the other had insulted him. We live, man and worm, in a time when almost everything can mean almost anything, for this is the age of gobbledygook, doubletalk, and gudda.

MORAL: A word to the wise is not sufficient if it doesn't make any sense.

From *Further Fables for Our Time*, published by Simon & Schuster. © 1956 James Thurber. Originally printed in *The New Yorker*.

1. The central idea of the fable is the
   - (A) frequent failure of language as a means of communication
   - (B) unstable nature of casual relationships
   - (C) richness of language, even in everyday situations
   - (D) unwillingness of people to listen to each other
   - (E) possibility of misunderstanding in any relationship

2. The silkworm intended "make" (line 6) as a synonym for

   (A) imply (B) arrange (C) start (D) draw (E) weave

3. The characters were insulted because the words "stuff" (line 4) and "make something out of it" (line 6) were misinterpreted as
   - (A) "nonsense" and "cause a disturbance"
   - (B) "material" and "weave a garment from it"
   - (C) "junk" and "use it as a reason for a quarrel"
   - (D) "garbage" and "make a mountain out of a molehill"
   - (E) "rubbish" and "take it for your own use"

GO ON TO THE NEXT PAGE

4. The effect of the phrase "man and worm" (line 10) is to

   (A) suggest that the narrator is hostile toward the two characters
   (B) demonstrate that human language is appropriate for a wide variety of situations
   (C) emphasize the close relationship among all living creatures
   (D) indicate the narrator's concern for sophisticated and unsophisticated creatures
   (E) suggest the gently satiric attitude of the narrator

5. The primary reason that the misunderstanding between the two is ironic is that

   (A) weavers and silkworms seldom talk to each other in such a way
   (B) neither the weaver nor the silkworm means to be hostile
   (C) the silkworm is a creature that is useful to people
   (D) the weaver and the silkworm are not wise
   (E) the weaver and the silkworm are using language incorrectly

6. The misunderstanding between the two characters might have been prevented if they had paid more attention to

   (A) grammar
   (B) sentence structure
   (C) imagery
   (D) tone
   (E) alliteration

GO ON TO THE NEXT PAGE

Questions 7-15. Read the following poem carefully before you choose your answers.

This world a hunting is:
The prey, poor man; the Nimrod fierce is death;
His speedy greyhounds are
Lust, Sickness, Envy, Care,
Strife that ne'er falls amiss,
With all those ills which haunt us while we
breathe.
Now if, by chance, we fly
Of these the eager chase,
Old Age with stealing pace
Casts up his nets, and there we panting die.

7. The poem is concerned primarily with the

(A) gradual coming of old age
(B) different forms that death can take
(C) inevitability of death
(D) cruelty of hunting
(E) nature of disease

8. In the context of the poem as a whole, the speaker's attitude toward "poor man" (line 2) can best be described as

(A) condescending
(B) mocking
(C) dispassionate
(D) sympathetic
(E) deferential

9. From the context we can conclude that "Nimrod" (line 2) refers to a

(A) predatory animal
(B) famous hunter
(C) diabolical old man
(D) fearless soldier
(E) dangerous weapon

10. Which of the following changes is introduced in line 6 ?

(A) The greyhounds become even more threatening.
(B) Man's chief enemy changes from fierce greyhounds to physical disorders.
(C) The emphasis is placed on man's struggles to defeat the hunters.
(D) The multiplicity of man's ills is suggested.
(E) The impersonal "man" (line 2) becomes the more personal "we."

GO ON TO THE NEXT PAGE

11. What is the effect of "by chance" (line 7) ?
    - (A) It stresses man's ineffectualness in influencing his own fate.
    - (B) It weakens the speaker's analysis in lines 1-6.
    - (C) It marks a shift in the speaker's attitude toward the hunting.
    - (D) It introduces the theme of man's good fortune in escaping harm.
    - (E) It suggests that man can be the hunter as well as the hunted.

12. Which of the following best describes the relationship between lines 7-8 and the rest of the poem?
    - (A) They are even more pessimistic than the rest of the poem.
    - (B) They mark a major shift in mood.
    - (C) They heighten tension by allowing for a moment of false optimism.
    - (D) They echo the gloomy tone of the opening lines.
    - (E) They reveal the speaker's complacency.

13. What is the effect of the personification of "Old Age" (lines 9-10) ?
    - (A) The essentially human qualities of aging are emphasized.
    - (B) A time of life is made especially threatening by depicting it as a determined enemy.
    - (C) The identity of "Nimrod" (line 2) becomes clearer.
    - (D) Old age fights against the allegorical greyhounds in the series "Lust, Sickness, Envy, Care,/Strife" (lines 4-5).
    - (E) Old age is rendered consolingly familiar and comprehensible by making it human.

14. In its context, "stealing" (line 9) suggests that old age is
    - (A) sluggish and grasping
    - (B) dishonest and mean
    - (C) sadistic and vicious
    - (D) slow and stealthy
    - (E) subtle and complex

15. Which of the following pairs of words does NOT correctly illustrate the contrast in content between the two parts of the poem (lines 1-6 and lines 7-10) ?
    - (A) "man" (line 2) and "Old Age" (line 9)
    - (B) "Nimrod" (line 2) and "Old Age" (line 9)
    - (C) "speedy" (line 3) and "stealing" (line 9)
    - (D) "greyhounds" (line 3) and "nets" (line 10)
    - (E) "we breathe" (line 6) and "we panting die" (line 10)

GO ON TO THE NEXT PAGE

Questions 16-26. Read the following passage carefully before you choose your answers.

Miss Sally Appleby,

Madam,

Understanding you have a parcel of heart, warranted sound, to be disposed of, shall be willing to treat for said commodity, on reasonable terms; doubt not, shall agree for same; shall wait of you for further information, when and where you shall appoint. This the needful from

Yours etc.

Gam. Pickle

This laconic epistle, simple and unadorned as it was, met with as cordial a reception from the person to whom it was addressed, as if it had been couched in the most elegant terms that delicacy of passion and cultivated genius could supply; nay, I believe, was the more welcome on account of its mercantile plainness; because when an advantageous match is in view, a sensible woman often considers the flowery professions and rapturous exclamations of love as ensnaring ambiguities, or at best impertinent preliminaries, that retard the treaty they are designed to promote; whereas Mr. Pickle removed all disagreeable uncertainty by descending at once to the most interesting particular.

16. It can be inferred from his letter that Pickle is

(A) a cold-hearted exploiter
(B) a lover too shy to say what he means
(C) an arrogant snob
(D) a man too rushed to enjoy life
(E) a thoroughgoing pragmatist

17. All of the following are true of the letter EXCEPT that its

(A) opening and closing courtesies suggest that the two people may not be well acquainted
(B) avoidance of the pronoun "I" makes it seem impersonal
(C) tone is insincere
(D) clipped phrases sound hurried
(E) purpose is practical

18. The narrator's comments (lines 12-27) about the letter are designed to

(A) dispel any favorable impression the reader might have of Pickle
(B) confirm the reader's expectation that Sally Appleby would be insulted by the letter
(C) distract the reader from the letter's offensive tone
(D) show the superiority of the narrator's taste to that of Pickle or Sally Appleby
(E) indicate that the letter is more appropriate than it might seem

GO ON TO THE NEXT PAGE

19. According to the narrator, Miss Appleby's reaction to the letter makes clear that she values

(A) success over happiness
(B) directness over decoration
(C) humility over assertiveness
(D) style over substance
(E) her welfare over that of others

20. The phrase "delicacy of passion" (line 16) means

(A) refinement of feeling
(B) concealment of emotion
(C) shyness and coyness
(D) feeble affection
(E) witty expression

21. The statement made in lines 18-24 is presented in which of the following ways?

(A) As a general truth that helps the reader understand the incident
(B) As a controversial statement requiring closer examination
(C) As an excuse made up by Pickle for his unconventional behavior
(D) As a cynical observation made by the narrator
(E) As a belief held by the rich, but not by the poor

22. As used by the narrator, the effect of such phrases as "elegant terms" (line 15), "delicacy of passion" (line 16), "flowery professions" (lines 20-21), and "rapturous exclamations" (line 21) is to

(A) indicate the narrator's appreciation of true love letters
(B) stress the narrator's contempt for emotion
(C) satirize the language of conventional love
(D) reveal the deeply sentimental nature of language
(E) mock Pickle's futile attempt at fine language

23. Which of the following best describes the effect of the words "advantageous" (line 19), "match" (line 19), "treaty" (line 23), and "promote" (line 24) ?

(A) They imply that the commercialism of marriage is degrading.
(B) They provide a contrast to the phrase "mercantile plainness" (line 18).
(C) They suggest that marriage is like a sporting contest.
(D) They echo the commercial and legal metaphors of Pickle's letter.
(E) They elaborate on the analogy between marital and international strife.

24. As it is used in the passage, the word "impertinent" (line 22) means

(A) distressing (B) rude (C) exaggerated (D) critical (E) irrelevant

25. The "most interesting particular" (lines 26-27) is best understood as a

(A) consummation of the marriage
(B) proposed marriage settlement
(C) date for the marriage
(D) token of eternal love
(E) reconciliation of the two lovers

26. The narrator's attitude toward a sensible woman's considerations in regard to marriage is best described as

(A) heavily ironic
(B) bitterly disapproving
(C) strongly defensive
(D) gently satirical
(E) somewhat shocked

GO ON TO THE NEXT PAGE

Questions 27-35. Read the following poem carefully before you choose your answers.

Kitchenette Building

We are things of dry hours and the involuntary plan,
Grayed in, and gray. "Dream" makes a giddy sound, not strong
Like "rent," "feeding a wife," "satisfying a man."

But could a dream send up through onion fumes
Its white and violet, fight with fried potatoes
And yesterday's garbage ripening in the hall,
Flutter, or sing an aria down these rooms

Even if we were willing to let it in,
Had time to warm it, keep it very clean,
Anticipate a message, let it begin?

We wonder. But not well! not for a minute!
Since Number Five is out of the bathroom now,
We think of lukewarm water, hope to get in it.

27. The best paraphrase of "dry hours" (line 1) is

(A) summer drought
(B) fruitless existence
(C) chronic fatigue
(D) sudden misfortune
(E) orderly lives

28. The kind of paradox in the phrase "involuntary plan" (line 1) most closely resembles that in which of the following?

(A) Careful disorder
(B) Spontaneous combustion
(C) Dangerous hobby
(D) Secret agreement
(E) Irrelevant information

29. As it is used in the poem, "giddy" (line 2) can be understood in all of the following senses EXCEPT

(A) dizzy (B) flighty (C) ephemeral (D) impractical (E) raucous

30. In the context of the poem, the opposition of "white and violet" (line 5) to "Grayed in, and gray" (line 2) suggests all of the following contrasts EXCEPT the

(A) attractiveness of dreams and the dullness of reality
(B) varied nature of dreams and the monotonous nature of routine duties
(C) purity and intensity of abstractions and the dinginess of concreteness
(D) beauty of the outside world and the drabness of the apartment
(E) poetic and the prosaic

GO ON TO THE NEXT PAGE

31. An aria (line 7) is unlikely to be heard because

(A) the speaker is too poor to attend the opera
(B) the speaker does not like loud or giddy noises
(C) the speaker is too tired to listen to music
(D) it would not be a pleasant diversion from the daily routine
(E) it would be too weak to compete with the sordidness of daily life

32. Lines 8-9 refer to the dream as though it were a

(A) dangerous vagrant
(B) valuable possession
(C) distant relative
(D) young creature requiring care
(E) mysterious but beneficent force

33. The primary effect of the change of tempo in line 11 is to suggest that the speaker

(A) is putting aside the temptation to dream and returning to the reality at hand
(B) is excited by the possibilities she has just imagined
(C) is unaccustomed to sustaining a pessimistic mood for any length of time
(D) is angry because she has missed the opportunity to get hot water
(E) recognizes the need for haste in finishing the chores so that important decisions can be made

34. The "onion fumes" (line 4), "garbage" (line 6), and "lukewarm water" (line 13) help to indicate that the

(A) speaker is indifferent to housekeeping
(B) speaker does not like the finer things in life
(C) speaker's life is ruled by necessities
(D) speaker's senses are very acute
(E) speaker is afraid of change and excitement

35. In this poem, the sequence "dream" (line 2) to "wonder" (line 11) to "hope" (line 13) emphasizes a progression from the

(A) divine to the profane
(B) improbable to the attainable
(C) permanent to the transient
(D) unpleasant to the pleasant
(E) present to the future

GO ON TO THE NEXT PAGE

Questions 36-44. Read the following passage carefully before you choose your answers.

Other faces there were, too, of men who (if the brevity of their remembrance, after death, can be augured from their little value in life) should have been represented in snow rather than marble. Posterity will be puzzled what to do with busts like these, the concretions and petrifactions of a vain self-estimate; but will find, no doubt, that they serve to build into stone walls, or burn into quicklime, as well as if the marble had never been blocked into the guise of human heads.

But it is an awful thing, indeed, this endless endurance, this almost indestructibility, of a marble bust! Whether in our own case, or that of other men, it bids us sadly measure the little, little time during which our lineaments are likely to be of interest to any human being. It is especially singular that Americans should care about perpetuating themselves in this mode. The brief duration of our families, as a hereditary household, renders it next to a certainty that the great-grandchildren will not know their father's grandfather, and that half a century hence, at furthest, the hammer of the auctioneer will thump its knockdown blow against his blockhead, sold at so much for the pound of stone! And it ought to make us shiver, the idea of leaving our features to be a dusty-white ghost among strangers of another generation, who will take our nose between their thumb and fingers (as we have seen men do by Caesar's), and infallibly break it off if they can do so without detection!

36. In this passage, marble busts become symbolic of

(A) man's foolish attempts to transcend time
(B) the extravagant aspirations of the artist
(C) the loneliness of man in his own time
(D) the hardness of man's heart
(E) nature's triumph over civilization

37. The "other faces" mentioned in line 1 should have been represented in snow because they

(A) were cold-hearted and arrogant
(B) did not wish to be remembered
(C) failed to remember their friends
(D) did not merit a permanent memorial
(E) were not respected by their friends

38. The speaker's tone in lines 7-11 is best described as

(A) arrogant and patronizing
(B) shocked and indignant
(C) mildly disappointed
(D) reluctantly approving
(E) contemptuously ironic

GO ON TO THE NEXT PAGE

39. As it is used in line 26, the word "blockhead" functions as a

(A) play on words
(B) literary allusion
(C) reference to the sculptor
(D) nonsense word
(E) paradoxical term

40. In the second paragraph, the speaker implies that American families are characterized by their

(A) contempt for foreigners
(B) lack of interest in their own past
(C) indifference to fine works of art
(D) overindulgence of their children and grandchildren
(E) eagerness to acquire and exhibit wealth

41. The "shiver" described in line 27 is occasioned by

(A) the coldness of our graves
(B) fear of the disrespect of those who come after us
(C) apprehension about what our ghosts will do
(D) horror at the corruption of our bodies
(E) the knowlege that we must come to dust

42. As it is used in line 28, the image of the ghost suggests something that is

(A) pitiful (B) ominous (C) vindictive (D) restless (E) ageless

43. In the second paragraph, the speaker characterizes posterity as

(A) pious (B) resentful (C) frugal (D) impudent (E) industrious

44. According to the passage, which of the following properties of marble is most important to those who have busts of themselves made?

(A) Beauty (B) Translucence (C) Usefulness (D) Coldness (E) Durability

GO ON TO THE NEXT PAGE

Questions 45-52. Read the following poem carefully before you choose your answers.

The Garden

En robe de parade.
Samain

Like a skein of loose silk blown against a wall
She walks by the railing of a path in Kensington Gardens,
And she is dying piece-meal
of a sort of emotional anaemia.

And round about there is a rabble
Of the filthy, sturdy, unkillable infants of the very poor.
They shall inherit the earth.

In her is the end of breeding.
Her boredom is exquisite and excessive.
She would like some one to speak to her,
And is almost afraid that I
will commit that indiscretion.

45. The woman in the poem is best described as a

(A) lonely social outcast
(B) feeble but kindly elderly woman
(C) devitalized aristocrat
(D) determined and ambitious social climber
(E) person who has lost her inherited money

46. Which of the following best represents the relationship between "she" in lines 1-4 and "infants" in lines 5-7 ?

(A) "skein" (line 1) and "poor" (line 6)
(B) "walks" (line 2) and "inherit" (line 7)
(C) "Kensington Gardens" (line 2) and "the earth" (line 7)
(D) "dying" (line 3) and "unkillable" (line 6)
(E) "piece-meal" (line 3) and "filthy" (line 6)

47. What is the effect of using the word "infants" (line 6) rather than "children" or simply "the very poor"?

(A) To suggest that "They" (line 7) seem particularly vulnerable and pathetic to "her" (line 8)
(B) To stress "her" (line 8) maternal sympathies
(C) To indicate that "They" (line 7) will be irresponsible in governing the earth they will eventually inherit
(D) To symbolize the universality of the problem of poverty
(E) To link the word to "inherit" (line 7) by alliteration

GO ON TO THE NEXT PAGE

48. Given the context of the poem, the poor are most likely to inherit the earth because they

(A) have been promised it
(B) are determined to have it
(C) are the only ones willing to accept it
(D) are stronger than those who control it now
(E) are the legal heirs of the present owners

49. In its context, the phrase "end of breeding" (line 8) conveys which of the following ideas?

I. Result of centuries of privilege
II. Epitome of refined manners
III. Termination of reproduction

(A) I only (B) II only (C) III only (D) I and II only (E) I, II, and III

50. "I" (line 11) can best be described as

(A) the critical observer
(B) a sympathetic friend
(C) her would-be lover
(D) a social activist
(E) a social snob

51. The attitude of "She" (line 10) toward "I" (line 11) is best described as

(A) hostile (B) ambivalent (C) indifferent (D) curious (E) receptive

52. In this poem, the woman functions as which of the following?

I. A symbol of the emptiness of modern life
II. The representative of a social class
III. The personification of the power of love

(A) I only (B) II only (C) I and III only (D) II and III only (E) I, II, and III

GO ON TO THE NEXT PAGE

Questions 53-60. Read the following passage carefully before you choose your answers.

But Leander got the last word. Opening Aaron's copy of Shakespeare, after it had begun to rain, Coverly found the place marked with a note in his father's hand. "Advice to my sons," it read. "Never put whisky into hot water bottle crossing borders of dry states or countries. Rubber will spoil taste. Never make love with pants on. Beer on whisky, very risky. Whisky on beer, never fear. Never eat apples, peaches, pears, etc., while drinking whisky except long French-style dinners, terminating with fruit. Other viands have mollifying effect. Never sleep in moonlight. Known by scientists to induce madness. Should bed stand beside window on clear night draw shades before retiring. Never hold cigar at right angles to fingers. Hayseed. Hold cigar at diagonal. Remove band or not as you prefer. Never wear red necktie. Provide light snorts for ladies if entertaining. Effects of harder stuff on frail sex sometimes disastrous. Bathe in cold water every morning. Painful but exhilarating. Also reduces horniness. Have haircut once a week. Wear dark clothes after 6 p.m. Eat fresh fish for breakfast when available. Avoid kneeling in unheated stone churches. Ecclesiastical dampness causes prematurely gray hair. Fear tastes like a rusty knife and do not let her into your house. Courage tastes of blood. Stand up straight. Admire the world. Relish the love of a gentle woman. Trust in the Lord."

53. With which of the following is Leander's advice most concerned?

(A) Practical knowledge and sensible living
(B) Fortitude and salvation
(C) Accomplishment and material success
(D) Determination and moral rectitude
(E) Wit and serenity

54. The first sentence suggests that the

(A) sons tried to be unlike their father in every way they could
(B) father was never able to communicate with his sons
(C) father was never more profound than in his note
(D) sons exercised great control over their own lives
(E) sons and father debated about the conduct of the sons' lives

55. The humor of the advice given in lines 5-7 ("Never. . . taste") depends primarily on the fact that Leander

(A) is aware that his sons enjoy whisky
(B) thinks it likely that his sons have hot water bottles
(C) assumes that his sons will be traveling
(D) assumes that his sons' cars will be searched
(E) is unconcerned about his sons' breaking the law

GO ON TO THE NEXT PAGE

56. Which of the following pieces of advice is most probably based on superstition?

(A) "Never make love with pants on." (lines 7-8)
(B) "Never eat [fruit] while drinking whisky." (lines 9-10)
(C) "Never sleep in moonlight." (lines 12-13)
(D) "Never hold cigar at right angles to fingers." (lines 15-16)
(E) "Bathe in cold water every morning." (line 21)

57. Which of the following pairs best points up the contrast in levels of diction in the passage?

(A) "viands" (line 12).."snorts" (line 19)
(B) "mollifying" (line 12).."entertaining" (line 19)
(C) "sleep" (line 12).."retiring" (line 15)
(D) "Painful" (line 21).."exhilarating" (line 22)
(E) "Fear" (line 27).."Courage" (line 29)

58. Leander's comment "Hayseed" (line 16) suggests that

(A) Leander has a favorite brand of cigar
(B) Leander thinks it undignified for gentlemen to smoke
(C) holding a cigar at right angles is a hazard
(D) holding a cigar at right angles is unrefined
(E) holding a cigar at right angles indicates aggressiveness

59. Leander writes, "Fear tastes like a rusty knife and do not let her into your house. Courage tastes of blood" (lines 27-29). All of the following are true of these sentences EXCEPT:

(A) They are metaphorical.
(B) They summarize the rest of the passage.
(C) They are aphoristic.
(D) They are abstractions following many specific and concrete statements.
(E) They serve as a transition to the serious closing statements.

60. Which of the following best characterizes the language in which Leander's advice is conveyed?

(A) Concise syntax
(B) Abundance of metaphors
(C) Florid diction
(D) Coherent organization
(E) Regular rhythm

S T O P

IF YOU FINISH BEFORE TIME IS CALLED, YOU MAY CHECK YOUR WORK ON THIS TEST ONLY. DO NOT WORK ON ANY OTHER TEST IN THIS BOOK.

How to Score the SAT II: Literature Subject Test

When you take the Literature Subject Test, your answer sheet will be "read" by a scanning machine that will record your responses to each question. Then a computer will compare your answers with the correct answers and produce your raw score. You get one point for each correct answer. For each wrong answer, you lose one-fourth of a point. Questions you omit (and any for which you mark more than one answer) are not counted. This raw score is converted to a College Board scaled score that is reported to you and to the college you specify. After you have taken this test, you can get an idea of what your score might be by following the instructions in the next two sections.

FINDING YOUR RAW TEST SCORE	
Step 1:	Table A lists the correct answers for all the questions on the SAT II: Literature Subject Test that is reproduced in this book. It also serves as a worksheet for you to calculate your raw score. • Compare your answers with those given in the table. • Put a check in the column marked "Right" if your answer is correct. • Put a check in the column marked "Wrong" if your answer is incorrect. • Leave both columns blank if you omitted the question.
Step 2:	Count the number of right answers and enter the total here: .... ________
Step 3:	Count the number of wrong answers and enter the total here: ...... ________
Step 4:	Divide the number of wrong answers by 4 and enter the result here: .... ________
Step 5:	Subtract the result obtained in Step 4 from the total you obtained in Step 2. Enter the result here: .... ________
Step 6:	Round the number obtained in Step 5 to the nearest whole number. Enter the result here: .... ________
The number you obtained in Step 6 is your raw score.	

TABLE A

Answers to the SAT II: Literature Subject Test, Form 3EAC, and Percentage of Students Answering Each Question Correctly

Question Number	Correct Answer	Right	Wrong	Percentage of Students Answering the Question Correctly*	Question Number	Correct Answer	Right	Wrong	Percentage of Students Answering the Question Correctly*
1	A			66	31	E			73
2	E			76	32	D			70
3	C			84	33	A			86
4	E			51	34	C			65
5	B			86	35	B			69
6	D			51	36	A			80
7	C			73	37	D			78
8	D			66	38	E			51
9	B			50	39	A			70
10	E			68	40	B			83
11	A			57	41	B			77
12	C			78	42	A			47
13	B			54	43	D			37
14	D			59	44	E			73
15	A			40	45	C			50
16	E			37	46	D			67
17	C			51	47	E			11
18	E			81	48	D			46
19	B			76	49	E			23
20	A			53	50	A			63
21	A			56	51	B			40
22	C			63	52	B			42
23	D			49	53	A			59
24	E			72	54	E			54
25	B			55	55	E			40
26	D			56	56	C			85
27	B			61	57	A			48
28	A			50	58	D			48
29	E			56	59	B			51
30	D			33	60	A			33

*These percentages are based on the analysis of the answer sheets for a random sample of 2,845 students who took this test in December 1982 and whose mean score was 523. They may be used as an indication of the relative difficulty of a particular question. Each percentage may also be used to predict the likelihood that a typical SAT II: Literature Subject Test candidate will answer correctly that question on this edition of this test.

Finding Your College Board Scaled Score

When you take SAT II: Subject Tests, the scores sent to the colleges you specify are reported on the College Board scale, which ranges from 200 to 800. You can convert your practice test score to a scaled score by using Table B. To find your scaled score, locate your raw score in the left-hand column of Table B; the corresponding score in the right-hand column is your College Board scaled score. For example, a raw score of 40 on this particular edition of the SAT II: Literature Subject Test corresponds to a College Board scaled score of 610.

Raw scores are converted to scaled scores to ensure that a score earned on any one edition of a particular Subject Test is comparable to the same scaled score earned on any other edition of the same Subject Test. Because some editions of tests may be slightly easier or more difficult than others, College Board scaled scores are adjusted so that they indicate the same level of performance regardless of the edition of the test taken and the ability of the group that takes it. Thus, for example, a score of 400 on one edition of a test taken at a particular administration indicates the same level of achievement as a score of 400 on a different edition of the test taken at a different administration.

When you take the SAT II: Subject Tests during a national administration, your scores are likely to differ somewhat from the scores you obtain on the tests in this book. People perform at different levels at different times for reasons unrelated to the tests themselves. The precision of any test is also limited because it represents only a sample of all the possible questions that could be asked.

TABLE B

Score Conversion Table
Literature Subject Test, Form 3EAC

Raw Score	College Board Scaled Score	Raw Score	College Board Scaled Score
60	800	25	480
59	780	24	470
58	770	23	470
57	760	22	460
56	750	21	450
55	740	20	440
54	730	19	430
53	720	18	420
52	710	17	420
51	700	16	410
50	690	15	400
49	680	14	390
48	670	13	380
47	660	12	370
46	660	11	370
45	650	10	360
44	640	9	350
43	630	8	340
42	620	7	330
41	620	6	320
40	610	5	320
39	600	4	310
38	590	3	300
37	580	2	290
36	570	1	280
35	570	0	270
34	560	−1	270
33	550	−2	260
32	540	−3	250
31	530	−4	240
30	520	−5	230
29	520	−6	220
28	510	−7	220
27	500	−8	210
26	490	−9 through −15	200

Reviewing Your Test Performance

After you have scored your test, you should take some time to consider the following points in relation to your performance on the test.

- *Did you run out of time before you reached the end of the test?*

  If you did, you may want to consider pacing yourself better. For example, you may have spent too much time working on one or two difficult questions. A better approach might have been to continue the test and return to those questions after you had attempted to answer the remaining questions on the test.

- *Did you take a long time reading the directions for the test?*

  The directions in this test are the same as those in the Literature Subject Tests now being administered. You will save time when you take the test if you become thoroughly familiar with them in advance.

- *How did you handle questions you were unsure of?*

  If you were able to eliminate one or more of the answer choices and you guessed from the remaining choices, then your approach probably worked to your advantage. On the other hand, omitting questions about which you have some knowledge or guessing answers haphazardly would probably be a mistake.

- *How difficult were the questions for you compared with other students who took the test?*

  By referring to Table A, you can find out how difficult each question was for the group of students who took this test. The right-hand column in the table tells you what percentage of this group answered the question correctly. A question that was answered correctly by almost everyone in the group is obviously an easy question. Question 5, for example, was answered correctly by 86 percent of the students in the sample. On the other hand, question 16 was answered correctly by only 37 percent.

  It is important to remember that these percentages are based on only one particular group of students; had this edition of the test been given to other groups of students at that time, the percentages would probably have been different.

  If you find that you missed several questions that would be considered easy, you may want to review those questions carefully. They may cover some aspect of the subject that you need to review. Perhaps you misunderstood the directions for one part of the test or you thought the questions were so easy that you did not spend as much time on them as you might have.

The SAT II: American History and Social Studies Subject Test

The SAT II: American History and Social Studies Subject Test consists of 90-95 multiple-choice questions. Its principal emphasis is on American history from pre-Columbian times to the present. A lesser emphasis is placed on basic social science concepts, methods, and generalizations as they are found in the study of history. The questions cover political, economic, social, intellectual, and cultural history as well as foreign policy. The test content and approximate percentages of questions covering that content are given below.

Content of the Test

Material Covered	Approximate Percentage of Test
Political History	32-36
Economic History	18-20
Social History	18-22
Intellectual and Cultural History	10-12
Foreign Policy	13-17
Social science concepts, methods and generalizations are incorporated in the material above.	

Periods Covered	
Pre-Columbian history to 1789	20
1790 to 1898	40
1899 to the present	40

Most of the test questions are based on material commonly taught in American history courses in secondary schools, although some of the material may be covered in other social studies courses. Knowledge gained from these courses or from outside reading could be helpful; however, the only essential preparation is a sound, one-year course in American history at the college-preparatory level. No one textbook or method of instruction is considered better than another. You can use a variety of approaches to content and chronology, including in-depth studies of limited topics, provided you do not ignore large historical periods and fundamental subject-matter areas.

Questions Used in the Test

The types of questions used in the test and the abilities they measure are described below. These abilities should not be thought of as mutually exclusive, since many questions test several abilities at the same time. Questions may be presented as separate items or in sets based on quotations, maps, pictures, graphs, or tables.

Directions: Each of the questions or incomplete statements below is followed by five suggested answers or completions. Select the one that is best in each case and then fill in the corresponding oval on the answer sheet.

Some questions require you to know facts, terms, concepts, and generalizations. They test your recall of basic information and your understanding of significant aspects of American history and the social studies. Question 1 is a sample of this type.

1. All of the following statements about the Puritans in seventeenth-century New England are true EXCEPT:

(A) They were a highly religious people who believed in predestination.
(B) They were tolerant of other religions and encouraged religious diversity.
(C) They preferred to be governed by local rather than by distant government authorities.
(D) They were primarily farmers, although some of them enjoyed considerable commercial success.
(E) They used slaves primarily as household servants rather than as farm laborers.

This question asks you to identify the exception in a series of otherwise true statements. Familiarity with the Puritans and knowledge of the Puritans' treatment of religious dissenters such as Anne Hutchinson and Roger Williams should lead you to (B), a statement that is not true, as the answer.

Questions posed in the negative, such as the one discussed above, occur in the test but never account for more than 25 percent of the test questions. Variations of this question format employ the capitalized words NOT or LEAST, as in the following examples: "Which of the following is NOT true?" "Which of the following is LEAST likely to occur?"

Some questions require you to analyze and interpret materials. Question 2, based on a chart, illustrates a question that tests your ability to analyze and interpolate.

POPULAR VOTE FOR PRESIDENTIAL ELECTORS, GEORGIA, 1848 AND 1852

	Democratic Electors	Whig Electors	Webster Electors
1848	44,809	47,538	——
1852	40,516	16,660	5,324

2. Using the table above, one might conclude that the most plausible explanation for the Georgia Democrats' victory in 1852, following their defeat in 1848, was that

(A) many new voters increased the turnout in 1852, to the advantage of the Democrats
(B) many voters abstained from voting in 1852, to the disadvantage of the Whigs
(C) Webster, who had not run in 1848, drew sufficient votes from the Whigs to cost them the election of 1852
(D) the Democrats, who had run a highly unpopular candidate in 1848, ran a highly popular candidate in 1852
(E) the Democrats cast fraudulent ballots to increase their share of the votes in 1852

To answer question 2, you must analyze the electoral data given for 1848 and 1852, noting that the voter turnout dropped dramatically in 1852 and that the Whigs suffered a much larger decline in voter turnout than did the Democrats. As a consequence, the Whigs lost their majority position. Options A, C, D, and E are not logically consistent with this data. For example, option C is incorrect because the table shows that the Democratic Electors received more votes than the Whig and Webster Electors combined. Option (B) is the correct answer because it is the only plausible explanation for the change in the fortunes of the Georgia Democrats.

Other questions test both your ability to analyze material as well as your ability to recall information related to the materials, or to make inferences and interpolations based on the material. Questions 3, 4, 5, and 6 are illustrations of questions that test a combination of interpretation and recall.

3. "What is man born for but to be a reformer, a remaker of what man has made; a renouncer of lies; a restorer of truth and good, imitating that great Nature which embosoms us all, and which sleeps no moment on an old past, but every hour repairs herself, yielding every morning a new day, and with every pulsation a new life?"

These sentiments are most characteristic of

(A) fundamentalism
(B) Social Darwinism
(C) pragmatism
(D) neoorthodoxy
(E) transcendentalism

Several elements in the quotation suggest which option is the correct answer. The emphasis that the quotation places on reform, on nature as a source of moral truth, and on the infinite possibilities open to people mark it as an example of the thought of the transcendentalist movement. This combination of elements is not pertinent to any of the other choices. Even if you do not know the source of the material, your understanding of the nature of transcendentalism should lead you to choose (E), the correct answer.

Questions 4-5 refer to the following map.

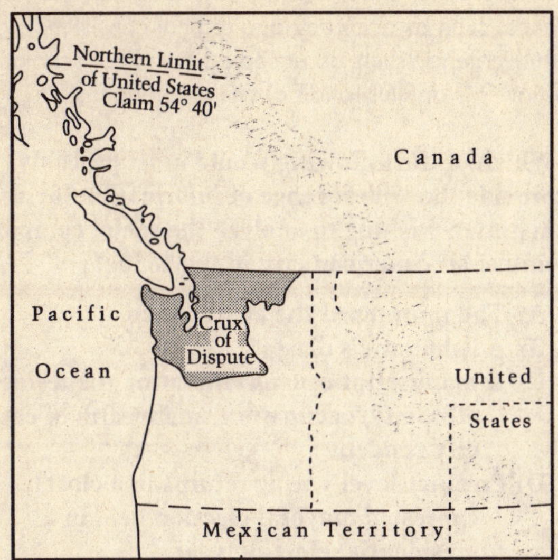

4. **The controversy with Great Britain over control of the shaded section was settled during the presidency of**

   (A) John Quincy Adams
   (B) James K. Polk
   (C) Franklin Pierce
   (D) James Buchanan
   (E) Andrew Johnson

5. **To the northwest of the area shown on the map is a continental territory purchased by Secretary of State William H. Seward from**

   (A) Great Britain
   (B) Canada
   (C) Russia
   (D) France
   (E) Spain

To answer question 4, you must interpret the map and recognize the shaded section as part of the Oregon territory. Since the Oregon dispute with Great Britain was settled during the presidency of James K. Polk, choice (B) is the correct answer.

To answer question 5, you must go beyond the content of the map in order to determine that the territory referred to in the question is Alaska. If you recall that Secretary of State Seward purchased the territory from Russia in 1867, you can choose the correct answer, (C).

Courtesy of the New-York Historical Society

6. **The point of view expressed by this cartoon would probably have met with the approval of**

   (A) Daniel Webster
   (B) James K. Polk
   (C) Martin Van Buren
   (D) Roger B. Taney
   (E) Stephen A. Douglas

To answer question 6, you must first note the anti-Jackson tone of the cartoon, which portrays King Andrew the First trampling the Constitution of the United States. You must then decide which of the choices given opposed Jackson's use of the veto to return important bills to Congress. Only the Whig Daniel Webster fits that description. The others were Democrats who either supported Andrew Jackson or were politically active at a later time.

Some questions require you to select or relate hypotheses, concepts, principles, or generalizations to given data. The questions may begin with concrete specifics and ask for the appropriate concept, or they may begin with a concept and apply it to particular problems or situations. Thus, you may need to use inductive and deductive reasoning. Questions 7 and 8 are examples of questions in this category.

7. **From 1870 to 1930, the trend in industry was for hours to be generally reduced, while both money wages and real wages rose. What factor was primarily responsible for this trend?**

   (A) A reduction in profit margins
   (B) Minimum wage laws
   (C) Restriction of the labor supply
   (D) Increased output per hour of work
   (E) Right-to-work legislation

The best answer to this question is choice (D). To arrive at this answer, you must be aware that the trend referred to in the question came about primarily because of technological advances that resulted in increased productivity. None of the other answer choices satisfactorily accounts for all the conditions described in the question.

8. **Which of the following wars of the United States would fit the description of a war neither lost nor won?**

   I. The War of 1812
   II. The Mexican War
   III. The Spanish-American War
   IV. The Second World War

   (A) I only
   (B) II only
   (C) I and III only
   (D) II and IV only
   (E) III and IV only

In answering question 8, you must recognize that a war not won, though not necessarily lost, is one in which a country either fails to achieve clear victory on the battlefield or fails to sign a peace treaty that is definitive and fulfills its goals. Only the War of 1812 is an illustration of the kind of war defined by the question. That war was ended by The Treaty of Ghent, which provided for the *Status quo ante bellum*, or a return to things as they had been before the war. Thus, (A) is the best answer.

Some questions require you to judge the value of data for a given purpose, either basing your judgment on internal evidence, such as accuracy and logical consistency, or on external criteria, such as accepted historical scholarship. Question 9 is an illustration of this kind of question.

9. **Which of the following would most probably provide the widest range of information for a historian wishing to analyze the social composition of an American city in the 1880s?**

   (A) The minutes of the city council
   (B) A debutante's diary
   (C) A manuscript census tabulating the residence, ethnicity, occupation, and wealth of each city resident
   (D) Precinct-level voting returns in a closely contested mayoral election held in a presidential election year
   (E) A survey of slum housing conditions carried out by a Social Gospel minister in the year following several epidemics

In answering this question, you must be able to eliminate from consideration choices that offer information about the city that is either irrelevant or less relevant than other options to understanding the social composition of the city (options A and D). You must also eliminate choices that offer relevant information but are limited to a particular section of the population of the city (options B and E). Option (C), the correct answer, contains the widest range of information about the social composition of a city.

SAT II:

American History and Social Studies Subject Test

The test that follows is representative of a typical SAT II: American History and Social Studies Subject Test. So that you may have an idea of what the national test administration will be like, try to take the test in this book under conditions as close as possible to those of the nationally administered test. It will probably help if you do the following.

- Set aside an hour for the test when you will not be interrupted, so that you can complete all of it in one sitting.
- Sit at a desk with no other papers or books. You can't take a dictionary, other books, or notes into the test room.
- Have a kitchen timer or clock in front of you for timing yourself.
- Tear out an answer sheet from the back of this book and fill it in just as you would on the day of the test. You can use one answer sheet for as many as three Subject Tests.
- Read the instructions that precede the test. When you take the test, you will be asked to read them before you begin answering questions.
- After you finish the test, read the sections on "How to Score the SAT II: American History and Social Studies Subject Test" and "Reviewing Your Test Performance," which follow the test.

FORM K-30AC

AMERICAN HISTORY AND SOCIAL STUDIES TEST

The top portion of the section of the answer sheet that you will use in taking the American History and Social Studies test must be filled in exactly as shown in the illustration below. Note carefully that you have to do all of the following on your answer sheet.

1. Print AMERICAN HISTORY AND SOCIAL STUDIES on the line under the words "Subject (print)."

2. In the shaded box labeled "Test Code" fill in four ovals:

   —Fill in oval 2 in the row labeled V.

   —Fill in oval 5 in the row labeled W.

   —Fill in oval 5 in the row labeled X.

   —Fill in oval C in the row labeled Y.

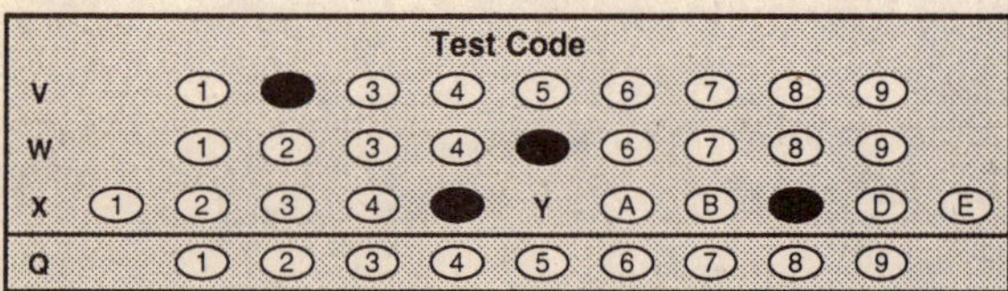

Subject (print)

AMERICAN HISTORY AND SOCIAL STUDIES

3. Please answer the two questions below by filling in the appropriate ovals in the row labeled Q on the answer sheet. The information you provide is for statistical purposes only and will not affect your score on the test.

Question I

How many semesters of American History have you taken from grade 9 to the present? (If you are taking American History this semester, count it as a full semester.) Fill in only one oval of ovals 1-4.

One semester or less	—Fill in oval 1.
Two semesters	—Fill in oval 2.
Three semesters	—Fill in oval 3.
Four or more semesters	—Fill in oval 4.

Question II

Which, if any, of the following social studies courses have you taken from grade 9 to the present? (Fill in ALL ovals that apply.)

One or more semesters of government	—Fill in oval 5.
One or more semesters of economics	—Fill in oval 6.
One or more semesters of geography	—Fill in oval 7.
One or more semesters of psychology	—Fill in oval 8.
One or more semesters of sociology or anthropology	—Fill in oval 9.

If you have taken none of these social studies courses, leave the oval 5 through 9 blank.

When the supervisor gives the signal, turn the page and begin the American History and Social Studies test. There are 100 numbered ovals on the answer sheet and 90 questions in the American History and Social Studies test. Therefore, use only ovals 1 to 90 for recording your answers.

AMERICAN HISTORY AND SOCIAL STUDIES TEST

Directions: Each of the questions or incomplete statements below is followed by five suggested answers or completions. Select the one that is best in each case and then fill in the corresponding oval on the answer sheet.

1. The first permanent colony established by the English in North America was

   (A) St. Augustine
   (B) Jamestown
   (C) Plymouth
   (D) Newfoundland
   (E) Boston

2. Which of the following were the four largest cities of British North America?

   (A) New York, Philadelphia, St. Louis, and Cincinnati
   (B) New York, Philadelphia, Charleston, and New Orleans
   (C) New York, Washington, Philadelphia, and Charleston
   (D) Savannah, Cincinnati, Chicago, and Boston
   (E) New York, Boston, Charleston, and Philadelphia

3. "We hold these truths to be self-evident, that all men are created equal, that they are endowed by their Creator with certain unalienable Rights, that among these are Life, Liberty and the pursuit of Happiness."

   In the words above, the signers of the Declaration of Independence declared their intellectual commitment to the

   (A) Enlightenment philosophy of natural rights
   (B) centuries-old heritage of English common law
   (C) Puritan ideal of a covenanted community
   (D) liberal idea of American exceptionalism
   (E) pioneer philosophy of egalitarianism

4. Which of the following best characterizes the dominant policy of the United States government toward American Indian tribes during the presidency of Andrew Jackson?

   (A) Detribalization and incorporation of individual American Indians as citizens of the states within which the tribal territory had been located
   (B) Federal protection of American Indians from excessive contact with White people by means of the "factory system" of trade
   (C) Strong support of missionary activity within existing tribal territory
   (D) Forced removal of all tribes east of the Mississippi to "permanent" tribal territory in the West
   (E) Creation of reservations in existing tribal territory where tribal rather than state law would apply

5. Harriet Tubman was known as the "Moses" of her people because she

   (A) helped slaves escape from the South
   (B) was instrumental in bringing about suffrage reform
   (C) advocated emigration to Africa for Black people
   (D) organized mass civil rights demonstrations
   (E) traveled as a lay minister preaching the gospel

GO ON TO THE NEXT PAGE

3OAC

Library of Congress

6. The nineteenth-century lithograph above is best described as a portrayal of the

   (A) ideal of American womanhood
   (B) character of the American Indian
   (C) spirit of Manifest Destiny
   (D) grandeur of the natural landscape
   (E) concern for conservation of natural resources

GO ON TO THE NEXT PAGE

7. Which of the following bears the closest relationship to whether or not a state seceded and joined the Confederacy?

   (A) The extent of its tobacco production
   (B) The extent of its reliance on slavery
   (C) The extent of its commercial activity
   (D) Its degree of access to river transportation
   (E) Its rate of population growth

8. From 1870 to 1970, the most persistent problem that periodically depressed agricultural prices in the United States was

   (A) scarcity of productive land
   (B) widespread lack of mechanized farming
   (C) frequent droughts and other unfavorable climatic conditions
   (D) overproduction and underconsumption of farm commodities
   (E) lack of government subsidies and technical aid

GO ON TO THE NEXT PAGE

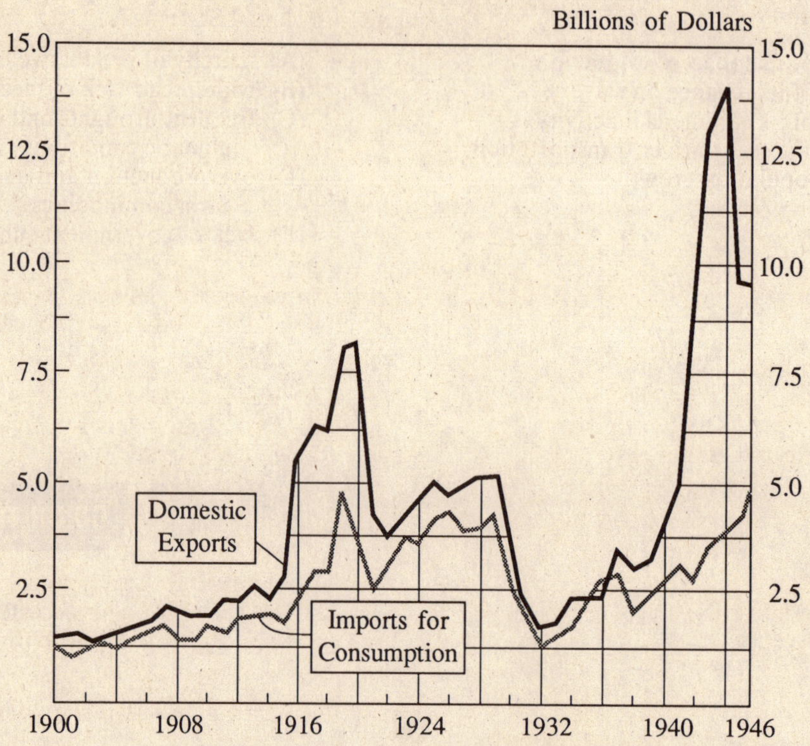

9. Which of the following best accounts for the fact that during two periods shown in the graph above the United States had a more favorable balance of trade than during any other period?

(A) The election of Republican Presidents
(B) Foreign demand for armaments and other wartime supplies
(C) The increased preference of Europeans for American products
(D) The rising value of the dollar
(E) The declining value of the dollar

GO ON TO THE NEXT PAGE

10. "It is our true policy to steer clear of permanent alliances with any portion of the foreign world. . . . Taking care always to keep ourselves by suitable establishments on a respectable defensive posture, we may safely trust to temporary alliances for extraordinary emergencies."

    Of the following, which President would have been LEAST likely to agree with the statement above?

    (A) George Washington
    (B) Thomas Jefferson
    (C) Abraham Lincoln
    (D) Warren G. Harding
    (E) Harry S Truman

11. During the seventeenth century, the buffalo-hunting technique of the American Indians of the Great Plains became more effective when they secured which of the following from areas under Spanish influence?

    (A) Horses
    (B) Repeating rifles
    (C) Guides to buffalo migration routes
    (D) Steel traps
    (E) Hunting dogs

12. Which of the following statements about women in colonial America is correct?

    (A) Women were elected to colonial legislatures.
    (B) Women usually retained control of the property that they had owned prior to marriage.
    (C) Many women remained single because of a shortage of men in the colonies.
    (D) Young women had as many opportunities for education as did young men.
    (E) Married women were legally represented by their husbands.

13. In the 1780's and 1790's, the United States sought the right to navigate the Mississippi River in order to

    (A) establish a western naval force against Spain
    (B) satisfy New England economic interests
    (C) take full advantage of the Louisiana Purchase
    (D) provide a cheaper trade route for the farm goods of the Ohio Valley
    (E) open lands west of the Mississippi to cotton production

14. During the first half of the nineteenth century, which of the following disqualified the most people from voting?

    (A) Residential requirements
    (B) Sexual and racial restrictions
    (C) Religious tests
    (D) Exclusion of the foreign-born
    (E) Literacy qualifications

15. Which of the following reasons is most commonly given by historians for the settlement of Irish immigrants in Eastern seaport cities in the 1830's and 1840's?

    (A) They hoped to return to Ireland as soon as they had made some money.
    (B) They were not experienced as farmers and therefore preferred to live in cities.
    (C) They did not have the capital to buy land and establish farms.
    (D) Restrictive legislation prevented them from living where they pleased.
    (E) They wanted to settle close to Catholic churches.

GO ON TO THE NEXT PAGE

16. Which of the following sources would be most likely to yield quantitative evidence to support the thesis that occupational choice in nineteenth-century America was significantly affected by sex and race?

    (A) Diaries kept by workers
    (B) Newspaper obituary notices
    (C) Speeches by business and industry leaders
    (D) Reports of the United States Census
    (E) Photographs of men and women at work

17. Of the following, which was the principal source of federal income between the Civil War and the First World War?

    (A) Income taxes collected from individuals
    (B) Income taxes collected from corporations
    (C) Tariffs imposed on imported goods
    (D) Fees from the Homestead Act
    (E) Taxes on inherited wealth

18. The most important and widely read novel about the Great Depression is

    (A) Zora Neal Hurston's *Their Eyes Were Watching God*
    (B) Upton Sinclair's *The Jungle*
    (C) John Steinbeck's *The Grapes of Wrath*
    (D) Pearl Buck's *The Good Earth*
    (E) William Faulkner's *The Sound and the Fury*

19. "Whereas, the successful prosecution of the war requires every possible protection against espionage to national-defense material, national-defense premises and national-defense utilities . . ."

    This 1942 executive order of Franklin D. Roosevelt, excerpted above, was used to

    (A) remove Japanese Americans from their homes on the West Coast
    (B) incarcerate German Americans suspected of being sympathetic to Hitler
    (C) prevent European refugees from entering the United States
    (D) quarantine members of the American Communist party
    (E) repatriate Italian Americans suspected of supporting Mussolini

20. The action of the United States Congress in overriding President Truman's veto of the Taft-Hartley bill is an example of which of the following in operation?

    (A) Judicial review
    (B) Checks and balances
    (C) Legislative compromise
    (D) Popular sovereignty
    (E) The power of impeachment

GO ON TO THE NEXT PAGE

Drawing by Claude; © 1956 The New Yorker Magazine, Inc.

21. This cartoon about life in the 1950's satirizes

    (A) American sentimentalism
    (B) increased affluence
    (C) the housing boom
    (D) family togetherness
    (E) middle-class conformity

GO ON TO THE NEXT PAGE

22. The "domino theory," used in reference to international affairs in the 1950's and 1960's, asserted that

(A) an economic depression in one nation increases the likelihood of similar depressions in neighboring nations
(B) military aid given to one nation increases the demand by neighboring nations for similar aid
(C) a communist takeover in one nation increases the likelihood of a communist takeover in a neighboring nation
(D) if economic aid is denied to one nation, it must also be denied to that nation's enemies
(E) if a political leader is assassinated, other political assassinations can be expected

23. The most important motivation behind Spanish conquests in the Americas was the desire to

(A) exploit a new source of slave labor
(B) convert the native population to Catholicism
(C) establish an exemplary religious community
(D) found permanent settlements
(E) enrich the Spanish treasury

24. Which of the following was the immediate response of the British government to the Boston Tea Party?

(A) Passage of the Declaratory Act
(B) Imposition of the Townshend duties
(C) Repeal of the Stamp Act
(D) Passage of the Coercive (Intolerable) Acts
(E) Enforcement of the Tea Act

25. Before 1820 most manufacturing in the United States took place in houses and small shops where

(A) coal was the chief form of fuel
(B) women and children often participated in the production process
(C) artisans, journeymen, and apprentices worked in assembly lines to facilitate quick production of goods
(D) artisans produced goods mainly for foreign export
(E) artisans used tools driven by waterpower

26. The term "spoils system" originated in the Jacksonian era in reference to the

(A) distribution of surplus federal revenues to the states
(B) use of political appointments for party purposes
(C) disadvantages of slave labor
(D) operations of the Second Bank of the United States
(E) corruption in programs for internal improvements

GO ON TO THE NEXT PAGE

27. The photograph above was probably taken in which of the following settings?

    (A) Massachusetts in the 1840's
    (B) Kentucky in the 1850's
    (C) Michigan in the 1860's
    (D) Kansas in the 1870's
    (E) Hawaii in the 1890's

GO ON TO THE NEXT PAGE

28. The first large-scale use of automated assembly-line production occurred with the

(A) manufacture of guns for the army during the Mexican War
(B) manufacture of clothes for the Union army during the Civil War
(C) development of the General Electric Company's electric light bulb around 1895
(D) development of the ladies' garment industry around 1910
(E) development of the Ford Motor Company's Model T around 1910

29. Between 1910 and 1960, one of the most pronounced population trends in the United States was the

(A) migration of people from rural to urban areas
(B) increased proportion of immigrants in the total population
(C) steady decline in the birth rate
(D) decline in life expectancy
(E) increasing preponderance of males in the total population

30. The concept of "containment" in United States foreign policy is most closely associated with the era of

(A) the Spanish-American War
(B) Dollar Diplomacy
(C) the Cold War
(D) the New Deal
(E) the Good Neighbor policy

31. Which of the following provided the legal basis for affirmative action programs on behalf of women and minority groups?

(A) *Roe* v. *Wade*
(B) The Taft-Hartley Act
(C) The proposal of the Equal Rights Amendment in 1972
(D) President Nixon's revenue-sharing program
(E) The Civil Rights Act of 1964

32. Which of the following was a major factor in the eventual success of the colonists in the American Revolution?

(A) United support of the American people for George Washington and his army
(B) Continuous superiority of American generals over British generals
(C) Outbreak of war in Europe, and Britain's need to concentrate its forces there
(D) French financial and military support of American troops
(E) Defeat of the British navy by the American navy

33. Between 1800 and 1860, American agriculture became increasingly productive primarily because of the

(A) advances in soil-conserving and soil-building techniques
(B) movement toward greater crop diversification
(C) extension of arable land and the introduction of new laborsaving machinery
(D) introduction of dry-farming techniques on the Great Plains
(E) eradication of the boll weevil and other destructive insects

GO ON TO THE NEXT PAGE

34. Which of the following writers was most closely associated with the Transcendentalist movement?

    (A) Edgar Allan Poe
    (B) Henry David Thoreau
    (C) Harriet Beecher Stowe
    (D) Herman Melville
    (E) Emily Dickinson

35. Which of the following was a consequence of the Kansas-Nebraska Act?

    (A) The demise of the Federalist party was hastened.
    (B) The Whig party was revived.
    (C) Proslavery and antislavery sentiment was intensified.
    (D) Stephen A. Douglas won the support of Free Soilers.
    (E) Nebraska was allowed to enter the Union as a slave state.

36. When Mark Twain coined the phrase "the Gilded Age" to describe the United States of the 1870's, he was referring to the

    (A) corruption and superficiality of life
    (B) progress of the arts since the Civil War
    (C) great wealth of the country
    (D) elaborate etiquette of public officials
    (E) reuniting of the North and the South

37. The Progressive movement was primarily a reflection of which of the following?

    (A) A belief that poor people should be taught to care for themselves
    (B) A desire to spread Christian teachings overseas
    (C) Concern over problems associated with urban and industrial growth
    (D) A belief that the growth of American business strengthened the rights of American citizens
    (E) A desire to win rights for Black Americans

The Only Way We Can Save Her

Carey Orr. *The Tribune* (Chicago), 1939.

38. All of the following elements in the cartoon above are intended to convey the cartoonist's isolationist sentiments EXCEPT the

    (A) depiction of Europe as a continent accustomed to war
    (B) presence of an ocean separating America from Europe
    (C) plea of Democracy to Uncle Sam
    (D) statement that America is the last remaining hope for democracy
    (E) costumes worn by Democracy and Uncle Sam

GO ON TO THE NEXT PAGE

39. The Scopes or "monkey" trial of 1925 is historically significant because it symbolized the conflict between

    (A) urban ethnic groups and rural nativists
    (B) modern scientific ideas and religious fundamentalism
    (C) economic developers and wildlife conservationists
    (D) parochial isolationists and cosmopolitan internationalists
    (E) literary freedom and Victorian constraints

40. Allied strategy after the United States entered the Second World War in 1941 called for

    (A) bringing Spain into the war against Germany and Italy
    (B) postponing an attack on Italy until the liberation of France
    (C) immediately opening a second front in Europe
    (D) concentrating on the defeat of Germany before the defeat of Japan
    (E) allowing the Soviet Union to carry the primary war effort against Japan

41. Periods of rapid economic growth in the United States have often been associated with expansion of particular industries. Which two of the following industries were associated with the economic growth of the 1950's?

    I. Railroad
    II. Coal
    III. Electronics
    IV. Chemical

    (A) I and II
    (B) I and III
    (C) II and III
    (D) II and IV
    (E) III and IV

42. César Chávez was important in the 1960's for his efforts to unionize

    (A) migrant agricultural workers
    (B) public employees
    (C) unskilled factory workers
    (D) school teachers
    (E) unskilled hotel and kitchen workers

43. In the middle of the sixteenth century, England became interested in colonizing the New World for all of the following reasons EXCEPT:

    (A) England's trade relationship with the Netherlands was jeopardized, and English merchants were therefore interested in developing new markets for cloth.
    (B) The accession of Queen Elizabeth I in 1558 led to the development of rivalry between Protestant England and Catholic Spain over the founding of colonies.
    (C) English adventurers such as Sir Humphrey Gilbert and Sir Walter Raleigh were eager to organize private expeditions to explore the New World for their own financial gain.
    (D) Colonies in North America would serve as way stations along proposed routes to the Far East.
    (E) English manufacturers saw the native population of North America as a source of labor for their factories.

44. A principal consequence of the first Great Awakening was the

    (A) uniting of the Congregationalists and the Presbyterians
    (B) proliferation of religious sects
    (C) weakening of the Methodists
    (D) broadening of manhood suffrage
    (E) strengthening of the mercantile system

45. During 1787 and 1788, Anti-Federalist arguments against ratification of the Constitution included all of the following EXCEPT:

    (A) The Constitution gave too much power to the central government.
    (B) The Constitutional Convention had exceeded its authority.
    (C) The Constitution failed to establish a state church.
    (D) The Constitution lacked guarantees of basic liberties.
    (E) The congressional districts were too large for representatives to know their constituents.

GO ON TO THE NEXT PAGE

46. United States foreign policy from 1794 to 1815 was primarily concerned with

(A) weakening British influence in the West Indies
(B) insuring American survival as an independent republic
(C) appeasing French hostility toward the United States
(D) thwarting Napoleon's ambitions for a North American empire
(E) aiding the French in their conflict with Britain

47. In the early nineteenth century, the first textile factories were located in New England for all of the following reasons EXCEPT

(A) proximity to raw materials
(B) easy access to a source of power
(C) proximity to markets
(D) an available labor force
(E) available investment capital

48. Reform movements in the 1840's sought all of the following EXCEPT

(A) establishment of insane asylums
(B) abolition of slavery
(C) promotion of temperance
(D) recognition of legal and political rights for women
(E) recognition of American Indians' citizenship rights

49. Which of the following best states the 1860 position of the Republican party concerning slavery?

(A) The principle of the Missouri Compromise should be revived and applied to new territories in the West.
(B) Slavery should be abolished with all deliberate speed.
(C) Slavery should be banned north of the Mason-Dixon Line.
(D) The extension of slavery into the western territories should be prevented.
(E) The status of slavery in the western territories should be determined by popular sovereignty.

50. All of the following statements about immigration to the United States in the nineteenth century are true EXCEPT:

(A) The number of immigrants was higher in the first half of the century than in the second half.
(B) The major European sources of immigration shifted during the century from Northern and Western Europe to Southern and Eastern Europe.
(C) More immigrants were male than female.
(D) More immigrants were unskilled than skilled.
(E) More immigrants settled in the North than in the South.

51. Which of the following challenged the political and social doctrines of Booker T. Washington and played an important role in the founding of the National Association for the Advancement of Colored People?

(A) George Washington Carver
(B) Frederick Douglass
(C) W. E. B. Du Bois
(D) Marcus Garvey
(E) A. Philip Randolph

52. Which of the following was NOT a major political issue during the 1920's?

(A) Prohibition and its enforcement
(B) Scandals in the administration of President Warren G. Harding
(C) The religion of Democratic presidential candidate Alfred E. Smith
(D) Proposals to dispose of agricultural surpluses during a period of reduced farm income
(E) Rearmament to meet the renewed military threat of Germany

GO ON TO THE NEXT PAGE

53. A major result of the New Deal was

    (A) an increase in the power of the federal government
    (B) a return to nineteenth-century laissez-faire policies
    (C) an increased emphasis on rugged individualism
    (D) a balanced budget and reduction of the federal deficit
    (E) a decrease in political party membership

54. The activity of Senator Joseph McCarthy of Wisconsin that was primarily responsible for making him a national political force between 1950 and 1954 was his

    (A) allegation of illegal activities by Alger Hiss
    (B) effort to win support for a national health service
    (C) assertion that the Hollywood movie industry was communist dominated
    (D) claim that communists had infiltrated the State Department
    (E) charge that the policies of the Republican party were responsible for the spread of communism in China and Eastern Europe

55. In enacting the seventeenth-century Navigation Acts, England sought to do all of the following EXCEPT

    (A) confine the profits of colonial trade to its own subjects
    (B) encourage colonial manufacturing
    (C) regulate the colonial production of staple crops
    (D) increase its customs receipts
    (E) increase its sea power

56. Black slavery came to be regarded as an essential institution in the colonial Chesapeake area when

    (A) the first Africans were brought to Virginia in 1619
    (B) settlers learned in the period 1615-1625 that tobacco culture was labor-intensive
    (C) the experience of the 1620's showed that Africans were less subject to New World diseases than were White indentured servants
    (D) contact with Latin American economies early in the seventeenth century demonstrated the profitability of slavery
    (E) the supply of indentured servants proved insufficient to meet the demands of tobacco production in the late seventeenth century

57. Which of the following is true of Roger Williams?

    (A) He believed in the divine right of kings.
    (B) He believed that all citizens should take a loyalty oath to the government under which they lived.
    (C) He founded Connecticut.
    (D) He believed that each person had the right to worship according to individual conscience.
    (E) He seized American Indian lands without providing any compensation.

58. Which of the following favored decentralized governmental powers and a society of self-sufficient free farmers?

    (A) John Jay
    (B) John Marshall
    (C) Thomas Jefferson
    (D) John Adams
    (E) Alexander Hamilton

59. The presidency of James K. Polk was dominated by the

    (A) banking question and the issue of cheap money
    (B) issue of fugitive slaves
    (C) conflict with Great Britain over the Oregon question
    (D) constitutional conflict over states' rights
    (E) Mexican War and its implications for the slavery issue

60. In the 1850's the doctrine of obedience to a higher law than the United States Constitution was most frequently invoked in connection with

    (A) temperance reform
    (B) the Know-Nothing campaign against Irish Catholic immigrants
    (C) the Fugitive Slave Law
    (D) the woman suffrage movement
    (E) the movement for the ten-hour workday

GO ON TO THE NEXT PAGE

61. United States Supreme Court decisions in the period 1877-1900 were effective in

(A) ensuring racial equality
(B) encouraging the growth of big business
(C) providing relief for small farmers and sharecroppers
(D) protecting the rights of labor unions in industrial disputes
(E) guaranteeing civil liberties

62. Which of the following forms of transportation contributed most to changing residential patterns in American cities during the late nineteenth and early twentieth centuries?

(A) Subways
(B) Streetcars
(C) Automobiles
(D) Gasoline buses
(E) Diesel locomotives

63. Which of the following is true of immigration restriction acts passed in the 1920's?

(A) They discriminated against immigrants from southern and eastern Europe.
(B) They were opposed by the labor unions.
(C) They were supported by the most recent immigrant groups.
(D) They were proposed by President Harding to placate the Ku Klux Klan.
(E) They did not really decrease the numbers who actually immigrated.

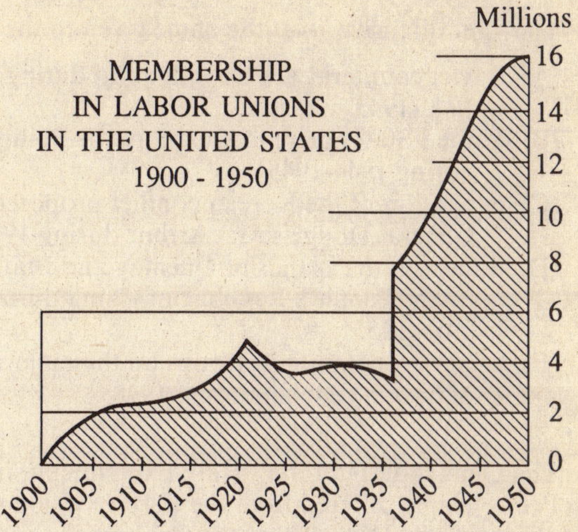

64. Which of the following bears the closest relationship to the changes depicted on the graph?

(A) The utilization of the techniques of mass production
(B) The movement of people from rural to urban areas
(C) The decline in the purchasing power of the dollar
(D) Military expenditures of the government
(E) The attitude of government toward unionization

GO ON TO THE NEXT PAGE

65. The "Tet offensive" was the name given to the
    (A) Soviet counterattack at Stalingrad during 1942-1943
    (B) United States drive to recapture the Philippines during 1944-1945
    (C) expansion of the Korean conflict proposed by General Douglas MacArthur during 1951
    (D) attack on the islands of Quemoy and Matsu by the People's Republic of China during 1954-1955
    (E) attack by communist troops on the major cities of South Vietnam during 1968

66. The Quaker design for a "Holy Experiment" in Pennsylvania differed from the Puritan vision of a "City upon a Hill" in that the Quakers
    (A) encouraged the dispersal of population throughout the colony as a strategy for rapid agricultural development
    (B) envisioned a community based on principles of economic and political equality
    (C) followed their religious principles by banning the institution of slavery
    (D) accepted religious diversity in the colony and recruited settlers from continental Europe as well as England
    (E) devised a constitution ensuring that the colony would be free of political dissension and religious conflict

67. The Proclamation Line of 1763 marked the
    (A) point beyond which British colonists were forbidden to settle
    (B) boundary of new British colonies in the Ohio Valley
    (C) division between French and English possessions in North America
    (D) farthest extent of Iroquois land claims
    (E) boundary of the Ohio Company's grant

68. Which of the following was true of the first national political parties in the United States?
    (A) Their establishment was provided for by the United States Constitution.
    (B) Their leaders were concerned about the disruptive nature of factional rivalries.
    (C) They were praised by Washington for their contribution to the political process.
    (D) They agreed on major foreign policy issues.
    (E) They referred to themselves as Whigs and Democrats.

69. John C. Calhoun's doctrine of nullification was based on all of the following principles EXCEPT:
    (A) Majority rule ought to be the bond of union.
    (B) The states are older than the Union.
    (C) The Constitution is a compact among sovereign states.
    (D) Judicial review is a form of federal usurpation.
    (E) The federal government is the agent of the states.

70. Which of the following best supports the thesis that the Civil War introduced the United States to modern "total war"?
    (A) The use of professional armed forces
    (B) The battle of Gettysburg
    (C) Sherman's March to the Sea
    (D) The battles of Bull Run
    (E) The use of spies

71. Which of the following was the Radical Republican position following the Civil War?
    (A) By seceding, the Southern states had reverted to provinces or territories of the Union.
    (B) Southern planters should play the major role in rebuilding the South.
    (C) Reconstruction should be left to the federal courts.
    (D) The Civil War was basically a rebellion of individual citizens.
    (E) The primary responsibility for Reconstruction belonged to the executive branch of the federal government.

GO ON TO THE NEXT PAGE

72. "Popular values and beliefs in the United States in the period 1865-1900 generally supported the spirit of American capitalism."

    All of the following can be used to support the hypothesis above EXCEPT

    (A) the popularity of Henry George's *Progress and Poverty* and Edward Bellamy's *Looking Backward*
    (B) the popularity of Horatio Alger stories
    (C) church leaders' sermons praising the achievements of men such as John D. Rockefeller and Andrew Carnegie
    (D) the emphasis on industrial advances in the exhibits shown at world fairs in Philadelphia (1876) and Chicago (1893)
    (E) the speeches that William McKinley gave during the presidential campaign of 1896

73. The Populists sought to obtain their goals through all of the following EXCEPT

    (A) expanding farm credit during the marketing season by means of the "subtreasury" plan
    (B) limiting the coinage of silver to insure against a possible inflation of prices
    (C) nationalizing banks, railroads, and utilities
    (D) gaining widespread adoption of the techniques and devices of direct democracy
    (E) linking southern and western farmers in a concerted political movement

74. The truth of an idea is found in the consequences to which it leads.

    Which of the following philosophies does the statement above reflect?

    (A) Conservatism
    (B) Pragmatism
    (C) Social Darwinism
    (D) Idealism
    (E) Transcendentalism

75. As part of its imperial expansion from 1895 to 1914, the United States fought an extended guerrilla war against local nationalists in

    (A) China
    (B) Cuba
    (C) Venezuela
    (D) Panama
    (E) the Philippines

76. At the peak of its strength, between 1900 and 1917, the Socialist movement in the United States was able to

    (A) bring about the defeat of William Howard Taft in the election of 1912
    (B) secure temporary nationalization of the coal and steel industries
    (C) gain control of the American Federation of Labor and elect some officials of the Industrial Workers of the World
    (D) win control of a number of city governments and elect some members of Congress and state legislators
    (E) reorient United States diplomacy toward better relations with Russia

77. One of the key elements in the success of Progressivism was

    (A) the oratory of protective-tariff advocates in the Senate
    (B) the muckrakers' mobilization of public opinion for the purpose of reform
    (C) a large Democratic majority in Congress ready to follow the President's lead
    (D) extensive support by women voters
    (E) a Congress willing to pass radical measures to alleviate the most serious depression in American history

78. Which of the following was NOT part of United States government policy during the First World War?

    (A) Liberty Bond campaigns
    (B) Censorship of the press
    (C) Diplomatic recognition of the Soviet Union
    (D) Passage of espionage legislation
    (E) Contracts and subsidies to the shipbuilding industry

GO ON TO THE NEXT PAGE

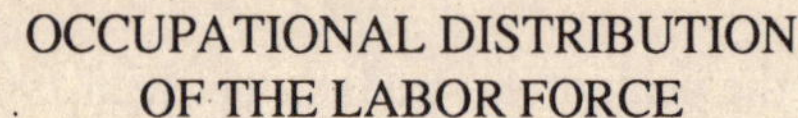

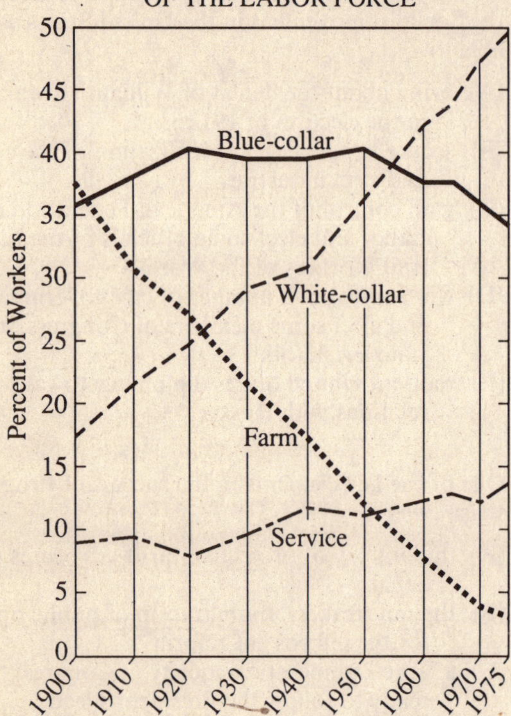

79. The graph above supports which of the following statements about the period 1900 to 1975 ?

    (A) Most white-collar workers were formerly farmers.
    (B) White-collar workers increasingly took jobs once held by blue-collar workers.
    (C) The standard of living rose for all workers except farm laborers.
    (D) The percentage of the labor force directly engaged in the production of goods declined.
    (E) Agricultural production fell dramatically.

80. Which of the following describes the Southern Christian Leadership Conference?

    (A) An organization committed to the advancement of Black civil rights
    (B) The religious wing of the White Citizens' Councils
    (C) The forerunner of the Moral Majority
    (D) An organization lobbying on behalf of religious education
    (E) An early leader of the anticommunist crusade of the 1950's

81. The Constitution states that all federal revenue bills

    (A) must originate in the House of Representatives
    (B) must be proposed by the President
    (C) must pass both the House and the Senate by a two-thirds majority
    (D) are exempt from the pocket veto
    (E) are subject to review and approval by the Treasury Department

82. "Here was a new generation, shouting the old cries, learning the old creeds, through a revery of long days and nights, destined finally to go out into that dirty gray turmoil to follow love and pride; a new generation dedicated more than the last to the fear of poverty and the worship of success; grown up to find all Gods dead, all wars fought, all faiths in man shaken."

    This statement of protest best expressed the mood of

    (A) the transcendentalists of the 1830's
    (B) Black southerners after the Civil War
    (C) the practitioners of the "genteel tradition" in the late nineteenth century
    (D) the Harlem Renaissance of the 1920's
    (E) the "lost generation" of the 1920's

83. All of the following are explicitly provided for in the Constitution EXCEPT

    (A) the right of free speech
    (B) the electoral college system
    (C) the power of judicial review
    (D) the right to bear arms
    (E) equal representation of each state in the Senate

GO ON TO THE NEXT PAGE

84. A United States citizen who was born in 1815 and died in 1885 might have done all of the following EXCEPT

(A) helped Texas achieve independence
(B) read the news of Custer's Last Stand
(C) traveled from coast to coast by train
(D) heard a lecture by Ralph Waldo Emerson
(E) voted for a Populist presidential candidate

85. Under the leadership of Samuel Gompers, the American Federation of Labor (AFL) did which of the following?

(A) Rejected the use of strikes.
(B) Strove to unionize unskilled workers.
(C) Formed a worker's political party.
(D) Organized skilled workers along craft lines.
(E) Stressed opportunities for wage workers to become industrialists.

86. The United States built the Panama Canal after

(A) backing the Panamanian revolution against Colombia
(B) winning a competitive bidding war with the French
(C) discovering a vaccine that prevented malaria
(D) signing a treaty with Colombia in 1903
(E) securing the help of the British in construction

87. "My party's in power in the city, and it's going to undertake a lot of public improvements. Well, I'm tipped off, say, that they're going to lay out a new park at a certain place. I see my opportunity and I take it. I go to that place and I buy up all the land I can in the neighborhood. Then the board of this or that makes its plan public, and there is a rush to get my land which nobody cared particular for before. Ain't it perfectly honest to charge a good price and make a profit on my investment and foresight? Of course it is. Well, that's honest graft."

This statement was most likely made by

(A) a populist
(B) a machine politician
(C) a mugwump
(D) a tenement owner
(E) an urban merchant

88. Which of the following is a progressive, rather than a regressive, form of taxation currently used in the United States?

(A) Graduated taxes on incomes
(B) Sales taxes on food
(C) Excise taxes on cigarettes
(D) Flat taxes on incomes
(E) Tariffs on manufactured goods

89. The principal reason for the increased migration of Black people to northern cities in the period 1914-1919 was the

(A) shortage of factory labor in the North brought about by a decline in European immigration
(B) improved working conditions in northern factories brought about by progressive reformers
(C) striking down of segregation laws in the North
(D) federal policies designed to encourage Black workers to leave the South for northern cities
(E) success of unions in organizing industrial workers

90. All of the following help explain the defeat of the Versailles Treaty in the Senate EXCEPT:

(A) Republicans sought to gain political advantage from the issue.
(B) Conservatives feared that the Soviet Union would boycott the League of Nations.
(C) The Senate was jealous of its role in foreign affairs.
(D) Senator Lodge and other Republicans disapproved of United States participation in the League of Nations as it was constituted.
(E) President Wilson refused to agree to substantive reservations to the treaty.

STOP

IF YOU FINISH BEFORE TIME IS CALLED, YOU MAY CHECK YOUR WORK ON THIS TEST ONLY.
DO NOT TURN TO ANY OTHER TEST IN THIS BOOK.

How to Score the SAT II: American History and Social Studies Subject Test

When you take the American History and Social Studies Subject Test, your answer sheet will be "read" by a scanning machine that will record your responses to each question. Then a computer will compare your answers with the correct answers and produce your raw score. You get one point for each correct answer. For each wrong answer, you lose one-fourth of a point. Questions you omit (and any for which you mark more than one answer) are not counted. This raw score is converted to a College Board scaled score that is reported to you and to the colleges you specify. After you have taken this test, you can get an idea of what your score might be by following the instructions in the next two sections.

FINDING YOUR RAW TEST SCORE

Step 1: Table A lists the correct answers for all the questions on the SAT II: American History and Social Studies Subject Test that is reproduced in this book. It also serves as a worksheet for you to calculate your raw score.

- Compare your answers with those given in the table.
- Put a check in the column marked "Right" if your answer is correct.
- Put a check in the column marked "Wrong" if your answer is incorrect.
- Leave both columns blank if you omitted the question.

Step 2: Count the number of right answers and enter the total here: .... ________

Step 3: Count the number of wrong answers and enter the total here: .... ________

Step 4: Divide the number of wrong answers by 4 and enter the result here: .... ________

Step 5: Subtract the result obtained in Step 4 from the total you obtained in Step 2. Enter the result here: .... ________

Step 6: Round the number obtained in Step 5 to the nearest whole number. Enter the result here: .... ________

The number you obtained in Step 6 is your raw score.

TABLE A

Answers to the SAT II: American History and Social Studies Subject Test, Form K-30AC, and Percentage of Students Answering Each Question Correctly

Question Number	Correct Answer	Right	Wrong	Percentage of Students Answering the Question Correctly*	Question Number	Correct Answer	Right	Wrong	Percentage of Students Answering the Question Correctly*
1	B			85	46	B			76
2	E			87	47	A			48
3	A			79	48	E			54
4	D			88	49	D			51
5	A			95	50	A			56
6	C			89	51	C			75
7	B			92	52	E			57
8	D			80	53	A			67
9	B			84	54	D			73
10	E			60	55	B			42
11	A			76	56	E			50
12	E			92	57	D			54
13	D			69	58	C			67
14	B			74	59	E			46
15	C			68	60	C			35
16	D			49	61	B			47
17	C			64	62	B			29
18	C			71	63	A			68
19	A			82	64	E			47
20	B			83	65	E			70
21	E			78	66	D			36
22	C			88	67	A			62
23	E			75	68	B			35
24	D			73	69	A			23
25	B			62	70	C			35
26	B			77	71	A			48
27	D			69	72	A			41
28	E			85	73	B			44
29	A			62	74	B			41
30	C			79	75	E			52
31	E			55	76	D			40
32	D			62	77	B			51
33	C			63	78	C			44
34	B			81	79	D			30
35	C			73	80	A			37
36	A			61	81	A			29
37	C			74	82	E			54
38	E			59	83	C			46
39	B			79	84	E			38
40	D			64	85	D			37
41	E			74	86	A			54
42	A			68	87	B			43
43	E			57	88	A			47
44	B			64	89	A			22
45	C			67	90	B			34

*These percentages are based on an analysis of the answer sheets of a random sample of 9,995 students who took the original form of this test in June 1992 and whose mean score was 565. They may be used as an indication of the relative difficulty of a particular question. Each percentage may also be used to predict the likelihood that a typical SAT II: American History and Social Studies Subject Test candidate will answer correctly that question on this edition of this test.

Finding Your College Board Scaled Score

When you take SAT II: Subject Tests, the scores sent to the colleges you specify are reported on the College Board scale, which ranges from 200 to 800. You can convert your practice test score to a scaled score by using Table B. To find your scaled score, locate your raw score in the left-hand column of Table B; the corresponding score in the right-hand column is your College Board scaled score. For example, a raw score of 60 on this particular edition of the SAT II: American History and Social Studies Subject Test corresponds to a College Board scaled score of 640.

Raw scores are converted to scaled scores to ensure that a score earned on any one edition of a particular Subject Test is comparable to the same scaled score earned on any other edition of the same Subject Test. Because some editions of tests may be slightly easier or more difficult than others, College Board scaled scores are adjusted so that they indicate the same level of performance regardless of the edition of the test taken and the ability of the group that takes it. Thus, for example, a score of 400 on one edition of a test taken at a particular administration indicates the same level of achievement as a score of 400 on a different edition of the test taken at a different administration.

When you take the SAT II: Subject Tests during a national administration, your scores are likely to differ somewhat from the scores you obtain on the tests in this book. People perform at different levels at different times for reasons unrelated to the tests themselves. The precision of any test is also limited because it represents only a sample of all the possible questions that could be asked.

TABLE B

Score Conversion Table
American History and Social Studies
Subject Test, Form K-30AC

Raw Score	College Board Scaled Score	Raw Score	College Board Scaled Score
90	800	33	480
89	800	32	470
88	800	31	470
87	790	30	460
86	790	39	450
85	780	28	450
84	780	27	440
83	770	26	440
82	760	25	430
81	760	24	420
80	750	23	420
79	750	22	410
78	740	21	410
77	740	20	400
76	730	19	400
75	720	18	390
74	720	17	380
73	710	16	380
72	710	15	370
71	700	14	370
70	690	13	360
69	690	12	350
68	680	11	350
67	680	10	340
66	670	9	340
65	670	8	330
64	660	7	330
63	650	6	320
62	650	5	310
61	640	4	310
60	640	3	300
59	630	2	300
58	620	1	290
57	620	0	280
56	610	−1	280
55	610	−2	270
54	600	−3	270
53	590	−4	260
52	590	−5	260
51	580	−6	250
50	580	−7	240
49	570	−8	240
48	570	−9	230
47	560	−10	230
46	550	−11	220
45	550	−12	210
44	540	−13	210
43	540	−14	200
42	530	−15	200
41	520	−16	200
40	520	−17	200
39	510	−18	200
38	510	−19	200
37	500	−20	200
36	500	−21	200
35	490	−22	200
34	480		

Reviewing Your Test Performance

After you have scored your test, you should take some time to consider the following points in relation to your performance on the test.

- *Did you run out of time before you reached the end of the test?*

  If you did, you may want to consider pacing yourself better. For example, you may have spent too much time working on one or two difficult questions. A better approach might have been to continue the test and return to those questions after you had attempted to answer the remaining questions on the test.

- *Did you take a long time reading the directions for the test?*

  The directions in this test are the same as those in the American History and Social Studies Subject Tests now being administered. You will save time when you read the directions on the test day if you become thoroughly familiar with them in advance.

- *How did you handle questions you were unsure of?*

  If you were able to eliminate one or more of the answer choices and you guessed from the remaining choices, then your approach probably worked to your advantage. On the other hand, omitting questions about which you have some knowledge or guessing answers haphazardly would probably be a mistake.

- *How difficult were the questions for you compared with other students who took the test?*

  By referring to Table A you can find out how difficult each question was for the particular group of students who took the original version of the test. The right-hand column in the table tells you what percentage of that group of students answered the question correctly. It is important to remember that these percentages are based on only one group of students; had this edition of the test been given to all students taking an American History and Social Studies Subject Test at that time, the percentages would probably have been different. A question that was answered correctly by almost everyone in the group, obviously, is an easy question. Question 5, for example, was answered correctly by 95 percent of the students in the sample. On the other hand, question 89 was answered correctly by only 22 percent of the students. If you find that you missed several questions that would be considered easy, you may want to review those questions carefully. They may cover some aspect of the subject that you need to review. Perhaps you misunderstood the directions for one part of the test or you thought the questions were so easy that you did not spend as much time on them as you might have.

The SAT II: World History Subject Test

The SAT II: World History Subject Test consists of 95 multiple-choice questions. The test is 60 minutes in length. The test measures your understanding of the development of major world cultures and your use of historical methodology. This methodology includes the application and weighing of evidence and the ability to interpret and generalize. Slightly more than half the test questions are devoted to Africa, Southwest Asia, South Asia, East Asia, and the Americas; the remainder cover Europe. Many of the questions are global in nature, i.e., they deal with major trends and concerns that have significance for all areas of the modern world (see the chart to the right). Some questions require familiarity with terms commonly used in the social sciences, understanding of cause-and-effect relationships, and knowledge of the history and geography necessary for understanding major historical developments. Other questions test your grasp of concepts essential to historical analysis, your capacity to interpret artistic materials, and your ability to assess quotations from speeches, documents, and other published materials. Questions based on maps, graphs, charts, or cartoons require the use of historical knowledge in interpreting data.

All historical fields — political and diplomatic, intellectual and cultural, and social and economic — are covered in the test.

Because secondary school programs differ, no one textbook or particular course of study is emphasized in the test. Test content lends itself to a variety of academic preparations. These include a course in world or global history, a course concentrating on either world cultures or area studies, or a course in European history taught against a global background.

Chronological Material Covered	Approximate Percentage of Test*
Prehistory and Civilizations to the year 500 C.E.*	10
500-1500 C.E.	20
1500-1900 C.E.	30
Post-1900 C.E.	30
Cross-chronological	10
Geographical Material Covered	
Europe	50
Middle East	10
Africa	10
South Asia	5
East Asia	10
The Americas (excluding the United States)	5
Global	10

*The SAT II: World History Subject Test uses the chronological designations B.C.E. (before the common era) and C.E. (common era). These labels correspond to B.C. (before Christ) and A.D. (anno Domini), which are used in some history textbooks.

Questions Used in the Test

The sample multiple-choice questions that follow illustrate the types of questions used in the test, their range of difficulty, and the abilities they measure. These abilities should not be thought of as mutually exclusive, since many questions test several abilities at the same time. Questions may be presented as separate items or in sets based on quotations, maps, pictures, graphs, or tables.

All questions in the SAT II: World History Subject Test are multiple-choice questions requiring you to choose the best response from the five choices offered. The directions that follow are identical to those that appear in the test.

Directions: Each of the questions or incomplete statements below is followed by five suggested answers or completions. Select the one that is best in each case and then fill in the corresponding oval on the answer sheet.

Questions 1 and 2 fall into the category of questions that require you to know social science terms, factual cause-and-effect relationships, geography, and other data necessary for understanding major historical developments.

1. **Which of the following was immediately responsible for precipitating the French Revolution?**

   (A) The threat of national bankruptcy
   (B) An attack upon the privileges of the middle class
   (C) The desire of the nobility for a written constitution
   (D) The suffering of the peasantry
   (E) The king's attempt to restore feudalism

To answer this question, you need to recall the circumstances that led in May 1789 to the first meeting of the French Estates-General in over a century and a half, an event that arrayed the Third Estate against the nobility and Louis XVI in the first stage of a political struggle that was to evolve into the French Revolution. With his debt-ridden government brought to a halt, the king, by mid-1788, was left with no other recourse than a promise to convene the Estates-General in the months ahead. The correct answer is (A).

Question 2 refers to the map below.

2. **The shaded area in the map above shows the extent of which of the following?**

   (A) Irrigation agriculture in 1000 B.C.E.
   (B) Greek colonization in 550 B.C.E.
   (C) Alexander the Great's empire in 323 B.C.E.
   (D) The Roman Empire in 117 C.E.
   (E) The Byzantine Empire in 565 C.E.

Question 2 tests your knowledge of both history and geography. To answer this question you must know something about the extent to which irrigated farming was practiced in Africa, Europe, and Southwest Asia three thousand years ago, and have a general idea of the extent of the territory controlled by four major ancient civilizations at specific points in time. (A) can be eliminated because irrigation in this early period would have been confined to the regions along the major rivers of the Middle East and Southwest Asia. (B) can be eliminated because Greek colonization was confined primarily to the eastern Mediterranean and did not extend as far north in Europe as shown in the shaded areas of the map. (C) can be eliminated because Alexander the Great's empire did not extend into either the western Mediterranean or northwestern Europe. (D), the correct answer, outlines the greatest extent of territory controlled by the Roman Empire under the Emperor Trajan in the second century C.E. (E) can be eliminated because the Byzantine Empire, with its capital in Constantinople, was confined primarily to the eastern Mediterranean area.

Questions 3-6 fall into the category of questions that test your understanding of concepts essential to history and social science, your capacity to interpret artistic materials, and your ability to assess quotations from speeches, documents, and other published materials.

3. **Which of the following was introduced into the diet of Europeans only after European contact with the Americas in the fifteenth century?**

   (A) Tea
   (B) Rice
   (C) Cinnamon
   (D) Sugar
   (E) Potatoes

To answer this question you need to have some basic information about what has come to be known as the "Columbian Exchange", i.e., the enormous biological transfer that occurred as a result of the fifteenth- and sixteenth-century European voyages of discovery. (A) can be ruled out because tea comes from China, not from the Americas, and was not widely used in Europe until the mid-seventeenth century. (B) can be eliminated because the origin of rice culture has been traced to India. Rice was introduced into southern Europe in medieval times. (C) can be eliminated because the cinnamon tree is native to South Asia and, like rice, has been known in Europe since medieval times. (D) can be eliminated because sugarcane originated in what is now known as New Guinea, followed human migration routes from Southeast Asia through Southwest Asia to Europe and, although rare and expensive, was known to the European aristocracy in medieval times. (E) is the correct answer. The potato is native to the Peruvian-Bolivian Andes and, after its "discovery" by the Europeans in the fifteenth century, became a staple of the European diet. The potato is now a major food crop worldwide.

Giraudon/Art Resource

4. The nineteenth-century wood block print above is associated with the culture of

(A) Japan
(B) India
(C) Iran
(D) Myanmar (Burma)
(E) Thailand

The correct answer choice to question 4 is (A) Japan. The scene depicted in this dramatic picture is world-famous. Although the spacial arrangement and perspective are generally East Asian and the title at the upper left-hand corner is written in Chinese characters, also used in Japan, there are a number of characteristics that identify the picture as Japanese. The dramatic subject matter, with Mount Fuji in the background, is Japanese. In addition, colorful wood-block prints depicting famous scenery, beautiful women, warriors, and well-known theater subjects were popular in Japan from the seventeenth to the nineteenth centuries because they were widely affordable. This work is by the nineteenth-century artist Hokusai.

Questions 5 and 6 refer to the following passage.

We have heard that in your country opium is prohibited with the utmost strictness and severity — this is a strong proof that you know full well how hurtful it is to humankind. Since then you do not permit it to injure your own country, you ought not to have the injurious drug transferred to another country, and above all others, how much less to the Middle Kingdom!

5. The author of the diplomatic dispatch above most probably lived in which of the following countries?

(A) Ghana
(B) The Netherlands
(C) Iran
(D) China
(E) Germany

The above discussion of the forced importation of opium suggests China's struggle against Great Britain, culminating in the Opium War of the mid-nineteenth century. The tone of the dispatch, expressing indignation at Great Britain's flaunting of Chinese law, is consistent with China's concern over growing opium addiction in China and with Chinese resistance to the British. From your study of China you will also remember that the Chinese used to refer to their country as the Middle Kingdom. (D) is the answer to question 5.

6. The country which went to war in the nineteenth century over the issue raised in the dispatch was

(A) France
(B) Egypt
(C) Great Britain
(D) India
(E) Japan

The answer to question 6 is (C) Great Britain. Great Britain was expanding its Asian trade and needed a product to exchange for Chinese goods. Opium from India was Great Britain's answer to this dilemma. The dispatch above was sent by a representative of the Chinese emperor to Queen Victoria shortly before the Opium War (1839-1842), in which China was defeated by the British and therefore was not able to enforce its prohibition against the importation of opium.

7. All of the following are "Pillars of Islam" EXCEPT

(A) giving alms for the support of society's poor
(B) praying four times a day in the direction of Mecca
(C) fasting for one month of the year
(D) making a pilgrimage to Mecca at least once during a lifetime
(E) attending mosque prayers daily

Question 7 asks you to identify the exception in a series of true statements. In other words, you are being asked to locate the *false* answer among the five options. To answer this question you need to draw on your knowledge of Islam. Options (A) through (D) are true because they refer to four of the five "Pillars of Islam." Option (E) is false because Muslims are not required to attend mosque prayers daily. The fifth pillar actually is the "profession of faith." In question (7) the correct answer choice is (E).

Questions posed in the negative, like this one, account for at most 25 percent of the test questions. Variations of this question format employ the capitalized words NOT or LEAST, as in the following examples: "Which of the following is NOT true?" "Which of the following is LEAST likely to occur?"

Questions based on graphs, charts, or cartoons require you to use historical knowledge in interpreting data. Questions 8-10 fall into this category.

ANNUAL PRODUCTION OF STEEL (in thousands of metric tons)				
Year				
1865	225	13	97	41
1870	286	68	169	83
1875	723	396	370	258
1880	1,320	1,267	660	388
1885	2,020	1,739	1,202	533
1890	3,637	4,346	2,161	566
1895	3,444	6,212	3,941	899
1900	5,130	10,382	6,645	1,565
1905	5,983	20,354	10,066	2,110
1910	6,374	26,512	13,698	3,506

8. Read from left to right, the column headings for the table above should be

(A) Great Britain, United States, Germany, and France
(B) Italy, Great Britain, Russia, and Germany
(C) Germany, Great Britain, Russia, and France
(D) Great Britain, United States, France, and Germany
(E) Germany, Russia, Great Britain, and United States

The correct answer choice is (A). To answer this question, you need to know in which country the industrial revolution began and which other countries caught up early or late. Great Britain was industrialized by 1850, the United States and Germany were next, and France, Italy, and Russia followed later in the nineteenth century.

Questions containing charts and graphs require careful study and therefore may be more time-consuming than other types of questions. Remember to budget your time accordingly.

Questions 9 and 10 are based on the August 1914 *Punch* cartoon below.

BRAVO, BELGIUM!

9. The "No Thoroughfare" sign in the cartoon is a reference to

(A) an international treaty guaranteeing the neutrality of Belgium
(B) the heavy defensive fortifications built by Belgium in the preceding decade
(C) a bilateral nonaggression pact between Belgium and Germany
(D) an alliance between Belgium and France
(E) the treacherous, swampy terrain on the Belgian-German border

10. This cartoon is a comment on Germany's attempt to

(A) acquire valuable mineral resources in Belgium
(B) invade France through Belgium
(C) force Belgium to repeal tariffs on German goods
(D) intimidate Belgium into signing a military alliance with Germany
(E) pressure Belgium into withdrawing from the Triple Alliance

In this question set you are asked to interpret a British political cartoon published during the tense diplomatic period before the outbreak of the First World War. The correct answer to question 9 is (A), which refers to treaties signed by the Great Powers in 1839 guaranteeing the neutrality of Belgium and Luxembourg in the event of war. The set's second question focuses on Belgium's resistance to the more powerful Germany's threat of aggression if Belgium, situated between Germany and France, will not give transit to German troops. The correct answer choice for question 10 is (B).

11. Which of the following statements would be most difficult for historians to prove true or false?

(A) There was little organized education in Europe during the Middle Ages.

(B) Greece contributed more to Western civilization than Rome.

(C) The invention of the steam engine influenced the way people lived.

(D) Russia is territorially the largest country in the world.

(E) The tourist industry in Europe increased markedly after the Second World War.

In a methodology question such as the one above, you must make the distinction between statements that are verifiable by fact and statements that are based on judgments. The latter are more difficult than the former to prove true or false because they are evaluations. In this question, choice (B) is the correct answer, since the assertion that Greece's contribution to Western Civilization was greater than Rome's requires the most justification. Choice (B) is the most opinionated of the statements and therefore the one most difficult to prove or disprove.

12. The term "green revolution" refers to

(A) protests against the placement of nuclear weapons in Europe

(B) ecological changes in the ocean because of algae growth

(C) increased agricultural output resulting from development of hybrid seeds and chemical fertilizers

(D) expanded irrigation farming made possible by the construction of large dams

(E) thinning of the atmospheric ozone layer resulting in changes in the growing season

The correct answer to question 12 is (C). To answer this question you need to know about modern scientific breakthroughs in agricultural research that have allowed countries like India, formerly subject to terrible famines, to become self-sufficient in grain production.

SAT II:

World History Subject Test

The test that follows is representative of a typical SAT II: World History Subject Test. It has already been administered. So that you may have an idea of what the national test administration will be like, try to take the test in this book under conditions as close as possible to those of the nationally administered test. It will probably help if you do the following.

- Set aside an hour for the test when you will not be interrupted, so that you can complete all of it in one sitting.
- Sit at a desk with no other papers or books. You can't take a dictionary, other books, or notes into the test room.
- Have a kitchen timer or clock in front of you for timing yourself.
- Tear out an answer sheet from the back of this book and fill it in just as you would on the day of the test. You can use one answer sheet for as many as three Subject Tests.
- Read the instructions that precede the test. When you take the test, you will be asked to read them before you begin answering questions.
- After you finish the test, read the sections on "How to Score the SAT II: World History Subject Test" and "Reviewing Your Test Performance," which follow the test.

FORM 3PAC

WORLD HISTORY TEST

The top portion of the section of the answer sheet that you will use in taking the World History test must be filled in exactly as shown in the illustration below. Note carefully that you have to do all of the following on your answer sheet.

1. Print WORLD HISTORY on the line under the words "Subject (print)."

2. In the shaded box labeled "Test Code" fill in four ovals:

   —Fill in oval 1 in the row labeled V.

   —Fill in oval 7 in the row labeled W.

   —Fill in oval 3 in the row labeled X.

   —Fill in oval D in the row labeled Y.

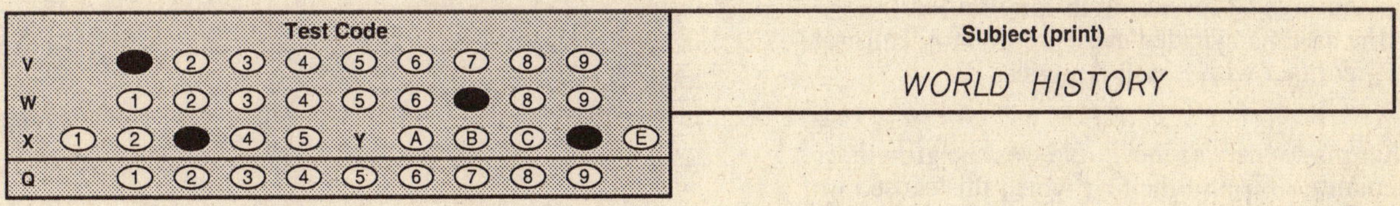

Test Code		Subject (print)
V	● 2 3 4 5 6 7 8 9	WORLD HISTORY
W	1 2 3 4 5 6 ● 8 9	
X	1 2 ● 4 5 Y A B C ● E	
Q	1 2 3 4 5 6 7 8 9	

3. Please answer the three questions below by filling in the appropriate ovals in the row labeled Q on the answer sheet. The information you provide is for statistical purposes only and will not affect your score on the test.

Question I

How many semesters of World History, World Cultures, or European History have you taken from grade 9 to the present? (If you are taking a course this semester, count it as a full semester.) Fill in only one oval of ovals 1-2.

- One semester or less —Fill in oval 1.
- Two semesters or more —Fill in oval 2.

Question II

For the courses in World History, World Cultures, or European History you have taken, which of the following geographical areas did you study? Fill in all of the ovals that apply.

- Africa —Fill in oval 3.
- Asia —Fill in oval 4.
- Europe —Fill in oval 5.
- Latin America —Fill in oval 6.
- Middle East —Fill in oval 7.

Question III

How recently have you studied World History, World Cultures, or European History?

- I am currently enrolled in or have just completed such a course. —Fill in oval 8.
- I have not studied this subject for 6 months or more. —Fill in oval 9.

When the supervisor gives the signal, turn the page and begin the World History test. There are 100 numbered ovals on the answer sheet and 95 questions in the World History test. Therefore, use only ovals 1 to 95 for recording your answers.

WORLD HISTORY TEST

Directions: Each of the questions or incomplete statements below is followed by five suggested answers or completions. Select the one that is best in each case and then fill in the corresponding oval on the answer sheet.

1. East Africa has been a rich source of information about the prehistoric life of humans because

   (A) the carbon-14 dating method can be used only in this region
   (B) fossils survive better in East Africa's warm climate than in colder regions
   (C) palm trees are especially suited for tree-ring dating
   (D) the fault system of the region has shifted enough to reveal fossils long buried
   (E) the area has yielded evidence of early cultural contact with South America

2. "What made the war inevitable was the growth of Athenian power and the fear which this caused in Sparta."

   The Greek historian quoted above was referring to the

   (A) Peloponnesian War
   (B) Trojan War
   (C) Indus campaign of Alexander the Great
   (D) invasion of Greece by Xerxes
   (E) First Punic War

Questions 3-5 refer to the figures below, numbered I-VI, which depict various architectural forms.

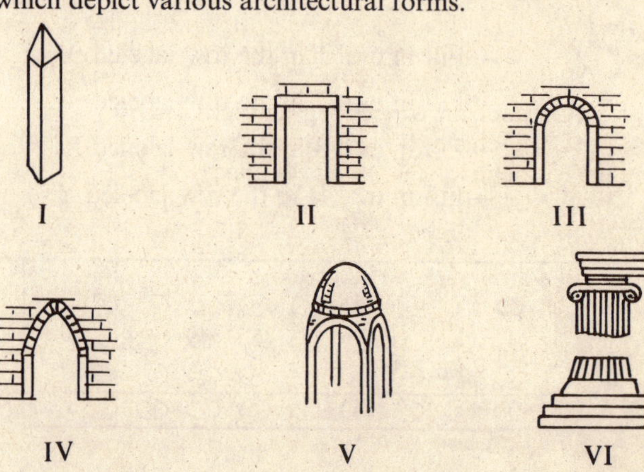

3. Which pair of forms was used in ancient Greek temples?

   (A) I and VI
   (B) II and VI
   (C) III and V
   (D) IV and V
   (E) V and VI

4. Which form was widely used by the Romans in their construction of aqueducts and sewers?

   (A) I
   (B) II
   (C) III
   (D) IV
   (E) VI

5. Which form was widely used throughout the Byzantine Empire, but is less often seen in Western Europe?

   (A) II
   (B) III
   (C) IV
   (D) V
   (E) VI

GO ON TO THE NEXT PAGE

6. "Upon this rock I will build my church; and the gates of hell shall not prevail against it. And I will give unto thee the keys of the kingdom of heaven, and whatsoever thou shalt bind on earth shall be bound in heaven; and whatsoever thou shalt loose on earth shall be loosed in heaven."

   The Biblical passage above provides the foundation for the

   (A) Donation of Constantine
   (B) Nicene Creed
   (C) doctrine of the forgiveness of sins
   (D) doctrine of predestination
   (E) doctrine of papal supremacy

7. Most adults in the Roman Empire worked primarily in which of the following areas?

   (A) The military
   (B) Crafts
   (C) Trade
   (D) Government bureaucracy
   (E) Agriculture

8. Which of the following helps to explain why Hernán Cortés and his troops entered Tenochtitlán, the Aztec capital, unopposed?

   (A) The Aztec emperor's inexperience as a military commander
   (B) The Aztec emperor's belief that Cortés possessed divine power
   (C) The location of the capital, which made an effective defensive strategy impossible
   (D) The Aztec emperor's absence from the capital when Cortés began his invasion
   (E) The conversion to Christianity of the majority of the capital's inhabitants

9. According to Descartes, the foundation of certainty in human knowledge is

   (A) revelation (B) convention (C) history (D) nature (E) reason

10. All of the following were part of the regular curriculum of a medieval university EXCEPT

    (A) the works of Copernicus
    (B) the works of Aristotle
    (C) Ptolemy's astronomical theories
    (D) Latin language and literature
    (E) Euclidean geometry

11. The Roman Empire was rescued from almost incessant civil war over the imperial succession by the administrative reforms of

    (A) Diocletian
    (B) Caracalla
    (C) Tiberius Gracchus
    (D) Tiberius
    (E) Domitian

12. Which of the following led to the division of Islam between the Sunnis and the Shi'ites (Shi'a) after the death of Muhammad in 632 A.D.?

    (A) Disputes over the forced conversion of conquered peoples to Islam
    (B) Theological debate over the question of free will versus predestination
    (C) The unequal status of Arab and non-Arab Muslims
    (D) Conflict over the rightful successor to Muhammad
    (E) Arguments over different interpretations of scripture

13. In the fourteenth century, the Roman Catholic church lost prestige among Europeans when the

    (A) French king forced the pope to move from Rome to Avignon
    (B) French queen ordered the massacre of thousands of French Protestants
    (C) Anabaptists succeeded in establishing prosperous communes
    (D) Church failed to prevent the Muslims from reconquering most of Spain
    (E) Normans almost conquered Rome

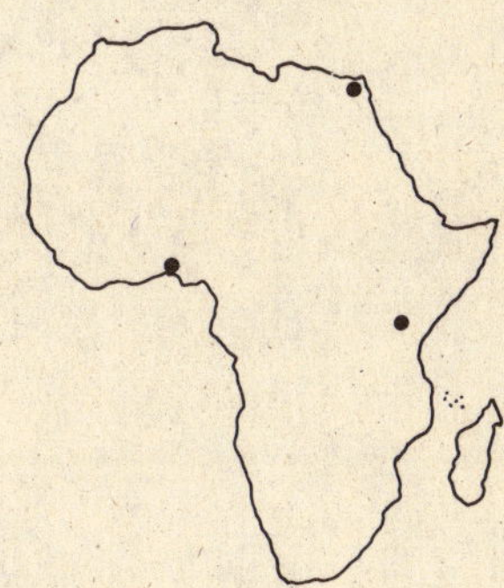

14. On the map above of Africa, the modern-day cities marked are

    (A) Dakar, Kinshasa, and Dar es Salaam
    (B) Conakry, Lusaka, and Johannesburg
    (C) Algiers, Khartoum, and Addis Ababa
    (D) Lagos, Cairo, and Nairobi
    (E) Abidjan, Kampala, and Windhoek

GO ON TO THE NEXT PAGE

SOCIAL AND ECONOMIC ORIGINS OF WOMEN WHO MARRIED ENGLISH PEERS, 1300-1500

Status	Heiress	Nonheiress	Total
Noble Family	135 (36%)	236 (64%)	371 (100%)
Non-noble Family	75 (36%)	134 (64%)	209 (100%)
Total	210	370	580

Number of Peers: 430

15. Which of the following statements can be supported by the table above?
    - (A) There were more noble than non-noble families in England.
    - (B) The percentage of heiresses married to peers varied by social class.
    - (C) Divorces were common among the English peerage.
    - (D) Peers were more likely to marry women of noble birth than of non-noble birth.
    - (E) Peers were not allowed to marry across class lines.

GO ON TO THE NEXT PAGE

16. "If a ruler himself is upright, all will go well without orders. But if he himself is not upright, even though he gives orders, they will not be obeyed."

    The quotation above is taken from

    (A) Confucius' *Analects*
    (B) Montesquieu's *The Spirit of the Laws*
    (C) *The Secret History of the Mongols*
    (D) Hobbes's *Leviathan*
    (E) Omar Khayyám's *Rubáiját*

17. Which of the following is true about medieval guilds?

    (A) They were regulated by the Church.
    (B) They were governed by the feudal nobility.
    (C) They controlled wages and prices.
    (D) They encouraged competition.
    (E) They sought to attract as many members as possible.

18. One of the immediate outcomes of the United States occupation of Japan following the Second World War was the

    (A) institution of Japan's first parliamentary form of government
    (B) demilitarization of Japan
    (C) electoral success of the Communist party
    (D) beginning of Japan's industrialization
    (E) opening of diplomatic relations between China and Japan

19. "We have demolished the facades of oppression, extortion, and humiliation. Today, O citizens, the Suez Canal has been nationalized."

    The quotation above is taken from a speech by

    (A) Ferdinand de Lesseps
    (B) Anwar Sadat
    (C) King Farouk
    (D) Mohammed Ali Jinnah
    (E) Gamal Abdel Nasser

GO ON TO THE NEXT PAGE

Questions 20-21 refer to the following passage.

I once more repeat, the sovereign represents the state; he and his people form but one body, which can only be happy as far as united by concord. The prince is to the nation he governs what the head is to the man; it is his duty to see, think, and act for the whole community. He is only the first servant of the state, who is obliged to act with probity and prudence; and to remain as totally disinterested as if he were each moment liable to render an account of his administration to his fellow citizens.

20. This passage sums up the spirit of

(A) the divine right of kings
(B) enlightened despotism
(C) a constitutional monarchy
(D) republicanism
(E) nationalism

21. The prince described in this quotation would probably have favored all of the following EXCEPT

(A) a rational and efficient civil service
(B) abolition of the peasants' manorial obligations
(C) universal suffrage
(D) improved agricultural productivity
(E) improved educational facilities

22. "Our Celestial Empire possesses all things in prolific abundance and lacks no product within its own borders. There was, therefore, no need to import the manufactures of outside barbarians."

The above was most likely written by

(A) the Holy Roman Emperor Rudolph I to the Mongol ruler Kublai Khan
(B) the Chinese Emperor Ch'ien-lung to King George III of England
(C) Pope Leo I to Attila the Hun
(D) Meiji Emperor Mutsuhito of Japan to President Grover Cleveland
(E) Mughal Emperor Bahadur Shah II to Queen Victoria of England

23. In the English Civil War, the leader of the New Model Army was

(A) Prince Rupert
(B) Charles II
(C) Oliver Cromwell
(D) the Earl of Essex
(E) John Lilburne

GO ON TO THE NEXT PAGE

Victoria and Albert Museum

24. The statue shown above is most closely associated with the culture of

(A) Sumer
(B) ancient China
(C) classical Greece
(D) Islamic North Africa
(E) Hindu India

GO ON TO THE NEXT PAGE

25. "By no means can a prudent ruler keep his word—and he does not—when to keep it works against himself and when the reasons that made him promise are annulled. . . . Never has a shrewd prince lacked justifying reasons to make his promise-breaking appear honorable."

    The statement above is drawn from the writings of

    (A) Bossuet
    (B) Grotius
    (C) Machiavelli
    (D) Metternich
    (E) Voltaire

26. Which of the following theorized that unchecked population growth would lead to disaster by outstripping the food supply?

    (A) Adam Smith
    (B) Thomas Hobbes
    (C) John Stuart Mill
    (D) Thomas Malthus
    (E) John Maynard Keynes

27. The Arab-Islamic conquests of the seventh century A.D. succeeded partly because the

    (A) peoples of Syria, Persia, and Egypt failed to support their rulers in repelling the Arab armies
    (B) Arabs scattered enemy forces by using gunpowder artillery
    (C) European rulers sent armies to fight on the side of the Arabs
    (D) long-standing Byzantine-Persian alliance broke down when the Arabs appeared
    (E) Christian and Jewish populations of Syria and Egypt quickly converted to Islam

28. In 1914 the only countries in Africa that were neither colonies nor protectorates of European powers were

    (A) Kenya and Angola
    (B) Nigeria and Sierra Leone
    (C) Egypt and the Sudan
    (D) Liberia and Ethiopia
    (E) Morocco and Tunisia

29. The financial crisis that France faced in the 1780's was brought on by increased government spending intended to

    (A) subsidize peasant farmers after two years of crop failure
    (B) suppress a popular revolt in France's Caribbean colonies
    (C) make up for the lowering of tariff barriers on foreign imports
    (D) pay for an invasion of Algeria to oust the Ottoman Turks
    (E) support a popular revolution in Britain's North American colonies

30. Which of the following led Henry VIII to break with the Roman Catholic church?

    (A) His acceptance of the theology of Martin Luther
    (B) His dissatisfaction with the low educational levels of the English clergy
    (C) His desire to seize lands held by the Church
    (D) Lord Chancellor Cardinal Wolsey's high-handedness
    (E) The pope's refusal to annul Henry's marriage to Catherine of Aragon

31. Which of the following emerged from the Reformation with a population divided almost equally between Protestantism and Catholicism?

    (A) Switzerland
    (B) The German states
    (C) England
    (D) The Italian city-states
    (E) Hungary

32. For centuries China's paramount concern in foreign relations has been the

    (A) security of its northern borders
    (B) threat to its shipping in the China Sea from pirates
    (C) tensions among peoples of the Indian subcontinent
    (D) colonization of Southeast Asia
    (E) status of European balance-of-power rivalries

33. Which of the following was true of the joint-stock company during the Commercial Revolution?

    (A) It was developed to reduce competition.
    (B) It sold shares to investors to raise capital.
    (C) It guaranteed profits to its investors.
    (D) It loaned money to monarchs.
    (E) It eliminated the need for insurance.

GO ON TO THE NEXT PAGE

34. The introduction of gunpowder weaponry in Europe in the fourteenth and fifteenth centuries led directly to the
    (A) reduction of the power of feudal lords by diminishing the importance of castles as defensive strongholds
    (B) reduction of the importance of the common infantry soldier in European warfare
    (C) reduction of the size of armies
    (D) consolidation of the Hapsburg's hold on the German states
    (E) ability of Eastern European kingdoms to repel the Ottoman Turks

35. The Committee of Public Safety was set up primarily to
    (A) provide representation for the workers in Paris
    (B) eliminate the bourgeoisie
    (C) redistribute confiscated church lands
    (D) provide protection from the brigands that were terrorizing France
    (E) protect the French Republic from its domestic and foreign enemies

36. Luther and Calvin were in agreement that
    (A) churches are best administered by bishops
    (B) churches should be stripped of all ornamentation
    (C) every individual has the right to worship God in his or her own way
    (D) people are saved by God's grace, not by good works
    (E) women should be ordained as ministers

37. Which of the following innovations contributed to increased agricultural productivity in medieval Europe?
    (A) Horse collars and moldboard plows
    (B) Hybridized seeds and fertilizers
    (C) Waterwheels and pumps
    (D) Sickles and seed drills
    (E) Barbed wire and enclosures

38. Shi'ite (Shi'a) Islam became Iran's official religion during the
    (A) Arab conquest of Persia in the seventh century
    (B) Safavid rule in the sixteenth century
    (C) territorial division of the Middle East following the First World War
    (D) 1920's when Reza Shah Pahlavi followed a policy of independence from the Arab nations
    (E) late 1940's when Israel was created

39. All of the following organizations were concerned with a struggle for national independence EXCEPT
    (A) Young Italy
    (B) the Viet Minh
    (C) the Fabian Society
    (D) Sinn Fein
    (E) the Indian National Congress

40. The largest volume of medieval European trade was in which of the following commodities?
    (A) Wine
    (B) Iron
    (C) Cotton
    (D) Wool
    (E) Olive oil

41. Which of the following former European colonies became independent before 1900 ?
    (A) Algeria
    (B) Brazil
    (C) India
    (D) Indochina
    (E) Ivory Coast

42. "The time will come when the sun will shine only on free men who know no other master but their reason; . . . when we shall . . . learn how to recognize and so to destroy, by force of reason, the first seeds of tyranny and superstition."

    The quotation above was most likely written in
    (A) Rome in the first century
    (B) England in the fifteenth century
    (C) Italy in the sixteenth century
    (D) France in the eighteenth century
    (E) Russia in the twentieth century

43. Which of the following would most likely have been viewed as heretical by Church authorities in the Middle Ages?
    (A) Denial of the spiritual authority of the priesthood
    (B) Criticism of the social order
    (C) Anti-Semitism
    (D) Ignorance of Christian doctrine
    (E) Continued failure to attend Church services regularly

GO ON TO THE NEXT PAGE

Questions 44-46 refer to the following artistic styles. In each question, identify the style of the work of art shown.

(A) Bauhaus
(B) Renaissance
(C) Pre-Raphaelite
(D) Byzantine
(E) Rococo

44.

GO ON TO THE NEXT PAGE

45.

46.

GO ON TO THE NEXT PAGE

47. All of the following occurred during the reign of Charlemagne EXCEPT

(A) his coronation as emperor by the pope
(B) the establishment of a palace school
(C) the expulsion of the Muslims from Spain
(D) the incorporation of northern Italy into the Frankish Kingdom
(E) the Frankish conquest of Saxony and Bavaria

48. The principal reason for the success of fifteenth-century European monarchs such as Louis XI of France, Henry VII of England, and Ferdinand and Isabella of Spain is that they

(A) established civil order
(B) introduced religious freedom
(C) introduced educational reforms
(D) shared power with the nobility
(E) emphasized social reforms

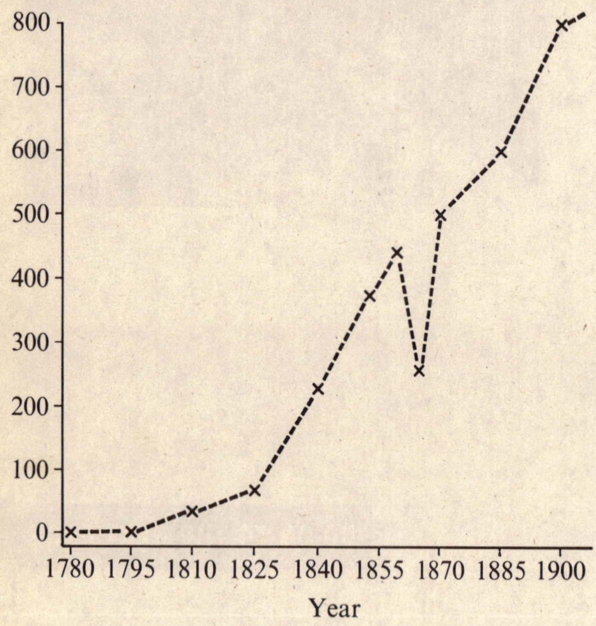

49. The graph above refers to which of the following aspects of the English economy?

(A) Work hours lost due to strikes led by trade unions, in hundreds of hours
(B) Production of coal, in millions of tons
(C) Value of imported grain, in thousands of pounds sterling
(D) Value of gross national product, in millions of pounds sterling
(E) Weight of imported raw cotton, in thousands of metric tons

50. At the time of their creation, the Italian Kingdom and the German Empire were each marked by

(A) a government responsible to a democratically elected parliament
(B) a social revolution that created an ethnically unified society
(C) a common religion that helped rally the people behind the central government
(D) a surge of liberalism that created a cohesive society
(E) the political dominance of one region over the rest of the nation

51. "The British were in Burma and the French in Indo-China, suspicious and distrustful of one another, neither allowing the other to move a step nearer."

This statement refers to

(A) a basic cause of the Opium War in the 1840's
(B) a result of the Treaty of Paris in 1763
(C) the situation in South Asia when the Mughal Empire was established
(D) a reason why Siam remained free and independent
(E) a reason for the extension of Dutch power in the East Indies

52. Max Weber's thesis that the Protestant Reformation encouraged the creation of a new set of attitudes and values leading to modern capitalism has been criticized on the ground that the same values and attitudes were found in medieval

(A) Italy
(B) France
(C) Poland
(D) England
(E) Scotland

GO ON TO THE NEXT PAGE

53. The renewed interest in folk arts and traditions associated with the Romantic era had the effect of

    (A) arousing national consciousness and increasing the feelings of nationalism
    (B) reducing interest in the cultures of Greece and Rome
    (C) reviving a preoccupation with the cultures of Egypt and Assyria
    (D) discouraging any widespread participation in the arts by the general public
    (E) broadening support for the rationalism of the Enlightenment

54. Estimates of the number of slaves sent from West Africa to the Western Hemisphere from the seventeenth through the nineteenth century would LEAST likely be derived from which of the following?

    (A) Logbooks of slave ships
    (B) Records of port cities
    (C) Trading-company records
    (D) Personal diaries of ship captains
    (E) Records of taxes paid by freed slaves

GO ON TO THE NEXT PAGE

The Leading Role of the Party.
A. Krauze, 1981.

55. The cartoon above reflects a critical view of the Communist party leadership in which of the following countries?

(A) The Soviet Union
(B) Poland
(C) Hungary
(D) Romania
(E) Bulgaria

GO ON TO THE NEXT PAGE

56. "Above all else, modern society requires rational management. Private wealth, property, and enterprise should be subject to an administration other than that of its owners. The ideal government consists of a large board of directors organizing and coordinating the activity of individuals and groups to achieve social harmony."

    The passage above reflects the views of

    (A) a Social Darwinist
    (B) a Marxist revolutionary
    (C) a Utopian socialist
    (D) a French philosophe
    (E) an English Chartist

57. An economic weakness of many of the Central American countries in the twentieth century has been their

    (A) mountainous topography that limits agricultural production
    (B) heavy investment in foreign manufacturing industries
    (C) chronic labor shortages caused by small population growth
    (D) overdependence on one or two cash crops for export
    (E) highly diversified industries that have no central focus

58. The European peace treaty that is best known for reestablishing monarchies and redrawing national borders to achieve a balance of power was concluded in

    (A) Berlin
    (B) Frankfurt
    (C) Vienna
    (D) Versailles
    (E) Westphalia

59. The Spanish monarchs Ferdinand and Isabella relied on the Inquisition in the late fifteenth century primarily to

    (A) ensure the religious orthodoxy of Jews and Muslims who had converted to Christianity
    (B) ensure the regular collection of taxes from commoners
    (C) identify the instigators of unrest fueled by food shortages in the countryside
    (D) combat the spread of Calvinism in the cities of Castile and Aragon
    (E) enforce celibacy and doctrinal orthodoxy among the clergy

60. The establishment of "people's republics" by revolutionaries in Central and Eastern Europe after the Second World War was made possible largely by the

    (A) implementation of wartime treaties
    (B) Italian military collapse and withdrawal
    (C) presence of Soviet military power
    (D) organization of locally sponsored national referendums
    (E) support of the United States and Great Britain

GO ON TO THE NEXT PAGE

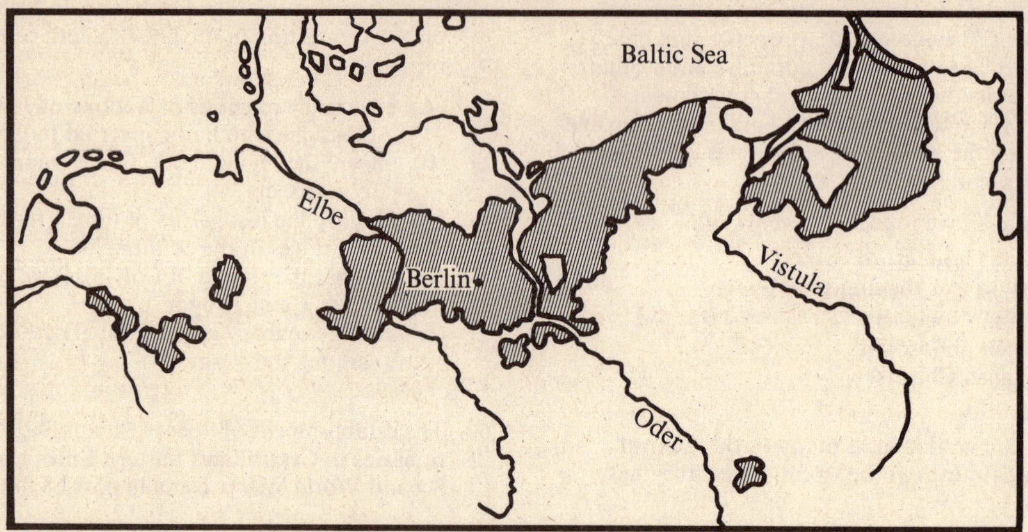

61. The shaded areas on the map above illustrate
    (A) the nucleus of the Hapsburg Empire in the fifteenth century
    (B) Brandenburg-Prussia in the late seventeenth century
    (C) Poland after the first partition in 1772
    (D) the division of Germany into two independent states after 1945
    (E) the extent of Soviet domination of Eastern Europe after 1960

GO ON TO THE NEXT PAGE

62. On the termination of Great Britain's rule in India, the most important factor determining the areas to be included in Pakistan rather than in India was

(A) the existence of a Muslim majority in the areas
(B) the British desire to accommodate the Indian princely states
(C) the outcome of a popular referendum on partition
(D) Gandhi's refusal to concede any areas in which Hindi was the major language
(E) the long-standing existence of Muslim kingdoms in the areas

63. Local government administration in France under Louis XIV was largely controlled by

(A) noble marshals
(B) *baillis* (bailiffs)
(C) ecclesiastical officers
(D) *intendants*
(E) regional *parlements*

64. Reading from left to right, which of the following represents the correct chronological order in which the countries listed achieved independence from European colonial rule?

(A) India, Ghana, Nigeria, Zimbabwe
(B) India, Zimbabwe, Nigeria, Ghana
(C) Ghana, Nigeria, India, Zimbabwe
(D) Nigeria, Zimbabwe, India, Ghana
(E) Zimbabwe, India, Ghana, Nigeria

65. In late-sixteenth- and early-seventeenth-century Japan, the consolidation of political power at the local level and the increased strength of the daimyo (feudal lord) was symbolized by the

(A) adoption of Western technology
(B) success of Jesuit missions in spreading Christianity
(C) establishment of numerous castle towns
(D) growing dependence on rice imported from China
(E) abolition of the land tax on the peasantry

66. In response to Hitler's aggression, the Second World War began in September 1939 with a declaration of war by

(A) Great Britain, France, and the United States against Germany and Italy
(B) Great Britain, France, and the Soviet Union against Germany, Italy, and Poland
(C) Great Britain, France, and Poland against Germany
(D) Poland and the Soviet Union against Germany and Italy
(E) the Soviet Union against Germany

67. Under Indira Gandhi, Indian foreign policy was characterized by

(A) continued tension with Pakistan
(B) general support for United States policies in Asia
(C) hostility toward the Soviet Union
(D) complete nonalignment in the tradition of Nehru
(E) friendship with China to ensure Indian control over Bangladesh

GO ON TO THE NEXT PAGE

68. Approximately 50 percent of the African terrain consists of

(A) deserts
(B) tropical rain forests
(C) savannas
(D) mountains
(E) tundras

69. Most nineteenth-century European anarchists upheld which of the following as the highest ideal?

(A) A world government capable of maintaining global peace and order
(B) A society of workers, farmers, and artisans free from centralized political control
(C) A strong state capable of guaranteeing social justice for all people
(D) An organized church that would be responsible for defining social morality
(E) Free compulsory education for all children from age five through age eighteen

70. Italy's invasion of Ethiopia and Japan's seizure of Manchuria demonstrated the ineffectiveness of the

(A) League of Nations
(B) North Atlantic Treaty Organization
(C) United Nations
(D) Rome-Berlin-Tokyo Axis
(E) Warsaw Pact

71. The organization that would most likely deal with a dispute between two African countries is the

(A) Organization of Petroleum Exporting Countries
(B) North Atlantic Treaty Organization
(C) Organization of African Unity
(D) Economic Community of West African States
(E) African Defense Council

72. "The species of domestic industry which his capital can employ, and of which the produce is likely to be of greatest value, every individual can, in his local situation, judge much better than any statesman or lawgiver can."

The statement above was written in the

(A) seventeenth century in an attack on the laissez-faire principles
(B) eighteenth century in an attack on mercantilism
(C) nineteenth century in favor of democracy
(D) nineteenth century on behalf of the ideas of utopian socialism
(E) twentieth century to help the election of British Labour party candidates

73. The main result of the Franco-Prussian War of 1870-1871 was

(A) the Prussian occupation of France until 1890
(B) the conversion of France from a republic to an empire
(C) a severe reduction of Prussian power
(D) a socialist revolution in Prussia
(E) the creation of the German Empire

74. Which of the following was a consequence of the aggressive foreign policy of Napoleon III of France between 1848 and 1870 ?

(A) Military victory over Prussia in the Franco-Prussian War
(B) Political crisis with Britain over control of the Upper Nile valley
(C) Seizure and colonization of the island of Haiti
(D) Installation of Archduke Maximilian as emperor of Mexico
(E) Invasion of Hungary in alliance with Austria

GO ON TO THE NEXT PAGE

75. Population growth in India in the twentieth century has been due chiefly to

(A) the success of Gandhi's campaign of non-violence
(B) an increase in the ratio of female to male births
(C) a decline in the death rate
(D) the emergence of industrialized centers
(E) government incentives for large families

76. Which of the following occurred in Western Europe as a consequence of the Great Depression?

(A) An increase in economic protectionism by Europe's leading nations
(B) An increase in speculation on major stock markets
(C) An expansion of free trade among the major European states
(D) A lessening of government involvement in national economies
(E) The creation of the International Monetary Fund

77. "From Stettin in the Baltic, to Trieste in the Adriatic, an iron curtain has descended across the continent. . . ."

Which of the following countries was west of the "iron curtain" in 1948 ?

(A) Belgium
(B) Bulgaria
(C) Czechoslovakia
(D) Poland
(E) Romania

78. The signing of the Soviet-Nazi Nonaggression Pact in 1939 paved the way for the

(A) Anschluss
(B) Spanish Civil War
(C) German invasion of Poland
(D) Russian invasion of Czechoslovakia
(E) remilitarization of the Rhineland

79. For English classical liberals, the main function of the state was to

(A) regulate working conditions
(B) provide a trained labor force through universal, compulsory education
(C) safeguard the environment against industrial pollution
(D) use tariffs to keep out unfair foreign competition
(E) protect private property

80. Karl Marx argued that the problems created by the Industrial Revolution would

(A) be solved by economic and social legislation
(B) be solved by a government run by industrial experts
(C) only be solved by the peaceful cooperation of all classes
(D) ultimately lead to violent revolution
(E) result in the elimination of all forms of authority

GO ON TO THE NEXT PAGE

Private collection, Switzerland

81. The 1907 painting by Picasso shown above reveals the influence of which of the following?

    (A) Chinese art
    (B) African art
    (C) Indian art
    (D) European medieval art
    (E) European Romantic art

GO ON TO THE NEXT PAGE

82. In post-Second World War Western Europe, which of the following economic sectors has experienced the most rapid growth in employment?

(A) Small business
(B) Mining
(C) Services
(D) Agriculture
(E) Heavy industry

83. The Boer War (1899-1902) was fought between

(A) France and Germany for control of territory in East Africa
(B) Spain and the Netherlands for control of the East Indies
(C) Great Britain and the Afrikaners for control of territory in South Africa
(D) Austria and Italy for control of Trieste
(E) Belgium and Portugal for control of Central Africa

84. Which of the following religions had their origin on the subcontinent of India?

I. Buddhism
II. Shintoism
III. Sikhism
IV. Jainism
V. Taoism

(A) II and III only
(B) I, III, and IV only
(C) I, III, and V only
(D) I, IV, and V only
(E) II, III, and IV only

85. Which of the following did NOT have a significant effect on British industrialization in the eighteenth century?

(A) A rising population
(B) A growing market for manufactured goods
(C) Government policies to limit industrial growth
(D) Increased agricultural productivity
(E) The movement of people from rural areas to the cities

86. Mustafa Kemal Atatürk is widely admired for his leadership of Turkey because he

(A) blocked a communist takeover after the Second World War
(B) drove the British out of Cyprus
(C) was principally responsible for establishing the modern Turkish republic
(D) was the moving force in the revival of traditional Islamic culture
(E) reestablished control over former Ottoman territories

87. In the mid-eighteenth century, slaves from West Africa were transported on European ships mainly to

(A) silver mines in Peru
(B) sugar plantations in the West Indies
(C) canal construction sites in the Middle East
(D) farms in New England
(E) logging sites in the Amazon valley

GO ON TO THE NEXT PAGE

88. Which of the following were newly industrialized countries that assumed increasingly important roles in world trade in the 1970's?

(A) Taiwan and South Korea
(B) Zaire and Guinea
(C) Bolivia and Peru
(D) Cambodia and Burma
(E) Afghanistan and Nepal

89. Otto von Bismarck's chief social legislation included

(A) equal pay for equal work for men and women
(B) health, accident, and old-age insurance
(C) factory safety laws
(D) freeing the remaining serfs in Prussia
(E) recognizing the shipyard union in Hamburg

90. Which of the following occurred in the People's Republic of China in the years between the death of Mao Tse-tung and the early 1980's?

(A) Population declined.
(B) Per capita income declined.
(C) Relations with the Soviet Union were normalized.
(D) Democratic rights were restored.
(E) Foreign trade rose.

91. Which of the following was among the goals of the Kennedy administration's Alliance for Progress?

(A) To use economic aid to prevent Marxist revolutions
(B) To create a common Latin American currency in order to promote trade
(C) To bring Latin America into the North Atlantic Treaty Organization
(D) To curtail arms sales to Latin American countries
(E) To promote rapid urbanization

92. Which of the following correctly describes Bangladesh?

(A) A modern Hindu revivalist movement in India
(B) A modern Muslim revivalist movement in India
(C) An independent Southeast Asian state that was created by the French after the First World War
(D) An independent Muslim state that was created by the partition of British India in 1947
(E) An independent state that emerged as a result of a civil war in Pakistan in the 1970's

GO ON TO THE NEXT PAGE

SHARES OF GROSS WORLD PRODUCT, 1960-1980
(percent)

	1960	1970	1980
European Economic Community	26.0	24.7	22.5
United States	25.9	23.0	21.5
USSR	12.5	12.4	11.4
Other Communist Countries	6.8	6.2	6.1
Other Developed Countries	10.1	10.3	9.7
Less-Developed Countries	11.1	12.3	14.8
Japan	4.5	7.7	9.0
China	3.1	3.4	4.5

93. The table above indicates that between 1960 and 1980, shares of the gross world product did which of the following?

(A) Decreased for all countries north of the equator.
(B) Decreased for members of the European Economic Community.
(C) Increased for countries within the Soviet sphere of influence.
(D) Increased for countries with democratic forms of government.
(E) Increased at a higher rate for less-developed countries than for Japan.

GO ON TO THE NEXT PAGE

94. Which of the following best describes the Brezhnev Doctrine?

(A) It affirmed the right of the Soviet Union to intervene in the affairs of Eastern Bloc countries in danger of deviating from socialism.
(B) It was an attempt to open new commercial and trading links with Western Europe.
(C) It was an example of the Soviet Union's attempt to comply with the Helsinki Agreement.
(D) It represented a radical shift of economic policy from a central planning mode to one based on individual and local initiatives.
(E) It provided for more troops and military installations along the Soviet-Chinese border.

95. Pope John XXIII was famous for his efforts to

(A) encourage lay organizations among Roman Catholics to oppose communism
(B) focus Roman Catholic efforts on opposing labor unions and socialist programs
(C) counter new theological trends among liberal Roman Catholic theologians
(D) establish the Latin mass as the basic sacrament of the Roman Catholic church
(E) bring Roman Catholic institutions into harmony with modern political and social changes

S T O P

IF YOU FINISH BEFORE TIME IS CALLED, YOU MAY CHECK YOUR WORK ON THIS TEST ONLY.
DO NOT WORK ON ANY OTHER TEST IN THIS BOOK.

How to Score the SAT II: World History Test

When you take an actual SAT II: World History Subject Test, your answer sheet will be "read" by a scanning machine that will record your responses to each question. Then a computer will compare your answers with the correct answers and produce your raw score. You get one point for each correct answer. For each wrong answer, you lose one-fourth of a point. Questions you omit (and any for which you mark more than one answer) are not counted. This raw score is converted to a College Board scaled score that is reported to you and to the colleges you specify. After you have taken this test, you can get an idea of what your score might be by following the instructions in the next two sections.

FINDING YOUR RAW SCORE

Step 1: Table A lists the correct answers for all the questions on the SAT II: World History Subject Test that is reproduced in this book. It also serves as a worksheet for you to calculate your raw score.

- Compare your answers with those given in the table.
- Put a check in the column marked "Right" if your answer is correct.
- Put a check in the column marked "Wrong" if your answer is incorrect.
- Leave both columns blank if you omitted the question.

Step 2: Count the number of right answers and enter the total here: .... ________

Step 3: Count the number of wrong answers and enter the total here: .... ________

Step 4: Divide the number of wrong answers by 4 and enter the result here: .... ________

Step 5: Subtract the result obtained in Step 4 from the total you obtained in Step 2. Enter the result here: .... ________

Step 6: Round the number obtained in Step 5 to the nearest whole number. Enter the result here: .... ________

The number you obtained in Step 6 is your raw score.

TABLE A

Answers to the SAT II: World History Subject Test, Form 3PAC, and Percentage of Students Answering Each Question Correctly

Question Number	Correct Answer	Right	Wrong	Percentage of Students Answering the Question Correctly*	Question Number	Correct Answer	Right	Wrong	Percentage of Students Answering the Question Correctly*
1	D			48	49	E			23
2	A			51	50	E			40
3	B			53	51	D			31
4	C			73	52	A			27
5	D			63	53	A			41
6	E			30	54	E			63
7	E			29	55	B			52
8	B			72	56	C			41
9	E			64	57	D			63
10	A			53	58	C			33
11	A			22	59	A			40
12	D			48	60	C			51
13	A			44	61	B			48
14	D			79	62	A			53
15	D			35	63	D			20
16	A			29	64	A			24
17	C			52	65	C			48
18	B			56	66	C			54
19	E			34	67	A			25
20	B			33	68	C			30
21	C			53	69	B			63
22	B			38	70	A			68
23	C			62	71	C			62
24	E			85	72	B			22
25	C			57	73	E			34
26	D			36	74	D			23
27	A			34	75	C			41
28	D			41	76	A			38
29	E			46	77	A			68
30	E			86	78	C			67
31	B			45	79	E			21
32	A			47	80	D			49
33	B			57	81	B			65
34	A			42	82	C			21
35	E			32	83	C			56
36	D			32	84	B			49
37	A			50	85	C			43
38	B			13	86	C			33
39	C			32	87	B			64
40	D			41	88	A			76
41	B			57	89	B			17
42	D			49	90	E			37
43	A			55	91	A			27
44	D			67	92	E			28
45	E			31	93	B			59
46	B			53	94	A			32
47	C			43	95	E			43
48	A			48					

*These percentages are based on an analysis of the answer sheets for a random sample of 1,952 students who took this form of the test in December 1993 and whose mean score was 545. They may be used as an indication of the relative difficulty of a particular question. Each percentage may also be used to predict the likelihood that a typical SAT II: World History Subject Test candidate will answer correctly that question on this edition of this test.

Finding Your College Board Scaled Score

When you take SAT II: Subject Tests, the scores sent to the colleges you specify are reported on the College Board scale, which ranges from 200 to 800. You can convert your practice test score to a scaled score by using Table B. To find your scaled score, locate your raw score in the left-hand column of Table B; the corresponding score in the right-hand column is your College Board scaled score. For example, a raw score of 47 on this particular edition of the SAT II: World History Subject Test corresponds to a College Board scaled score of 590.

Raw scores are converted to scaled scores to ensure that a score earned on any one edition of a particular Subject Test is comparable to the same scaled score earned on any other edition of the same Subject Test. Because some editions of tests may be slightly easier or more difficult than others, College Board scaled scores are adjusted so that they indicate the same level of performance regardless of the edition of the test taken and the ability of the group that takes it. Thus, for example, a score of 400 on one edition of a test taken at a particular administration indicates the same level of achievement as a score of 400 on a different edition of the test taken at a different administration.

When you take the SAT II: Subject Tests during a national administration, your scores are likely to differ somewhat from the scores you obtain on the tests in this book. People perform at different levels at different times for reasons unrelated to the tests themselves. The precision of any test is also limited because it represents only a sample of all the possible questions that could be asked.

TABLE B

Score Conversion Table
World History Subject Test, Form 3PAC

Raw Score	College Board Scaled Score	Raw Score	College Board Scaled Score
95	800	35	520
94	800	34	510
93	800	33	510
92	800	32	510
91	800	31	500
90	800	30	500
89	800	29	490
88	800	28	490
87	800	27	490
86	800	26	480
85	800	25	480
84	790	24	470
83	790	23	470
82	790	22	460
81	780	21	460
80	770	20	450
79	770	19	450
78	760	18	450
77	750	17	440
76	740	16	440
75	740	15	430
74	730	14	430
73	720	13	420
72	720	12	420
71	710	11	410
70	710	10	410
69	700	9	400
68	700	8	390
67	690	7	380
66	690	6	380
65	680	5	370
64	680	4	360
63	670	3	360
62	670	2	350
61	660	1	350
60	660	0	340
59	650	−1	330
58	650	−2	320
57	640	−3	310
56	640	−4	310
55	630	−5	300
54	630	−6	290
53	620	−7	280
52	610	−8	270
51	610	−9	260
50	600	−10	250
49	600	−11	250
48	590	−12	240
47	590	−13	230
46	580	−14	220
45	570	−15	210
44	570	−16	200
43	560	−17	200
42	560	−18	200
41	550	−19	200
40	550	−20	200
39	540	−21	200
38	540	−22	200
37	530	−23	200
36	530	−24	200

Reviewing Your Test Performance

After you have scored your test, you should take some time to consider the following points in relation to your performance on the test.

- *Did you run out of time before you reached the end of the test?*

  If you did, you may want to consider pacing yourself better. For example, you may have spent too much time working on one or two difficult questions. A better approach might have been to continue the test and return to those questions after you had attempted to answer the remaining questions on the test.

- *Did you take a long time reading the directions for the test?*

  The directions in this test are the same as those in the World History Subject Tests now being administered. You will save time when you read the directions on the test day if you become thoroughly familiar with them in advance.

- *How did you handle questions you were unsure of?*

  If you were able to eliminate one or more of the answer choices and you guessed from the remaining choices, then your approach probably worked to your advantage. On the other hand, omitting questions about which you have some knowledge or guessing answers haphazardly would probably be a mistake.

- *How difficult were the questions for you compared with other students who took the test?*

By referring to Table A, you can find out how difficult each question was for the group of students who took this test. The right-hand column in the table tells you what percentage of this group answered the question correctly. A question that was answered correctly by almost everyone in the group is obviously an easy question. Question 30, for example, was answered correctly by 86 percent of the students in the sample. On the other hand, question 11 was answered correctly by only 22 percent.

It is important to remember that these percentages are based on only one particular group of students; had this edition of the test been given to other groups of students at that time, the percentages would probably have been different.

If you find that you missed several questions that would be considered easy, you may want to review those questions carefully. They may cover some aspect of the subject that you need to review. Perhaps you misunderstood the directions for one part of the test or you thought the questions were so easy that you did not spend as much time on them as you might have.

The SAT II: Mathematics Subject Tests

The two Subject Tests in Mathematics are currently Mathematics Level I and Mathematics Level IIC. Mathematics Level IC will be introduced in June 1995.

Mathematics Level I is a broad survey test composed of 50 multiple-choice questions that can be answered without the use of a calculator. Students are not permitted to use a calculator on this test. The Mathematics Level I test is intended for students who have taken three years of college-preparatory mathematics (two years of algebra and a year of geometry). This test contains questions in algebra; geometry; basic trigonometry; algebraic functions; elementary statistics, including counting problems, data interpretation, and measures of central tendency (mean, median, and mode); and other miscellaneous topics, including logic, elementary number theory, and arithmetic and geometric sequences. Students are not expected to have studied every topic on the test.

Mathematics Level IIC is also composed of 50 multiple-choice questions, some of which require the use of at least a scientific calculator. It is intended for students who have taken college-preparatory mathematics for more than three years (two years of algebra, a year of geometry, and elementary functions (precalculus) and/or trigonometry). The Level IIC test contains questions in algebra; geometry; trigonometry; functions; statistics, including probability, permutations, and combinations; and other miscellaneous topics, including logic and proof, elementary number theory, sequences, and limits. Students are not expected to have studied every topic on the test.

The questions on the Level IIC test are classified into three categories with respect to calculator use:

Category (1) Calculator inactive — there is no advantage (perhaps even a disadvantage) to using a calculator.

Category (2) Calculator neutral — these problems could be solved without a calculator, but a calculator may be useful.

Category (3) Calculator active — a calculator is very helpful or necessary to solve these problems.

Approximately 40 percent of the questions are in category 1 and 60 percent are in categories 2 and 3. Therefore, it is not necessary to use a calculator to solve every question on the Level IIC test. Knowing when and how to use a calculator is important when taking the Level IIC test.

Mathematics Level IC will be introduced in June 1995. This test will cover the same content as the Mathematics Level I Subject Test but will require the use of at least a scientific calculator. Approximately 60 percent of the questions on Mathematics Level IC will be in category 1; about 40 percent will be in categories 2 and 3.

Calculators: STUDENTS CURRENTLY ARE NOT PERMITTED TO USE A CALCULATOR ON ANY SUBJECT TEST OTHER THAN THE MATHEMATICS LEVEL IIC TEST.

Students will be permitted to use almost any scientific or graphing calculator on the Mathematics Level IIC Test. This excludes pocket organizers, "hand-held" mini-computers, laptop computers, models with QWERTY (i.e., typewriter) keypads, models with paper tapes, models that make noise or "talk," and calculators that require an external power source such as an electrical outlet. Calculators may not be shared by students.

You should be thoroughly familiar with the operation of the calculator you plan to use on the test. Your degree of familiarity with the calculator may affect how well you do on the test.

To minimize the chance of a calculator malfunction, you should verify prior to the test that your calculator is in good working order. Test center staff cannot assist you if your calculator malfunctions. No calculators will be available at the test center for your use.

Comparisons between the Tests

The content of the Level I test overlaps somewhat that of the Level IIC test, especially in questions on elementary algebra, coordinate geometry, statistics, and basic trigonometry. Some questions may be appropriate for both of these tests. However, the emphasis on the Level IIC test is on more advanced content, with a greater percentage of questions devoted to trigonometry, elementary functions, and precalculus topics. A significant percentage of questions on Level I is devoted to plane geometry, a topic not tested directly on Level IIC; the geometry questions on Level IIC cover topics such as coordinate geometry in two or three dimensions, transformations, and solid geometry. The trigonometry questions on Level I are primarily limited to right triangle trigonometry and the fundamental relationships among the trigonometric ratios, whereas the Level IIC test places more emphasis on the properties and graphs of the trigonometric functions, the inverse trigonometric functions, trigonometric equations and identities, and the laws of sines and cosines.

If you have had preparation in trigonometry and elementary functions, have attained grades of B or better in your mathematics courses, and have skill in knowing when and how to use a scientific or graphing calculator, you should select the Level IIC test. (Students who are sufficiently prepared to take the Level IIC test, but who elect to take the Level I test in hopes of receiving high scores, may not do as well as they expect.) No student taking Level I or Level IIC is expected to have studied every topic on the test.

In general, because the content measured by the Level I and Level IIC tests differs considerably, your score on one of these Mathematics Subject Tests should not be used to predict your score on the other.

The chart below shows approximately how the questions in each test are distributed among the major curriculum areas. Comparison of the percentages for the levels should help you decide which test you are better prepared to take.

Topics Covered	Approximate Percentage of Test	
	Level I	**Level IIC**
Algebra	30	18
Geometry		
Plane Geometry	20	—
Solid Geometry	6	8
Coordinate Geometry	12	12
Trigonometry	8	20
Functions	12	24
Statistics	6	6
Miscellaneous	6	12

Questions Used in the Tests

As much as possible, test questions are constructed so that they can be understood by all students regardless of the mathematics curriculums and textbooks they have studied. Symbolism has been kept simple; for example, the symbol PQ may be used to denote a line, a ray, a segment, or the measure (length) of a segment; the particular interpretation of the symbol is indicated by its context in the problem.

The five-choice completion question is written either in an incomplete statement or as a question. In its simplest application, this type of question poses a problem that has a unique solution.

A special type of five-choice completion question is used in some tests to allow for the possibility of several correct answers. In such situations, you should evaluate each response independently of the others in order to select the most appropriate combination. (See examples 4, 12, and 20.)

The sample questions that follow illustrate the kinds of mathematical knowledge and techniques required for the tests; they do not describe the specific content of any test.

The best test-taking approach is to solve each problem and then look for the choice that best fits the answer you obtained. Trying to work each problem by testing each of the choices is time consuming and, in many instances, will not work. However, you should look at all the answer choices before answering the question, since the form of the answer choices may help point out the best approach to solve the problem.

Sample Questions

Mathematics Level I

Directions: For each of the following problems, decide which is the BEST of the choices given. Then fill in the corresponding oval on the answer sheet.

Notes: (1) Figures that accompany problems in this test are intended to provide information useful in solving the problems. They are drawn as accurately as possible EXCEPT when it is stated in a specific problem that its figure is not drawn to scale. All figures lie in a plane unless otherwise indicated.

(2) Unless otherwise specified, the domain of any function f is assumed to be the set of all real numbers x for which $f(x)$ is a real number.

(3) Reference information that may be useful in answering the questions in this test can be found below.

Reference Information: The following information is for your reference in answering some of the questions in this test.

Volume of a right circular cone with radius r and height h: $V = \frac{1}{3}\pi r^2 h$

Lateral Area of a right circular cone with circumference of the base c and slant height ℓ: $S = \frac{1}{2}c\ell$

Volume of a sphere with radius r: $V = \frac{4}{3}\pi r^3$

Surface Area of a sphere with radius r: $S = 4\pi r^2$

Volume of a pyramid with base area B and height h: $V = \frac{1}{3}Bh$

Algebra

1. **The rental cost of a certain video game is \$6 per day for each of the first 2 days and \$3 per day for each succeeding day. Which of the following is an expression for the cost, in dollars, of renting this video game for n days, if $n > 2$?**

   (A) $5n$
   (B) $6 + 3(n - 2)$
   (C) $12 + 3n$
   (D) $12 + (3n - 2)$
   (E) $12 + 3(n - 2)$

For the first two days the rental cost is \$12. For the remaining $(n - 2)$ days the rental cost is $3(n - 2)$ dollars. Thus, the total cost, in dollars, of renting the video game for n days is $12 + 3(n - 2)$, which is choice (E).

2. **Which of the following equations has the same solution(s) as $|x + 1| = 3$?**

   (A) $2x = 4$
   (B) $3x = -12$
   (C) $x^2 = 4$
   (D) $x^2 + 2x - 8 = 0$
   (E) $x^2 + 4x + 4 = 0$

If $|x + 1| = 3$, then $x + 1 = 3$ or $x + 1 = -3$, which yields $x = 2$ or $x = -4$. You need to find an equation with two solutions. Choices (A) and (B) can be eliminated since they each have one solution. Choice (C) yields $x = \pm 2$. Choice (D) factors to $(x - 2)(x + 4) = 0$, which yields $x = 2$ or $x = -4$. Choice (E) factors to $(x + 2)^2 = 0$, which yields $x = -2$. The correct choice is (D).

Plane Geometry

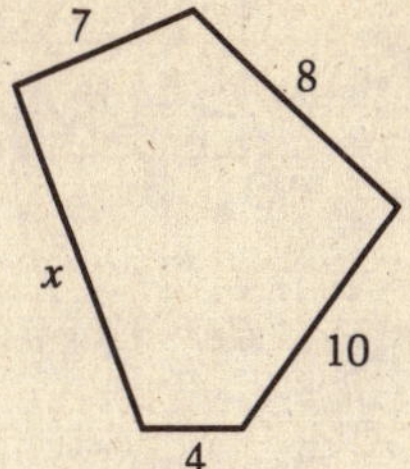

Figure 1

Note: Figure not drawn to scale.

3. **In Figure 1, a pentagon has four of its sides with lengths 4, 7, 8, and 10. If the length x of the fifth side is also an integer, then the greatest possible value of x is**

   (A) 16
   (B) 22
   (C) 26
   (D) 28
   (E) 30

In order for the pentagon to exist, x must be less than the sum of the lengths of the other four sides. Since this sum is 29 and x is an integer, the greatest possible value of x is 28, and the correct choice is (D). The note that the figure is not drawn to scale means that the lengths of the sides given in the figure are not to scale. For example, the side labeled 8 may not be drawn exactly twice the length of the side marked 4.

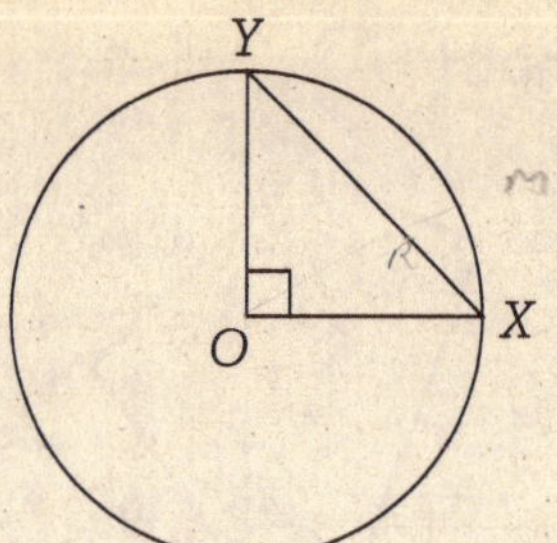

Figure 2

4. In Figure 2, X and Y are points on the circle with center O. Point M (not shown) is a point on the minor arc XY such that OM intersects chord XY at point R (not shown). If the length of segment OX is 5, which of the following must be true?

I. The length of segment XY is $5\sqrt{2}$.
II. The length of segment XR equals the length of segment RY.
III. The length of segment OM is 5.

(A) I only
(B) II only
(C) III only
(D) I and II
(E) I and III

In this type of question, each of three statements, labeled I, II, and III, must be considered independently based on the information given. First, consider statement I. From the figure we know $OX \perp OY$. Since segments OX and OY are both radii and segment OX has length 5, segment OY also has length 5. Thus, chord XY is the hypotenuse of an isosceles right triangle and has length $5\sqrt{2}$, and statement I is true.

In statement II, we know that R is the point where segment OM intersects segment XY. If M is closer to Y, then R is also closer to Y, and if M is closer to X, R is closer to X. Thus, it *cannot* be concluded that the length of segment XR must equal the length of segment RY.

In statement III, since we know the circle has radius 5 and that segment OM is a radius of the circle, statement III is true. Therefore, the correct choice is (E) because statements I and III *must* be true.

Coordinate Geometry

5. If one vertex of a square in the xy-plane has coordinates (0,0), how many other vertices of the square must lie on either the x-axis or the y-axis?

(A) None
(B) One
(C) Two
(D) Three
(E) Four

For this question it may be helpful to draw a figure:

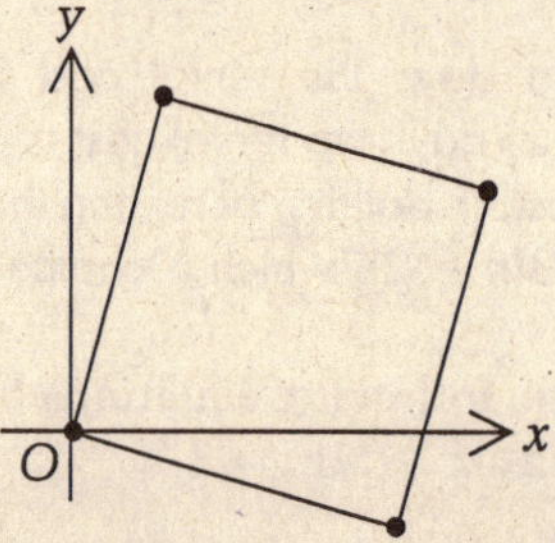

The figure above shows a square with no other vertices on the axes. Therefore, the correct choice is (A) since none of the other three vertices must be on the axes.

6. Which of the following shaded regions could be the graph of $\begin{cases} y \leq 3x - 2 \\ x \geq 0 \end{cases}$?

(A)

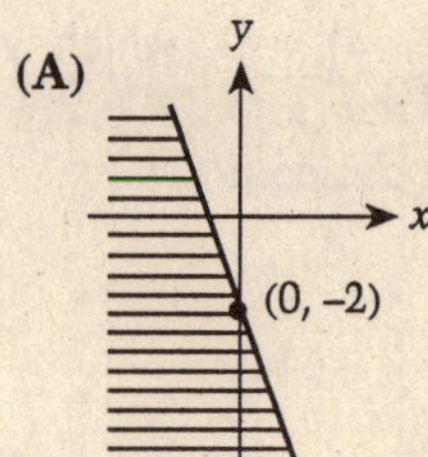

(B)

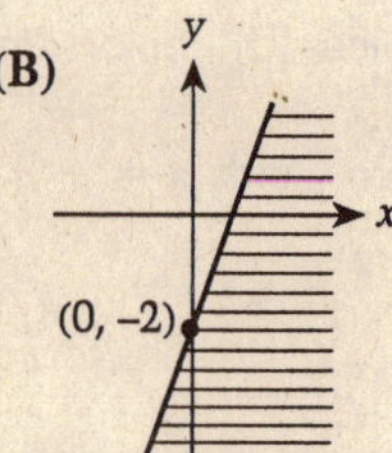

(C)

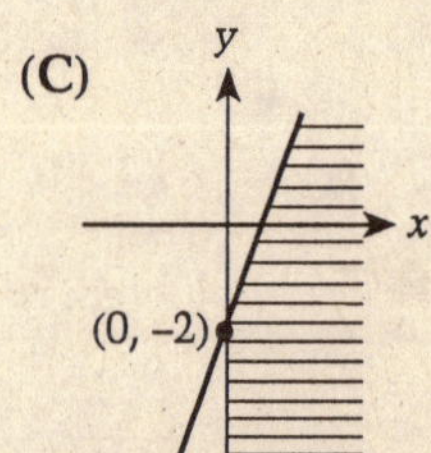

(D)

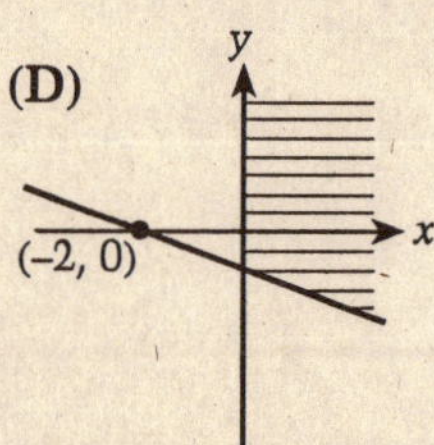

(E)

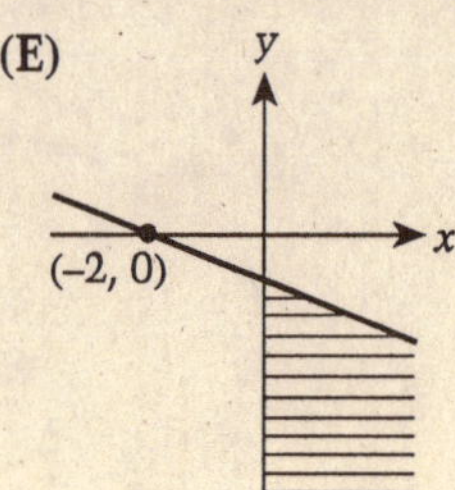

This problem can be solved by sketching the graph of each inequality and then determining the region that represents their intersection.

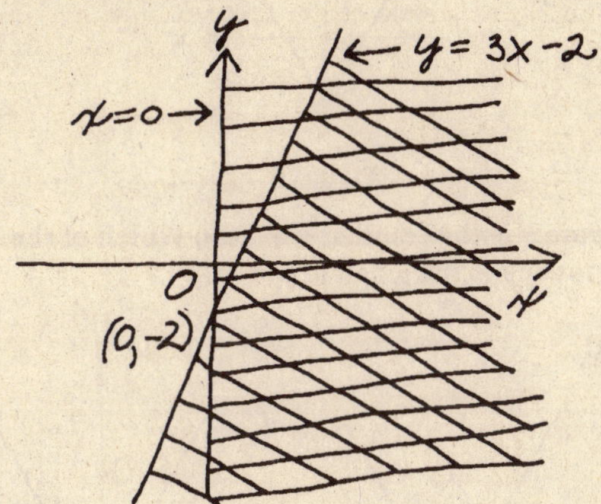

The boundary of the half-plane represented by the inequality $y < 3x - 2$ is the line with equation $y = 3x - 2$. The boundary of the half-plane represented by the inequality $x > 0$ is the line with equation $x = 0$, which is the y-axis. The solution is the region where $y \leq 3x - 2$ and $x \geq 0$. The intersection of these half-planes is represented by choice (C).

Solid Geometry

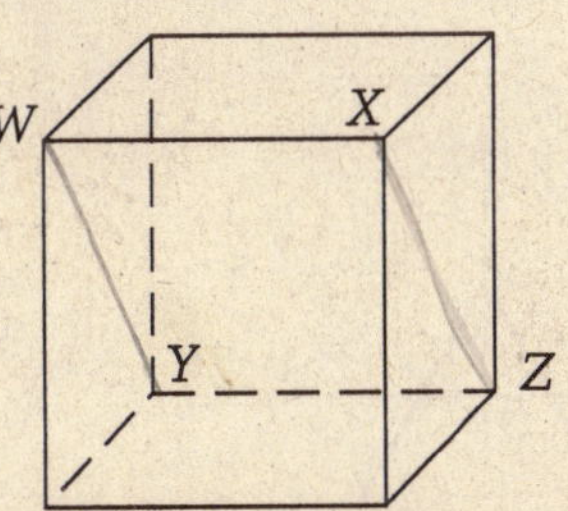

Figure 3

7. The cube in Figure 3 has a volume of 1 cubic meter. A cut is made along the plane that contains points W, X, Y, and Z so that two separate identical pieces are formed. How much greater than the surface area of the original cube is the combined surface area of the two pieces, in square meters?

(A) $\sqrt{2}$
(B) 2
(C) $2\sqrt{2}$
(D) $2 + \sqrt{2}$
(E) 4

If the volume of the cube is 1 cubic meter, the length of an edge of the cube is 1 meter. After you cut along the plane $WXZY$, as shown in the figure below, the combined surface area of the two pieces is the same as the surface area of the cube plus the surface area of the two identical faces $WXZY$.

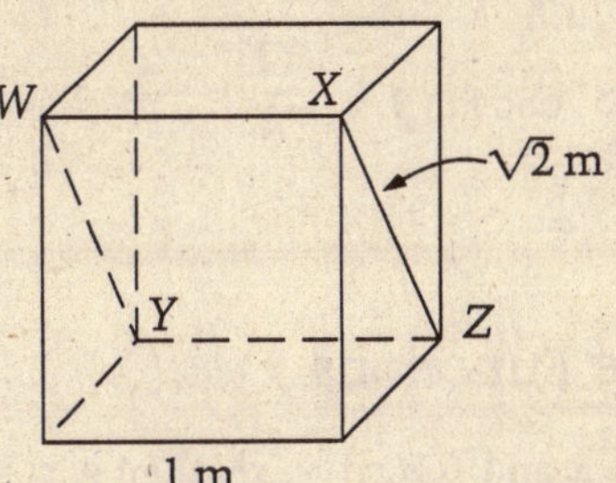

Since each of these faces is 1 meter wide, and $\sqrt{1^2 + 1^2} = \sqrt{2}$ meters long, each has an area of $\sqrt{2}$ square meters. Therefore, the combined surface area of the two pieces is $2\sqrt{2}$ square meters greater than the surface area of the original cube. The correct choice is (C).

Trigonometry

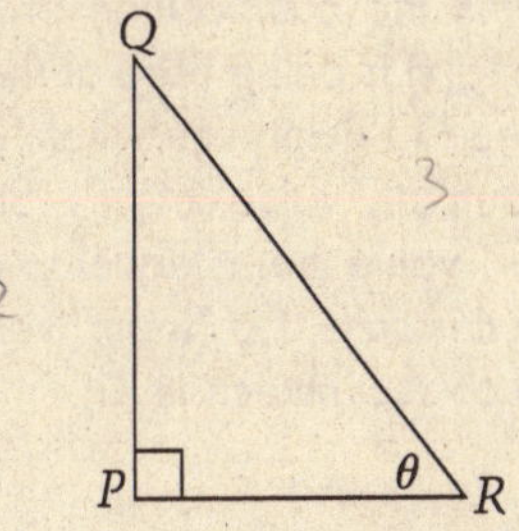

Figure 4

8. In Figure 4, if $\frac{PQ}{QR} = \frac{2}{3}$, then $\tan\theta =$

(A) $\frac{2}{5}$
(B) $\frac{2}{\sqrt{5}}$
(C) $\frac{3}{\sqrt{5}}$
(D) $\frac{\sqrt{5}}{2}$
(E) $\frac{\sqrt{5}}{3}$

The tangent of an acute angle in a right triangle is defined as the ratio of the length of the side opposite the angle to the length of the side adjacent to the angle. You can find the length of the adjacent side PR by using the Pythagorean theorem. By letting the length of PQ be 2 and the length of QR be 3, $(PQ)^2 + (PR)^2 = (QR)^2$ or $4 + (PR)^2 = 9$. Thus $PR = \sqrt{5}$, and $\tan\theta = \frac{PQ}{PR} = \frac{2}{\sqrt{5}}$. The correct choice is (B).

Algebraic Functions

9. If $f(x) = x$ and $f(g(x)) = x^2$, then $g(x) =$

(A) $\frac{1}{x^3}$

(B) $\frac{1}{x}$

(C) x

(D) x^2

(E) x^3

This problem involves the composition of two functions, f and g. In this case, $g(x)$ is being used as the "input" value in function f. You need to determine what "input" value of f will yield an "output" value of x^2. Since $f(x) = x$, f assigns an "output" value that is equal to its corresponding "input" value. In this case, the "input" value must be x^2. Thus, $g(x) = x^2$; the correct choice is (D).

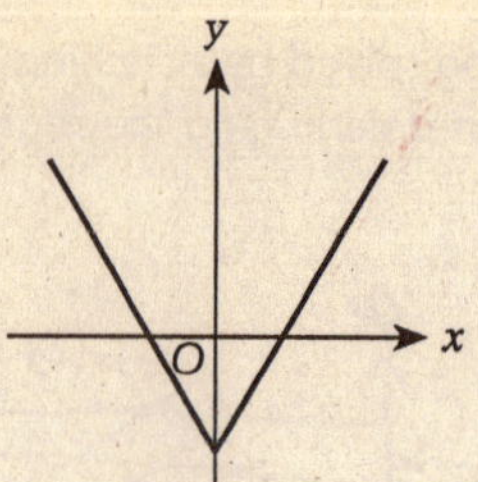

Figure 5

10. Figure 5 is the graph of $y = f(x)$. Which of the following is the graph of $y = |f(x)|$?

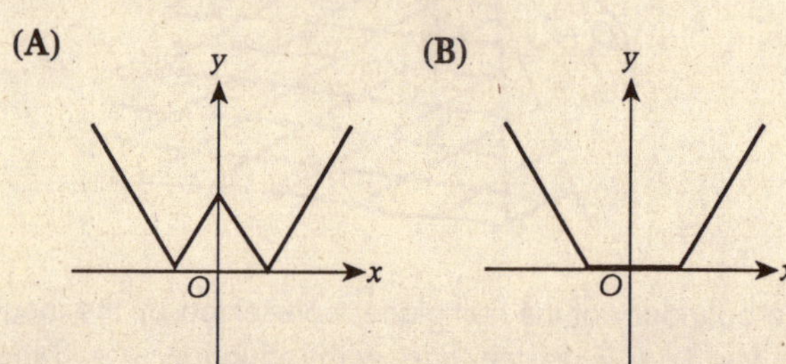

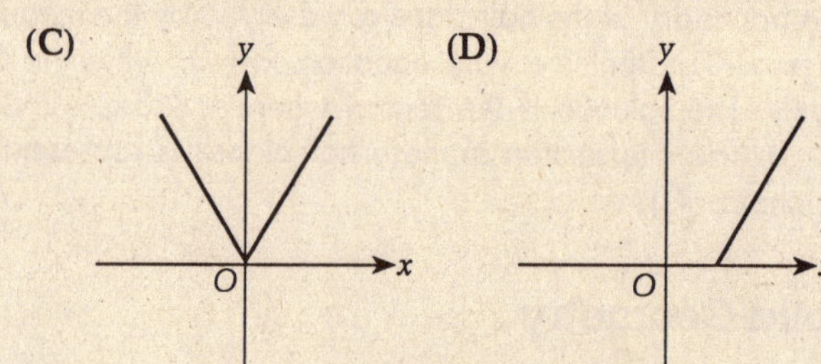

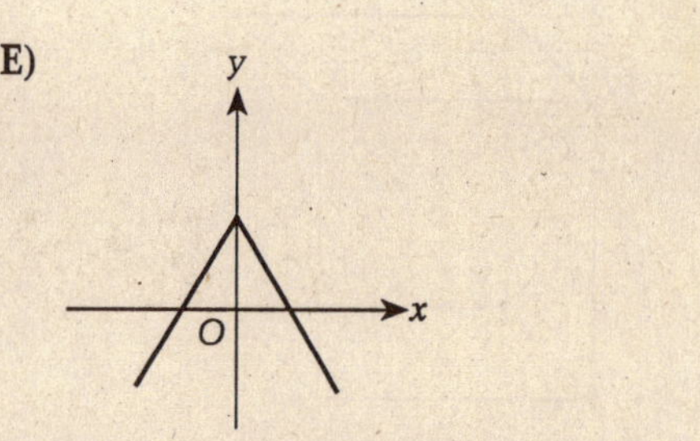

This problem can be solved by using the fact that the absolute value of any number is greater than or equal to 0. Since $|x| = -x$ when x is negative, all values of $|f(x)|$ where $f(x) < 0$ will be transformed to $-f(x)$ by the definition of absolute value. Thus the portion of the graph below the x-axis in Figure 5 (that is, where $y = f(x) < 0$) would be reflected in that axis to become positive. The correct choice is (A).

Elementary Statistics

Office	Name
President	
Vice President	
Secretary	

11. **From among 5 people, a committee must select one person for each of the 3 offices of a club shown in the table above. No person can be selected for more than one office. In how many ways can the table be completed?**

    (A) 120
    (B) 60
    (C) 20
    (D) 10
    (E) 6

There are 5 different people who can be president. Once the president is selected, there are 4 possibilities for vice president. Once these two offices are selected, there are 3 possibilities for secretary. The total number of ways the table can be completed is $5 \times 4 \times 3 = 60$, which is choice (B).

Miscellaneous

12. **For all positive real numbers, let $a \odot b$ be defined as $a \odot b = \dfrac{ab}{a+b}$. Which of the following must be true for all positive real numbers a and b ?**

    I. $a \odot b = b \odot a$

    II. $a \odot 1 = a$

    III. $a \odot a = \dfrac{a}{2}$

    (A) I only
    (B) II only
    (C) III only
    (D) I and III only
    (E) I, II, and III

In statement I, $a \odot b = \dfrac{ab}{a+b}$ and $b \odot a = \dfrac{ba}{b+a}$. Since $ab = ba$ and $a + b = b + a$, statement I is true. In statement II, $a \odot 1 = \dfrac{a \times 1}{a+1} = \dfrac{a}{a+1}$. Since $\dfrac{a}{a+1}$ is not equal to a for any positive value of a, statement II is false. In statement III, $a \odot a = \dfrac{a \times a}{a+a} = \dfrac{a^2}{2a} = \dfrac{a}{2}$. Thus, statement III is true and the correct choice is (D).

Mathematics Level IIC

Directions: For each of the following problems, decide which is the BEST of the choices given. If the exact numerical value is not one of the choices, select the choice that best approximates this value. Then fill in the corresponding oval on the answer sheet.

Notes: (1) A calculator will be necessary for answering some (but not all) of the questions in this test. For each question you will have to decide whether or not you should use a calculator. The calculator you use must be at least a scientific calculator; programmable calculators and calculators that can display graphs are permitted.

(2) For some questions in this test you may have to decide whether your calculator should be in the radian mode or the degree mode.

(3) Figures that accompany problems in this test are intended to provide information useful in solving the problems. They are drawn as accurately as possible EXCEPT when it is stated in a specific problem that its figure is not drawn to scale. All figures lie in a plane unless otherwise indicated.

(4) Unless otherwise specified, the domain of any function f is assumed to be the set of all real numbers x for which $f(x)$ is a real number.

(5) Reference information that may be useful in answering the questions in this test can be found below.

Reference Information: The following information is for your reference in answering some of the questions in this test.

Volume of a right circular cone with radius r and height h: $V = \frac{1}{3}\pi r^2 h$

Lateral Area of a right circular cone with circumference of the base c and slant height ℓ: $S = \frac{1}{2}c\ell$

Volume of a sphere with radius r: $V = \frac{4}{3}\pi r^3$

Surface Area of a sphere with radius r: $S = 4\pi r^2$

Volume of a pyramid with base area B and height h: $V = \frac{1}{3}Bh$

Algebra

13. If $2^x = 3$, what does 3^x equal?

(A) 5.7
(B) 5.2
(C) 2.0
(D) 1.8
(E) 1.6

A calculator is useful for this problem. To solve for x, you can take the natural log of both sides of the equation.

$$\ln 2^x = \ln 3$$
$$x \ln 2 = \ln 3$$
$$x = \frac{\ln 3}{\ln 2} = \frac{1.0986}{0.6931} \approx 1.5850$$
$$3^x = 5.7045$$

Since the directions to this test state, "If the exact numerical value is not one of the choices, select the choice that best approximates this value," the correct answer choice is (A).

You can also solve this problem by using a graphing calculator. First, graph $y_1 = 2^x$ and $y_2 = 3^x$. Using the trace feature, trace the graph of $y_1 = 2^x$ until you get a y-value that is close to 3 (for example, $y = 2.9875$ when $x = 1.5789$). Using the trace feature on the graph of $y_2 = 3^x$, find the y-value for the point where $x = 1.5789$. At this point $y = 5.6669$, which also rounds to 5.7.

Solid Geometry

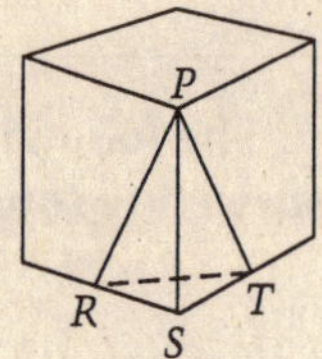

Figure 6

14. In Figure 6, R and T are the midpoints of two adjacent edges of the cube. If the length of each edge of the cube is h, what is the volume of the pyramid $PRST$?

(A) $\frac{h^3}{24}$

(B) $\frac{h^3}{12}$

(C) $\frac{h^3}{8}$

(D) $\frac{h^3}{6}$

(E) $\frac{h^3}{4}$

The formula for the volume of a pyramid and several other formulae are given in the reference information at the beginning of the test. The volume of a pyramid is $\frac{1}{3}Bh$, where B is the area of the base of the pyramid and h is its height. It may be helpful to mark the figure to indicate those parts whose lengths are given or that can be deduced.

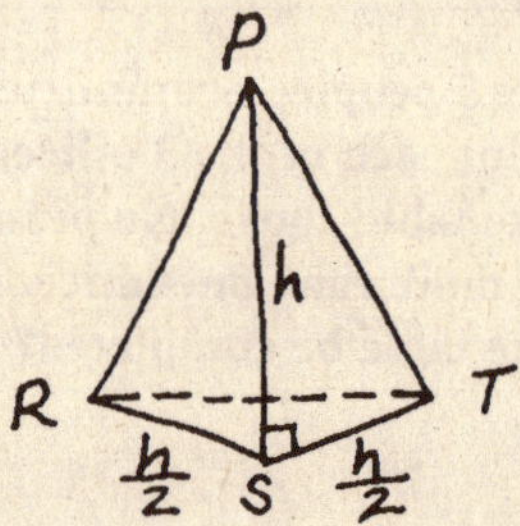

Since segment PS is perpendicular to the triangular base RST, its length h is the height of the pyramid $PRST$. R and T are the midpoints of the two adjacent edges of the cube; therefore the lengths of segments RS and ST are both $\frac{h}{2}$. Since $\triangle RST$ is a right triangle, its area is $\left(\frac{1}{2}\right)\left(\frac{h}{2}\right)\left(\frac{h}{2}\right) = \frac{h^2}{8}$. Thus the volume of $PRST$ is $\left(\frac{1}{3}\right)\left(\frac{h^2}{8}\right)(h) = \frac{h^3}{24}$ and the correct choice is (A).

Coordinate Geometry

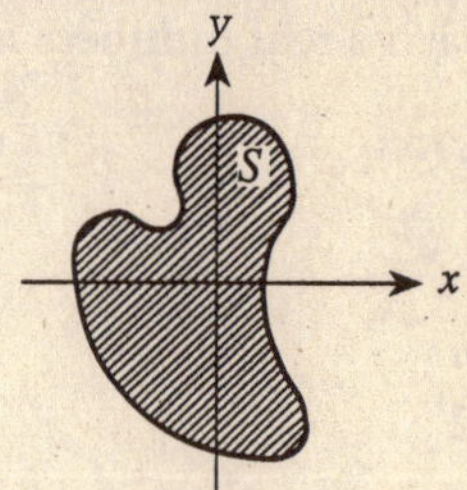

Figure 7

15. A region T is defined in terms of the region S in Figure 7 above as follows:

$(x - 1, y + 4)$ is in T if and only if (x, y) is in S.

If region S has area 10, what is the area of region T?

(A) 40
(B) 30
(C) 20
(D) $10\sqrt{2}$
(E) 10

By definition of T, each point of S corresponds to a point of T that is 1 unit to the left and 4 units up. Therefore, T is obtained by translating S 1 unit to the left and 4 units up. This translation preserves shape and area. Therefore, choice (E) is correct.

Trigonometry

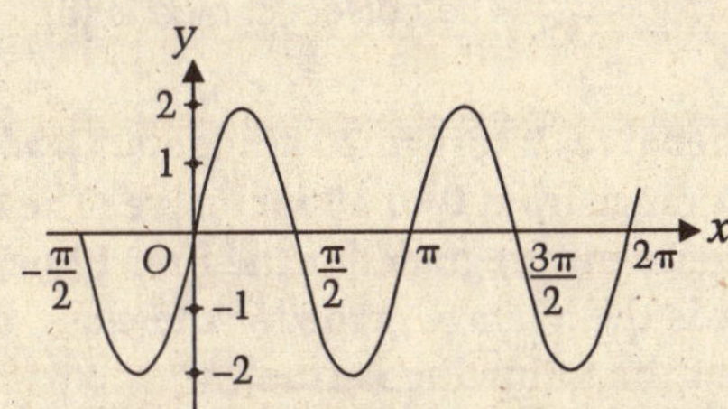

Figure 8

16. Which of the following equations has the graph shown in Figure 8?

(A) $y = \sin\frac{x}{2} + 1$

(B) $y = \sin 2x$

(C) $y = 2\sin\frac{x}{2}$

(D) $y = 2\sin x$

(E) $y = 2\sin 2x$

The graph in Figure 8 is the graph of a sine function with amplitude 2 and period π. Therefore, the equation of the graph shown in Figure 8 is $y = 2\sin 2x$, which is choice (E).

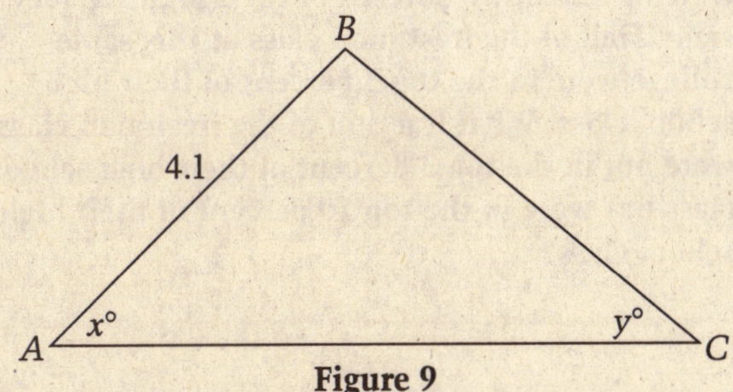

Figure 9

Note: Figure not drawn to scale.

17. In the triangle in Figure 9, $x = 36$ and $y = 30$. What is the length of side BC?

(A) 3.5
(B) 3.8
(C) 4.8
(D) 5.1
(E) 7.5

This problem can be solved by using the law of sines with the calculator in degree mode.

$$\frac{\sin 30^\circ}{4.1} = \frac{\sin 36^\circ}{\text{length of side } BC}$$

The length of side $BC = \frac{(4.1)\sin 36^\circ}{\sin 30^\circ}$, which is approximately equal to 4.82. The correct choice is (C).

Elementary Functions

18. The total cost, in dollars, of a telephone call that is m minutes in length from City R to City T is given by the function $f(m) = 1.06(0.75 \times \lceil m \rceil + 1)$, where $m > 0$ and $\lceil m \rceil$ is the least integer greater than or equal to m. What is the total cost of a 5.5-minute telephone call from City R to City T?

(A) \$4.77
(B) \$5.04
(C) \$5.25
(D) \$5.56
(E) \$5.83

To solve this question, you need to evaluate $f(5.5) = 1.06\,(0.75\,\lceil 5.5 \rceil + 1)$. Since 6 is the least integer greater than 5.5, $\lceil 5.5 \rceil = 6$. Thus, $f(5.5) = 1.06\,(0.75\,(6) + 1) = 5.83$. The correct choice is (E).

19. If $f(x) = 10^x$, where x is a real number, and if the inverse function of f is denoted by f^{-1}, then what is $\frac{f^{-1}(a)}{f^{-1}(b)}$ where $a > 1$ and $b > 1$?

(A) $\log_{10}a - \log_{10}b$

(B) $\log_{10}(a - b)$

(C) $\frac{\log_{10}a}{\log_{10}b}$

(D) $\frac{10^b}{10^a}$

(E) None of the above

Since the inverse of the exponential function $f(x) = 10^x$ is the logarithmic function $f^{-1}(x) = \log_{10}x$, $\frac{f^{-1}(a)}{f^{-1}(b)} = \frac{\log_{10}a}{\log_{10}b}$ and the correct choice is (C).

20. If $f(x) = \frac{1-x}{x-1}$ for all $x \neq 1$, which of the following statements must be true?

I. $f(3) = f(2)$
II. $f(0) = f(2)$
III. $f(0) = f(4)$

(A) None
(B) I only
(C) II only
(D) II and III only
(E) I, II, and III

Realizing that $\frac{1-x}{x-1} = -1$ for all $x \neq 1$ greatly simplifies this problem. Since $f(0)$, $f(2)$, $f(3)$, and $f(4)$ are all equal to -1, statements I, II, and III are all true and the correct choice is (E). If you do not realize $f(x) = -1$, you can easily substitute the numbers in f. Using a calculator may actually be a disadvantage to you if you spend time substituting the numbers into an expression of this kind to find the answer with the calculator. However, if you have a graphing calculator, you can graph $f(x) = \frac{1-x}{x-1}$ and see that the graph is a horizontal line crossing the y-axis at -1. Therefore, $f(x) = -1$ for all values of x except 1.

Statistics

21. The probability that R hits a certain target is $\frac{3}{5}$ and, independently, the probability that T hits it is $\frac{5}{7}$. What is the probability that R hits the target and T misses it?

(A) $\frac{4}{35}$

(B) $\frac{6}{35}$

(C) $\frac{3}{7}$

(D) $\frac{21}{25}$

(E) $\frac{31}{35}$

Since the two events are independent, the probability that R hits the target and T misses it is the product of the two probabilities. The former probability is given. Since the probability that T hits the target is $\frac{5}{7}$, the probability that T misses the target is $1 - \frac{5}{7}$ or $\frac{2}{7}$. Therefore $P = \left(\frac{3}{5}\right)\left(\frac{2}{7}\right) = \frac{6}{35}$. The correct choice is (B).

22. A teacher gives a test to 20 students. Grades on the test range from 0 to 10 inclusive. The average (arithmetic mean) grade for the first 12 papers is 6.5. If x is the average grade for the class, then which of the following is true?

(A) $0.33 \leq x \leq 6.50$
(B) $3.25 \leq x \leq 6.50$
(C) $3.90 \leq x \leq 6.50$
(D) $3.90 \leq x \leq 7.90$
(E) $4.00 \leq x \leq 7.90$

Since the average grade of the first 12 papers is 6.5, the sum of these grades is 12(6.5) or 78. The least possible sum of the grades for the other 8 papers is 0 and the maximum possible sum is 80. Therefore the average grade for the class is between $\frac{78+0}{20} = 3.90$ and $\frac{78+80}{20} = 7.90$ inclusive. The correct choice is (D). A calculator may be useful in solving this problem but is not necessary.

Miscellaneous

23. Two-thirds of the freshman class at a college were in the top 10 percent of their high school class. Half of the freshman class at this same college were in the top 3 percent of their high school class. What fraction of the freshman class were not in the top 3 percent of their high school class but were in the top 10 percent of their high school class?

(A) $\frac{1}{6}$

(B) $\frac{3}{10}$

(C) $\frac{1}{3}$

(D) $\frac{7}{10}$

(E) $\frac{5}{6}$

Since $\frac{1}{2}$ of the freshman class were in the top 3 percent of their high school class and $\frac{2}{3}$ of the class were in the top 10 percent of their high school class, then $\frac{2}{3} - \frac{1}{2}$ or $\frac{1}{6}$ of the freshman class were not in the top 3 percent but were in the top 10 percent of their high school class. The correct choice is (A).

It may also be helpful to sketch a figure:

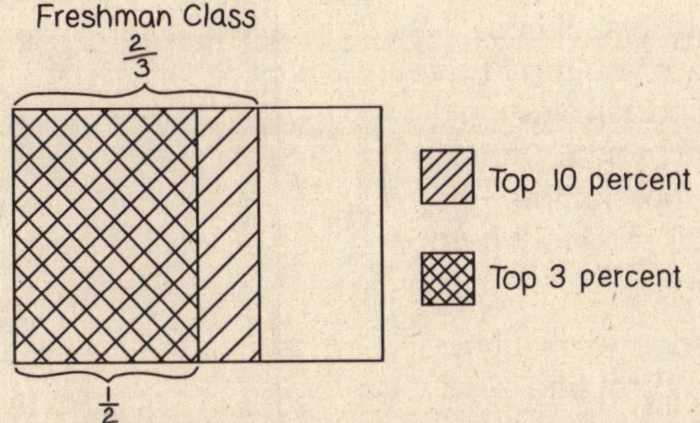

The fraction that is in the top 10 percent but not in the top 3 percent is $\frac{2}{3} - \frac{1}{2} = \frac{1}{6}$.

24. If $f(x) = \frac{x^2 - 16}{x - 4}$, what value does $f(x)$ approach as x approaches 4 ?

(A) 0
(B) 4
(C) 8
(D) 16
(E) It does not approach a single number.

Since $\frac{x^2 - 16}{x - 4} = \frac{(x - 4)(x + 4)}{x - 4}$, the values of the function $\frac{x^2 - 16}{x - 4}$ are equal to $x + 4$ for all values of x except 4. As x approaches 4 the values of the function approach 8. The correct choice is (C). You could use a calculator to help you arrive at this answer by substituting numbers very close to 4, such as 3.99 and 4.01, into the function $\frac{x^2 - 16}{x - 4}$ and see how the function behaves. If you have a graphing calculator, you could graph $f(x) = \frac{x^2 - 16}{x - 4}$ and trace the graph to obtain the answer.

SAT II:

Mathematics Level I Subject Test

The test that follows is representative of a typical SAT II: Mathematics Level I Subject Test. It has already been administered. So that you may have an idea of what the national test administration will be like, try to take the test in this book under conditions as close as possible to those of the nationally administered test. It will probably help if you do the following.

- Set aside an hour for the test when you will not be interrupted, so that you can complete all of it in one sitting.
- Sit at a desk with no other papers or books. You can't take a calculator, dictionary, other books, or notes into the test room.
- Have a kitchen timer or clock in front of you for timing yourself.
- Tear out an answer sheet from the back of this book and fill it in just as you would on the day of the test. You can use one answer sheet for as many as three Subject Tests.
- Read the instructions that precede the test. When you take the test, you will be asked to read them before you begin answering questions.
- After you finish the test, read the sections on "How to Score the SAT II: Mathematics Level I Subject Test" and "Reviewing Your Test Performance," which follow the test.

FORM 3JAC2

MATHEMATICS LEVEL I TEST

The top portion of the section of the answer sheet that you will use in taking the Mathematics Level I test must be filled in exactly as shown in the illustration below. Note carefully that you have to do all of the following on your answer sheet.

1. Print MATHEMATICS LEVEL I on the line under the words "Subject (print)."

2. In the shaded box labeled "Test Code" fill in four ovals:

   —Fill in oval 1 in the row labeled V.

   —Fill in oval 1 in the row labeled W.

   —Fill in oval 5 in the row labeled X.

   —Fill in oval A in the row labeled Y.

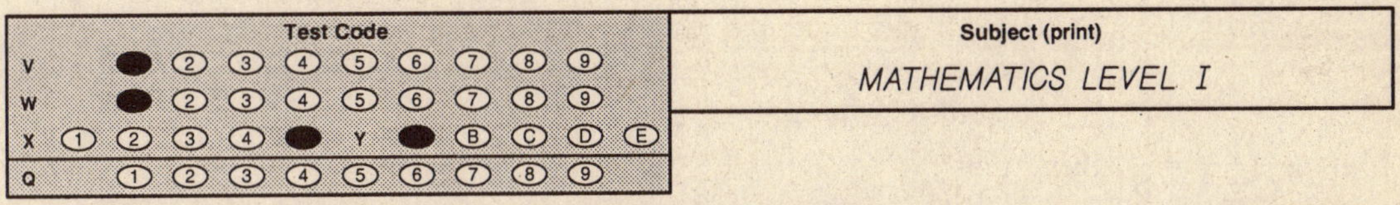

Test Code											Subject (print)
V	●	2	3	4	5	6	7	8	9		MATHEMATICS LEVEL I
W	●	2	3	4	5	6	7	8	9		
X	1	2	3	4	●	Y ●	B	C	D	E	
Q	1	2	3	4	5	6	7	8	9		

3. Please answer either Part I or Part II below by filling in the specified ovals in row Q that correspond to the courses you have taken or are presently taking. FILL IN ALL OVALS THAT APPLY. The information that you provide is for statistical purposes only and will not affect your score on the test.

   Students who are enrolled in the sequential mathematics program (Course I, Course II, Course III) used in New York State should proceed to Part II.

Part I Which of the following describe a mathematics course you have taken or are taking? (Fill in ALL ovals that apply.)

- Algebra I or Elementary Algebra —Fill in oval 1.
- Geometry —Fill in oval 2.
- Algebra II or Intermediate Algebra —Fill in oval 3.
- Elementary Functions (Precalculus) and/or Trigonometry —Fill in oval 4.
- Advanced Placement Mathematics (Calculus AB or Calculus BC) —Fill in oval 9.

Answer Part II only if you are or were enrolled in the sequential mathematics program (Course I, Course II, Course III) used in New York State.

Part II Which of the following describe a mathematics course you have taken or are taking? (Fill in ALL ovals that apply.)

- Course I —Fill in oval 5.
- Course II —Fill in oval 6.
- Course III —Fill in oval 7.
- A course beyond course III (not Advanced Placement Calculus AB or BC) —Fill in oval 8.
- Advanced Placement Mathematics (Calculus AB or Calculus BC) —Fill in oval 9.

When the supervisor gives the signal, turn the page and begin the Mathematics Level I test. There are 100 numbered ovals on the answer sheet and 50 questions in the Mathematics Level I test. Therefore, use only ovals 1 to 50 for recording your answers.

MATHEMATICS LEVEL I TEST

For each of the following problems, decide which is the BEST of the choices given. Then fill in the corresponding oval on the answer sheet.

Notes: (1) Figures that accompany problems in this test are intended to provide information useful in solving the problems. They are drawn as accurately as possible EXCEPT when it is stated in a specific problem that its figure is not drawn to scale. All figures lie in a plane unless otherwise indicated.

(2) Unless otherwise specified, the domain of any function f is assumed to be the set of all real numbers x for which $f(x)$ is a real number.

(3) Reference information that may be useful in answering the questions in the test can be found on the page preceding question 1.*

USE THIS SPACE FOR SCRATCHWORK.

1. If $\frac{1}{2x - 1} = \frac{1}{9}$, then $x =$

(A) 3 (B) 4 (C) 5 (D) 6 (E) 10

2. The least positive integer that is divisible by 3, 6, and 7 is

(A) 126 (B) 84 (C) 63 (D) 42 (E) 21

3. In Figure 1, if the length of $ST = 2y - 4$ and the length of RS is half the length of ST, what is the length of RT?

(A) $3y - 4$
(B) $3y - 6$
(C) $3y + 2$
(D) $6y - 12$
(E) $6y + 4$

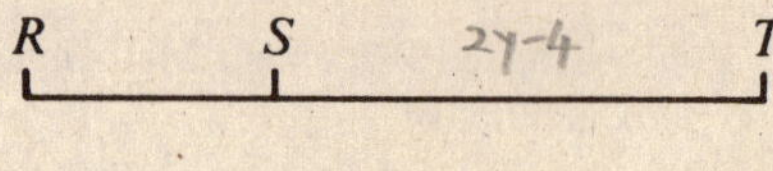

Figure 1

4. If $y = x^2$ and $x = 3k$, what is the value of y when $k = 2$?

(A) 36 (B) 18 (C) 12 (D) 6 (E) $\sqrt{6}$

*In the actual test, the reference information is located on the page preceding question 1. In this book, the reference information can be found on page 130.

GO ON TO THE NEXT PAGE

USE THIS SPACE FOR SCRATCHWORK.

5. In Figure 2, the sides of quadrilateral $ABCD$ are extended as shown. What is the sum of the degree measures of the marked angles?

   (A) 300 (B) 330 (C) 360 (D) 450 (E) 540

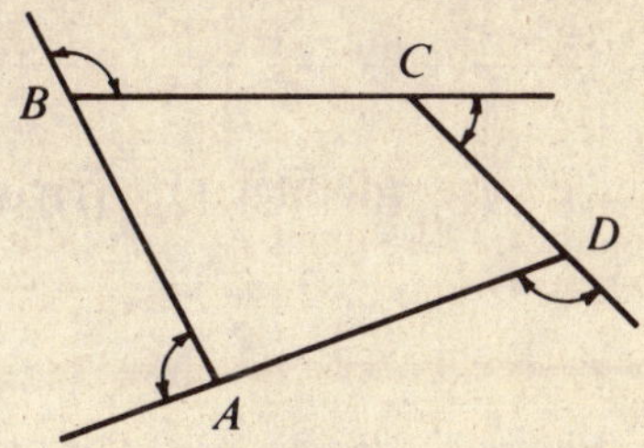

Figure 2

6. For $x \neq -2$, $\dfrac{2x^2 + 5x + 2}{x + 2} =$

   (A) $x + 1$
   (B) $2x + 1$
   (C) $2x + 2$
   (D) $x^2 + 1$
   (E) $x^2 + 2$

7. In which of the following figures does the shaded region represent the set of all points $(x,\ y)$ for which $|x| \leqq 1$?

(A)

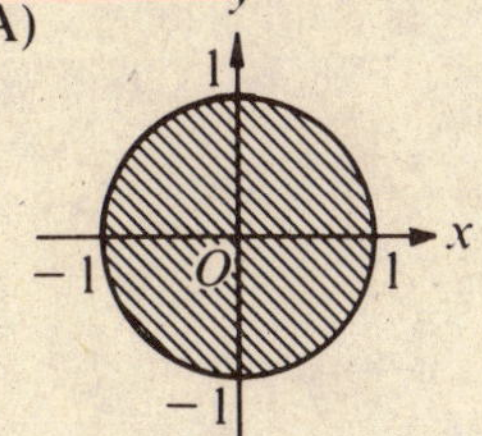

(B)

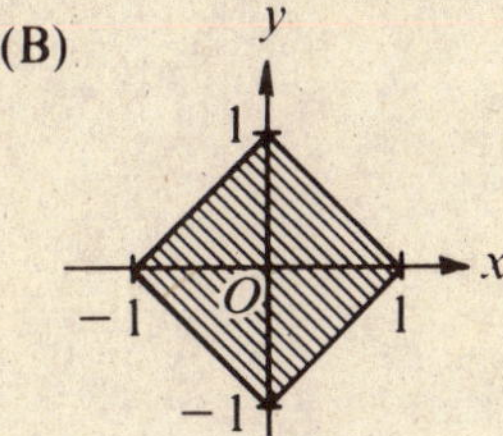

(C)

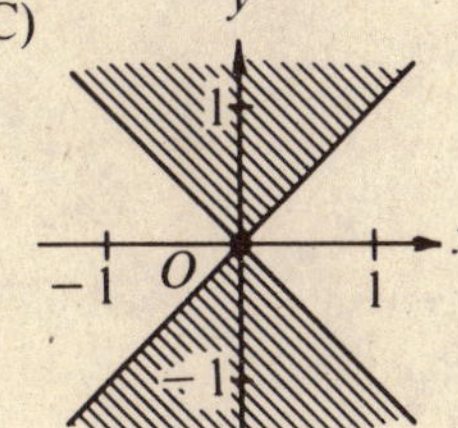

(D)

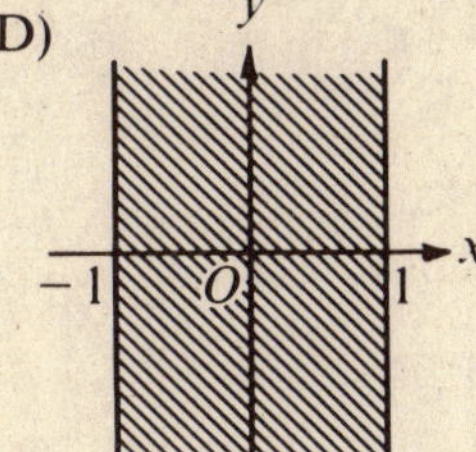

(E)

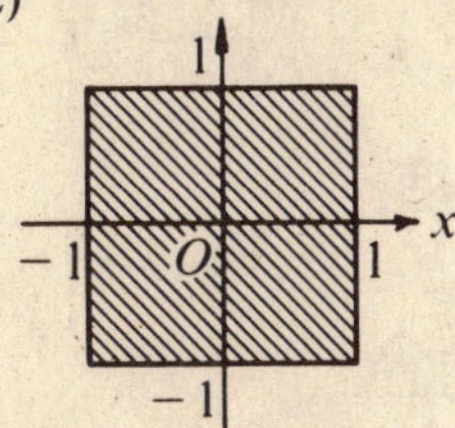

GO ON TO THE NEXT PAGE

USE THIS SPACE FOR SCRATCHWORK.

8. $\dfrac{3^2-1}{3+1}+\dfrac{4^2-1}{4+1}+\dfrac{5^2-1}{5+1}+\dfrac{6^2-1}{6+1}=$

(A) 8 (B) 10 (C) 12 (D) 14 (E) 22

9. In Figure 3, triangles are to be constructed using three of the five points shown on the square grid as vertices. Of the following triangles, which will have the least area?

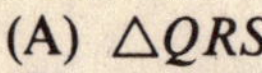

(A) $\triangle QRS$
(B) $\triangle QST$
(C) $\triangle PQR$
(D) $\triangle PQT$
(E) $\triangle PRT$

Figure 3

10. $||-1|-|-3||=$

(A) 4 (B) 2 (C) 0 (D) -2 (E) -4

GO ON TO THE NEXT PAGE

USE THIS SPACE FOR SCRATCHWORK.

11. An operation ⊛ is defined for all positive real numbers x and y by the equation $x \circledast y = x^y$. If $2 \circledast m = 64$, then $m =$

(A) 2 (B) 4 (C) 6 (D) 8 (E) 32

12. A man traveled from his home to a nearby town. He went $\frac{1}{3}$ of the way by foot, 4 kilometers by car, and $\frac{2}{5}$ of the way by bus. How many kilometers did he travel?

(A) 12 (B) 15 (C) 18 (D) 24 (E) 30

13. If $x + y = 5$ and $x - y = 7$, then $xy =$

(A) -1 (B) -6 (C) 6 (D) 12 (E) 35

14. If $a + 3b = 5c - e$, then, in terms of c and e, $a + 3b + 3 =$

(A) $5c - e + 3$
(B) $5c - e - 3$
(C) $5c + 2e$
(D) $8c + 2e$
(E) $15c - 3e$

15. If $x - 2(3 - x) = 2(x - 1) - 2$, then $x =$

(A) -1 (B) 0 (C) 1 (D) 2 (E) 3

GO ON TO THE NEXT PAGE

USE THIS SPACE FOR SCRATCHWORK.

16. If a square has perimeter 28, then its area is

(A) 784 (B) 196 (C) 49 (D) 28 (E) $2\sqrt{7}$

17. If $f(x) = 1 - x^2$ and $g(x) = 2x + 5$, then $g(f(2)) =$

(A) -80 (B) -3 (C) -1 (D) 1 (E) 9

18. Eight pounds of apples, 3 pounds of oranges, and 1 pound of pears are put into a large empty container. How many more pounds of oranges must be added to make the mixture in the container 50 percent oranges by weight?

(A) $\frac{3}{2}$ (B) 2 (C) 3 (D) 5 (E) 6

19. The slope of the line $y - 5 = \frac{2}{3}(x + 7)$ is

(A) -7 (B) -5 (C) $\frac{2}{3}$ (D) $\frac{3}{2}$ (E) 5

20. If $x \neq 0$, then $\dfrac{175 \text{ percent of } x}{0.175 \text{ percent of } x} =$

(A) $\frac{1}{1{,}000}$ (B) $\frac{1}{100}$ (C) 10 (D) 100 (E) 1,000

GO ON TO THE NEXT PAGE

USE THIS SPACE FOR SCRATCHWORK.

21. If $x^3 - 3x^2 + x - 3 = (x - 3)\ P(x)$, where $P(x)$ is a polynomial in x, then $P(x) =$

(A) x^2
(B) $x^2 - 1$
(C) $x^2 + 1$
(D) $x^2 - x - 1$
(E) $x^2 + x + 1$

22. The numbers 3, 5, and 7 are three consecutive odd numbers that are prime. How many other triplets of consecutive odd numbers greater than 1 consist entirely of primes?

(A) None
(B) One
(C) Two
(D) Three
(E) More than three

23. Which of the following is a counterexample to the statement "$\sqrt{n}$ is irrational for all real numbers n"?

(A) 34 (B) 25 (C) 11 (D) 8 (E) 2

24. If $f(x) = 1 - x^3$, then $f(-1) =$

(A) -2 (B) -1 (C) 0 (D) 1 (E) 2

25. If the origin is the midpoint of the line segment between the points $(1, 2)$ and (x, y), then $(x, y) =$

(A) $\left(\frac{1}{2}, 1\right)$

(B) $(1, -2)$

(C) $(-1, 2)$

(D) $(-1, -2)$

(E) $(-2, 1)$

GO ON TO THE NEXT PAGE

USE THIS SPACE FOR SCRATCHWORK.

26. If $2^{x^2} \cdot 2^{2x} \cdot 2 = 512$ and $x > 0$, then $x =$

(A) 9 (B) 4 (C) 3 (D) 2 (E) 1

27. If $i^2 = -1$, then all of the following expressions have equal value EXCEPT

(A) $i + i^3$
(B) $i^2 + i^4$
(C) $i^5 + i^7$
(D) $(4i)^2 - 16$
(E) $(-7i)^2 + 49$

28. Which of the following lines is parallel to the line $y = 2x + 3$?

(A) $y = -2x + 3$

(B) $y = -\frac{1}{2}x + 3$

(C) $y = \frac{1}{2}x + \frac{1}{3}$

(D) $y = x + 3$

(E) $y = 2x + \frac{1}{3}$

29. What is the maximum number of diagonals that can be drawn on the faces of a cube so that no two diagonals have a point in common?

(A) Two (B) Three (C) Four (D) Five (E) Six

30. If points (0, 0), (3, 5), (8, 0), and $(5, k)$ are the vertices of a parallelogram, then $k =$

(A) 8 (B) 5 (C) 3 (D) −3 (E) −5

GO ON TO THE NEXT PAGE

USE THIS SPACE FOR SCRATCHWORK.

31. Which of the following is equivalent to $\{x: x > 4 \text{ or } x < 0\}$?

(A) $\{x: |x + 2| > 6\}$
(B) $\{x: |x - 2| > 2\}$
(C) $\{x: |x + 2| < 2\}$
(D) $\{x: |x - 2| < 2\}$
(E) $\{x: 2 < x + 2 < 6\}$

32. A circle has three chords with the following lengths:

I. 3.05
II. 3.50
III. 0.305

Which of the following is a list of these chords in order of increasing distance from the center of the circle?

(A) II, I, III
(B) I, II, III
(C) II, III, I
(D) III, I, II
(E) III, II, I

33. The average (arithmetic mean) grade of 2 students on a geometry test was 82. The average grade of 3 other students on the same test was 72. What was the average grade of all 5 students on the test?

(A) 74 (B) 76 (C) 77 (D) 78 (E) 80

34. If $f(x) = 2x + 1$ for $0 \leqq x \leqq 3$, then which of the following sets is the range of f?

(A) $\{y: 0 \leqq y \leqq 3\}$
(B) $\{y: 0 \leqq y \leqq 6\}$
(C) $\{y: 0 \leqq y \leqq 7\}$
(D) $\{y: 1 \leqq y \leqq 6\}$
(E) $\{y: 1 \leqq y \leqq 7\}$

GO ON TO THE NEXT PAGE

USE THIS SPACE FOR SCRATCHWORK.

35. If $f(x) = \sqrt{x+1}$ and $g(x) = x^2 - 3$, which of the following could be the graph of $y = g(f(x))$?

(A)

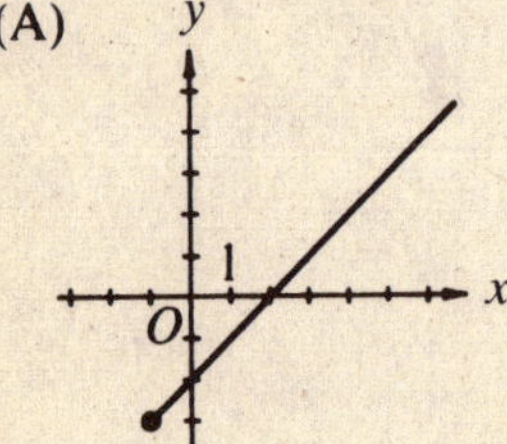

(B)

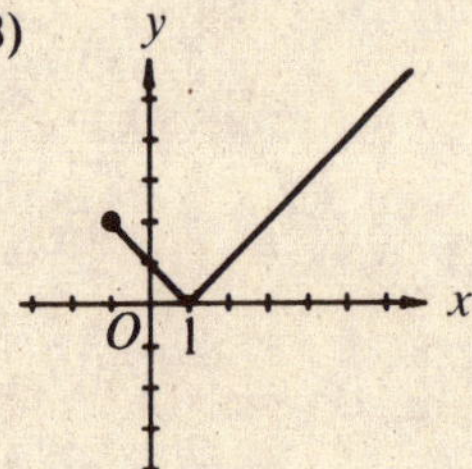

(C)

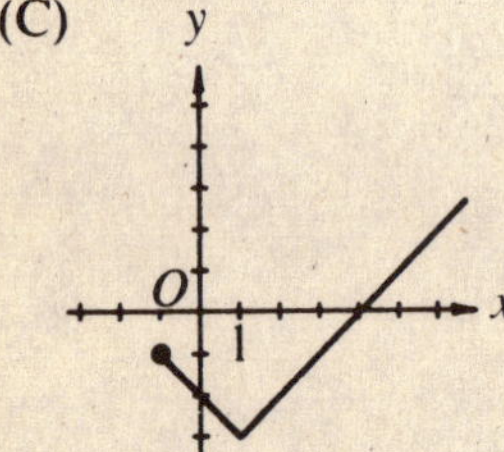

(D)

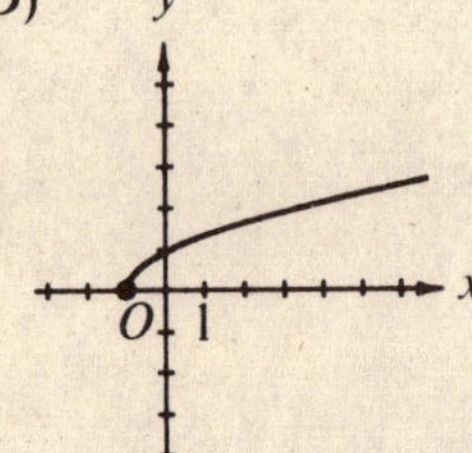

(E)

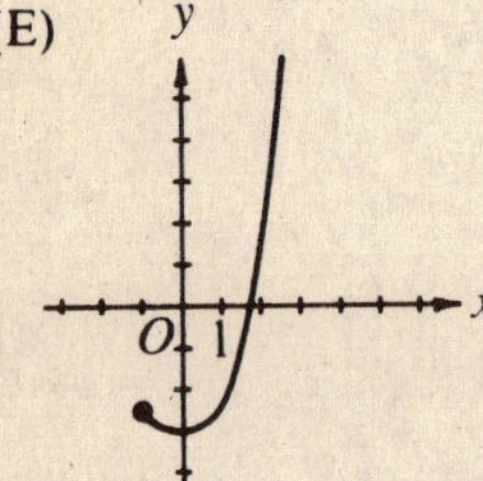

36. $2\cos^2\theta + 2\sin^2\theta =$

(A) 0 (B) 1 (C) 2 (D) 3 (E) 4

37. The maximum value of the function defined by $f(x) = 2 - x^2$ over the interval $-1 \leqq x \leqq 2$ is

(A) -2 (B) 0 (C) 1 (D) 2 (E) 3

GO ON TO THE NEXT PAGE

USE THIS SPACE FOR SCRATCHWORK.

38. If $f(x) = x^2 - 3x$ and $g(x) = x^2 + 2x - 15$, then for $x \neq 3$ and $x \neq -5$, $\dfrac{f(x)}{g(x)} =$

(A) $\dfrac{1}{x+5}$

(B) $\dfrac{x}{x+5}$

(C) $x^4 - 21x^2 + 45x$

(D) $x^2 + 5x$

(E) $\dfrac{x+5}{x}$

39. In Figure 4, if $a = 2b$ and $b = \dfrac{c}{2}$, what is the volume of the rectangular solid in terms of c?

(A) $\dfrac{c^2}{2}$ (B) $2c^2$ (C) c^3 (D) $\dfrac{c^3}{2}$ (E) $\dfrac{c^3}{4}$

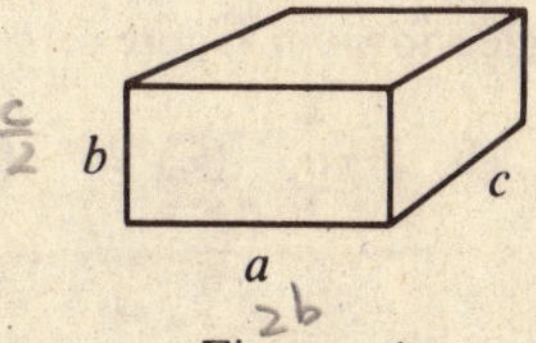

Figure 4

40. If a point with coordinates (2, 3) is on a graph that is symmetric with respect to the x-axis, which of the following are coordinates of a point that must also be on this graph?

(A) $(-2, -3)$
(B) $(-2, 3)$
(C) $(2, -3)$
(D) $(3, -2)$
(E) $(3, 2)$

41. In Figure 5, the circle and the square have centers at O. If the area of the circle is one-half the area of the square, what is the ratio $\dfrac{a}{b}$?

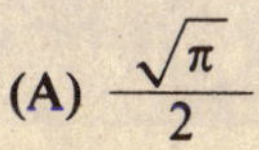 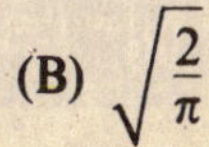 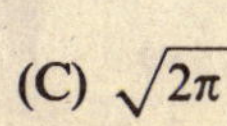

(A) $\dfrac{\sqrt{\pi}}{2}$ (B) $\sqrt{\dfrac{2}{\pi}}$ (C) $\sqrt{2\pi}$ (D) $\dfrac{\pi}{2}$ (E) $\dfrac{2}{\pi}$

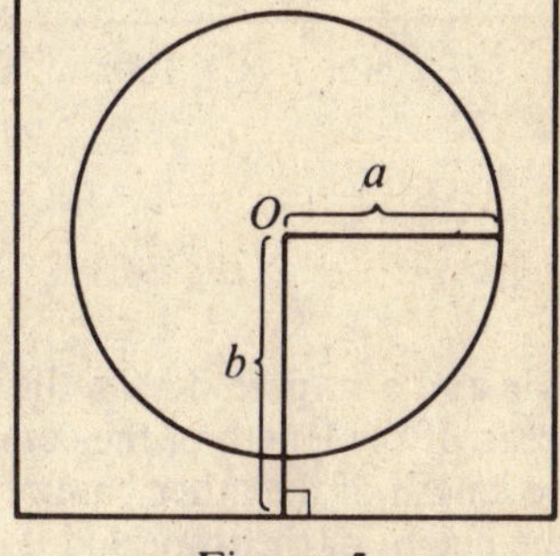

Figure 5

GO ON TO THE NEXT PAGE

USE THIS SPACE FOR SCRATCHWORK.

42. Let A be the larger acute angle in a triangle with sides of lengths 3, 4, and 5, and let B be the larger acute angle in a triangle with sides of lengths 5, 12, and 13. Which of the following statements must be true?

    I. $\sin A < \sin B$
    II. $\cos A < \cos B$
    III. $\tan A < \tan B$

    (A) None
    (B) I and II only
    (C) I and III only
    (D) II and III only
    (E) I, II, and III

43. In the triangle shown in Figure 6, $b =$

    (A) $a\sqrt{2}$ (B) $2\sqrt{a}$ (C) $2a$ (D) $\sqrt{a}$ (E) $\sqrt{2}$

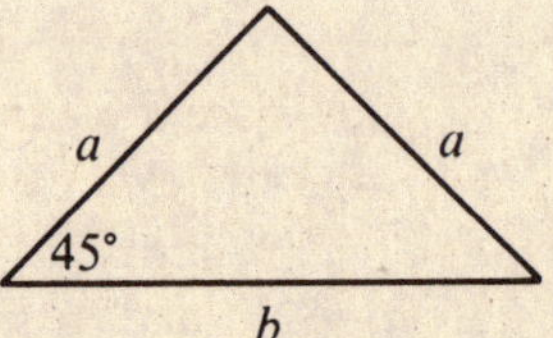

Figure 6

44. If $0° < x < 90°$, then $\dfrac{\sin x}{\tan x \cos x} =$

    (A) $\dfrac{1}{\sin x}$ (B) $\cos x$ (C) -1 (D) 0 (E) 1

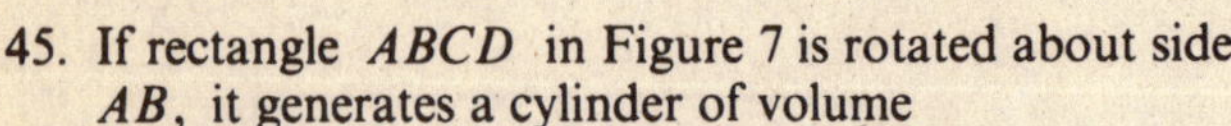

45. If rectangle $ABCD$ in Figure 7 is rotated about side AB, it generates a cylinder of volume

    (A) 40π (B) 50π (C) 100π (D) 200π (E) 320π

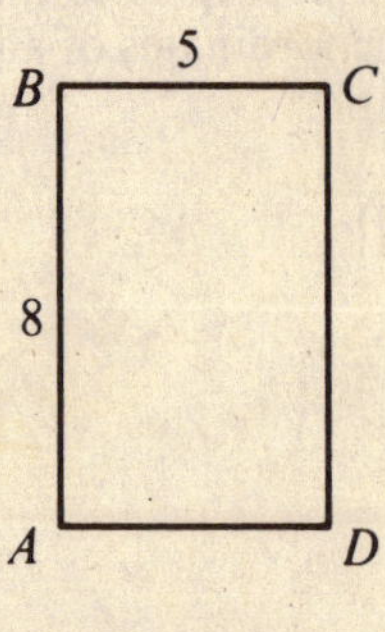

Figure 7

46. A triangle and a trapezoid have the same base and equal areas. If the length of the common base is twice the length of the other base of the trapezoid, and if the height of the trapezoid is h, what is the height of the triangle in terms of h?

    (A) $3h$ (B) $2h$ (C) $\frac{3}{2}h$ (D) $\frac{2}{3}h$ (E) $\frac{1}{2}h$

GO ON TO THE NEXT PAGE

USE THIS SPACE FOR SCRATCHWORK.

47. If $a + b = ac$, where a and b are nonzero integers, which of the following statements are always true?

    I. c is an integer.
    II. If $b = ae$ and e is an integer, then c is an integer.
    III. If a and c are positive, then b is positive.

    (A) II only
    (B) III only
    (C) I and II only
    (D) II and III only
    (E) I, II, and III

48. Figure 8 shows two adjacent squares, each with side x. With P as center and PR as radius, an arc is drawn as shown. What is the area of the shaded region in terms of x?

    (A) $\dfrac{x^2(\pi - 2)}{4}$
    (B) $\dfrac{x^2(\pi - 3)}{6}$
    (C) $\dfrac{x^2(\pi - 8)}{8}$
    (D) $\dfrac{x^2(\pi - 4)}{8}$
    (E) $\dfrac{x^2(\pi - 4)}{4}$

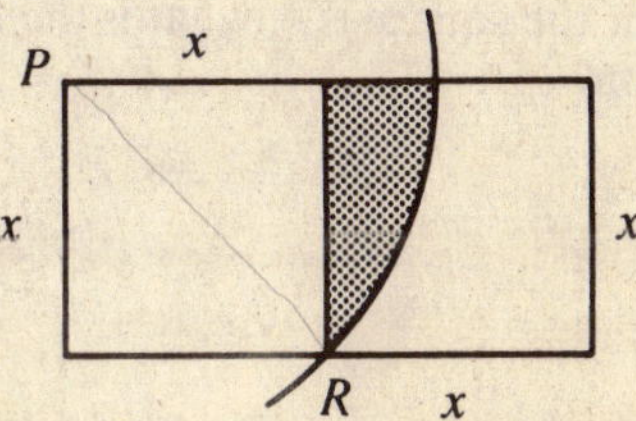

Figure 8

GO ON TO THE NEXT PAGE

USE THIS SPACE FOR SCRATCHWORK.

49. If $|x| = |y|$, which of the following must be true?

(A) x and y are both positive numbers.
(B) $x = y$ only
(C) $x = y$ or $-x = -y$
(D) $x = y$ or $x = -y$
(E) $x = -y$ or $y = -x$

50. Figure 9 shows a regular octagon (eight-sided polygon) with four of its sides on the sides of a square. If the length of a side of the square is 1, what is the length of a side of the octagon?

Figure 9

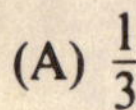
(A) $\frac{1}{3}$

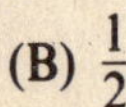
(B) $\frac{1}{2}$

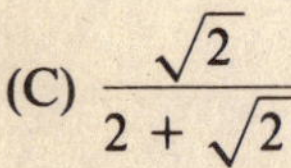
(C) $\frac{\sqrt{2}}{2+\sqrt{2}}$

(D) $\frac{1}{2+\sqrt{2}}$

(E) $\frac{\sqrt{2}}{4}$

STOP

IF YOU FINISH BEFORE TIME IS CALLED, YOU MAY CHECK YOUR WORK ON THIS TEST ONLY. DO NOT TURN TO ANY OTHER TEST IN THIS BOOK.

How to Score the Mathematics Level I Test

When you take the Mathematics Subject Test, Level I, your answer sheet will be "read" by a scanning machine that will record your responses to each question. Then a computer will compare your answers with the correct answers and produce your raw score. You get one point for each correct answer. For each wrong answer, one-fourth of a point is subtracted to correct for random guessing. Questions you omit are not counted. This raw score is converted to a College Board scaled score that is reported to you and to the colleges you specify. After you have taken the practice test, you can get an idea of what your score might be by following the instructions in the next two sections.

FINDING YOUR RAW TEST SCORE

Step 1: Table A lists the correct answers for all the questions on the SAT II: Mathematics Level I Subject Test that is reproduced in this book. It also serves as a worksheet for you to calculate your raw score.

- Compare your answers with those given in the table.
- Put a check in the column marked "Right" if your answer is correct.
- Put a check in the column marked "Wrong" if your answer is incorrect.
- Leave both columns blank if you omitted the question.

Step 2: Count the number of right answers and enter the total here: .... ________

Step 3: Count the number of wrong answers and enter the total here: .... ________

Step 4: Divide the number of wrong answers by 4 and enter the result here: .... ________

Step 5: Subtract the result obtained in Step 4 from the total you obtained in Step 2. Enter the result here: .... ________

Step 6: Round the number obtained in Step 5 to the nearest whole number. Enter the result here: .... ________

The number you obtained in Step 6 is your raw test score.

TABLE A

Answers to the SAT II: Mathematics Level I Subject Test, Form 3JAC2, and Percentage of Students Answering Each Question Correctly

Question Number	Correct Answer	Right	Wrong	Percentage of Students Answering the Question Correctly*	Question Number	Correct Answer	Right	Wrong	Percentage of Students Answering the Question Correctly*
1	C			93	26	D			64
2	D			92	27	D			26
3	B			89	28	E			57
4	A			92	29	C			43
5	C			84	30	E			38
6	B			79	31	B			32
7	D			54	32	A			46
8	D			91	33	B			47
9	A			93	34	E			54
10	B			78	35	A			48
11	C			82	36	C			41
12	B			60	37	D			41
13	B			75	38	B			70
14	A			75	39	D			57
15	D			71	40	C			43
16	C			90	41	B			12
17	C			74	42	C			22
18	E			70	43	A			43
19	C			83	44	E			52
20	E			58	45	D			25
21	C			47	46	C			16
22	A			65	47	A			08
23	B			70	48	A			11
24	E			76	49	D			21
25	D			71	50	C			07

*These percentages are based on an analysis of the answer sheets for a random sample of 3,995 students who took this form of the test in December 1987 and whose mean score was 536. They may be used as an indication of the relative difficulty of a particular question. Each percentage may also be used to predict the likelihood that a typical SAT II: Mathematics Level I Subject Test candidate will answer correctly that question on this edition of this test.

Finding Your College Board Scaled Score

When you take SAT II: Subject Tests, the scores sent to the colleges you specify are reported on the College Board scale, which ranges from 200 to 800. You can convert your practice test score to a scaled score by using Table B. To find your scaled score, locate your raw score in the left-hand column of Table B; the corresponding score in the right-hand column is your College Board scaled score. For example, a raw score of 40 on this particular edition of the SAT II: Mathematics Level I Subject Test corresponds to a College Board scaled score of 680.

Raw scores are converted to scaled scores to ensure that a score earned on any one edition of a particular Subject Test is comparable to the same scaled score earned on any other edition of the same Subject Test. Because some editions of tests may be slightly easier or more difficult than others, College Board scaled scores are adjusted so that they indicate the same level of performance regardless of the edition of the test taken and the ability of the group that takes it. Thus, for example, a score of 400 on one edition of a test taken at a particular administration indicates the same level of achievement as a score of 400 on a different edition of the test taken at a different administration.

When you take the SAT II: Subject Tests during a national administration, your scores are likely to differ somewhat from the scores you obtain on the tests in this book. People perform at different levels at different times for reasons unrelated to the tests themselves. The precision of any test is also limited because it represents only a sample of all the possible questions that could be asked.

TABLE B

Score Conversion Table
Mathematics Level I Subject Test, Form 3JAC2

Raw Score	College Board Scaled Score	Raw Score	College Board Scaled Score
50	800	15	450
49	780	14	440
48	770	13	430
47	760	12	430
46	740	11	420
45	730	10	410
44	720	9	400
43	710	8	390
42	700	7	380
41	690	6	370
40	680	5	370
39	670	4	360
38	660	3	350
37	650	2	340
36	640	1	340
35	630	0	330
34	610	−1	320
33	600	−2	310
32	590	−3	300
31	580	−4	300
30	570	−5	290
29	560	−6	280
28	550	−7	270
27	550	−8	260
26	540	−9	260
25	530	−10	250
24	520	−11	240
23	510	−12	230
22	510		
21	500		
20	490		
19	480		
18	480		
17	470		
16	460		

Reviewing Your Test Performance

After you have scored your test, you should take some time to consider the following points in relation to your performance on the test.

- *Did you run out of time before you reached the end of the test?*

  If you did, you may want to consider pacing yourself better. For example, you may have spent too much time working on one or two difficult questions. A better approach might have been to continue the test and return to those questions after you had attempted to answer the remaining questions on the test.

- *Did you take a long time reading the directions for the test?*

  The directions in this test are the same as those in the Mathematics Level I Subject Tests now being administered. You will save time when you take the test if you become thoroughly familiar with them in advance.

- *How did you handle questions you were unsure of?*

  If you were able to eliminate one or more of the answer choices and you guessed from the remaining choices, then your approach probably worked to your advantage. On the other hand, omitting questions about which you have some knowledge or guessing answers haphazardly would probably be a mistake.

- *How difficult were the questions for you compared with other students who took the test?*

  By referring to Table A, you can find out how difficult each question was for the group of students who took this test. The right-hand column in the table tells you what percentage of this group answered the question correctly. A question that was answered correctly by almost everyone in the group is obviously an easy question. Question 1, for example, was answered correctly by 93 percent of the students in the sample. On the other hand, question 46 was answered correctly by only 16 percent.

  It is important to remember that these percentages are based on only one particular group of students; had this edition of the test been given to other groups of students at the time, the percentages would probably have been different.

  If you find that you missed several questions that would be considered easy, you may want to review those questions carefully. They may cover some aspect of the subject that you need to review. Perhaps you misunderstood the directions for one part of the test or you thought the questions were so easy that you did not spend as much time on them as you might have.

SAT II:

Mathematics Level IIC Subject Test

The test that follows is representative of a typical SAT II: Mathematics Level IIC Subject Test. It has already been administered. So that you may have an idea of what the national test administration will be like, try to take the test in this book under conditions as close as possible to those of the nationally administered test. It will probably help if you do the following.

- Set aside an hour for the test when you will not be interrupted, so that you can complete all of it in one sitting.
- Sit at a desk with no other papers or books. You can't take a dictionary, other books, or notes into the test room.
- Have a kitchen timer or clock in front of you for timing yourself.
- Tear out an answer sheet from the back of this book and fill it in just as you would on the day of the test. You can use one answer sheet for as many as three Subject Tests.
- Read the instructions that precede the test. When you take the test, you will be asked to read them before you begin answering questions.
- After you finish the test, read the sections on "How to Score the SAT II: Mathematics Level IIC Subject Test" and "Reviewing Your Test Performance," which follow the test.

FORM 3PBC

MATHEMATICS LEVEL IIC TEST

The top portion of the section of the answer sheet that you will use in taking the Mathematics Level IIC test must be filled in exactly as shown in the illustration below. Note carefully that you have to do all of the following on your answer sheet.

1. Print MATHEMATICS LEVEL IIC on the line under the words "Subject (print)."

2. In the shaded box labeled "Test Code" fill in four ovals:

   —Fill in oval 5 in the row labeled V.

   —Fill in oval 3 in the row labeled W.

   —Fill in oval 5 in the row labeled X.

   —Fill in oval E in the row labeled Y.

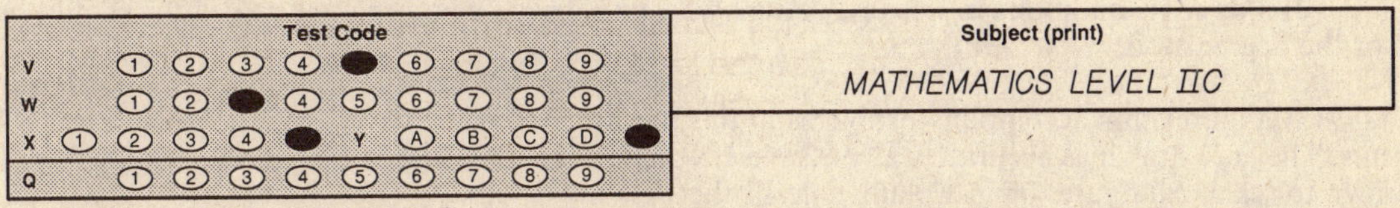

Test Code										Subject (print)
V		1	2	3	4	●	6	7	8	9	MATHEMATICS LEVEL IIC
W		1	2	●	4	5	6	7	8	9	
X	1	2	3	4	●	Y	A	B	C	D	●
Q		1	2	3	4	5	6	7	8	9	

3. Please answer either Part I or Part II below by filling in the specified ovals in row Q that correspond to the courses you have taken or are presently taking. FILL IN ALL OVALS THAT APPLY. The information that you provide is for statistical purposes only and will not affect your score on the test.

   Students who are enrolled in the sequential mathematics program (Course I, Course II, Course III) used in New York State should proceed to Part II.

Part I Which of the following describes a mathematics course you have taken or are taking? (Fill in ALL ovals that apply.)

- Algebra I or Elementary Algebra —Fill in oval 1.
- Geometry —Fill in oval 2.
- Algebra II or Intermediate Algebra —Fill in oval 3.
- Elementary functions (Precalculus) and/or Trigonometry —Fill in oval 4.
- Advanced Placement Mathematics (Calculus AB or Calculus BC) —Fill in oval 9.

Answer Part II only if you are or were enrolled in the sequential mathematics program (Course I, Course II, Course III) used in New York State.

Part II Which of the following describes a mathematics course you have taken or are taking? (Fill in ALL ovals that apply.)

- Course I —Fill in oval 5.
- Course II —Fill in oval 6.
- Course III —Fill in oval 7.
- A course beyond course III (not Advanced Placement Calculus AB or BC) —Fill in oval 8.
- Advanced Placement Mathematics (Calculus AB or Calculus BC) —Fill in oval 9.

When the supervisor gives the signal, turn the page and begin the Mathematics Level IIC test. There are 100 numbered ovals on the answer sheet and 50 questions in the Mathematics Level IIC test. Therefore, use only ovals 1 to 50 for recording your answers.

MATHEMATICS LEVEL IIC

Time—60 minutes

For each of the following problems, decide which is the BEST of the choices given. If the exact numerical value is not one of the choices, select the choice that best approximates this value. Then fill in the corresponding oval on the answer sheet.

Notes: (1) A calculator will be necessary for answering some (but not all) of the questions in this test. For each question you will have to decide whether or not you should use a calculator. The calculator you use must be at least a scientific calculator; programmable calculators and calculators that can display graphs are permitted.

(2) For some questions in this test you may have to decide whether your calculator should be in the radian mode or the degree mode.

(3) Figures that accompany problems in this test are intended to provide information useful in solving the problems. They are drawn as accurately as possible EXCEPT when it is stated in a specific problem that its figure is not drawn to scale. All figures lie in a plane unless otherwise indicated.

(4) Unless otherwise specified, the domain of any function f is assumed to be the set of all real numbers x for which $f(x)$ is a real number.

(5) Reference information that may be useful in answering the questions in this test can be found on the page preceding question 1.*

USE THIS SPACE FOR SCRATCHWORK.

1. If $\sqrt[5]{4-3x} = 3$, what is the value of x?

(A) −82.33
(B) −79.67
(C) −1.75
(D) 0.92
(E) 82.33

2. If $f(a, b) = \dfrac{a+b}{2}$, which of the following is equal to $f(4, 8)$?

(A) $f(0, 6)$
(B) $f(1, 6)$
(C) $f(2, 4)$
(D) $f(2, 16)$
(E) $f(3, 9)$

*In the actual test, the reference information is located on the page preceding question 1. In this book, the reference information can be found on page 135.

GO ON TO THE NEXT PAGE

MATHEMATICS LEVEL IIC TEST—*Continued*

USE THIS SPACE FOR SCRATCHWORK.

3. $\frac{6!}{3!5!} =$

   (A) 60 (B) 24 (C) 6 (D) 1 (E) $\frac{1}{60}$

4. The graph of which of the following equations has a slope of $\frac{1}{2}$?

   (A) $y = \frac{1}{2}$

   (B) $y = 2x$

   (C) $y = 2x + 1$

   (D) $y = x + \frac{1}{2}$

   (E) $y = \frac{x}{2} + 1$

5. If $f(x) = x + \sqrt{x}$ and $g(x) = f(f(x))$, then $g(1.7) =$

   (A) 1.7
   (B) 3.0
   (C) 4.7
   (D) 6.9
   (E) 9.0

GO ON TO THE NEXT PAGE

MATHEMATICS LEVEL IIC TEST—*Continued*

USE THIS SPACE FOR SCRATCHWORK.

6. For all $m \neq 0$, $\dfrac{1 - \frac{1}{m}}{\frac{1}{m}} =$

(A) 1

(B) $m - 1$

(C) $\dfrac{m - 1}{m}$

(D) $\dfrac{1 - m}{m}$

(E) $m - \dfrac{1}{m}$

7. The graph of $y = bx - 1$ has points in the first quadrant if and only if

(A) $b \neq 0$
(B) $b < -1$
(C) $-1 < b < 1$
(D) $0 < b < 1$
(E) $b > 0$

8. If $\tan x = 5$, then $\dfrac{\tan x}{\cot x} =$

(A) $\frac{1}{5}$ (B) 1 (C) 5 (D) 10 (E) 25

GO ON TO THE NEXT PAGE

MATHEMATICS LEVEL IIC TEST—*Continued*

USE THIS SPACE FOR SCRATCHWORK.

9. If $\dfrac{a + bc}{we + f} = g$ and if $efg \neq 0$, which of the following is equal to w?

(A) $\dfrac{a + bc - fg}{eg}$

(B) $\dfrac{a + bc - g}{e}$

(C) $\dfrac{a - bc + fg}{eg}$

(D) $\dfrac{a + bc - f}{eg}$

(E) $\dfrac{a + bc - eg}{fg}$

10. If the probability of a certain event occurring is $\dfrac{4}{9}$, what is the probability of this event not occurring?

(A) $\dfrac{4}{13}$ (B) $\dfrac{4}{9}$ (C) $\dfrac{5}{9}$ (D) $\dfrac{9}{13}$ (E) $\dfrac{9}{4}$

11. If $x^4 - 19 = 19$ and $x \geq 0$, then $x =$

(A) 0
(B) 2.08
(C) 2.48
(D) 4.36
(E) 6.16

GO ON TO THE NEXT PAGE

MATHEMATICS LEVEL IIC TEST—*Continued*

USE THIS SPACE FOR SCRATCHWORK.

12. In Figure 1, if $\theta = 38°$, what is the value of t?

    (A) 0.15
    (B) 0.20
    (C) 2.46
    (D) 3.13
    (E) 3.15

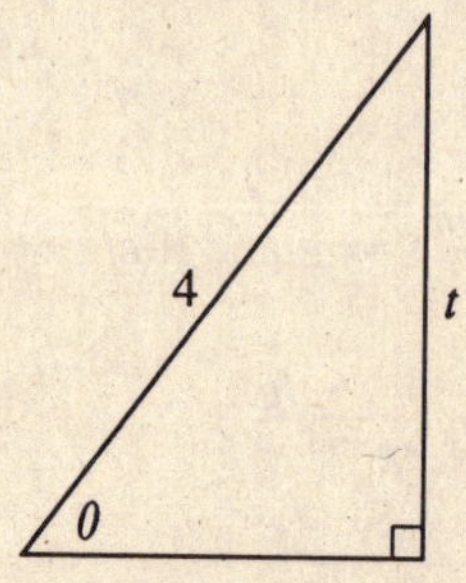

Figure 1

Note: Figure not drawn to scale.

13. Joe has a test average of 87 in mathematics. If his test average makes up 70 percent of his overall grade and the final exam makes up the remaining 30 percent, what must be his final exam score to give him an overall grade of exactly 90 ?

    (A) 91
    (B) 93
    (C) 95
    (D) 97
    (E) 99

14. An operation is defined on pairs of integers by $(a, b) \triangledown (c, e) = (a - c, b - e)$. If $[(1, 2) \triangledown (-3, 6)] \triangledown (x, y) = (1, 1)$, then $(x, y) =$

    (A) $(5, -5)$
    (B) $(3, -7)$
    (C) $(3, -5)$
    (D) $(3, 5)$
    (E) $(-3, 5)$

GO ON TO THE NEXT PAGE

MATHEMATICS LEVEL IIC TEST—*Continued*

USE THIS SPACE FOR SCRATCHWORK.

15. If $\cos t = \frac{5}{6}$, what is the value of $\cos 2t$?

(A) 0.92
(B) 0.39
(C) 0.28
(D) 0.15
(E) −0.83

16. Which of the following is a zero of $f(x) = 2x^2 - 3x - 1$?

(A) −1.00
(B) 0.28
(C) 0.50
(D) 1.78
(E) 3.56

17. What is the number of digits in the number obtained by multiplying 12,121,212 by 3,579 ?

(A) 4
(B) 9
(C) 10
(D) 11
(E) 12

GO ON TO THE NEXT PAGE

MATHEMATICS LEVEL IIC TEST—*Continued*

USE THIS SPACE FOR SCRATCHWORK.

18. If $\log_x 3 = 9$, then $x =$

(A) 0.50
(B) 1.13
(C) 1.22
(D) 2.00
(E) 2.08

19. Which of the following is a point at which the ellipse $\frac{x^2}{5} + \frac{y^2}{15} = 1$ intersects the x-axis?

(A) (2.2, 0)
(B) (3.9, 0)
(C) (4.5, 0)
(D) (5.0, 0)
(E) (15.0, 0)

20. The function f is given by $f(x) = x - [x]$, where $[x]$ is defined to be the greatest integer that is less than or equal to x. If $1 \leq x < 2$, then f is also given by $f(x) =$

(A) $x - 2$ (B) $x - 1$ (C) x (D) $x + 1$ (E) $x + 2$

GO ON TO THE NEXT PAGE

MATHEMATICS LEVEL IIC TEST—*Continued*

USE THIS SPACE FOR SCRATCHWORK.

21. In Figure 2, $r \sin \theta =$

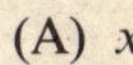

(A) x

(B) y

(C) $\frac{x}{y}$

(D) $\frac{y}{x}$

(E) $x + y$

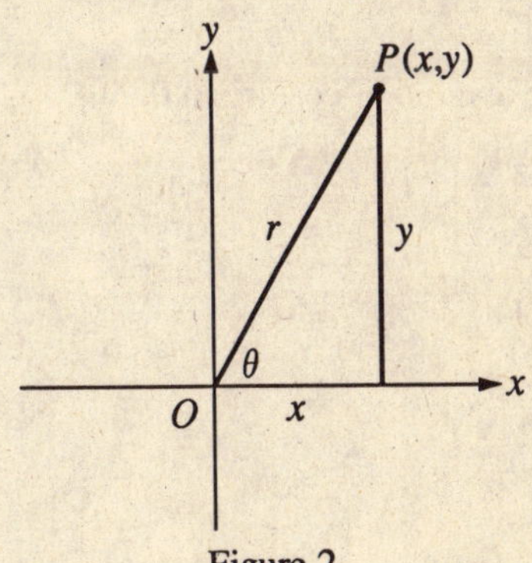

Figure 2

22. What is the remainder when $2x^4 - 3x^2 - x + 3$ is divided by $x + 1$?

(A) -3
(B) -1
(C) 1
(D) 2
(E) 3

23. In Figure 3, what is the length of segment AC?

(A) 4.47
(B) 5.00
(C) 5.39
(D) 6.23
(E) 9.00

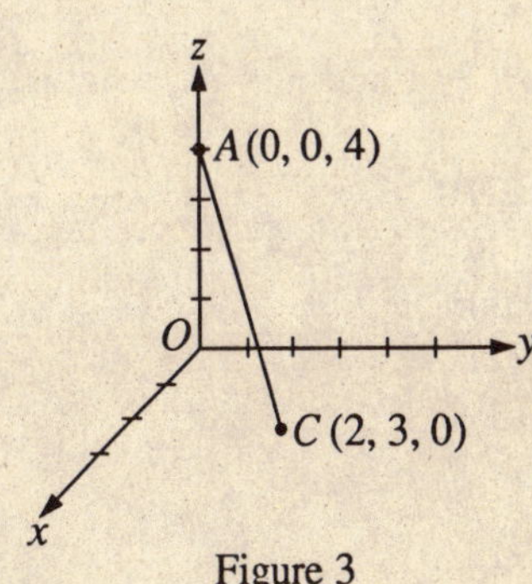

Figure 3

GO ON TO THE NEXT PAGE

USE THIS SPACE FOR SCRATCHWORK.

24. What is a value of cos(arcsin 0.90) ?

(A) 0.44
(B) 0.58
(C) 0.67
(D) 0.71
(E) 0.90

25. What is the area of a triangle whose vertices are $(\sqrt{2}, 0)$, $(2, \sqrt{10})$, and $(5, 0)$?

(A) 3.59
(B) 5.67
(C) 7.91
(D) 11.18
(E) 11.34

26. If $x = \sqrt{t} - 1$ and $y = t^2$, what is y in terms of x?

(A) $(x + 1)^4$
(B) $(x - 1)^4$
(C) $(x + 1)^2$
(D) $(x - 1)^2$
(E) $x^2 + 1$

GO ON TO THE NEXT PAGE

MATHEMATICS LEVEL IIC TEST—*Continued*

USE THIS SPACE FOR SCRATCHWORK.

27. What is the maximum value of $f(x) = 4 - (x - 1)^2$?

(A) 1
(B) 3
(C) 4
(D) 5
(E) 16

28. If a certain product now worth \$450 increases in value at the rate of 8 percent per year, how much will it be worth 6 years from now?

(A) \$630
(B) \$661
(C) \$666
(D) \$714
(E) \$771

29. The 1st term of an arithmetic sequence is 3 and the 5th term is 17. What is the 150th term of the sequence?

(A) 420.2
(B) 521.5
(C) 524.5
(D) 528.0
(E) 698.3

GO ON TO THE NEXT PAGE

MATHEMATICS LEVEL IIC TEST—*Continued*

USE THIS SPACE FOR SCRATCHWORK.

30. The cosine of an angle is one-half the sine of the same angle. What is the tangent of this angle?

(A) 0
(B) $\frac{1}{2}$
(C) 1
(D) 2
(E) It cannot be determined from the information given.

31. The graph in Figure 4 could be a portion of the graph of which of the following functions?

I. $f(x) = x^3 + ax^2 + bx + c$
II. $g(x) = x^5 + ax^3 + bx + c$
III. $h(x) = x^7 + ax^6 + bx^5 + cx^4 + dx^3 + ex^2 + fx + g$

(A) I only
(B) II only
(C) III only
(D) II and III only
(E) I, II, and III

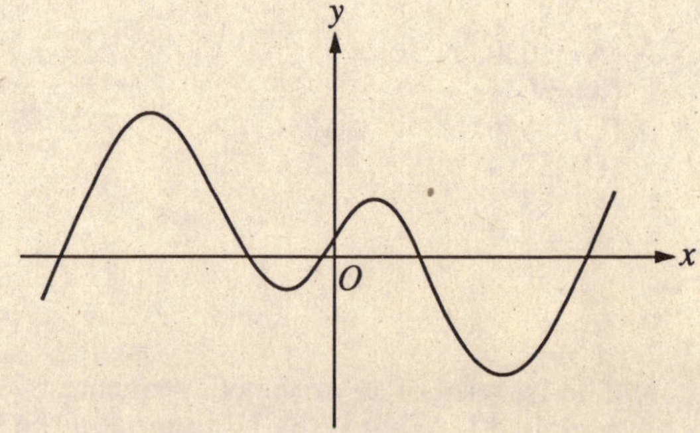

Figure 4

32. A right circular cylinder has radius 3 and height 3. If A and B are two points on its surface, what is the maximum straight-line distance between A and B?

(A) $3\sqrt{6}$ (B) $3\sqrt{5}$ (C) 6 (D) $3\sqrt{3}$ (E) $3\sqrt{2}$

GO ON TO THE NEXT PAGE

MATHEMATICS LEVEL IIC TEST—*Continued*

USE THIS SPACE FOR SCRATCHWORK.

33. What is the degree measure of the smallest positive angle θ for which $6\sin^2\theta - \sin\theta - 2 = 0$?

(A) 9.6°
(B) 19.5°
(C) 30°
(D) 41.8°
(E) 90°

34. The graph of $x^2 - y^2 - 2x - 4y - 4 = 0$ is a hyperbola centered at

(A) $(-1, -2)$
(B) $(-1, 2)$
(C) $(1, -2)$
(D) $(1, 2)$
(E) $(2, 1)$

35. Which of the following could be a portion of the graph of $f(x) = \frac{e^x + e^{-x}}{2}$?

(A)
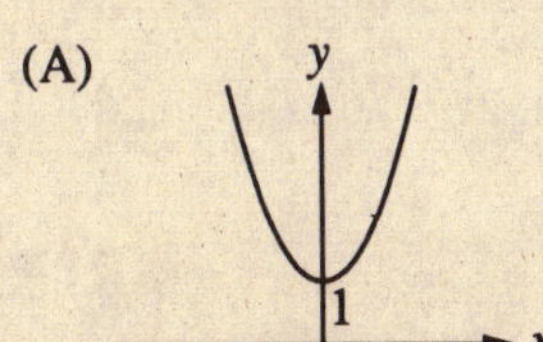

(B)
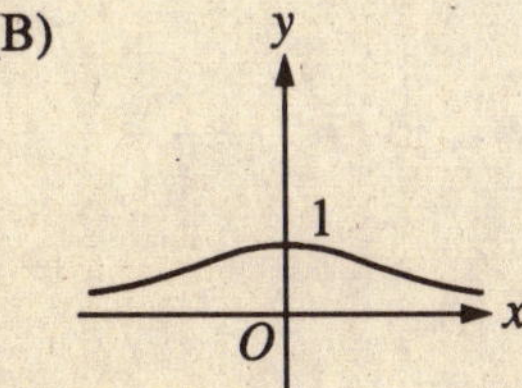

(C)
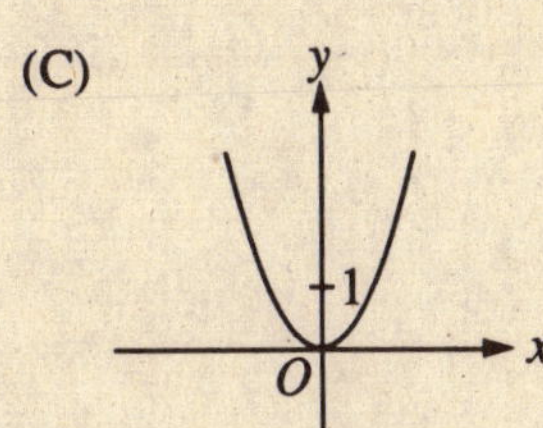

(D)
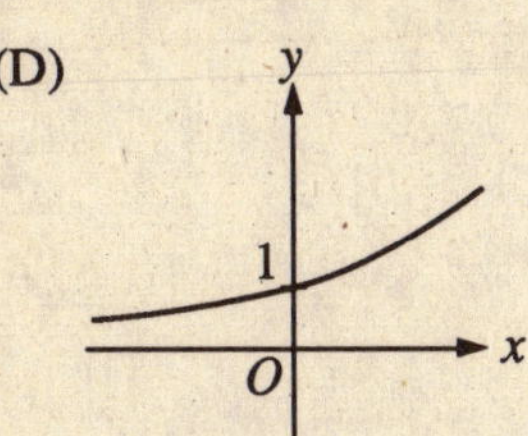

(E)
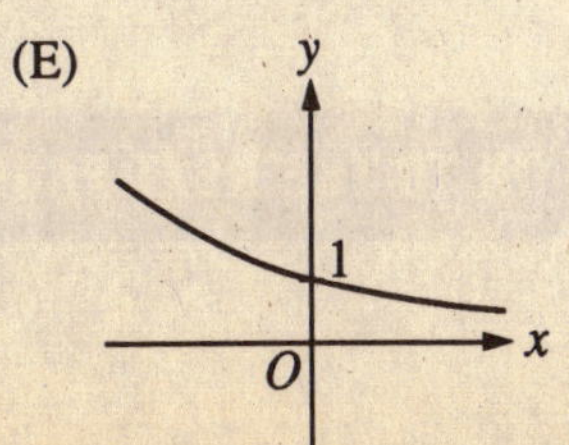

GO ON TO THE NEXT PAGE

MATHEMATICS LEVEL IIC TEST—*Continued*

USE THIS SPACE FOR SCRATCHWORK.

36. If $\frac{p}{r}$ is an integer, which of the following must also be an integer?

(A) $p - r$ (B) $p + 2r$ (C) $\frac{r}{p}$ (D) pr (E) $\frac{2p}{r}$

37. A function f has the property that whenever $x_2 > x_1$, then $f(x_2) \geq f(x_1)$. Which of the following could be the graph of f?

(A)

(B)

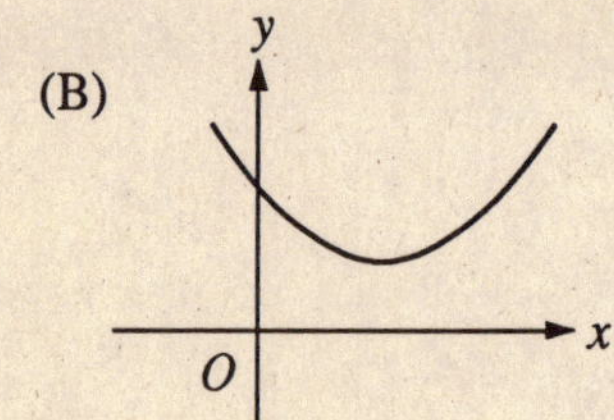

(C)

(D)

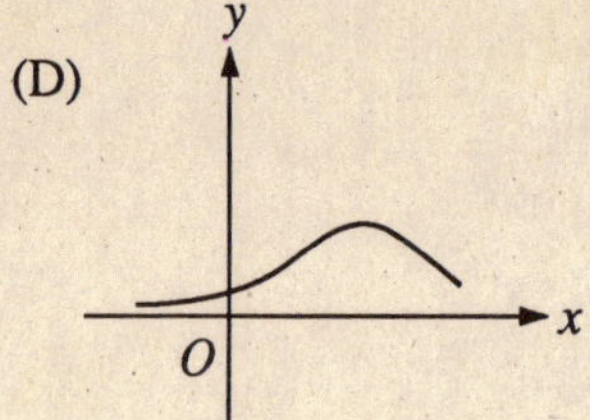

(E)

GO ON TO THE NEXT PAGE

MATHEMATICS LEVEL IIC TEST—*Continued*

USE THIS SPACE FOR SCRATCHWORK.

38. The two circles $x^2 + y^2 = 1$ and $(x - \sqrt{2})^2 + (y - \sqrt{2})^2 = 1$ are tangent to each other. What are the coordinates of the point of tangency?

(A) (0, 0.71)
(B) (0.5, 0.5)
(C) (0.71, 0)
(D) (0.71, 0.71)
(E) (1.41, 1.41)

39. What is $\lim_{x \to -2} \dfrac{2x^2 + 3x - 2}{x^2 - 4}$?

(A) 1.25
(B) 1.0
(C) 0.5
(D) 0
(E) The limit does not exist.

40. A function f is an even function if, for all values of x in the domain, $f(-x) = f(x)$. Which of the following is an even function?

(A) $f(x) = 2^x$
(B) $f(x) = x^2 + x$
(C) $f(x) = x$
(D) $f(x) = \sin x$
(E) $f(x) = \cos x$

GO ON TO THE NEXT PAGE

MATHEMATICS LEVEL IIC TEST—*Continued*

USE THIS SPACE FOR SCRATCHWORK.

41. Two cars start from the same point P and travel along separate straight highways. If these two highways originate at P, forming an angle of 80°, how many miles apart are the two cars after each has traveled 110 miles?

(A) 86
(B) 141
(C) 156
(D) 191
(E) 220

42. The shaded portion in Figure 5 shows the graph of

(A) $(y - \frac{1}{2}x)(y + x) \geq 0$

(B) $(y - 2x)(y + x) \leq 0$

(C) $(y - 2x)(y + x) \geq 0$

(D) $(y + 2x)(y - x) \leq 0$

(E) $(y + 2x)(y - x) \geq 0$

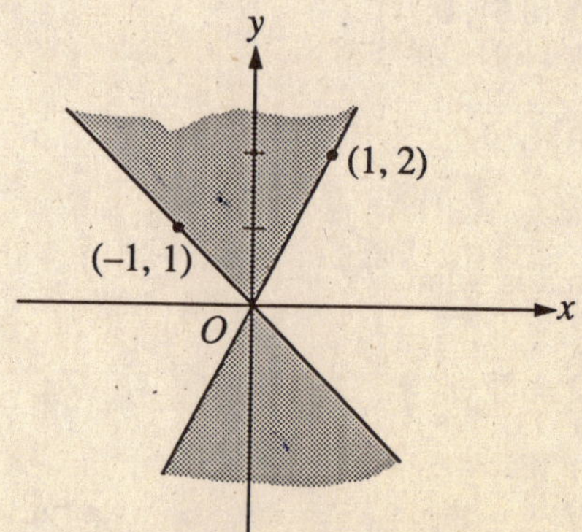

Figure 5

43. If $f(n) = \frac{1}{e^n}$, what is the least integer n such that $f(n) < 0.0001$?

(A) 9
(B) 10
(C) 11
(D) 12
(E) 13

GO ON TO THE NEXT PAGE

MATHEMATICS LEVEL IIC TEST—*Continued*

USE THIS SPACE FOR SCRATCHWORK.

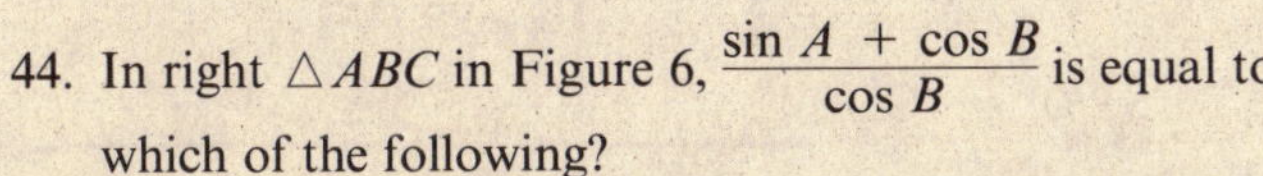

44. In right $\triangle ABC$ in Figure 6, $\dfrac{\sin A + \cos B}{\cos B}$ is equal to which of the following?

(A) 2 (B) $\dfrac{a+c}{c}$ (C) $\dfrac{2a}{b}$ (D) $\dfrac{2b}{c}$ (E) $\dfrac{2a}{c}$

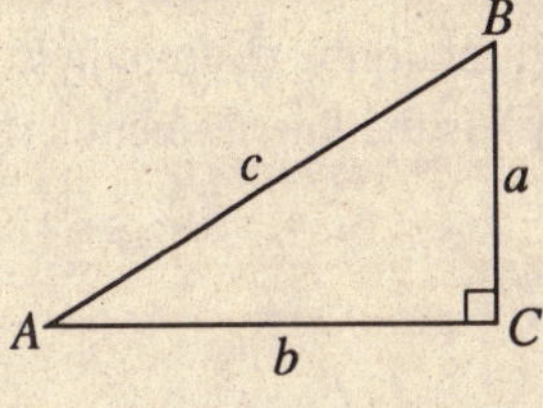

Figure 6

45. What is the volume, in cubic centimeters, of a rectangular solid that has faces with areas 2, 4, and 8 square centimeters?

(A) 128 (B) 64 (C) 32 (D) 16 (E) 8

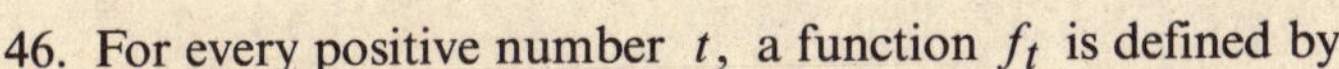

46. For every positive number t, a function f_t is defined by

$$f_t(x) = \begin{cases} 1, & x < 0 \\ 1 - \left(\dfrac{1}{t}\right)x, & 0 \le x \le t \\ 0, & x > t. \end{cases}$$

If $t > 5$, then $f_t(2) =$

(A) 0 (B) 1 (C) $\dfrac{5-t}{t}$ (D) $\dfrac{t+5}{t}$ (E) $\dfrac{t-2}{t}$

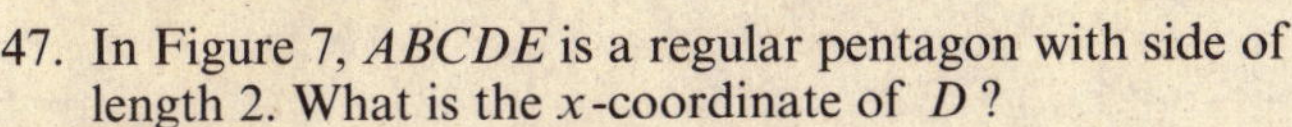

47. In Figure 7, $ABCDE$ is a regular pentagon with side of length 2. What is the x-coordinate of D?

(A) 2.62
(B) 3.62
(C) 3.73
(D) 3.90
(E) 4.90

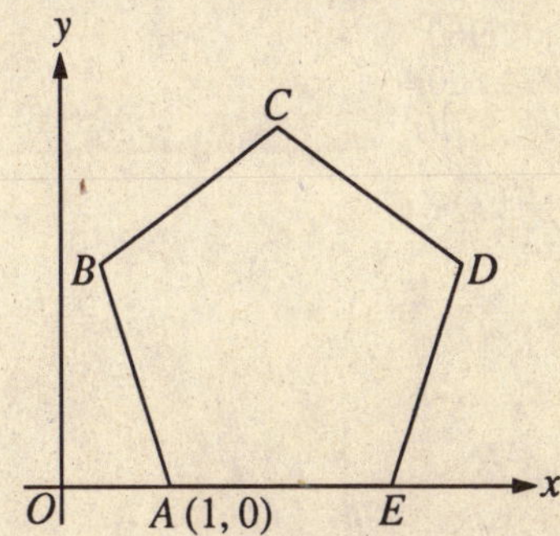

Figure 7

GO ON TO THE NEXT PAGE

MATHEMATICS LEVEL IIC TEST—*Continued*

USE THIS SPACE FOR SCRATCHWORK.

48. If f is the function with domain [0, 12] and range [0, 1] whose graph is the line segment shown in Figure 8, what is $f^{-1}(0.4)$?

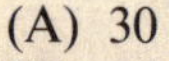

(A) 30
(B) 4.8
(C) 2.5
(D) 0.25
(E) 0.033

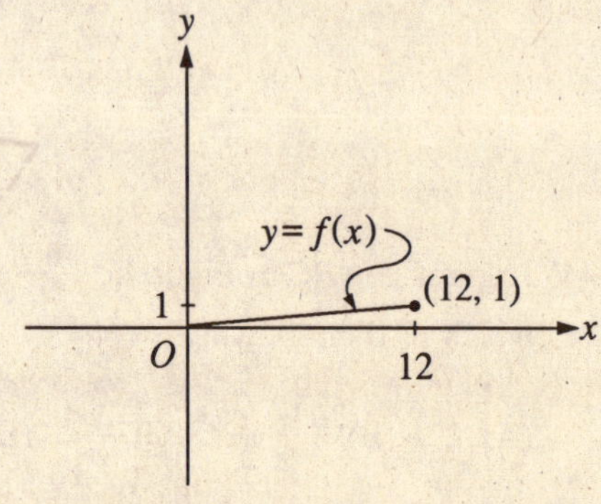

Figure 8

49. What does $|3 + 5i|$ equal ?

(A) 0.80
(B) 1.67
(C) 3.97
(D) 5.83
(E) 8.00

50. A committee of 3 mathematics majors and 4 history majors is to be chosen from a group of 20 mathematics majors and 16 history majors, respectively. How many different committees can be formed?

(A) 12
(B) 320
(C) 2,960
(D) 2,074,800
(E) 2.86×10^{15}

STOP

IF YOU FINISH BEFORE TIME IS CALLED, YOU MAY CHECK YOUR WORK ON THIS TEST ONLY. DO NOT TURN TO ANY OTHER TEST IN THIS BOOK.

How to Score the Mathematics Level IIC Test

When you take the Mathematics Subject Test, Level IIC, your answer sheet will be "read" by a scanning machine that will record your responses to each question. Then a computer will compare your answers with the correct answers and produce your raw score. You get one point for each correct answer. For each wrong answer, you lose one-fourth of a point. Questions you omit (and any for which you mark more than one answer) are not counted. This raw score is converted to a College Board scaled score that is reported to you and to the colleges you specify. After you have taken the practice test, you can get an idea of what your score might be by following the instructions in the next two sections.

FINDING YOUR RAW TEST SCORE

Step 1: Table A lists the correct answers for all the questions on the SAT II: Mathematics Level IIC Subject Test that is reproduced in this book. It also serves as a worksheet for you to calculate your raw score.

- Compare your answers with those given in the table.
- Put a check in the column marked "Right" if your answer is correct.
- Put a check in the column marked "Wrong" if your answer is incorrect.
- Leave both columns blank if you omitted the question.

Step 2: Count the number of right answers and enter the total here: .... ________

Step 3: Count the number of wrong answers and enter the total here: .... ________

Step 4: Divide the number of wrong answers by 4 and enter the result here: .... ________

Step 5: Subtract the result obtained in Step 4 from the total you obtained in Step 2. Enter the result here: .... ________

Step 6: Round the number obtained in Step 5 to the nearest whole number. Enter the result here: .... ________

The number you obtained in Step 6 is your raw test score.

TABLE A									
Answers to the SAT II: Mathematics Level IIC Subject Test, Form 3PBC, and Percentage of Students Answering Each Question Correctly									
Question Number	**Correct Answer**	**Right**	**Wrong**	**Percentage of Students Answering the Question Correctly***	**Question Number**	**Correct Answer**	**Right**	**Wrong**	**Percentage of Students Answering the Question Correctly***
1	B			86	26	A			69
2	E			86	27	C			55
3	D			93	28	D			66
4	E			94	29	C			44
5	C			80	30	D			61
6	B			90	31	D			40
7	E			77	32	B			47
8	E			84	33	D			60
9	A			70	34	C			38
10	C			95	35	A			33
11	C			91	36	E			63
12	C			92	37	C			48
13	D			82	38	D			43
14	C			80	39	A			37
15	B			80	40	E			61
16	D			72	41	B			61
17	D			69	42	C			23
18	B			76	43	B			46
19	A			74	44	A			72
20	B			70	45	E			45
21	B			88	46	E			39
22	E			59	47	B			32
23	C			65	48	B			27
24	A			86	49	D			16
25	B			54	50	D			27

*These percentages are based on an analysis of the answer sheets for a random sample of 3,040 students who took this form of the test in June 1993 and whose mean score was 670. They may be used as an indication of the relative difficulty of a particular question. Each percentage may also be used to predict the likelihood that a typical SAT II: Mathematics Level IIC Subject Test candidate will answer correctly that question on this edition of this test.

Finding Your College Board Scaled Score

When you take SAT II: Subject Tests, the scores sent to the colleges you specify are reported on the College Board scale, which ranges from 200 to 800. You can convert your practice test score to a scaled score by using Table B. To find your scaled score, locate your raw score in the left-hand column of Table B; the corresponding score in the right-hand column is your College Board scaled score. For example, a raw score of 40 on this particular edition of the SAT II: Mathematics Level IIC Subject Test corresponds to a College Board scaled score of 770.

Raw scores are converted to scaled scores to ensure that a score earned on any one edition of a particular Subject Test is comparable to the same scaled score earned on any other edition of the same Subject Test. Because some editions of tests may be slightly easier or more difficult than others, College Board scaled scores are adjusted so that they indicate the same level of performance regardless of the edition of the test taken and the ability of the group that takes it. Thus, for example, a score of 400 on one edition of a test taken at a particular administration indicates the same level of achievement as a score of 400 on a different edition of the test taken at a different administration.

When you take the SAT II: Subject Tests during a national administration, your scores are likely to differ somewhat from the scores you obtain on the tests in this book. People perform at different levels at different times for reasons unrelated to the tests themselves. The precision of any test is also limited because it represents only a sample of all the possible questions that could be asked.

TABLE B			
Score Conversion Table Mathematics Level IIC Subject Test, Form 3PBC			
Raw Score	**College Board Scaled Score**	**Raw Score**	**College Board Scaled Score**
50	800	15	560
49	800	14	540
48	800	13	530
47	800	12	520
46	800	11	500
45	800	10	490
44	800	9	470
43	800	8	460
42	790	7	440
41	780	6	430
40	770	5	410
39	760	4	400
38	750	3	380
37	740	2	370
36	730	1	360
35	720	0	340
34	710	−1	330
33	700	−2	310
32	690	−3	300
31	690	−4	280
30	680	−5	270
29	670	−6	250
28	660	−7	240
27	650	−8	220
26	640	−9	210
25	630	−10	200
24	630	−11	200
23	620	−12	200
22	610		
21	600		
20	590		
19	590		
18	580		
17	570		
16	560		

Reviewing Your Test Performance

After you have scored your test, you should take some time to consider the following points in relation to your performance on the test.

- *Did you run out of time before you reached the end of the test?*

  If you did, you may want to consider pacing yourself better. For example, you may have spent too much time working on one or two difficult questions. A better approach might have been to continue the test and return to those questions after you had attempted to answer the remaining questions on the test.

- *Did you take a long time reading the directions for the test?*

  The directions in this test are the same as those in the Mathematics Level IIC Subject Tests now being administered. You will save time when you take the test if you become thoroughly familiar with them in advance.

- *How did you handle questions you were unsure of?*

  If you were able to eliminate one or more of the answer choices and you guessed from the remaining choices, then your approach probably worked to your advantage. On the other hand, omitting questions about which you have some knowledge or guessing answers haphazardly would probably be a mistake.

- *How difficult were the questions for you compared with other students who took the test?*

  By referring to Table A, you can find out how difficult each question was for the group of students who took this test. The right-hand column in the table tells you what percentage of this group answered the question correctly. A question that was answered correctly by almost everyone in the group is obviously an easy question. Question 3, for example, was answered correctly by 93 percent of the students in the sample. On the other hand, question 31 was answered correctly by only 40 percent.

  It is important to remember that these percentages are based on only one particular group of students; had this edition of the test been given to other groups of students at the time, the percentages would probably have been different.

  If you find that you missed several questions that would be considered easy, you may want to review those questions carefully. They may cover some aspect of the subject that you need to review. Perhaps you misunderstood the directions for one part of the test or you thought the questions were so easy that you did not spend as much time on them as you might have.

The SAT II: Biology Subject Test

The SAT II: Biology Subject Test consists of 95 multiple-choice questions. The test content is based on the assumption that you have had a one-year course in general biology at a level suitable for college preparation. The test covers the topics listed in the chart to the right. Different aspects of each topic are stressed from year to year. However, because high school courses differ, both in the percentage of time devoted to each major topic and in the specific subtopics covered, it is likely that most students will encounter some questions on topics unfamiliar to them.

Because such courses typically rely on good reasoning and mathematical skills, students who take the Biology Subject Test should also have had a course in algebra that enables them to understand simple algebraic concepts, including ratios and direct and indirect proportions, and to apply such concepts to solving word problems.

The test is designed to be independent of the particular instructional approach of the course you have taken, as long as you are able to recall and understand the major concepts of biology and to apply the principles you have learned to solve specific problems in biology. You should also be able to organize and interpret results obtained by observation and experimentation and to draw conclusions or make inferences from experimental data, including data presented in graphic and/or tabular form. Laboratory experience is a significant factor in developing reasoning and problem-solving skills. Although testing of laboratory skills in a multiple-choice test is necessarily limited, reasonable experience in the laboratory is an asset in helping you prepare for the test.

You will not be allowed to use electronic calculators during the test. Numerical calculations are limited to simple arithmetic. In this test, the metric system of units is used.

Topics Covered	**Approximate Percentage of Test**
Cellular and Molecular Biology Cell structure and organization, mitosis, photosynthesis, cellular respiration, enzymes, molecular genetics, biosynthesis, biological chemistry	30
Ecology Energy flow, nutrient cycles, populations, communities, ecosystems, biomes	15
Classical Genetics Meiosis, Mendelian genetics, inheritance patterns	10
Organismal Biology Structure, function, and development of organisms (with emphasis on plants and animals), animal behavior	30
Evolution and Diversity Origin of life, evidence of evolution, natural selection, speciation, patterns of evolution, classification and diversity of prokaryotes, protists, fungi, plants and animals	15

Skills Specifications	
Knowledge of Fundamental Concepts: remembering specific facts; demonstrating straightforward knowledge of information and familiarity with terminology	35
Application: understanding concepts and reformulating information into other equivalent forms; applying knowledge to unfamiliar and/or practical situations; solving problems using mathematical relationships	35
Interpretation: inferring and deducing from qualitative and quantitative data and integrating information to form conclusions; recognizing unstated assumptions	30

Questions Used in the Test

Classification Questions

Each set of classification questions has five lettered choices in the heading that are used in answering all of the questions in the set. The choices may be statements that refer to concepts, principles, organisms, substances, or observable phenomena; or they may be graphs, pictures, equations, formulas, or experimental settings or situations. The questions themselves may be presented in one of these formats or in the question format directly. To answer each question, first consider all the choices. The directions for this type of question specifically state that you should not eliminate a choice simply because it is the correct answer to a previous question.

Because the same five choices are applicable to several questions, classification questions usually require less reading than other types of multiple-choice questions. Therefore, this type of question is a quick means, in terms of testing time, of determining how well you have mastered the topics represented in the choices. The degree of mastery required to answer a question correctly depends largely on the sophistication of the set of questions. One set may test recall; another may ask you to apply your knowledge to a specific situation or to translate information from one form to another (descriptive, graphical, mathematical). Thus several types of skills can be tested by this type of question.

Following are directions for and an example of a classification set.

Directions: Each set of lettered choices below refers to the numbered statements immediately following it. Select the one lettered choice that best fits each statement and then fill in the corresponding oval on the answer sheet. A choice may be used once, more than once, or not at all in each set.

Questions 1-3

(A) Decomposers (e.g., bacteria)
(B) Producers (e.g., grasses)
(C) Primary consumers (e.g., mice)
(D) Secondary consumers (e.g., snakes)
(E) Tertiary consumers (e.g., hawks)

1. **Organisms that comprise the greatest mass of living substance (biomass) in a terrestrial food chain**
2. **Organisms that convert nitrogen-containing organic molecules into nitrates**
3. **Organisms that would be the first to experience adverse effects if significant amounts of carbon dioxide were withdrawn from the biosphere**

The questions in this group deal with ecology and, in particular, with the identification of the proper trophic level for the organisms described in each question. To answer question 1 correctly, you need to know that terrestrial-based food chains begin with the capture of the sun's energy by autotrophic organisms, typically the green plants that carry on photosynthesis. These are the producers that provide the energy (in the form of chemical energy) for subsequent links in a food chain. Only a small fraction of the energy at any trophic level in a food chain can be passed on effectively to the next level, resulting in a steady draining of energy from the ecosystem. The producers, of which grasses are an example, are the first trophic level and, as a group of organisms, they have the greatest amount of energy. Hence, producers account for the greatest biomass of all organisms in a terrestrial food chain. Therefore the answer to question 1 is (B).

For question 2, you need to know that matter is recycled in an ecosystem. Organic molecules from dead organisms are broken down into inorganic compounds by microorganisms specifically adapted for such decomposition, that is, the decomposers. The inorganic compounds, of which the nitrates are an example, are thereby made available to producers such as the green plants for synthesis of fresh organic matter. Thus, (A) is the answer to question 2.

For question 3, you need to know that carbon dioxide is a raw material for photosynthesis. If its supply were severely limited, the first organisms to be affected would be those at the beginning of the food chain, that is, the producers that carry on photosynthesis. Thus, (B) is the answer to question 3.

Five-Choice Completion Questions

The five-choice completion question is written either as an incomplete statement or as a question. In its simplest application, this type of question poses a problem that intrinsically has a unique solution. It is also appropriate when: (1) the problem presented is clearly delineated by the wording of the question so that you are asked to choose not a universal solution but the best of the solutions offered; (2) the problem requires you to evaluate the relevance of five plausible, or even scientifically accurate, options and to select the one most pertinent; (3) the problem has several pertinent solutions and you are required to select the one *inappropriate* solution. In the latter case, the correct answer to the question is the choice that is *least* applicable to the situation described by the question. Such questions will normally contain a word in capital letters such as NOT, EXCEPT, or LEAST. (Question 5 is an example of this type of question.)

A special type of five-choice completion question allows for the possibility of multiple correct answers. Unlike many quantitative problems that have a unique solution, some questions have more than one correct response. For these questions, you must evaluate each response independently of the others in order to select the most appropriate combination. In questions of this type, several (usually three to five) statements labeled by Roman numerals are given with the question. One or more of these statements may answer the question correctly. The statements are followed by five lettered choices, each consisting of some combination of the Roman numerals that label the statements. You must select from among the five lettered choices the one combination of statements that best answers the question. In the test, questions of this type are intermixed among the more standard five-choice completion questions. (Question 6 is an example of this type of question.)

The five-choice completion questions can also be organized in sets, each of which pertains to a diagram (with labeled parts) common to all the questions in the set. Each question in a diagram-referenced set has its own group of five lettered choices that may refer either directly to some of the labeled parts in the diagram or to a function associated with those structures. This type of question is particularly useful for testing your knowledge of the morphology of plants and animals and your understanding of the relationships of structure to function. Questions of a diagram-based set are generally not as complex as questions in the sets on laboratory experimental situations. (Questions 7-9 are examples of the diagram-based type of question.)

The five-choice completion question is also used with other introductory material (such as a summary of an experiment, an outline of a problem, a graph, a chart) to assess your ability to use learned concepts and to apply them to unfamiliar laboratory or experimental situations. (Question 4 is an example of this type of question.) When the experimental data or other scientific problems to be analyzed are comparatively long, several five-choice completion questions may be organized into sets in which the material that precedes each set is common to all questions in the set. This type of question allows you to respond to several questions based on scientific information that may take considerable testing time to read and comprehend. However, you don't have to know the answer to one question in order to answer correctly a subsequent question in the same set. Each question is independent of the others and refers directly to the common material given for the entire set.

Sets of questions describing laboratory or experimental situations test your understanding of a problem in greater depth than is generally possible with some other formats. In particular, sets test your ability to: (1) identify a problem, (2) evaluate experimental situations, (3) suggest hypotheses, (4) interpret data, (5) make inferences and draw conclusions, (6) check the logical consistency of hypotheses based on relevant observations, and (7) select appropriate procedures for further investigation of the problem described. In the SAT II: Biology Subject Test, questions pertaining to laboratory or experimental situations are grouped together in the latter part of the test. (Questions 11-13 are examples of this type of question.)

Directions: Each of the questions or incomplete statements below is followed by five suggested answers or completions. Select the one that is best in each case and then fill in the corresponding oval on the answer sheet.

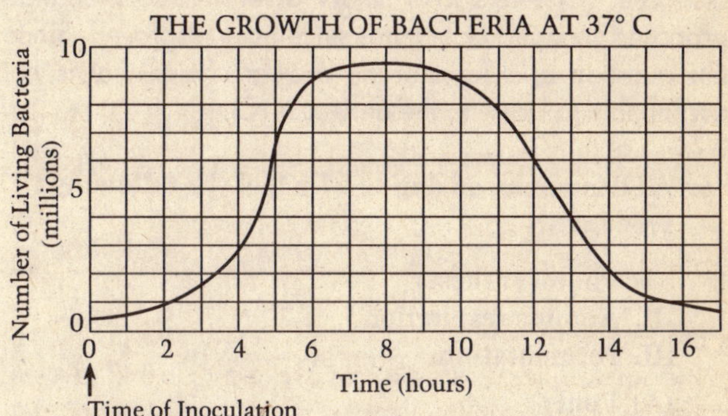

4. In the graph above, the time when the number of living bacteria is increasing at the greatest rate occurs

(A) during the first 2 hours
(B) between the 2nd and the 4th hour
(C) between the 4th and the 6th hour
(D) between the 6th and the 10th hour
(E) between the 11th and the 13th hour

This is a straightforward question that tests your ability to interpret experimental data given in graphical form. The number of bacteria is increasing at the greatest rate for the part of the curve that has the steepest positive slope. This occurs between the 4th and 6th hour after the inoculation of bacteria to the medium. Thus the answer is (C).

5. Darwin's theory of evolution by natural selection incorporated all of the following EXCEPT

(A) hereditary variation
(B) high reproductive potential
(C) inheritance of acquired characteristics
(D) struggle for existence
(E) differential survival

For this question, you must know the premises upon which Darwin based his explanation of evolutionary change in terms of natural selection. Darwin observed that variation exists among individuals in a species. He also recognized hereditary variation was a major factor in evolutionary change. Thus (A) is true. Darwin also observed that all organisms have high reproductive capacity under optimal conditions; that is, organisms have a high capacity for population growth. Thus (B) is also true. Darwin further pointed out that the food supply for any population is necessarily limited and that this results in continual competition among organisms of the same kind; that is, a struggle for existence occurs. Therefore, (D) is also true. Finally,

Darwin pointed out that organisms possessing favorable variations for a given environment will be able to survive better than those with less favorable variations; that is, there is a difference among organisms of a species in their ability to leave more offspring in the next generation. Thus (E) is also true. (C) refers to a theory of evolutionary change proposed by Lamarck that has since been disproved. Since this question asks for the one answer choice that is *not* attributable to Darwin, the answer is (C).

6. **ATP is produced during which of the following processes?**

   I. **Photosynthesis**
   II. **Aerobic respiration**
   III. **Fermentation**

   (A) **I only**
   (B) **II only**
   (C) **I and III only**
   (D) **II and III only**
   (E) **I, II, and III**

This is a question on cellular and molecular biology that asks you to consider whether ATP is produced by more than one metabolic pathway. Each of the processes designated by a Roman numeral must be evaluated independently. In photosynthesis, solar energy captured by chlorophyll-containing plants creates a flow of electrons that results in the synthesis of ATP. Thus I is correct. Aerobic respiration, the process by which glucose is broken down to CO_2 and H_2O in the presence of O_2, is the most efficient mechanism by which cells produce the ATP they need to carry on their other metabolic activities. Thus II is also correct. Fermentation also involves the breakdown of glucose but without O_2. Under these conditions, substances such as lactic acid or ethyl alcohol and CO_2 are produced, together with limited quantities of ATP. Although the carbon-containing end products of fermentation still have much of the energy contained in the original glucose, fermentation permits a cell to produce some ATP under anaerobic conditions. Thus III is also correct and the answer to the question is (E).

Questions 7-9

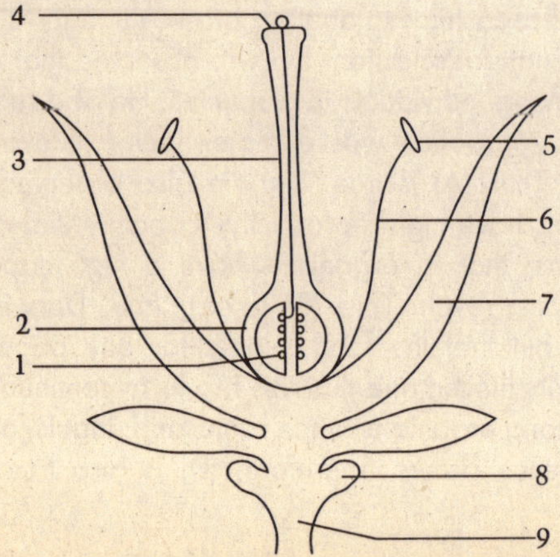

7. **Commonly, the fruit is derived from**

   (A) 2
   (B) 4
   (C) 7
   (D) 8
   (E) 9

8. **Pollination involves a transfer of pollen from**

   (A) 4 to 1
   (B) 4 to 2
   (C) 4 to 5
   (D) 5 to 4
   (E) 5 to 9

9. **The structures most directly involved in the formation of haploid cells through meiosis are**

   (A) 1 and 5
   (B) 1 and 7
   (C) 3 and 4
   (D) 1, 7, and 8
   (E) 4, 7, and 9

These questions refer to the diagram of a flowering plant. To answer these questions correctly, you need to identify the structures labeled in the diagram and associate each of them with their correct functions.

To answer question 7 correctly, you need to know that the fruit is derived from the ovary of the plant and that the ovary is the structure labeled 2 in the diagram. The answer is (A).

Question 8 deals with the process of pollination in angiosperms, which involves the transfer of pollen from the anther, the tip of the stamen, to the stigma, the tip of the pistil. In the diagram, the anther is labeled 5 and the stigma is labeled 4, so the answer is (D).

Question 9 asks you to identify the structures of a flowering plant in which meiosis occurs, producing the haploid cells necessary for reproduction. The egg cells are produced in the ovules (structure 1) located inside the ovary and the pollen grains are formed in the anther (structure 5). Thus the answer is (A).

10. **What would be the sequence of bases on the messenger RNA formed from a DNA base sequence of AAG-ATG?**

   (A) AAG-ATG
   (B) UUC-UAC
   (C) UUG-UAC
   (D) TTC-TAG
   (E) TUC-UAC

This question requires knowledge of the basic structure of nucleic acids and of the process by which information is transcribed from DNA to RNA. A molecule of DNA consists of a double strand of units called nucleotides, each of which is composed of a five-carbon sugar bonded to a phosphate group and a nitrogenous base. In DNA, the nitrogenous bases are adenine = A, guanine = G, cytosine = C, and thymine = T. The sequence of bases is such that an A on one strand is always paired with a T on the complementary strand, whereas a G is always paired with a C. When the two strands in DNA uncouple, RNA can be synthesized along one strand. RNA, however, contains uracil = U instead of thymine so that for every adenine in the DNA strand, a uracil nucleotide would be added to the growing RNA strand. Thus the DNA strand given in the question, AAG-ATG, would give rise to the base sequences of UUC-UAC in the RNA formed. The answer is (B).

Directions: Each group of questions below concerns a laboratory or experimental situation. In each case, first study the description of the situation. Then choose the one best answer to each question following it and fill in the corresponding oval on the answer sheet.

Questions 11-13

In a breeding experiment using gray and white mice of unknown genotypes, the following results were obtained.

	Parents			Offspring	
Cross	Female		Male	Gray	White
I	Gray	×	White	82	78
II	Gray	×	Gray	118	39
III	White	×	White	0	50
IV	Gray	×	White	74	0

11. Heterozygous gray female parents occur in

(A) cross I only
(B) cross II only
(C) cross IV only
(D) crosses I and II only
(E) crosses II and IV only

12. If two gray progeny of cross IV mate with each other, what is the probability that any of their offspring will be gray?

(A) 100%
(B) 75%
(C) 50%
(D) 25%
(E) 0%

13. If the gray female from cross IV were mated with the gray male from cross II, then which of the following would most likely be true?

(A) All of the offspring would be gray.
(B) All of the offspring would be white.
(C) Half of the offspring would be gray.
(D) One-quarter of the offspring would be gray.
(E) One-quarter of the offspring would be white.

Questions 11-13 are on heredity. They refer to the experiment described in the introductory material. You are asked to draw conclusions from the results of the experiment and to predict the results of further experimentation on the basis of the information obtained.

Question 11 asks you to determine which gray female parents were heterozygous. First you must realize from the ratio of offspring obtained in all the crosses that gray coat color is dominant over white in these mice. Next, you should note that no white offspring were obtained in cross IV. Thus the gray female in this cross was homozygous gray. In cross I, approximately 50 percent of the offspring were gray. Therefore, the gray female, mated with a white male, must have been heterozygous. In cross II, a gray female was mated with a gray male, and a 3:1 ratio of gray to white offspring was obtained. Therefore both gray female and gray male parents were heterozygous. Thus heterozygous females occurred only in crosses I and II. (D) is the answer.

Question 12 assumes that two gray progeny of cross IV were mated with each other. Since this progeny resulted from a cross between a gray female and a white male and no white offspring were produced, you can conclude that the female parent was homozygous gray and that all the offspring are heterozygous gray. Therefore, the mating of the gray progeny of cross IV will produce offspring in the ratio of 3 gray to 1 white. The probability, therefore, of an offspring of this cross being gray is 75 percent. The answer is (B).

Question 13 asks you to predict the results of a cross between the gray female from cross IV and the gray male from cross II. From the data given, you can determine that the gray female in cross IV is homozygous, and the male in cross II is heterozygous. Thus you could expect that all of the offspring from such a mating would be gray. The answer is (A).

SAT II:

Biology Subject Test

The test that follows is representative of a typical SAT II: Biology Subject Test. So that you may have an idea of what the national test administration will be like, try to take the test in this book under conditions as close as possible to those of the nationally administered test. It will probably help if you do the following.

- Set aside an hour for the test when you will not be interrupted, so that you can complete all of it in one sitting.
- Sit at a desk with no other papers or books. You can't take a calculator, dictionary, other books, or notes into the test room.
- Have a kitchen timer or clock in front of you for timing yourself.
- Tear out an answer sheet from the back of this book and fill it in just as you would on the day of the test. You can use one answer sheet for as many as three Subject Tests.
- Read the instructions that precede the test. When you take the test, you will be asked to read them before you begin answering questions.
- After you finish the test, read the sections on "How to Score the SAT II: Biology Subject Test" and "Reviewing Your Test Performance," which follow the test.

FORM K-3JAC2

BIOLOGY TEST

The top portion of the section of the answer sheet that you will use in taking the Biology test must be filled in exactly as shown in the illustration below. Note carefully that you have to do all of the following on your answer sheet.

1. Print BIOLOGY on the line under the words "Subject (print)."

2. In the shaded box labeled "Test Code" fill in four ovals:

   —Fill in oval 2 in the row labeled V.

   —Fill in oval 1 in the row labeled W.

   —Fill in oval 1 in the row labeled X.

   —Fill in oval A in the row labeled Y.

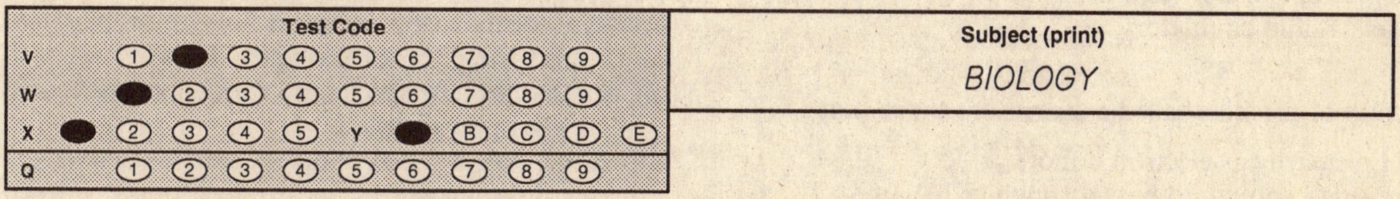

Test Code											Subject (print)
V		1	●	3	4	5	6	7	8	9	*BIOLOGY*
W		●	2	3	4	5	6	7	8	9	
X	●	2	3	4	5	Y	●	B	C	D	E
Q		1	2	3	4	5	6	7	8	9	

3. Please answer the questions below by filling in the appropriate ovals in the row labeled Q on the answer sheet. The information you provide is for statistical purposes only and will not affect your score on the test.

Question I

How many semesters of biology have you taken in high school? (If you are taking biology this semester, count it as a full semester.) Fill in only one oval of ovals 1-3.

- One semester or less —Fill in oval 1.
- Two semesters —Fill in oval 2.
- Three semesters or more —Fill in oval 3.

Question II

How recently have you studied biology?

- I am currently enrolled in or have just completed a biology course. —Fill in oval 4.
- I have not studied biology for 6 months or more. —Fill in oval 5.

Question III

Which of the following best describes your background in algebra? (If you are taking an algebra course this semester, count it as a full semester.) Fill in only one oval of ovals 6-7.

- One semester or less —Fill in oval 6.
- Two semesters or more —Fill in oval 7.

Question IV

Are you currently taking Advanced Placement Biology? If you are, fill in oval 8.

Leave oval 9 blank.

When the supervisor gives the signal, turn the page and begin the Biology test. There are 100 numbered ovals on the answer sheet and 95 questions in the Biology test. Therefore, use only ovals 1 to 95 for recording your answers.

BIOLOGY TEST

Part A

Directions: Each of the questions or incomplete statements below is followed by five suggested answers or completions. Select the one that is best in each case and then fill in the corresponding oval on the answer sheet.

1. Behavioral responses of animals are most directly regulated by which of the following systems?

   (A) Digestive and excretory
   (B) Endocrine and nervous
   (C) Muscular and integumentary
   (D) Reproductive and respiratory
   (E) Skeletal and circulatory

2. The group of proteins called enzymes are those that

   (A) act primarily as electron donors
   (B) are small enough to pass through cell membranes
   (C) act primarily as structural units
   (D) are specific in their reactions with substrates
   (E) are most active at 4° C

3. Which molecule is most abundant in living organisms?

   (A) Carbon dioxide
   (B) Water
   (C) Hemoglobin
   (D) Cholesterol
   (E) Glucose

4. Typically, asexual reproduction results in

   (A) offspring with a $1n$ (haploid) chromosome number
   (B) offspring genetically different from the parent
   (C) offspring genetically identical to the parent
   (D) polyploid species
   (E) complete or incomplete metamorphosis

5. Which of the following statements regarding evolution is FALSE ?

   (A) Chemical changes in gene makeup, called mutations, sometimes produce new phenotypes.
   (B) The environment tends to favor or select some traits over others.
   (C) New combinations of genes are continually producing new phenotypes.
   (D) Sometimes new species are formed as a result of geographic isolation.
   (E) Individuals but not populations change over evolutionary time.

6. Arthropods that have wings include which of the following?

   I. Arachnid
   II. Insect
   III. Crustacean

   (A) I only
   (B) II only
   (C) I and III only
   (D) II and III only
   (E) I, II, and III

7. For the following vertebrates, which is the correct sequence of evolution?

   (A) Bony fish, reptiles, birds, amphibians
   (B) Amphibians, birds, bony fish, reptiles
   (C) Bony fish, birds, amphibians, reptiles
   (D) Reptiles, birds, bony fish, amphibians
   (E) Bony fish, amphibians, reptiles, birds

GO ON TO THE NEXT PAGE

8. Ovulation is the process by which

    (A) sperm cells are ejaculated
    (B) an ovule in a flower is penetrated by a pollen tube
    (C) an egg is implanted in the wall of the uterus
    (D) an egg discards its surrounding membranes
    (E) an egg is released from the ovary

9. Glucose is normally stored in animal cells in the form of

    (A) glycogen
    (B) cellulose
    (C) cholesterol
    (D) monosaccharides
    (E) disaccharides

10. Adenosine triphosphate (ATP) functions directly in all of the following EXCEPT

    (A) RNA synthesis
    (B) glycolysis
    (C) protein synthesis
    (D) the contractile process
    (E) osmosis

11. Which of the following is more primitive than a pine tree but more advanced than a moss?

    (A) A fungus (B) A fern (C) A rose
    (D) A green alga (E) A cactus

12. In the development of the frog, which of the following is the correct sequence following fertilization?

    (A) Cleavage, gastrula, larva, blastula
    (B) Cleavage, blastula, gastrula, larva
    (C) Cleavage, blastula, larva, gastrula
    (D) Blastula, cleavage, gastrula, larva
    (E) Blastula, larva, gastrula, cleavage

13. The blue whale is the largest animal in the ocean. It feeds on very small, herbivorous crustaceans called krill. From this information, which of the following is the best conclusion that can be made concerning the position of the blue whale in this food chain?

    (A) It is the top consumer because it is the largest species present.
    (B) It is the bottom consumer because it requires so much bulk in its diet.
    (C) It is a secondary consumer because the krill that it devours is a primary consumer.
    (D) It is an omnivore because it must support itself.
    (E) It is a herbivore because there are not enough krill to support the huge populations of whales.

14. Which of the following organisms often function as decomposers in most forest ecosystems?

    (A) Cyanobacteria (blue-green algae)
    (B) Green plants
    (C) Vertebrates
    (D) Fungi
    (E) Protozoa

GO ON TO THE NEXT PAGE

15. Brown Male (I) × Black Female (I) → Offspring {9 Black, 8 Brown}

Same Brown Male (I) × Black Female (II) → Offspring {15 Black, 0 Brown}

One brown male guinea pig was crossed with two black females as illustrated in the diagram above. Which of the following statements is most likely to be true?

(A) All three parents were heterozygous.
(B) All three parents were homozygous.
(C) Female (I) is heterozygous.
(D) All progeny of female II are homozygous.
(E) All black guinea pigs are heterozygous.

16. A major difference in the structures of proteins, fats, and carbohydrates is that only proteins always contain

(A) carbon (B) hydrogen (C) oxygen
(D) sodium (E) nitrogen

17. Salts can enter living cells by which of the following?

I. Osmosis
II. Diffusion
III. Active transport

(A) I only
(B) II only
(C) I and II only
(D) II and III only
(E) I, II, and III

18. The principal function of thyroxine produced by the thyroid gland is to

(A) stimulate the maturation of gametes
(B) stimulate insulin production
(C) stimulate general metabolism
(D) promote sexual differentiation
(E) inhibit growth

GO ON TO THE NEXT PAGE

19. Cheetahs have been called the fastest animals on earth. They can achieve a burst of speed up to 110 km/hr. According to Darwin's theory of evolution, what is the best explanation for how such a capability might have evolved?

    (A) Fast-running cheetahs were more likely to survive and reproduce than those that ran more slowly.
    (B) Fast-running cheetahs were more likely to maintain constant body temperature than those that ran more slowly.
    (C) The more cheetahs ran, the stronger and faster they became.
    (D) Cheetahs show a preference for prey that run fast.
    (E) Individual cheetahs learned to associate fast running with survival

20. Representatives of a family of organisms are <u>less</u> alike than are the members of a

    (A) genus (B) order (C) class
    (D) phylum (E) kingdom

21. The gene for height in a plant is represented by *T* for tall and its recessive allele is represented by *t* for dwarf. A mating between parents of genotypes *TT* and *tt* would produce offspring with which of the following phenotypes?

    (A) 100% tall
    (B) 75% tall, 25% dwarf
    (C) 50% tall, 50% dwarf
    (D) 25% tall, 75% dwarf
    (E) 100% dwarf

22. All of the following are adaptations that directly enable terrestrial plants to maintain water balance EXCEPT

    (A) waxy cuticle (B) xylem (C) stomata
    (D) root hairs (E) chloroplasts

23. Which of the following statements does NOT represent a water-conservation advantage of a burrow-dwelling animal that inhabits the desert?

    (A) Burrowing animals dig their burrows rapidly when in danger.
    (B) Animals in burrows are less active than they would be outside the burrows.
    (C) Food carried into burrows is a source of moisture.
    (D) Due to body evaporation, humidity is higher inside the burrow than it is outside.
    (E) Temperatures in burrows are more constant than are temperatures on desert surfaces.

24. During which of the following processes is the largest amount of chemical energy in glucose converted to the energy of chemical bonds in ATP ?

    (A) Aerobic respiration
    (B) Hydrolysis
    (C) Photosynthesis
    (D) Fermentation
    (E) The emulsification of fats

25. Which of the following is thought to be responsible for the appearance of large amounts of oxygen gas in the Earth's atmosphere?

    (A) Protein synthesis
    (B) Nitrification
    (C) Photosynthesis
    (D) Chemosynthesis
    (E) Fermentation

26. When there are no limiting factors to restrain population growth, the population numbers are expected to

    (A) increase exponentially
    (B) increase at a constant rate
    (C) stabilize as the births equal the deaths
    (D) change unpredictably
    (E) decrease as a result of mutations

GO ON TO THE NEXT PAGE

27. The plant tissue that is meristematic and consequently produces new tissues during each growing season is the

(A) xylem (B) phloem (C) cambium
(D) cortex (E) epidermis

28. Liverworts and mosses are classified as belonging to which of the following phyla?

(A) Tracheophyta
(B) Mycophyta
(C) Rhodophyta
(D) Chlorophyta
(E) Bryophyta

29. In *Drosophila*, normal wing is dominant to wingless. In an experiment, a normal-winged male whose father was wingless was crossed with a wingless female. What percentage of the offspring would be expected to have normal wings?

(A) 0%
(B) 25%
(C) 50%
(D) 75%
(E) 100%

30. In humans, an egg develops into a male offspring if it

(A) contains a Y chromosome and is fertilized by a sperm containing an X chromosome
(B) contains a Y chromosome and is fertilized by a sperm containing a Y chromosome
(C) contains an X chromosome and is fertilized by a sperm containing an X chromosome
(D) contains an X chromosome and is fertilized by a sperm containing a Y chromosome
(E) develops parthenogenetically

31. In which of the following organisms is radial symmetry best illustrated?

(A) Planarian
(B) Jellyfish
(C) Roundworm
(D) Spider
(E) Millipede

32. Mutualism is represented by all of the following examples EXCEPT

(A) tapeworms in dogs
(B) *E. coli* in humans
(C) cellulose-fermenting bacteria in cows
(D) root-nodule bacteria of beans
(E) protozoa in termites

33. Mitosis and meiosis are similar in that both

(A) are preceded by the replication of DNA during interphase
(B) require two successive cell divisions
(C) involve the reduction of chromosome number
(D) yield the same number of cells
(E) occur in somatic cells

34. Which of the following structures secrete substances responsible for the development of secondary sex characteristics in a mammalian male?

(A) Penis
(B) Sperm ducts
(C) Prostate gland
(D) Testes
(E) Ureters

35. Stomata in plant leaves aid photosynthesis by enhancing the entrance of

(A) H_2O
(B) O_2
(C) light
(D) minerals in solution
(E) CO_2

36. Actin and myosin are important proteins associated with the

(A) synthesis of glycogen
(B) polymerization of DNA
(C) formation of lysosomes
(D) production of hemoglobin
(E) contraction of muscles

GO ON TO THE NEXT PAGE

37. All of the following provide evidence for a common origin of life EXCEPT
    (A) species-specific traits and adaptations
    (B) genetic code for protein synthesis
    (C) ATP as cellular energy
    (D) the twenty amino acids that are used to make proteins
    (E) the cell, which is the basic unit of structure and function

38. Which of the following men predicted that the increase in the human population would become a major problem?
    (A) Robert Koch
    (B) Thomas Malthus
    (C) Louis Pasteur
    (D) Walter Reed
    (E) Edward Jenner

39. A meadow was studied for 25 years. In the first year, the land was grassy, and the grasshopper sparrow was the dominant bird. Twenty-five years later, the land was covered with shrubs. The grasshopper sparrow was no longer present, but cardinals and warblers were observed. These observations illustrate the process of
    (A) divergent evolution
    (B) speciation
    (C) predation
    (D) succession
    (E) migration

40. Green plants that trap and digest insects grow well in certain volcanic clay soils. This evidence suggests that these green plants are adapted to compensate for soils that are likely to be deficient in
    (A) calcium carbonate
    (B) oxygen
    (C) soluble carbon
    (D) hydrogen sulfide
    (E) nitrogen

41. Zebras and Thomson's gazelles can usually coexist in the same ecosystem because
    (A) they are different species
    (B) they do not occupy the same niche
    (C) their relationship is mutualistic
    (D) their populations are controlled by immigration
    (E) they have different courtship patterns

42. Features typical of flowering plants adapted to a desert environment include which of the following?

    I. A taproot system
    II. Leaves with thick cuticles
    III. Leaves reduced to spines

    (A) II only
    (B) III only
    (C) I and II only
    (D) II and III only
    (E) I, II, and III

43. Which of the following correctly expresses the relationship between genes and the products that genes control?
    (A) RNA→trait→gene→protein
    (B) Protein→DNA→RNA→trait
    (C) DNA→RNA→protein→trait
    (D) Trait→RNA→DNA→protein
    (E) DNA→protein→RNA→trait

44. If a DNA-coding triplet for an amino acid is TAC, which of the following would be the complementary coding triplet in messenger RNA ?

    (A) TAC (B) CAT (C) AUG
    (D) TUG (E) ATG

45. Which of the following animals first adapted successfully to life on land through the development of the membranes that prevent water loss from embryos?
    (A) Lobe-finned fishes
    (B) Trilobites
    (C) Amphibians
    (D) Reptiles
    (E) Mammals

GO ON TO THE NEXT PAGE

Questions 46-50 refer to the diagram below of a neural pathway to striated muscle.

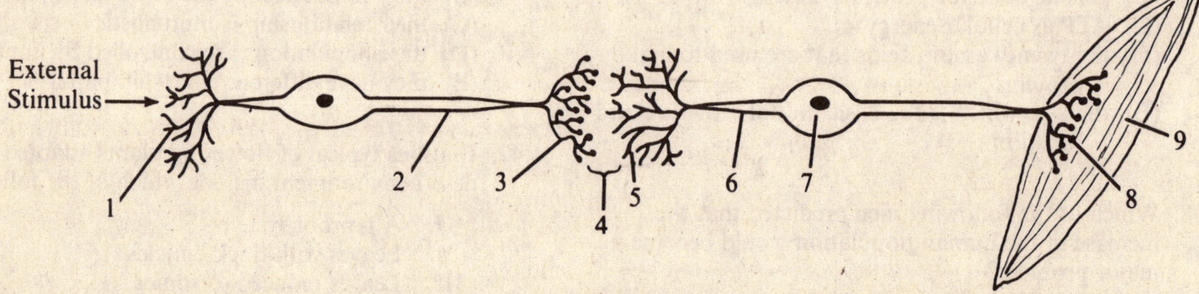

46. Structure 5 is known as
    (A) an axon
    (B) a dendrite
    (C) a nucleus
    (D) a myelin sheath
    (E) a Schwann cell

47. Of the following, which occurs at structure 3 ?
    (A) Initiation of the impulse
    (B) Flow of electricity to the next neuron
    (C) Synthesis of ions
    (D) Muscular contraction
    (E) Release of neurotransmitter

48. Of the following, which carries the impulse away from the cell body of a neuron?
    (A) 1
    (B) 2
    (C) 4
    (D) 6
    (E) 9

49. Which structure has sites on the surface of its membrane to receive a neurotransmitter?
    (A) 1
    (B) 2
    (C) 3
    (D) 5
    (E) 8

50. The synapse is indicated by
    (A) 2
    (B) 3
    (C) 4
    (D) 6
    (E) 7

GO ON TO THE NEXT PAGE

Questions 51-54 refer to the following diagram of a portion of the human female anatomy.

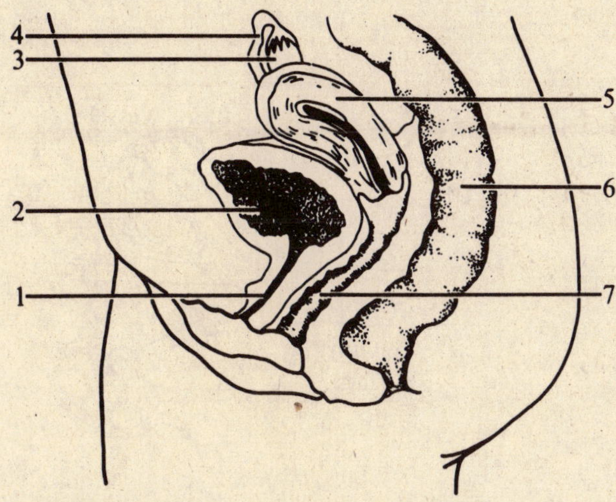

51. Fertilization normally occurs in structure

(A) 1
(B) 3
(C) 4
(D) 5
(E) 7

52. The hormone progesterone is produced in structure

(A) 2
(B) 3
(C) 4
(D) 5
(E) 7

53. During pregnancy, the placenta is located in structure

(A) 3
(B) 4
(C) 5
(D) 6
(E) 7

54. A cesarean section is a surgical procedure performed to open structure

(A) 1
(B) 2
(C) 3
(D) 5
(E) 7

GO ON TO THE NEXT PAGE

Part B

Directions: Each set of lettered choices below refers to the numbered statements immediately following it. Select the one lettered choice that best fits each statement and then fill in the corresponding oval on the answer sheet. A choice may be used once, more than once, or not at all in each set.

Questions 55-57

(A)
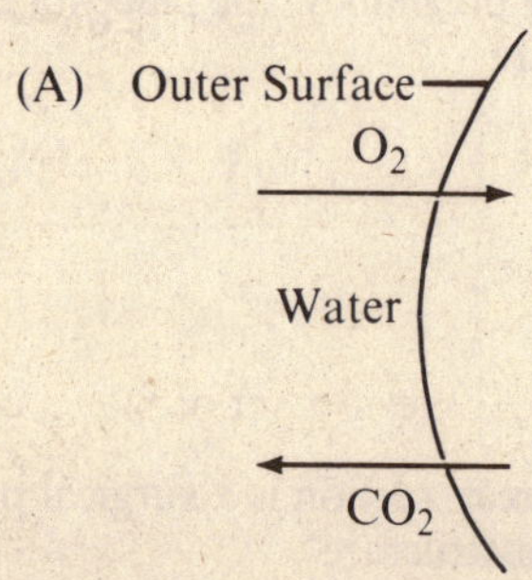

(B)
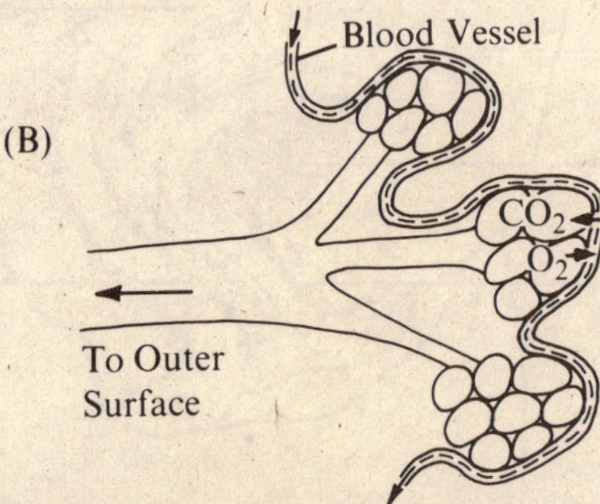

(C)
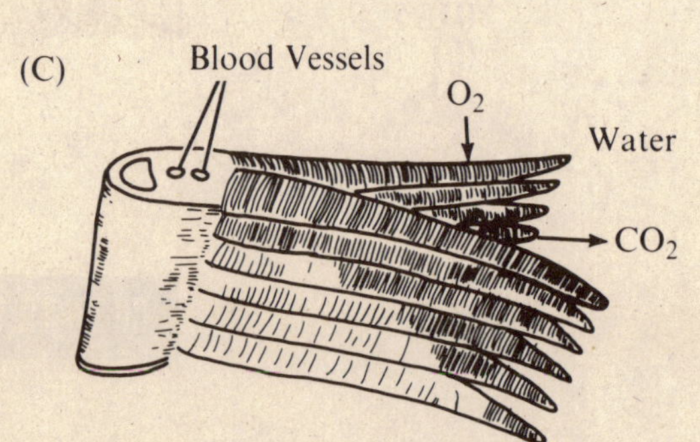

(D)
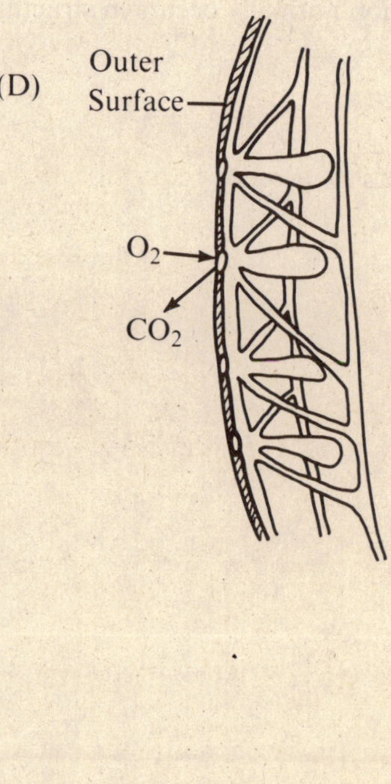

(E)
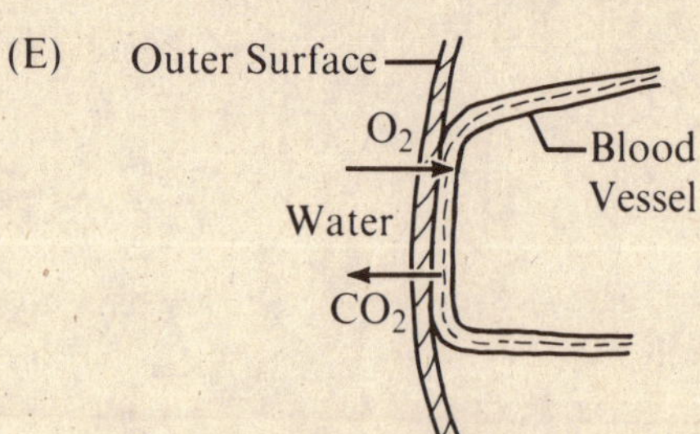

55. The gas-exchange system of humans

56. The gas-exchange system of trout

57. The gas-exchange system of protozoa

GO ON TO THE NEXT PAGE

Questions 58-60

(A) Mitochondria
(B) Lysosomes
(C) Golgi apparatus
(D) Ribosomes
(E) Chloroplasts

58. Contain enzymes of the Krebs cycle

59. Involved in intracellular digestion

60. Involved in packaging secretory products

Questions 61-64

(A) Mutation
(B) Reproductive isolation
(C) Hybridization
(D) Protective coloration
(E) Convergent evolution

61. A shore plant crossed with a mountain plant produces a plant that can live in a larger range of localities than either parent.

62. In a normal flock of sheep, a lamb with short, bowed legs is born.

63. Black moths are more numerous than light moths in industrial areas where the tree bark has been blackened by soot and the lichens on the trees have been killed by pollution.

64. A flowering plant that blooms in April cannot pollinate one that blooms in August.

Questions 65-67

(A) Starch
(B) Nucleic acid
(C) Cellulose
(D) Glycogen
(E) Lipid

65. A substance that cannot be digested by most animals

66. A substance that is incorporated into cell membranes

67. The major constituent of plant cell walls

GO ON TO THE NEXT PAGE

Questions 68-70 refer to the following graphs representing the growth of bacteria after being inoculated in nutrient media.

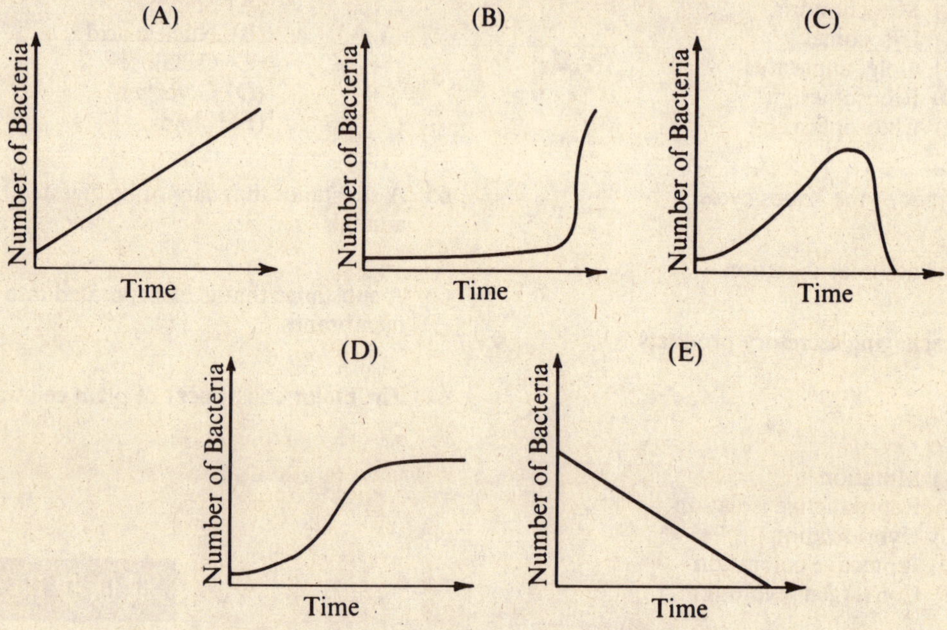

68. Represents the expected growth curve when a limited but constant food supply is provided and wastes are adequately removed

69. Represents a bacterial population allowed to become established and then exposed to lethal bacteriophage

70. Represents a bacterial population inoculated into a culture medium, refrigerated for several days, and then incubated at optimum temperature

GO ON TO THE NEXT PAGE

Questions 71-73

(A)
```
        CH3
        |         O
        |       //
H2N—C—C
        |       \
        |        OH
        H
```

(B)
```
           CH2OH
            |
     H      C——O       H
     |     /      \    |
     C          OH   H     C
     |  \   |   |  / |
    OH   C——C     OH
         |     |
         H     OH
```

(C)
```
      H   H
      |   |
  H—C—C—OH
      |   |
      H   H
```

(D)
```
H     H
  \  /
   O
```

(E)
```
     H   H   H   H    O
     |   |   |   |   //
 H—C—C—C—C—C
     |   |   |   |    \
     H   H   H   H     OH
```

71. An inorganic compound

72. An amino acid

73. A building block of a polysaccharide

GO ON TO THE NEXT PAGE

Part C

Directions: Each group of questions below concerns a laboratory or experimental situation. In each case, first study the description of the situation. Then choose the one best answer to each question following it and fill in the corresponding oval on the answer sheet.

Questions 74-77

During a study of the food chain that is found in a pond ecosystem, an analysis of a pond sample gave the following results.

Name of Organism	Number Present
Bass	Two
Frog	Forty
Phytoplankton	Thousands
Insect Larvae	Hundreds

74. Which of the following are consumer organisms found in the pond sample described above?

(A) Insect larvae only
(B) Phytoplankton only
(C) Frog and bass only
(D) Frog, insect larvae, and bass
(E) Frog, phytoplankton, and bass

75. Several different algal species were found among the phytoplankton. Which level in this food chain do these species represent?

(A) Primary consumer
(B) Secondary consumer
(C) Top carnivore
(D) Herbivore
(E) Producer

76. If frogs feed on the insect larvae, then what is the role of the frogs in this food chain?

(A) Primary consumer
(B) Secondary consumer
(C) Top carnivore
(D) Herbivore
(E) Producer

GO ON TO THE NEXT PAGE

77. Which of the following diagrams best represents the analysis of the pond's water sample as a pyramid of numbers?

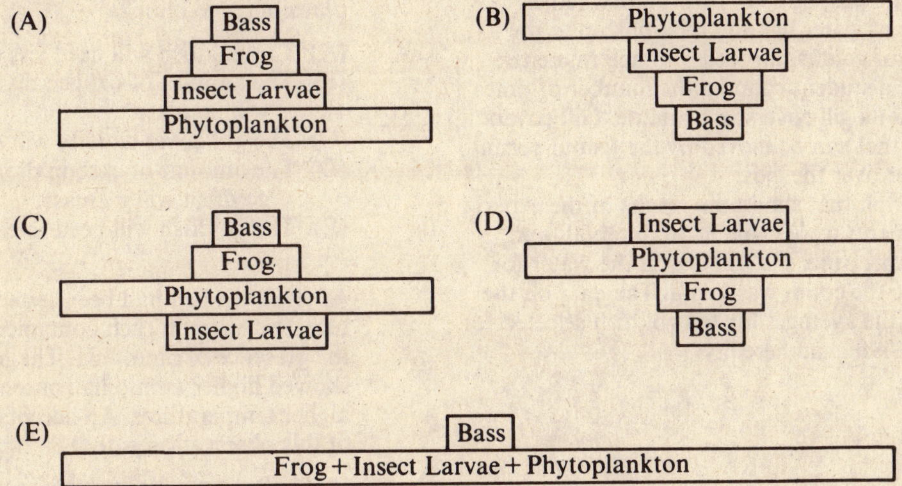

(E) Bass / Frog + Insect Larvae + Phytoplankton

Questions 78-79

A student plans to test animals for the fear of falling from high places. This can be done by the use of a device that has a plate of heavy glass covering two different levels lined with similar checkered cloth. One level is immediately under the glass; the other is 25 centimeters below the glass. The animal visually perceives a drop in elevation, but by touch feels the supportive glass flooring.

Several species are tested, including ducklings, kittens, and young rats and mice, none of which has had prior experience with a drop in elevation. The student finds that the animals are reluctant to walk out on the glass flooring above the lower level.

78. Overall, the observations suggest that the fear of falling is

(A) learned in these animals
(B) a conditioned reflex in these animals
(C) instinctive in the animals tested
(D) present only in young animals
(E) common to both warm- and cold-blooded animals

79. In each case, the sense that is most influential in determining the animal's behavior is

(A) smell
(B) proprioception
(C) touch
(D) hearing
(E) vision

GO ON TO THE NEXT PAGE

Questions 80-82

An experiment was set up to determine whether the temperature of water has any relationship to the respiration rate of goldfish. In order to determine the respiration rate, a student counted the number of times a goldfish closed its gill covers in 1 minute. Gill covers are bony plates that can be moved by the fish to permit the flow of water over the gills.

Below is a graph that shows the results of the experiment. Measurements were made at 10° intervals and, at each new temperature, the fish was in the water for 5 minutes before the count was taken. The data on the graph represent the averages for ten goldfish selected for comparable age, size, and heredity.

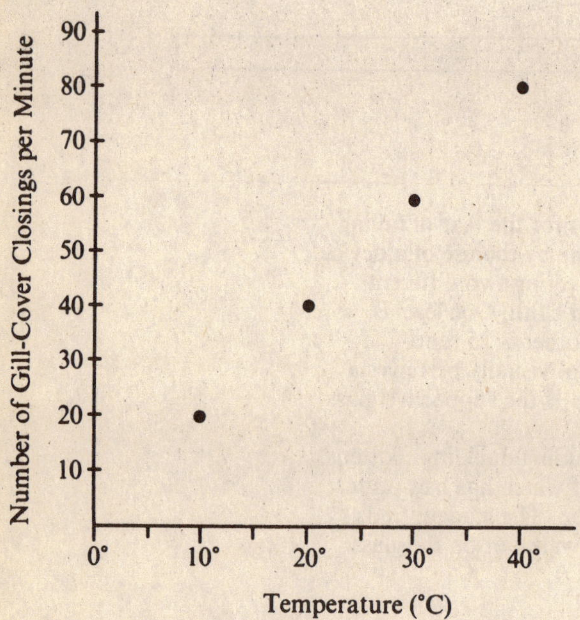

80. Within experimental error, it appears from the graph that, as the number of degrees Celsius doubles, the rate of gill-cover closings

(A) decreases by a factor of 2
(B) decreases linearly
(C) increases exponentially
(D) increases by a factor of 2
(E) shows no distinct relationship to temperature

81. As the temperature of the water increases in the experiment shown, which of the following is a plausible prediction?

(A) The goldfish will need less oxygen.
(B) The amount of oxygen dissolved in the water will increase.
(C) The gill-cover activity will decrease.
(D) The amount of carbon dioxide released by the goldfish will increase.
(E) The goldfish will need to consume less food.

82. After all ten fish had been tested at each temperature, the water in each container was checked for the presence of ammonia. The results of this showed higher ammonia concentrations at the higher temperatures. An acceptable interpretation of this observation is that

(A) ammonia is less soluble in warm water than in cold water
(B) excretory rates increase with increasing metabolism
(C) ammonia excretion is not temperature dependent
(D) excretory rates decrease with increasing temperature
(E) as the concentration of dissolved oxygen increases, the concentration of ammonia also increases

GO ON TO THE NEXT PAGE

Questions 83-85 refer to an experiment that is designed to investigate the effect of sugar concentration on the rate of fermentation in yeast. Six flasks are filled, each with a different concentration of sugar solution. The six concentrations, starting with 0 percent, are indicated on the graph below. Each flask is inoculated with the same amount of live yeast and then stoppered. The carbon dioxide, CO_2, produced in each flask is collected and measured after 24 hours. The results are shown in the graph below.

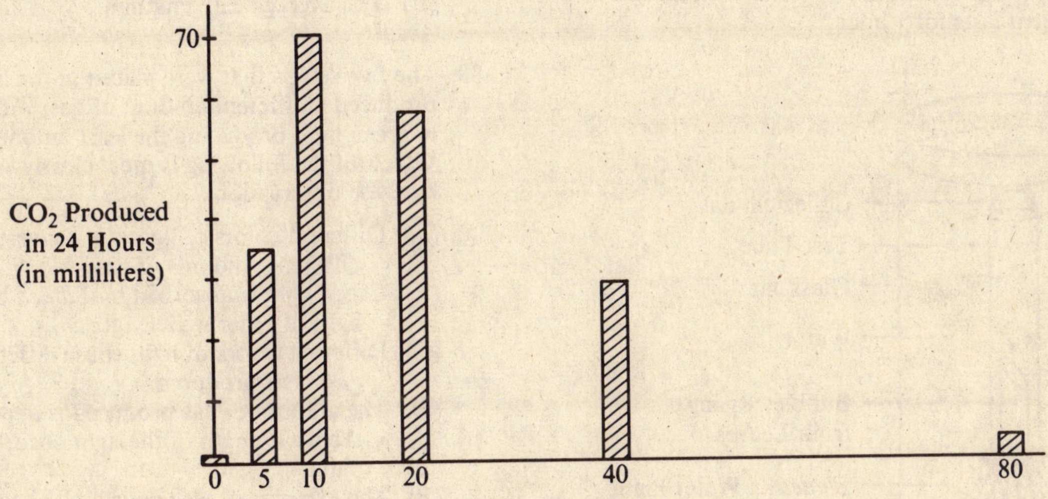

83. The optimal sugar concentration for yeast fermentation is

    (A) 5%
    (B) 10%
    (C) 20%
    (D) 40%
    (E) 80%

84. Which of the following best represents the chemical reaction that takes place in this experiment?

    (A) Glucose → 2 lactic acid
    (B) Glucose + 6 O_2 → 6 H_2O + 6 CO_2
    (C) Glucose → 2 ethyl alcohol + 2 CO_2
    (D) 6 H_2O + 6 CO_2 → glucose + 6 O_2
    (E) Glucose + 6 O_2 → 2 ethyl alcohol + 2 CO_2

85. It can be inferred from the graph that concentrations of sugar above 20 percent will

    (A) stimulate respiration
    (B) increase alcohol production
    (C) inhibit yeast activity
    (D) decrease oxygen production
    (E) increase CO_2 production

GO ON TO THE NEXT PAGE

Questions 86-88

In order to test the effects of different wavelengths of light on photosynthesis, a student makes six setups similar to the one illustrated below. One is placed in the dark. The other five are illuminated with violet, blue, green, orange, and red light, respectively. In all cases, the experiment lasts for 1 hour.

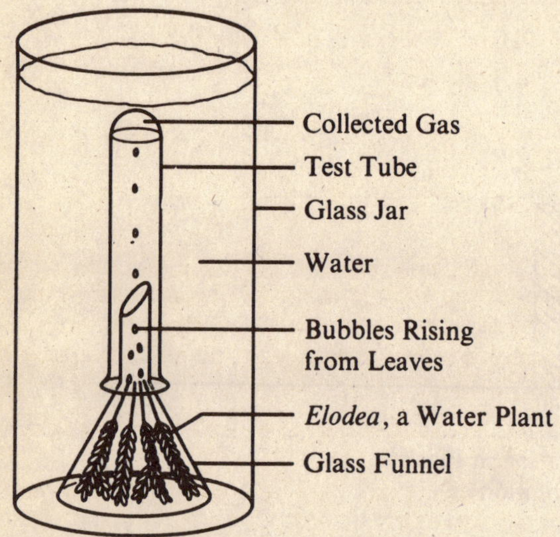

86. The purpose of placing one setup in the dark is to
    (A) test the effects of cosmic rays
    (B) study the dark reactions of photosynthesis
    (C) establish a control for the experiment
    (D) allow the *Elodea* to regenerate glucose
    (E) keep some *Elodea* available for repeating the experiment

87. For this experiment, it is most important that which of the following be the same in each setup?
    (A) The total area of leaf surface
    (B) The dry weight of each plant
    (C) The numbers of plants
    (D) The diameters of the plant stems
    (E) The average leaf lengths

88. The five setups that were placed in the light each produced a different amount of gas, with the setup in green light producing the least amount of gas. Which of the following is most clearly suggested by these observations?
    (A) Different colors of light are converted into different amounts of gas.
    (B) Green light is absorbed by *Elodea* better than light of other wavelengths.
    (C) Different colors of light cause different kinds of gas to be produced.
    (D) The amount of gas produced is dependent on the wavelength of the light absorbed by the plant.
    (E) The experiment was poorly planned.

GO ON TO THE NEXT PAGE

Questions 89-91

BASAL METABOLIC RATE IN VARIOUS SPECIES OF ADULT ANIMALS AS A FUNCTION OF BODY WEIGHT

Animal	Average Metabolic Rate (kcal/day)	Average Weight (kg)	Average Metabolic Rate (kcal/kg/day)
Mouse	3.82	0.018	212
Dog	773	15	51.5
Human	2,054	64	32.1
Pig	2,444	128	19.1
Horse	4,983	441	11.3

89. Which of the animals listed utilizes the greatest amount of food per unit of weight?
    (A) Mouse
    (B) Dog
    (C) Human
    (D) Pig
    (E) Horse

90. Which animal listed could probably survive the longest if given its own weight of usable food energy?
    (A) Mouse
    (B) Dog
    (C) Human
    (D) Pig
    (E) Horse

91. From the table above, it can be determined that the difference in the daily metabolic rate between a 100-kilogram adult human and a 100-kilogram adult pig is which of the following?
    (A) The human utilizes 13 kilocalories per day more than the pig.
    (B) The pig utilizes 13 kilocalories per day more than the human.
    (C) The human utilizes 1,300 kilocalories per day more than the pig.
    (D) The pig utilizes 1,300 kilocalories per day more than the human.
    (E) There is no significant difference in the daily metabolic rates of a human and a pig with the same mass.

GO ON TO THE NEXT PAGE

Questions 92-95

The following pedigree traces the appearance of an abnormal recessive trait in several families.

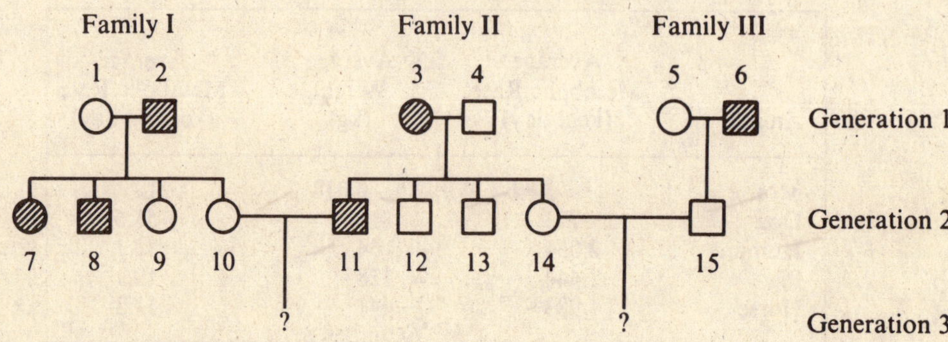

Key

- Female with normal trait
- Male with normal trait
- Female with abnormal trait
- Male with abnormal trait

92. Based on the pedigree above, which of the following statements is NOT true?

    (A) Individual 1 is heterozygous.
    (B) Individual 7 received a gene from each parent for the trait.
    (C) Individual 9 is homozygous.
    (D) A child born to individuals 10 and 11 has a 50% chance of showing the trait.
    (E) Individual 14 is a carrier of the trait.

93. The genotype of which of the following individuals is not known?

    (A) Individual 2
    (B) Individual 4
    (C) Individual 5
    (D) Individual 8
    (E) Individual 12

94. Based on the pedigree above, what is the probability that a child born to individuals 14 and 15 will have the abnormal trait?

    (A) 0 (B) $\frac{1}{4}$ (C) $\frac{1}{2}$ (D) $\frac{9}{16}$ (E) $\frac{3}{4}$

95. Of the following, which provides evidence that the abnormal trait is NOT sex-linked?

    (A) Some daughters of individuals 1 and 2 are normal for the trait.
    (B) Some sons of individuals 3 and 4 are normal for the trait.
    (C) Half the individuals in generation 1 have the trait.
    (D) Both sexes have the abnormal condition of the trait.
    (E) The trait appears in every generation.

STOP

IF YOU FINISH BEFORE TIME IS CALLED, YOU MAY CHECK YOUR WORK ON THIS TEST ONLY. DO NOT TURN TO ANY OTHER TEST IN THIS BOOK.

How to Score the SAT II: Biology Subject Test

When you take the Biology Subject Test, your answer sheet will be "read" by a scanning machine that will record your responses to each question. Then a computer will compare your answers with the correct answers and produce your raw score. You get one point for each correct answer. For each wrong answer, one-fourth of a point is subtracted to correct for random guessing. Questions you omit are not counted. Your raw score is converted to a College Board scaled score that is reported to you and to the colleges you specify. After you have taken this test, you can get an idea of what your score might be by following the instructions in the next two sections.

FINDING YOUR RAW SCORE

Step 1: Table A lists the correct answers for all the questions on the SAT II: Biology Subject Test that is reproduced in this book. It also serves as a worksheet for you to calculate your raw score.

- Compare your answers with those given in the table.
- Put a check in the column marked "Right" if your answer is correct.
- Put a check in the column marked "Wrong" if your answer is incorrect.
- Leave both columns blank if you omitted the question.

Step 2: Count the number of right answers and enter the total here: .... ________

Step 3: Count the number of wrong answers and enter the total here: ...... ________

Step 4: Divide the number of wrong answers by 4 and enter the result here: .... ________

Step 5: Subtract the result obtained in Step 4 from the total you obtained in Step 2. Enter the result here: .... ________

Step 6: Round the number obtained in Step 5 to the nearest whole number. Enter the result here: .... ________

The number you obtained in Step 6 is your raw score.

TABLE A

Answers to the SAT II: Biology Subject Test, Form K-3JAC2, and Percentage of Students Answering Each Question Correctly

Question Number	Correct Answer	Right	Wrong	Percentage of Students Answering the Question Correctly*	Question Number	Correct Answer	Right	Wrong	Percentage of Students Answering the Question Correctly*
1	B			87	51	C			45
2	D			72	52	B			62
3	B			84	53	C			78
4	C			81	54	D			54
5	E			79	55	B			75
6	B			80	56	C			72
7	E			79	57	A			69
8	E			87	58	A			43
9	A			63	59	B			56
10	E			66	60	C			65
11	B			68	61	C			62
12	B			49	62	A			88
13	C			63	63	D			81
14	D			67	64	B			83
15	C			66	65	C			49
16	E			58	66	E			47
17	D			43	67	C			72
18	C			50	68	D			34
19	A			77	69	C			81
20	A			60	70	B			76
21	A			71	71	D			63
22	E			69	72	A			48
23	A			72	73	B			44
24	A			60	74	D			61
25	C			77	75	E			70
26	A			59	76	B			70
27	C			42	77	A			75
28	E			38	78	C			79
29	C			66	79	E			71
30	D			68	80	D			78
31	B			52	81	D			70
32	A			56	82	B			63
33	A			58	83	B			74
34	D			50	84	C			30
35	E			49	85	C			67
36	E			48	86	C			68
37	A			46	87	A			54
38	B			44	88	D			69
39	D			48	89	A			63
40	E			43	90	E			50
41	B			47	91	C			21
42	E			47	92	C			47
43	C			55	93	C			46
44	C			55	94	B			52
45	D			38	95	B			19
46	B			65					
47	E			51					
48	B			61					
49	D			52					
50	C			75					

*These percentages are based on an analysis of the answer sheets for a random sample of 1,860 students who took this form of the test in May 1988 and whose mean score was 541. They may be used as an indication of the relative difficulty of a particular question. Each percentage may also be used to predict the likelihood that a typical SAT II: Biology Subject Test candidate will answer correctly that question on this edition of this test.

Finding Your College Board Scaled Score

When you take SAT II: Subject Tests, the scores sent to the colleges you specify are reported on the College Board scale, which ranges from 200 to 800. You can convert your practice test score to a scaled score by using Table B. To find your scaled score, locate your raw score in the left-hand column of Table B; the corresponding score in the right-hand column is your College Board scaled score. For example, a raw score of 60 on this particular edition of the SAT II: Biology Subject Test corresponds to a College Board scaled score of 590.

Raw scores are converted to scaled scores to ensure that a score earned on any one edition of a particular Subject Test is comparable to the same scaled score earned on any other edition of the same Subject Test. Because some editions of tests may be slightly easier or more difficult than others, College Board scaled scores are adjusted so that they indicate the same level of performance regardless of the edition of the test taken and the ability of the group that takes it. Thus, for example, a score of 400 on one edition of a test taken at a particular administration indicates the same level of achievement as a score of 400 on a different edition of the test taken at a different administration.

When you take the SAT II: Subject Tests during a national administration, your scores are likely to differ somewhat from the scores you obtain on the tests in this book. People perform at different levels at different times for reasons unrelated to the tests themselves. The precision of any test is also limited because it represents only a sample of all the possible questions that could be asked.

TABLE B

Score Conversion Table
Biology Subject Test, Form K-3JAC2

Raw Score	College Board Scaled Score	Raw Score	College Board Scaled Score
95	800	40	480
94	790	39	470
93	780	38	470
92	770	37	460
91	770	36	460
90	760	35	450
89	760	34	440
88	750	33	440
87	750	32	430
86	740	31	430
85	730	30	420
84	730	29	420
83	720	28	410
82	720	27	400
81	710	26	400
80	710	25	390
79	700	24	390
78	690	23	380
77	690	22	380
76	680	21	370
75	680	20	370
74	670	19	360
73	670	18	350
72	660	17	350
71	650	16	340
70	650	15	340
69	640	14	330
68	640	13	330
67	630	12	320
66	630	11	310
65	620	10	310
64	620	9	300
63	610	8	300
62	600	7	290
61	600	6	290
60	590	5	280
59	590	4	270
58	580	3	270
57	580	2	260
56	570	1	260
55	560	0	250
54	560	−1	250
53	550	−2	240
52	550	−3	230
51	540	−4	230
50	540	−5	220
49	530	−6	220
48	520	−7	210
47	520	−8	210
46	510	−9 through −24	200
45	510		
44	500		
43	500		
42	490		
41	480		

Reviewing Your Test Performance

After you have scored your test, you should take some time to consider the following points in relation to your performance on the test.

- *Did you run out of time before you reached the end of the test?*

  If you did, you may want to consider pacing yourself better. For example, you may have spent too much time working on one or two difficult questions. A better approach might have been to continue the test and return to those questions after you had attempted to answer the remaining questions on the test.

- *Did you take a long time reading the directions for the test?*

  The directions in this test are the same as those in the Biology Subject Tests now being administered. You will save time when you read the directions on the test day if you become thoroughly familiar with them in advance.

- *How did you handle questions you were unsure of?*

  If you were able to eliminate one or more of the answer choices and you guessed from the remaining choices, then your approach probably worked to your advantage. On the other hand, omitting questions about which you have some knowledge or guessing answers haphazardly would probably be a mistake.

- *How difficult were the questions for you compared with other students who took the test?*

  By referring to Table A, you can find out how difficult each question was for the group of students who took this test. The right-hand column in the table tells you what percentage of this group answered the question correctly. A question that was answered correctly by almost everyone in the group is obviously an easy question. Question 1, for example, was answered correctly by 87 percent of the students in the sample. On the other hand, question 95 was answered correctly by only 19 percent.

  It is important to remember that these percentages are based on only one particular group of students; had this edition of the test been given to other groups of students at that time, the percentages would probably have been different.

  If you find that you missed several questions that would be considered easy, you may want to review those questions carefully. They may cover some aspect of the subject that you need to review. Perhaps you misunderstood the directions for one part of the test or you thought the questions were so easy that you did not spend as much time on them as you might have.

The SAT II: Chemistry Subject Test

The Chemistry Subject Test consists of 85 multiple-choice questions. The test content is based on the assumption that you have had a one-year introductory course in chemistry at a level suitable for college preparation. The test covers the topics and skills listed in the charts below and to the right. Different aspects of each topic are stressed from year to year. However, because high school courses differ, both in the percentage of time devoted to each major topic and in the specific subtopics covered, it is likely that most students will encounter questions on topics unfamiliar to them.

The test is designed to be independent of the particular instructional approach of the course you have taken. You should be able to recall and understand the major concepts of chemistry and to apply the principles you have learned to solve specific problems in chemistry. You also should be able to organize and interpret results obtained by observation and experimentation and to draw conclusions or make inferences from experimental data, including data presented in graphic and/or tabular form. Laboratory experience is a significant factor in developing reasoning and problem-solving skills. Although laboratory skills can be tested only in a limited way in a multiple-choice test, reasonable laboratory experience is an asset in helping you prepare for the test. Your preparation in mathematics should enable you to handle simple algebraic relationships and to apply these to solving word problems. You should be familiar with the concepts of ratio and direct and inverse proportions, scientific notation, and exponential functions.

A periodic table indicating the atomic numbers and atomic masses of the elements is provided for all Saturday, Sunday, and make-up administrations.

You will not be allowed to use calculators during the test. Numerical calculations are limited to simple arithmetic. In this test, the metric system of units is used.

Skills Specifications	Approximate Percentage of Test
Recall of Knowledge: remembering fundamental concepts and specific information; demonstrating familiarity with terminology	20
Application of Knowledge: applying a single principle to unfamiliar and/or practical situations to obtain a qualitative result or solve a quantitative problem	45
Synthesis of Knowledge: inferring and deducing from qualitative and/or quantitative data; integrating two or more relationships to draw conclusions or solve problems	35

Topics Covered	Approximate Percentage of Test
I. ATOMIC AND MOLECULAR STRUCTURE	
• Atomic Theory and Structure, including periodic relationships	10
• Nuclear Reactions	3
• Chemical Bonding and Molecular Structure	11
II. STATES OF MATTER	
• Kinetic Molecular Theory of Gases	9
• Solutions, including concentration units, solubility, conductivity, and colligative properties	6
III. REACTION TYPES	
• Acids and Bases	9
• Oxidation-reduction, including electrochemical cells	7
IV. STOICHIOMETRY: Including the mole concept, Avogadro's number, empirical and molecular formulas, percentage composition, stoichiometric calculations, and limiting reagents	11
V. EQUILIBRIUM AND REACTION RATES: Equilibrium, including mass action expressions, ionic equilibria, and Le Chatelier's principle; factors affecting rates of reaction	7
VI. THERMODYNAMICS: Including energy changes in chemical reactions, randomness, and criteria for spontaneity	5
VII. DESCRIPTIVE CHEMISTRY: Physical and chemical properties of elements and their more familiar compounds, including simple examples from organic chemistry; periodic properties	15
VIII. LABORATORY: Equipment, procedures, observations, safety, calculations, and interpretation of results	7

Note: Every edition of the Chemistry Subject Test contains approximately five questions on equation balancing and/or predicting products of chemical reactions. These are distributed among the various content categories.

Questions Used in the Test

Classification Questions

Each set of classification questions has, in the heading, five lettered choices that you will use to answer all of the questions in the set. The choices may be statements that refer to concepts, principles, substances, or observable phenomena; or they may be graphs, pictures, equations, numbers, or experimental settings or situations. The questions themselves may also conform to one of these formats or may be given in the question format directly. To answer each question, you should select the choice in the heading that is most appropriate to it. Consider all of the choices before answering a question. The directions for this type of question specifically state that you should not eliminate a choice simply because it is the correct answer to a previous question.

Because the same five choices are applicable to several questions, the classification questions usually require less reading than other types of multiple-choice questions. Therefore, this type of question is a quick means, in terms of testing time, of determining how well you have mastered the topics represented in the choices. The degree of mastery required to answer a question correctly depends on the sophistication of the set of questions. One set may test your ability to recall information; another set may ask you to apply information to a specific situation or to translate information from one form to another (descriptive, graphical, mathematical). Thus, several types of skills can be tested by a question of this type.

Following are the directions for and an example of a classification set.

Directions: Each set of lettered choices below refers to the numbered statements immediately following it. Select the one lettered choice that best fits each statement and then fill in the corresponding oval on the answer sheet. A choice may be used once, more than once, or not at all in each set.

Questions 1-3 refer to the following aqueous solutions:

(A) 0.1 *M* HCl
(B) 0.1 *M* NaCl
(C) 0.1 *M* $HC_2H_30_2$
(D) 0.1 *M* CH_3OH
(E) 0.1 *M* KOH

1. **Is weakly acidic**
2. **Has the highest pH**
3. **Reacts with an equal volume of 0.05 *M* $Ba(OH)_2$ to form a solution with pH = 7**

These three questions belong to the topic category of acids and bases and require you to apply knowledge in this area to the particular solutions specified in the five choices.

To answer the first question, you must recognize which of the choices above are acid solutions. Only (A) and (C) satisfy this requirement. Choice (B) refers to a neutral salt solution, (D) is a solution of an alcohol, and (E) is a basic solution. Both (A) and (C) are acidic solutions, but (A) is a strong acid that is completely ionized in aqueous solution, while (C) is only partially ionized in aqueous solution. Since the concentrations of all the solutions are the same, you do not need to consider this factor. The hydrogen ion concentration of a 0.1-molar acetic acid solution is considerably smaller than 0.1-molar. The hydrogen ion concentration in (A) is equal to 0.1-molar. Thus (C) is a weakly acidic solution and is the answer to the question.

To answer the second question, you need to understand the pH scale, which is a measure of the hydrogen ion concentration in solution and is defined as $pH = -\log [H^+]$. The higher the pH, the lower the hydrogen ion concentration and the more basic the solution. Among the choices given above, (E) is the most basic solution and is the answer to this question.

To answer the third question, you need to know that acids react with bases to form salts and water. Since the question refers to equal volumes of each solution, assume 1 liter of each solution is available. Barium hydroxide solution is a strong base, i.e., is completely ionized in water, and 1 liter of 0.05 *M* Ba $(OH)_2$ provides 0.1 mole of OH^- ions in solution. When 1 liter of this solution is added to 1 liter of either 0.1 *M* NaCl, 0.1 *M* CH_3OH, or 0.1 *M* KOH no reactions occur and the resulting solutions remain basic, i.e., the pH will be greater than 7 in each case. When 0.1 mole OH^- ions reacts with 0.1 mole of acetic acid, the resulting solution will also be basic and have a pH greater than 7 because acetic acid is a weak acid, i.e., is incompletely ionized in water. The acetic acid reacts with the OH^- ions as follows:

$$HC_2H_3O_2 + OH^- \rightleftarrows C_2H_3O_2^- + H_2O$$

The acetate salt formed hydrolyzes in water yielding a solution containing more OH^- ions than H^+ ions. When 1 liter of 0.05 *M* $Ba(OH)_2$ reacts with 1 liter of 0.1 *M* HCl, there is a reaction between 0.1 mole OH^- ions and 0.1 mole H^+ to form 0.1 mole H_2O. The resulting solution contains Ba^{2+} ions and Cl^- ions and equal concentrations of OH^- and H^+ ions. The solution formed is neutral and the pH is 7. Thus (A) is the answer to the question.

Relationship Analysis Questions

This type of question consists of a specific statement or assertion (Statement I) followed by an explanation of the assertion (Statement II). The question is answered by determining if the assertion and the explanation are each true statements and if so, whether the explanation (or reason) provided does in fact properly explain the statement given in the assertion.

This type of question tests your ability to identify proper cause-and-effect relationships. It probes whether you can assess the correctness of the original assertion and then evaluate the truth of the "reason" proposed to justify it. The analysis required by this type of question provides you with an opportunity to demonstrate developed reasoning skills and the scope of your understanding of a particular topic.

<u>Directions:</u> Each question below consists of two statements, I in the left-hand column and II in the right-hand column. For each question, determine whether statement I is true or false <u>and</u> whether statement II is true or false and fill in the corresponding T or F ovals on your answer sheet. <u>Fill in oval CE only if statement II is a correct explanation of statement I.</u>

EXAMPLES:

	I		II
EX 1.	**H_2SO_4 is a strong acid**	**BECAUSE**	**H_2SO_4 contains sulfur.**
EX 2.	**An atom of oxygen is electrically neutral**	**BECAUSE**	**an oxygen atom contains an equal number of protons and electrons.**

SAMPLE ANSWERS

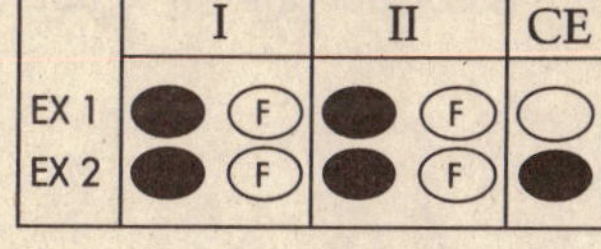

	I		II
4.	**The electrolysis of a concentrated solution of sodium chloride produces chlorine**	**BECAUSE**	**sodium chloride is a covalent compound.**

The above question has several components. Statement I, the assertion, has to do with an oxidation-reduction reaction, more specifically, an electrochemical reaction. This statement is true because the electrolysis of a concentrated sodium chloride solution yields chlorine gas at the anode (oxidation) and hydrogen gas at the cathode (reduction). The electrolytic solution gradually becomes alkaline with the accumulation of hydroxide ions (i.e., OH^- ions) as the reaction proceeds.

Statement II, the reason, is false because the type of chemical bonding in sodium chloride is ionic. According to the directions for answering this question type, you should fill in the corresponding T and F ovals on your answer sheet.

	I		II
5.	**Atoms of different elements can have the same mass number**	**BECAUSE**	**atoms of each element have a characteristic number of protons in the nucleus.**

This is a question on atomic structure. The sum of the number of protons plus the number of neutrons contained in the nucleus of an atom is the mass number. However, atoms of the same element may have different numbers of neutrons in their nuclei and thus have different masses. Such atoms, which have the same number of protons but different numbers of neutrons, are called isotopes of an element ($^{12}_{6}C$ and $^{14}_{6}C$, for example). The existence of isotopes makes it possible for atoms of different elements, that is, with different numbers of protons, to have the same total mass or mass number ($^{14}_{6}C$ and $^{14}_{7}N$, for example). Thus Statement I is true. Statement II is also true because the number of protons in the nucleus of an atom is a characteristic feature that identifies each element. But it is not the reason that explains the existence of isotopes and so does not properly explain Statement I. Thus, to answer this question, you should fill in both T ovals for this question, but not the CE oval.

	I		II
6.	**When the system $CO(g) + Cl_2(g) = COCl_2(g)$ is at equilibrium and the pressure on the system is increased by decreasing the volume at constant temperature, more $COCl_2(g)$ will be produced**	**BECAUSE**	**an increase of pressure on a system will be relieved when the system shifts to a smaller total number of moles of gas.**

Statement I is true because whenever stress is applied to a system at equilibrium the system will tend to shift to relieve the stress (Le Chatelier's principle). In the system described, the stress is caused by an increase in pressure resulting from a decrease in the volume and will be relieved by the reaction of some CO and Cl_2 to form more $COCl_2$. The new equilibrium that will be established will contain a smaller total number of moles of gas, thereby reducing the pressure stress. This is the explanation given in Statement II, which is not only true but also correctly explains the phenomenon described in Statement I. Thus, to answer this question correctly you should fill in both T ovals as well as the CE oval for this question.

Five-choice Completion Questions

The five-choice completion question is widely used in objective tests and is probably the type of question with which you are most familiar. It is written either as an incomplete statement or as a question. In its simplest application, this type of question poses a problem that intrinsically has a unique solution. It is also appropriate when: (1) the problem presented is clearly delineated by the wording of the question so that you are asked to choose not a universal solution but the best of the solutions offered; (2) the problem is such that you are required to evaluate the relevance of five plausible, or even scientifically accurate, options and to select the one most pertinent; (3) the problem has several pertinent solutions and you are required to select the one inappropriate solution that is presented. In the latter case, the correct answer to the question is the choice that is *least* applicable to the situation described by the question. Such questions normally contain a word in capital letters such as NOT, LEAST, or EXCEPT.

A special type of five-choice completion question is used in some tests, including the SAT II: Chemistry Subject Test, to allow for the possibility of multiple correct answers. Unlike many quantitative problems that must by their nature have a unique solution, some questions have more than one correct response. For these questions, you must evaluate each response independently of the others in order to select the most appropriate combination. In questions of this type several (usually three to five) statements labeled by Roman numerals are given with the question. One or more of these statements may correctly answer the question. The statements are followed by five lettered choices (A to E) each consisting of some combination of the Roman numerals that label the statements. You must select from among the five lettered choices the one combination of statements that best answers the question. In the test, questions of this type are intermixed among the more standard five-choice completion questions. (Question 8 is an example of this type of question.)

The five-choice completion question also tests problem-solving skills. With this type of question you may be asked to convert the information given in a word problem into graphical form or to select and apply the mathematical relationship necessary to solve the scientific problem. Alternatively, you may be asked to interpret experimental data, graphical stimulus, or mathematical expressions. Thus, the five-choice completion question can be adapted to test several kinds of skills.

When the experimental data or other scientific problems to be analyzed are comparatively extensive, it is often convenient to organize several five-choice completion questions into sets, that is, direct each question in a set to the same material. This practice allows you to answer several questions based on the same material, compensating for the testing time required to read and interpret a large amount of scientific information. In no case, however, is the answer to one question necessary for answering a subsequent question correctly. Each question in a set is independent of the others and refers only to the material given for the entire set.

Directions: Each of the questions or incomplete statements below is followed by five suggested answers or completions. Select the one that is best in each case and fill in the corresponding oval on the answer sheet.

7. **The hydrogen ion concentration of a solution prepared by diluting 50 milliliters of 0.100-molar HNO_3 with water to 500 milliliters of solution is**

   (A) 0.0010 *M*
   (B) 0.0050 *M*
   (C) 0.010 *M*
   (D) 0.050 *M*
   (E) 1.0 *M*

This is a question that concerns solution concentrations. One way to solve the problem is through the use of ratios. In this question, a solution of nitric acid is diluted 10-fold; therefore, the concentration of the solution will decrease by a factor of 10, that is, from 0.100-molar to 0.010-molar. Alternatively, you could calculate the number of moles of H^+ ions present and divide this value by 0.50 liter: $(0.100 \times 0.050)/0.5 = M$ of the diluted solution. In either case, the correct answer is (C).

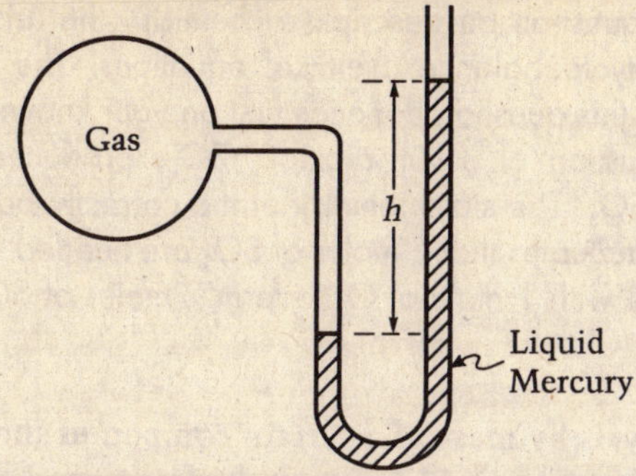

8. **The bulb of the open-end manometer shown above contains a gas. True statements about this system include which of the following?**

    I. **Only atmospheric pressure is exerted on the exposed mercury surface in the right side of the tube.**
    II. **The gas pressure is greater than atmospheric pressure.**
    III. **The difference in the height, *h*, of mercury levels is equal to the pressure of the gas.**

    (A) II only
    (B) III only
    (C) I and II only
    (D) I and III only
    (E) I, II, and III

This is a laboratory-oriented question pertaining to the measurement of gas pressures. It demands higher-level analytical skills that involve drawing conclusions from results obtained in an experiment. To answer this question correctly, you must first understand that, in an open type of manometer, the air exerts pressure on the column of liquid in the open side of the U-tube and the gas being studied exerts pressure on the other side of the U-tube. It is clear then that statement I is true since the data given show that the manometer is open-ended and its right side is exposed to the atmosphere. Statement II is also a true statement because the level of liquid mercury is higher in the right side, which is exposed to the atmosphere, than in the left side, which is exposed to the gas. Thus the gas pressure is greater than atmospheric pressure. Statement III is not a correct statement because the pressure of the gas in the bulb, expressed in millimeters of mercury, is equal to the difference in height, *h*, of the two mercury levels, plus the atmospheric pressure. Thus only statements I and II are correct and the answer to the question is (C).

9. **A thermometer is placed in a test tube containing a melted pure substance. As slow cooling occurs, the thermometer is read at regular intervals until well after the sample has solidified. Which of the following types of graphs is obtained by plotting temperature <u>versus</u> time for this experiment?**

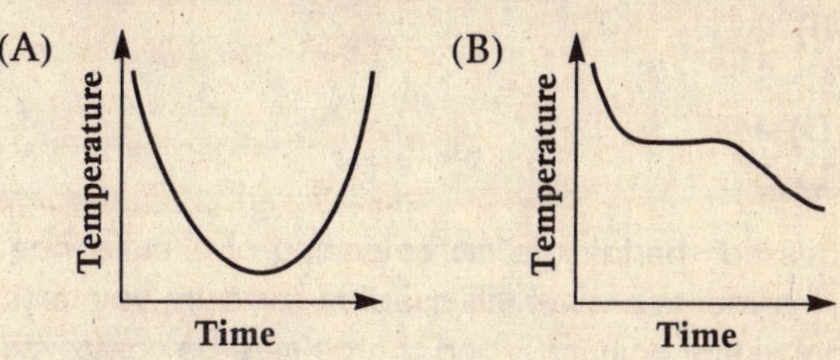

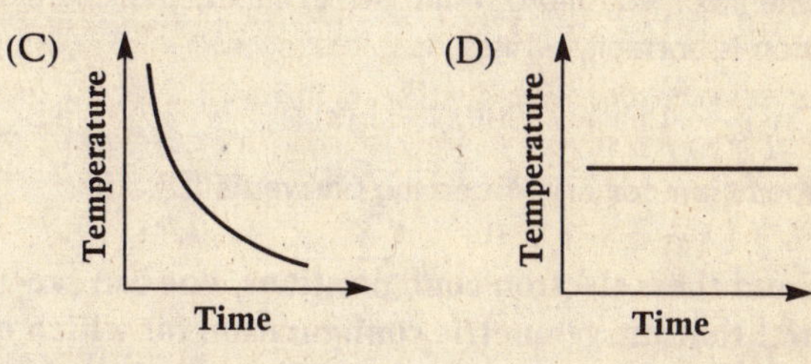

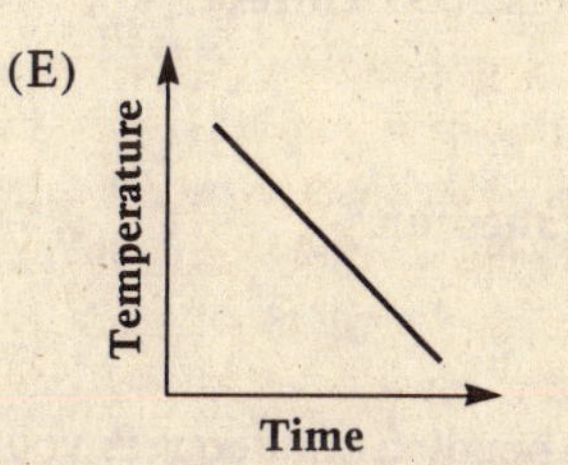

This is a question on states of matter. You must convert the description of the physical phenomenon given in the question to graphical form. When a liquid is cooled slowly, its temperature will decrease with time. Thus the first portion of a graph depicting this phenomenon must show a decrease when temperature is plotted against time. When a pure liquid substance reaches its fusion (melting) point, continued cooling will release heat with time as the substance solidifies. During this period there is no drop in temperature. After the substance has completely solidified, further cooling will cause an additional drop in temperature. The only graph above that accurately depicts the events described is (B), which is the answer.

$\ldots Cu^{2+} + \ldots I^- \rightarrow \ldots CuI(s) + \ldots I_2(s)$

10. When the equation above is balanced and all coefficients are reduced to lowest whole-number terms, the coefficient for I^- is

(A) 1
(B) 2
(C) 3
(D) 4
(E) 5

This question pertains to the balancing of chemical equations. In order to answer this question correctly, you need to recognize that both mass and charge must be conserved in any chemical equation. With this in mind, the chemical equation is correctly written as

$$2\,Cu^{2+} + 4\,I^- \rightarrow 2\,CuI(s) + I_2(s)$$

The coefficient for I^- is 4 and the answer is (D).

11. From their electron configurations, one can predict that the geometric configuration for which of the following molecules is NOT correct?

(A) PF_3 trigonal planar
(B) CF_4 tetrahedral
(C) $CHCl_3$ irregular tetrahedron
(D) OF_2 bent (v-shaped)
(E) HF linear

This is a question on chemical bonding and requires you to apply the principles of molecular bonding. Each of the molecules given is correctly paired with the term describing its molecular geometry except (A). The geometry of PF_3 is not trigonal planar, but trigonal pyramidal, because this geometry corresponds to a maximum possible separation of the electron pairs around the central atom, phosphorus, and therefore yields the most stable configuration; the central atom of the molecule is surrounded by three single bonds and one unshared electron pair. Thus the answer is (A). Note that this is the type of question that asks you to identify the *one* solution to the problem that is *inappropriate*.

$\ldots SO_2 + \ldots O_2 \rightarrow \ldots ?$

12. According to the reaction above, how many moles of SO_2 are required to react completely with 1 mole of O_2?

(A) 0.5 mole
(B) 1 mole
(C) 2 moles
(D) 3 moles
(E) 4 moles

This is a question on descriptive chemistry that also tests your ability to balance chemical equations. The correct answer to this question depends first on your knowing that the combustion of sulfur dioxide, SO_2, produces sulfur trioxide, SO_3. The stoichiometry of the correctly balanced equation indicates that 2 moles of SO_2 are needed to react completely with 1 mole of O_2 to form 2 moles of SO_3. The answer is (C).

13. Analysis by mass of a certain compound shows that it contains 14.4 percent hydrogen and 85.6 percent carbon. Which of the following is the most informative statement that can properly be made about the compound on the basis of these data?

(A) It is a hydrocarbon.
(B) Its empirical formula is CH_2.
(C) Its molecular formula is C_2H_4.
(D) Its molar mass is 28 grams.
(E) It contains a triple bond.

This is a question on stoichiometry that tests the important skill of scientific reasoning based on experimental evidence. The question states that 100 percent of the composition of the compound analyzed can be accounted for with the elements hydrogen and carbon. Thus, this compound is a hydrocarbon and (A) is a correct statement. It is not the correct answer to the question, however, because you can deduce more specific conclusions about this compound from the information given. The relative percentage composition provides evidence that the atomic ratio of carbon to hydrogen in the compound must be 85.6/12.0 : 14.4/1.0 or 1:2. Therefore, you can conclude that the empirical formula for the compound is CH_2, a hydrocarbon. Thus (B) is a better answer than (A). Since you do not know the total number of moles of the compound used for analysis, you cannot calculate the molar mass or derive the molecular formula for this compound. Thus (C) and (D) cannot be determined from the information given and so they are not correct answers to the question. It is known, however, that a substance with an empirical formula of CH_2 cannot have a triple bond. Therefore, (E) is incorrect. The best answer to the question is (B).

SAT II:

Chemistry Subject Test

The test that follows is representative of a typical SAT II: Chemistry Subject Test. So that you may have an idea of what the national test administration will be like, try to take the test in this book under conditions as close as possible to those of the nationally administered test. It will probably help if you do the following.

- Set aside an hour for the test when you will not be interrupted, so that you can complete all of it in one sitting.
- Sit at a desk with no other papers or books. You can't take a calculator, dictionary, other books, or notes into the test room.
- Have a kitchen timer or clock in front of you for timing yourself.
- Tear out an answer sheet from the back of this book and fill it in just as you would on the day of the test. You can use one answer sheet for as many as three Subject Tests.
- Read the instructions that precede the test. When you take the test, you will be asked to read them before you begin answering questions.
- After you finish the test, read the sections on "How to Score the SAT II: Chemistry Subject Test" and "Reviewing Your Test Performance," which follow the test.

FORM 3KAC2 (reformatted)

CHEMISTRY TEST

The top portion of the section of the answer sheet that you will use in taking the Chemistry test must be filled in exactly as shown in the illustration below. Note carefully that you have to do all of the following on your answer sheet.

1. Print CHEMISTRY on the line under the words "Subject (print)."

2. In the shaded box labeled "Test Code" fill in four ovals:

   —Fill in oval 2 in the row labeled V.

   —Fill in oval 2 in the row labeled W.

   —Fill in oval 4 in the row labeled X.

   —Fill in oval D in the row labeled Y.

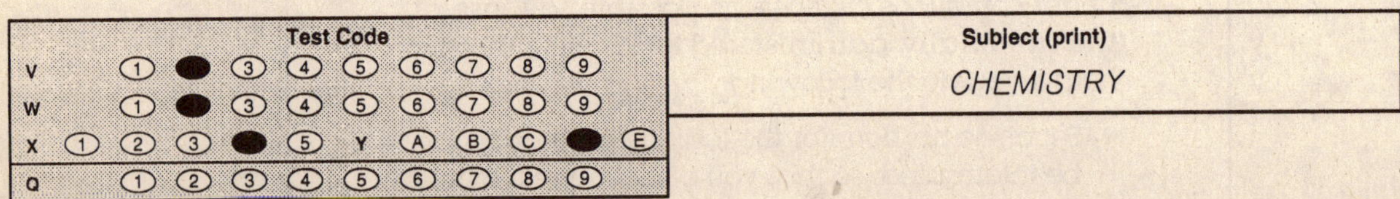

3. Please answer the questions below by filling in the appropriate ovals in the row labeled Q on the answer sheet. <u>The information you provide is for statistical purposes only and will not affect your score on the test.</u>

<u>Question I</u>

How many semesters of chemistry have you taken in high school? (If you are taking chemistry this semester, count it as a full semester.) Fill in only <u>one</u> oval of ovals 1-3.

- Onc semester or less —Fill in oval 1.
- Two semesters —Fill in oval 2.
- Three semesters or more —Fill in oval 3.

<u>Question II</u>

How recently have you studied chemistry?

- I am currently enrolled in or have just completed a chemistry course. —Fill in oval 4.
- I have not studied chemistry for 6 months or more. —Fill in oval 5.

<u>Question III</u>

Which of the following best describes your preparation in algebra? (If you are taking an algebra course this semester, count it as a full semester.) Fill in only <u>one</u> oval of ovals 6-8.

- One semester or less —Fill in oval 6.
- Two semesters —Fill in oval 7.
- Three semesters or more —Fill in oval 8.

<u>Question IV</u>

Are you currently taking Advanced Placement Chemistry? If you are, fill in oval 9.

When the supervisor gives the signal, turn the page and begin the Chemistry test. There are a total of 85 questions in the Chemistry test (1-69 plus 101-116 on the special section at the bottom left hand of the answer sheet.)

CHEMISTRY TEST

Material in the following table may be useful in answering the questions in this examination.

DO NOT DETACH FROM BOOK.

PERIODIC CHART OF THE ELEMENTS

1 H 1.0079																	2 He 4.003
3 Li 6.941	4 Be 9.012											5 B 10.81	6 C 12.011	7 N 14.007	8 O 16.00	9 F 19.00	10 Ne 20.179
11 Na 22.99	12 Mg 24.30											13 Al 26.98	14 Si 28.09	15 P 30.974	16 S 32.06	17 Cl 35.453	18 Ar 39.948
19 K 39.10	20 Ca 40.08	21 Sc 44.96	22 Ti 47.90	23 V 50.94	24 Cr 52.00	25 Mn 54.94	26 Fe 55.85	27 Co 58.93	28 Ni 58.70	29 Cu 63.55	30 Zn 65.38	31 Ga 69.72	32 Ge 72.59	33 As 74.92	34 Se 78.96	35 Br 79.90	36 Kr 83.80
37 Rb 85.47	38 Sr 87.62	39 Y 88.91	40 Zr 91.22	41 Nb 92.91	42 Mo 95.94	43 Tc (97)	44 Ru 101.1	45 Rh 102.91	46 Pd 106.4	47 Ag 107.868	48 Cd 112.41	49 In 114.82	50 Sn 118.7	51 Sb 121.75	52 Te 127.60	53 I 126.90	54 Xe 131.30
55 Cs 132.91	56 Ba 137.33	57 *La 138.91	72 Hf 178.49	73 Ta 180.95	74 W 183.85	75 Re 186.21	76 Os 190.2	77 Ir 192.2	78 Pt 195.09	79 Au 196.97	80 Hg 200.59	81 Tl 204.37	82 Pb 207.2	83 Bi 208.98	84 Po (209)	85 At (210)	86 Rn (222)
87 Fr (223)	88 Ra (226)	89 †Ac (227)															

*Lanthanum Series

58 Ce 140.12	59 Pr 140.91	60 Nd 144.24	61 Pm (145)	62 Sm 150.4	63 Eu 152.0	64 Gd 157.25	65 Tb 158.93	66 Dy 162.50	67 Ho 164.93	68 Er 167.26	69 Tm 168.93	70 Yb 173.04	71 Lu 174.97

†Actinium Series

90 Th 232.0	91 Pa 231.0	92 U 238.03	93 Np 237.0	94 Pu (244)	95 Am (243)	96 Cm (247)	97 Bk (247)	98 Cf (251)	99 Es (252)	100 Fm (257)	101 Md (258)	102 No (259)	103 Lr (260)

DO NOT DETACH FROM BOOK.

CHEMISTRY TEST

Note: For all questions involving solutions and/or chemical equations, assume that the system is in water unless otherwise stated.

Part A

Directions: Each set of lettered choices below refers to the numbered statements or formulas immediately following it. Select the one lettered choice that best fits each statement or formula and then fill in the corresponding oval on the answer sheet. A choice may be used once, more than once, or not at all in each set.

Questions 1-5

(A) Buret
(B) Calorimeter
(C) Manometer
(D) Geiger counter
(E) Voltmeter

1. Equipment needed to determine the half-life of carbon-14

2. Equipment needed for measuring the vapor pressure of a liquid

3. Equipment needed for measuring the volume of a solution that is delivered

4. Equipment needed to determine the heat of reaction

5. Equipment needed for measuring the potential of a cell

Questions 6-9

(A) Boiling point
(B) Rate of reaction
(C) Molecular mass
(D) Molarity
(E) Density

6. Can be expressed as grams per milliliter

7. Can be expressed as grams per mole

8. Does NOT vary with changes of temperature and pressure

9. Is a quantity necessary to determine the molecular formula of a compound

Questions 10-12

(A) Fe^{2+}
(B) Cl
(C) K^{+}
(D) Cs
(E) Au

10. Has the electron configuration $1s^2 2s^2 2p^6 3s^2 3p^6 3d^6$

11. Has a noble gas electron configuration

12. Has electrons in *f* orbitals

Questions 13-16

(A) Ionic substance
(B) Nonpolar covalent substance
(C) Polar covalent substance
(D) Macromolecular substance
(E) Metallic substance

13. Methyl alcohol, CH_3OH

14. Carbon tetrachloride, CCl_4

15. Cesium

16. Strontium chloride

GO ON TO THE NEXT PAGE

Questions 17-19

(A) Arrhenius acid
(B) Arrhenius base
(C) Buffer
(D) Indicator
(E) Salt

17. At 25° C, produces an aqueous solution with pH > 7

18. At 25°C, produces an aqueous solution with $[H^+] > 1.0 \times 10^{-7}$ moles per liter

19. Has different colors in its acidic and basic forms

Questions 20-23 refer to the following experimental setup that was used to generate various gases.

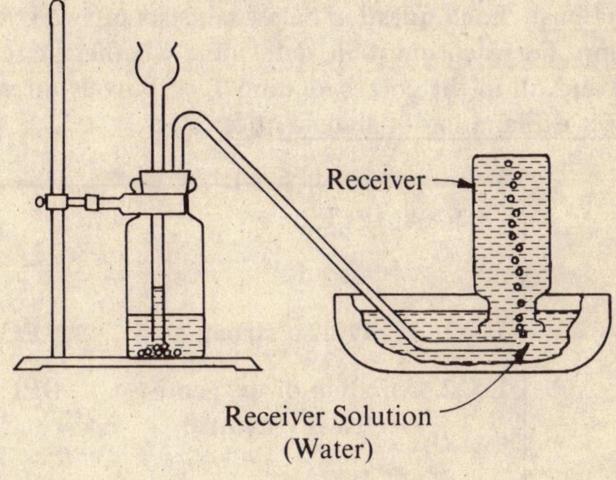

(A) HCl
(B) NH_3
(C) N_2
(D) H_2
(E) CO_2

20. The evolved gas is not very soluble in the water and the water remains neutral. When ignited in air, the gas burns with a blue flame.

21. The evolved gas dissolves readily in the water to give a strongly acidic solution.

22. The evolved gas is very soluble in the water and gives a basic solution.

23. The evolved gas is slightly soluble in the water and gives a weakly acidic solution. The gas does not burn in air.

GO ON TO THE NEXT PAGE

Part B

Directions: Each question below consists of two statements, I in the left-hand column and II in the right-hand column. For each question, determine whether statement I is true or false and whether statement II is true or false and fill in the corresponding T or F ovals on your answer sheet. Fill in oval CE only if statement II is a correct explanation of statement I.

EXAMPLES:

	I		II
EX 1.	H_2SO_4 is a strong acid	BECAUSE	H_2SO_4 contains sulfur.
EX 2.	An atom of oxygen is electrically neutral	BECAUSE	an oxygen atom contains an equal number of protons and electrons.

SAMPLE ANSWERS

	I		II		CE
EX 1	●	Ⓕ	●	Ⓕ	○
EX 2	●	Ⓕ	●	Ⓕ	●

	I		II
101.	Oxygen is an element	BECAUSE	oxygen exists in the form of diatomic molecules at room temperature and atmospheric pressure.
102.	A saturated solution may be quite dilute	BECAUSE	some substances have a very low solubility.
103.	^{14}C is an isotope of ^{14}N	BECAUSE	^{14}C and ^{14}N have the same mass number.
104.	A catalyst accelerates a chemical reaction	BECAUSE	a catalyst decreases the activation energy for a chemical reaction.
105.	An endothermic reaction has a positive $\triangle H$ value	BECAUSE	in an endothermic reaction, the total enthalpy (heat content) of the products is greater than that of the reactants.
106.	Molten potassium chloride is a good electrical conductor	BECAUSE	the melting process frees the ions in potassium chloride from their fixed positions in the crystal lattice.
107.	Hydrogen chloride is a polar substance	BECAUSE	hydrogen and chlorine have the same electronegativity.
108.	Ice is less dense than liquid water	BECAUSE	water molecules are nonpolar.

GO ON TO THE NEXT PAGE

	I		II
109.	A 0.1-molar solution of acetic acid is a poorer electrical conductor than a 0.1-molar solution of hydrochloric acid	BECAUSE	at the same concentration, the number of acetic acid molecules that ionize in water is less than the number of hydrogen chloride molecules that ionize in water.
110.	Covalent bonds are broken when sugars are dissolved in water	BECAUSE	in molecules with covalent bonds, electrons are shared by two or more atoms.
111.	Sodium chloride is used effectively to melt snow and ice	BECAUSE	sodium chloride melts at a high temperature.
112.	The O^{2-} ion and the neon atom have similar chemical properties	BECAUSE	the O^{2-} ion and the neon atom have the same number of electrons.
113.	At low temperatures and high pressures gases tend to condense	BECAUSE	gases expand to fill the container in which they are placed.
114.	The compound sodium hydrogen carbonate, $NaHCO_3$, can act as either a Brönsted base or a Brönsted acid	BECAUSE	the hydrogen carbonate ion can either accept or donate a proton.
115.	Fluorine is a weaker oxidizing agent than chlorine	BECAUSE	fluorine atoms are larger than chlorine atoms.
116.	A solution with $pH = 5$ has a higher concentration of hydronium ions than one with $pH = 3$	BECAUSE	pH is defined as $-\log [H^+]$.

RETURN TO THE SECTION OF YOUR ANSWER SHEET YOU STARTED FOR CHEMISTRY AND ANSWER QUESTIONS 24-69.

GO ON TO THE NEXT PAGE

Part C

Directions: Each of the questions or incomplete statements below is followed by five suggested answers or completions. Select the one that is best in each case and then fill in the corresponding oval on the answer sheet.

24. What volume of a 0.500-molar solution of hydrochloric acid is required to neutralize 60.0 milliliters of a 1.50-molar potassium hydroxide solution?

(A) 360. ml
(B) 180. ml
(C) 120. ml
(D) 60.0 ml
(E) 20.0 ml

25. $\ldots Al_2(C_2O_4)_3(s) \xrightarrow{\Delta} \ldots Al_2O_3(s) + \ldots CO(g) + \ldots CO_2(g)$

According to the equation for the reaction represented above, what is the mole ratio of CO to CO_2 that is produced by the decomposition of aluminum oxalate?

(A) 1 mole CO : 1 mole CO_2
(B) 1 mole CO : 2 moles CO_2
(C) 1 mole CO : 3 moles CO_2
(D) 2 moles CO : 1 mole CO_2
(E) 3 moles CO : 1 mole CO_2

26. $\ldots LiAlH_4(s) + \ldots BCl_3(\ell) \rightarrow \ldots B_2H_6(g) + \ldots LiCl(s) + \ldots AlCl_3(s)$

When the equation for the reaction represented above is balanced and all coefficients are reduced to lowest whole-number terms, the coefficient of B_2H_6 is

(A) 1
(B) 2
(C) 3
(D) 4
(E) 5

GO ON TO THE NEXT PAGE

27. $2\,Al(s) + Fe_2O_3(s) \rightarrow Al_2O_3(s) + 2\,Fe(s)$

According to the equation for the reaction represented above, which of the following statements is true?

(A) If 2 moles of aluminum are used, 1 mole of iron is produced.
(B) If 1 mole of aluminum is used, 0.5 mole of Fe_2O_3 is consumed.
(C) If 1 mole is aluminum is used, 1 mole of Al_2O_3 is produced.
(D) If 0.5 mole of aluminum is used, 1 mole of Al_2O_3 is produced.
(E) If 0.5 mole of aluminum is used, 0.5 mole of Fe_2O_3 is consumed.

28. Which of the following combinations of particles represents an ion of net charge − 1 and of mass number 80 ?

(A) 44 neutrons, 35 protons, 36 electrons
(B) 44 neutrons, 36 protons, 35 electrons
(C) 44 neutrons, 36 protons, 36 electrons
(D) 45 neutrons, 35 protons, 35 electrons
(E) 45 neutrons, 35 protons, 36 electrons

29. The colored complexes of the transition elements have color because they

(A) have very high formation constants
(B) absorb light of some visible wavelengths
(C) absorb light of some ultraviolet wavelengths
(D) have unpaired electrons
(E) are soluble in water

30. $C_2H_4(g) + 3\,O_2(g) \rightarrow 2\,CO_2(g) + 2\,H_2O(\ell)$

When 100 grams of O_2 are allowed to react completely with 1.0 mole of C_2H_4 according to the equation above, which of the following results?

(A) Some C_2H_4 remains unreacted.
(B) Some O_2 remains unreacted.
(C) Only CO_2 and H_2O are present when the reaction has run to completion.
(D) Less than 2 moles of CO_2 is formed.
(E) The partial pressure of O_2 falls to zero.

31. $\ldots Ag^+ + \ldots S^{2-} \rightarrow$

When the equation for the reaction represented above is completed and balanced by the use of lowest whole-number coefficients, the coefficient for Ag^+ is

(A) 1
(B) 2
(C) 3
(D) 4
(E) 6

32. The oxidation state of nitrogen is most positive in which of the following compounds?

(A) NO_3^-
(B) NO_2^-
(C) N_2O
(D) N_2
(E) NH_3

33. $\ldots MgCO_3(s) + \ldots H_3O^+ \rightarrow$

Products of the reaction represented above include which of the following?

I. $Mg(s)$
II. $H_2O(\ell)$
III. $CO_2(g)$

(A) I only
(B) III only
(C) I and III only
(D) II and III only
(E) I, II, and III

34. Of the following, the field of organic chemistry is LEAST concerned with the study of

(A) petroleum products
(B) alloys
(C) polymers
(D) carbohydrates
(E) alcohols

GO ON TO THE NEXT PAGE

35. According to quantum mechanics, correct statements concerning the electron in the hydrogen atom include which of the following?

    I. It moves in a definite orbit around the nucleus.
    II. It is associated with definite energy levels.
    III. It occupies a fixed position in space with reference to the nucleus.

    (A) I only
    (B) II only
    (C) I and III only
    (D) II and III only
    (E) I, II, and III

36. The conversion of $Cr_2O_7^{2-}$ to Cr^{3+} during a chemical reaction is an example of

    (A) hydrolysis (B) displacement
    (C) neutralization (D) reduction
    (E) oxidation

37. Oxidation-reduction processes include all of the following EXCEPT the

    (A) burning of wood
    (B) rusting of iron
    (C) generation of power by a storage battery
    (D) combustion of gasoline in an automobile engine
    (E) conduction of an electric current in a copper wire

38. Characteristic features of naturally radioactive elements include which of the following?

    I. The emission of α or β particles or γ rays
    II. A characteristic half-life
    III. Spontaneous decay

    (A) I only
    (B) I and II only
    (C) I and III only
    (D) II and III only
    (E) I, II, and III

39. What mass of lead nitrate, $Pb(NO_3)_2$, (formula weight = 331) is needed to make 100 milliliters of a 1.00-molar solution?

    (A) 438 grams
    (B) 331 grams
    (C) 269 grams
    (D) 53.8 grams
    (E) 33.1 grams

40. $H_2(g) + I_2(g) + 51.9 \text{ kilojoules} \rightarrow 2\,HI(g)$

    Which of the following can be expected to increase the rate of the reaction given by the equation above?

    I. Adding some helium gas
    II. Adding a catalyst
    III. Increasing the temperature

    (A) I only
    (B) III only
    (C) I and II only
    (D) II and III only
    (E) I, II, and III

41. An example of a network solid is

    (A) limestone, $CaCO_3$
    (B) table salt, NaCl
    (C) diamond, C
    (D) dry ice, CO_2
    (E) iodine, I_2

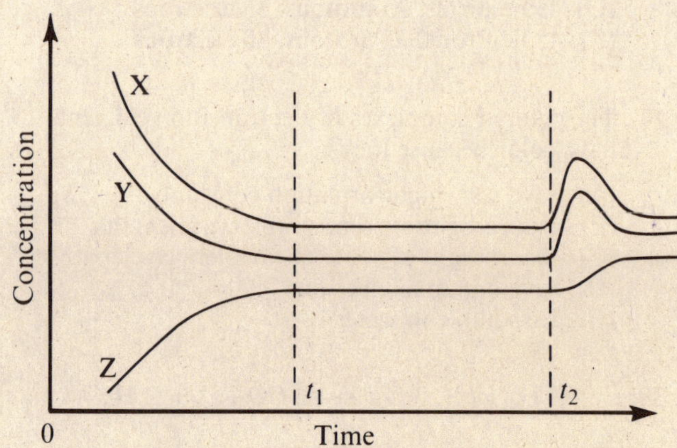

42. $X(g) + Y(g) \rightleftharpoons Z(g)$

    The diagram above shows that the reaction between X and Y to form Z had come to equilibrium at time t_1. The equilibrium shifts that occurred after time t_2 were most likely caused by which of the following?

    (A) Adding more X and Y to the equilibrium mixture
    (B) Adding only more X to the equilibrium mixture
    (C) Adding only more Y to the equilibrium mixture
    (D) Increasing the temperature
    (E) Increasing the pressure

GO ON TO THE NEXT PAGE

Questions 43-44 refer to the following situation.

A 5-mole sample of oxygen gas is added to a vessel that contains 1 mole of hydrogen gas and that is maintained at a constant temperature. No chemical reaction occurs. The volume of the vessel remains unchanged.

43. The ratio of the pressure exerted by the oxygen gas to the pressure exerted by the hydrogen gas is

(A) 6 : 1
(B) 5 : 1
(C) 4 : 1
(D) 1 : 1
(E) 1 : 5

44. After the gases are uniformly mixed, the partial pressure exerted on the walls of the vessel by the hydrogen gas is

(A) $\frac{1}{5}$ the original pressure
(B) the same as before the addition of the oxygen
(C) twice the original pressure
(D) 5 times the original pressure
(E) 6 times the original pressure

45. For a particular compound, which of the following pairs can represent the empirical and the molecular formula, respectively?

(A) CH_3 and C_3H_6
(B) CH_2 and C_2H_2
(C) CH_2 and C_3H_9
(D) CH and C_6H_6
(E) CH and CH_4

46. $$H_2O(\ell) \rightarrow H_2O(g)$$

Correct statements concerning the process above occurring at 100°C include which of the following?

I. The vaporization process is endothermic.
II. The randomness of the system increases during vaporization.
III. The average potential energy of the vapor molecules is greater than that of the liquid molecules.

(A) I only
(B) III only
(C) I and III only
(D) II and III only
(E) I, II, and III

47. Which of the following statements about the halogens is true?

(A) They all form X^- ions.
(B) They have the lowest ionization (potential) energies of the elements in their respective periods.
(C) They are all solids.
(D) They are among the best reducing agents.
(E) They all react with water to form basic solutions.

GO ON TO THE NEXT PAGE

48. On the basis of the acid dissociation constants given below, it can be determined that which of the following is the weakest acid?

(A)	$HCN \rightleftharpoons H^+ + CN^-$	$K = 4 \times 10^{-10}$
(B)	$HC_2H_3O_2 \leftrightharpoons H^+ + C_2H_3O_2^-$	$K = 1.8 \times 10^{-5}$
(C)	$HF \leftrightharpoons H^+ + F^-$	$K = 6.7 \times 10^{-4}$
(D)	$H_3PO_4 \leftrightharpoons H^+ + H_2PO_4^-$	$K = 7.1 \times 10^{-3}$
(E)	$H_2CO_3 \leftrightharpoons H^+ + HCO_3^-$	$K = 4.4 \times 10^{-7}$

49. The structure of CH_4, the methane molecule, is best described as

(A) linear (B) trigonal (C) planar
(D) square (E) tetrahedral

50. A drying agent is not suitable for removing the water vapor from a sample of gas with which the drying agent reacts chemically. Which of the following gases can properly be dried by means of NaOH ?

(A) CO_2 (B) SO_2 (C) HBr
(D) O_2 (E) HCl

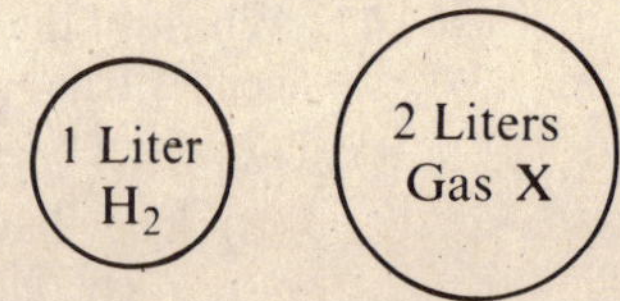

51. Both of the gas samples represented above are at the same temperature and pressure. The mass of H_2 in the one-liter container is 0.20 gram. The mass of X in the two-liter container is 8 grams. The molecular weight of X is

(A) 10 (B) 20 (C) 40 (D) 60 (E) 80

GO ON TO THE NEXT PAGE

Questions 52-54 pertain to the reaction represented by the following equation:

$$2\ NO(g) + O_2(g) \rightleftharpoons 2\ NO_2(g) + 150 \text{ kilojoules}$$

52. The equilibrium constant for the reaction is given by the expression

(A) $\frac{[2\ NO_2]}{[2\ NO][O_2]}$

(B) $\frac{[NO]^2[O_2]}{[NO_2]^2}$

(C) $\frac{[2\ NO_2]}{[2\ NO] + [O_2]}$

(D) $\frac{[NO_2]^2}{[NO]^2[O_2]}$

(E) $\frac{[2\ NO][O_2]}{[2\ NO_2]}$

53. Suppose that 0.80 mole of NO is converted to NO_2. The amount of heat evolved would be

(A) 150 kJ
(B) 130 kJ
(C) 80. kJ
(D) 60. kJ
(E) 30. kJ

54. If 60 grams of NO and 60 grams of O_2 are available, what is the maximum amount of NO_2 that can be produced? (Molecular weights: NO = 30., NO_2 = 46)

(A) 46 grams
(B) 60. grams
(C) 92 grams
(D) 120 grams
(E) 180 grams

55. Which of the following oxides dissolves in water to form a strongly acidic solution?

(A) Na_2O
(B) CaO
(C) Al_2O_3
(D) ZnO
(E) SO_3

56. At 23° C, 200 milliliters of an ideal gas exerts a pressure of 750 millimeters of mercury. The volume of the gas at 0° C and 760 millimeters of mercury is found from which of the following expressions?

(A) $200 \times \frac{760}{750} \times \frac{273}{296}$ ml

(B) $200 \times \frac{750}{760} \times \frac{0}{23}$ ml

(C) $200 \times \frac{760}{750} \times \frac{23}{0}$ ml

(D) $200 \times \frac{760}{750} \times \frac{296}{273}$ ml

(E) $200 \times \frac{750}{760} \times \frac{273}{296}$ ml

GO ON TO THE NEXT PAGE

57. $MnO_4^- + 5\,Fe^{2+} + 8\,H^+ \rightarrow Mn^{2+} + 5\,Fe^{3+} + 4\,H_2O(\ell)$

In the equation for the reaction represented above, which of the following indicates the reduction that takes place?

(A) $Fe^{2+} + e^- \rightarrow Fe^{3+}$
(B) $Fe^{3+} + e^- \rightarrow Fe^{2+}$
(C) $Fe^{2+} \rightarrow Fe^{3+} + e^-$
(D) $2\,H^+ + O^{2-} \rightarrow H_2O(\ell) + 2\,e^-$
(E) $MnO_4^- + 8\,H^+ + 5\,e^- \rightarrow Mn^{2+} + 4\,H_2O(\ell)$

Electron removed	1st Electron	2nd Electron	3rd Electron	4th Electron	5th Electron	6th Electron
Ionization energy (potential), kilojoules per mole	733	1,450	7,730	10,538	13,618	18,101

58. The ionization energies (potentials) for the removal of different electrons from an atom of an element in the gas phase are shown above. An atom of this element is most likely to form an ion that has a charge of

(A) +1 (B) +2 (C) +3 (D) +4 (E) +5

59. Of the following ground state electron configurations, the one that represents the element of lowest first ionization energy (potential) is

(A) $1s^2\,2s^2\,2p^5$
(B) $1s^2\,2s^2\,2p^6$
(C) $1s^2\,2s^2\,2p^6\,3s^1$
(D) $1s^2\,2s^2\,2p^6\,3s^2$
(E) $1s^2\,2s^2\,2p^6\,3s^2\,3p^1$

60. A 250-gram sample of a hydrated salt was heated at 110° C until all water was driven off. The remaining solid weighed 160 grams. From these data, the percent of water by weight in the original sample can be correctly calculated as

(A) $\frac{160}{340} \times 100$ (B) $\frac{90}{340} \times 100$ (C) $\frac{160}{250} \times 100$

(D) $\frac{90}{250} \times 100$ (E) $\frac{90}{160} \times 100$

GO ON TO THE NEXT PAGE

61. A 0.001-molar solution of which of the following has a hydrogen ion concentration of 1×10^{-3} molar?

(A) $HC_2H_3O_2$
(B) HCl
(C) $NaHCO_3$
(D) NaH
(E) NaOH

62. $$H_2O(\ell) + S^{2-} \rightleftharpoons HS^- + OH^-$$

In the equation for the reaction represented above, the species acting as acids (proton donors) are

(A) $H_2O(\ell)$ and OH^-
(B) $H_2O(\ell)$ and HS^-
(C) OH^- and HS^-
(D) HS^- and S^{2-}
(E) $H_2O(\ell)$ and S^{2-}

63. One species of element X has an atomic number of 9 and a mass number of 19; one species of element Y has an atomic number of 10 and a mass number of 19. Which of the following statements about these two species is true?

(A) They are isotopes.
(B) They are isomers.
(C) They are isoelectronic.
(D) They contain the same number of neutrons in their atoms.
(E) They contain the same total number of protons plus neutrons in their atoms.

64. Some solid crystalline compounds slowly change to the gaseous state when left at room temperature in an open container. Which of the following is true about this phenomenon?

(A) It is accompanied by an increase in temperature.
(B) It is accompanied by an absorption of heat by the solid.
(C) It is the result of a chemical reaction with air.
(D) It is best described as fusion.
(E) It is observed only with ice.

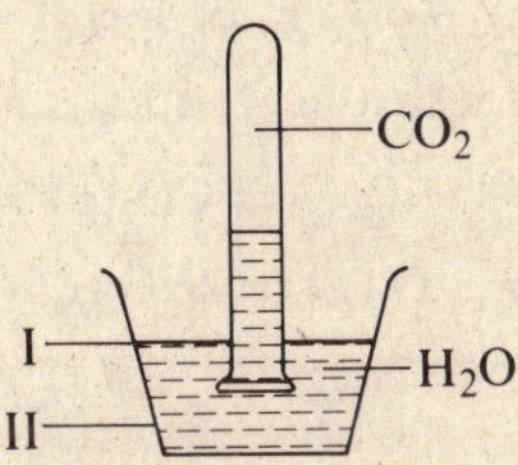

65. A test tube of carbon dioxide gas is inverted over water, as shown above. The gas becomes more soluble in the water if the

(A) water is heated
(B) gas is heated
(C) lip of the tube is moved to level I
(D) lip of the tube is moved to level II
(E) amount of gas in the tube is reduced

GO ON TO THE NEXT PAGE

66. A molecule of which of the following compounds contains a double bond?

    (A) C_3H_8
    (B) C_2H_6
    (C) C_2H_4
    (D) C_2H_6O
    (E) CH_4

67. Each of the following systems is at equilibrium in a closed container. A decrease in the total volume of each container increases the number of moles of product(s) for which system?

    (A) $Fe_3O_4(s) + 4H_2(g) \rightleftharpoons 3Fe(s) + 4H_2O(g)$

    (B) $H_2(g) + Cl_2(g) \rightleftharpoons 2HCl(g)$

    (C) $CO(g) + H_2O(g) \rightleftharpoons CO_2(g) + H_2(g)$

    (D) $2NO(g) + O_2(g) \rightleftharpoons 2NO_2(g)$

    (E) $2NH_3(g) \rightleftharpoons N_2(g) + 3H_2(g)$

68. $Cl_2(g) + 2\,Br^-\ \text{(excess)} \rightarrow$

    When 1 mole of chlorine gas reacts completely with excess KBr solution, as shown above, the products obtained are

    (A) 1 mole of Cl^- ions and 1 mole of Br
    (B) 1 mole of Cl^- ions and 2 moles of Br
    (C) 1 mole of Cl^- ions and 1 mole of Br_2
    (D) 2 moles of Cl^- ions and 1 mole of Br_2
    (E) 2 moles of Cl^- ions and 2 moles of Br_2

69. All of the following statements about ammonia, NH_3, are true EXCEPT:

    (A) It has a characteristic odor.
    (B) It is a liquid at room temperature.
    (C) It is readily soluble in water.
    (D) Its aqueous solution has a pH above 7.
    (E) It reacts readily with acids.

STOP

IF YOU FINISH BEFORE TIME IS CALLED, YOU MAY CHECK YOUR WORK ON THIS TEST ONLY. DO NOT TURN TO ANY OTHER TEST IN THIS BOOK.

How to Score the SAT II: Chemistry Subject Test

When you take the Chemistry Subject Test, your answer sheet will be "read" by a scanning machine that will record your response to each question. Then a computer will compare your answers with the correct answers and produce your raw score. You get one point for each correct answer. For each wrong answer, one-fourth of a point is subtracted to correct for random guessing. Questions you omit are not counted. Your raw score is converted to a College Board scaled score that is reported to you and to the colleges you specify. After you have taken the practice test, you can get an idea of what your score might be by following the instructions in the next two sections.

FINDING YOUR RAW TEST SCORE

Step 1: Table A lists the correct answers for all the questions on the SAT II: Chemistry Subject Test that is reproduced in this book. It also serves as a worksheet for you to calculate your raw score.

- Compare your answers with those given in the table.
- Put a check in the column marked "Right" if your answer is correct.
- Put a check in the column marked "Wrong" if your answer is incorrect.
- Leave both columns blank if you omitted the question.

Step 2: Count the number of right answers and enter the total here: .... ________

Step 3: Count the number of wrong answers and enter the total here: .... ________

Step 4: Divide the number of wrong answers by 4 and enter the result here: .... ________

Step 5: Subtract the result obtained in Step 4 from the total you obtained in Step 2. Enter the result here: .... ________

Step 6: Round the number obtained in Step 5 to the nearest whole number. Enter the result here: .... ________

The number you obtained in Step 6 is your raw test score.

TABLE A

Answers to the SAT II: Chemistry Subject Test, Form 3KAC2 reformatted, and Percentage of Students Answering Each Question Correctly

Question Number	Correct Answer	Right	Wrong	Percentage of Students Answering the Question Correctly*	Question Number	Correct Answer	Right	Wrong	Percentage of Students Answering the Question Correctly*
1	D			76	46	E			39
2	C			67	47	A			45
3	A			78	48	A			51
4	B			89	49	E			74
5	E			75	50	D			22
6	E			75	51	C			36
7	C			54	52	D			41
8	C			48	53	D			38
9	C			72	54	C			48
10	A			74	55	E			49
11	C			64	56	E			37
12	E			71	57	E			24
13	C			38	58	B			29
14	B			50	59	C			30
15	E			71	60	D			47
16	A			55	61	B			31
17	B			56	62	B			31
18	A			43	63	E			47
19	D			82	64	B			32
20	D			32	65	D			21
21	A			73	66	C			43
22	B			54	67	D			16
23	E			46	68	D			29
24	B			57	69	B			18
25	A			64					
26	B			69	101	T,T			71
27	B			79	102	T,T,CE			46
28	E			75	103	F,T			44
29	B			48	104	T,T,CE			58
30	B			53	105	T,T,CE			56
31	B			80	106	T,T,CE			47
32	A			45	107	T,F			54
33	D			28	108	T,F			43
34	B			66	109	T,T,CE			53
35	B			40	110	F,T			41
36	D			45	111	T,T			43
37	E			51	112	F,T			28
38	E			47	113	T,T			65
39	E			60	114	T,T,CE			53
40	D			69	115	F,F			42
41	C			53	116	F,T			43
42	A			58					
43	B			74					
44	B			39					
45	D			68					

*These percentages are based on an analysis of the answer sheets for a random sample of 3,285 students who took Form 3KAC2 in January 1988 and whose mean score was 546. They may be used as an indication of the relative difficulty of a particular question. Each percentage may also be used to predict the likelihood that a typical SAT II: Chemistry Subject Test candidate will answer correctly that question on this edition of this test.

Finding Your College Board Scaled Score

When you take SAT II: Subject Tests, the scores sent to the colleges you specify are reported on the College Board scale, which ranges from 200 to 800. You can convert your practice test score to a scaled score by using Table B. To find your scaled score, locate your raw score in the left-hand column of Table B; the corresponding score in the right-hand column is your College Board scaled score. For example, a raw score of 60 on this particular edition of the SAT II: Chemistry Subject Test corresponds to a College Board scaled score of about 680.

Raw scores are converted to scaled scores to ensure that a score earned on any edition of a particular Subject Test is comparable to the same scaled score earned on any other edition of the same Subject Test. Because some editions of tests may be slightly easier or more difficult than others, College Board scaled scores are adjusted so that they indicate the same level of performance regardless of the edition of the test taken and the ability of the group that takes it. Thus, for example, a score of 400 on one edition of a test taken at a particular administration indicates the same level of achievement as a score of 400 on a different edition of the test taken at a different administration.

When you take the SAT II: Subject Tests during a national administration, your score is likely to differ somewhat from the scores you obtain on the tests in this book. People perform at different levels at different times for reasons unrelated to the tests themselves. The precision of any test is also limited because it represents only a sample of all the possible questions that could be asked.

TABLE B

Score Conversion Table
Chemistry Subject Test, Form 3KAC2

Raw Score	College Board Scaled Score	Raw Score	College Board Scaled Score
85	800	30	500
84	800	29	500
83	800	28	490
82	800	27	490
81	800	26	480
80	800	25	470
79	800	24	470
78	790	23	460
77	780	22	460
76	780	21	450
75	770	20	440
74	770	19	440
73	760	18	430
72	750	17	430
71	750	16	420
70	740	15	410
69	740	14	410
68	730	13	400
67	730	12	400
66	720	11	390
65	710	10	380
64	710	9	380
63	700	8	370
62	700	7	370
61	690	6	360
60	680	5	350
59	680	4	350
58	670	3	340
57	670	2	340
56	660	1	330
55	650	0	320
54	650	−1	320
53	640	−2	310
52	640	−3	310
51	630	−4	300
50	620	−5	290
49	620	−6	290
48	610	−7	280
47	610	−8	280
46	600	−9	270
45	590	−10	260
44	590	−11	260
43	580	−12	250
42	580	−13	250
41	570	−14	240
40	560	−15	230
39	560	−16	230
38	550	−17	220
37	550	−18	220
36	540	−19	210
35	530	−20 through −21	200
34	530		
33	520		
32	520		
31	510		

Reviewing Your Test Performance

After you have scored your test, you should take some time to consider the following points in relation to your performance on the test.

- *Did you run out of time before you reached the end of the test?*

  If you did, you may want to consider pacing yourself better. For example, you may have spent too much time working on one or two difficult questions. A better approach might have been to continue the test and return to those questions after you had attempted to answer the remaining questions on the test.

- *Did you take a long time reading the directions for the test?*

  The directions in this test are the same as those in the Chemistry Subject Tests now being administered. You will save time when you read the directions on the test day if you become thoroughly familiar with them in advance.

- *How did you handle questions you were unsure of?*

  If you were able to eliminate one or more of the answer choices and you guessed from the remaining choices, then your approach probably worked to your advantage. On the other hand, omitting questions about which you have some knowledge or guessing answers haphazardly would probably be a mistake.

- *How difficult were the questions for you compared with other students who took the test?*

  By referring to Table A, you can find out how difficult each question was for the group of students who took this test. The right-hand column in the table tells you what percentage of this group answered the question correctly. A question that was answered correctly by almost everyone in the group is obviously an easy question. Question 4, for example, was answered correctly by 89 percent of the students in the sample. On the other hand, question 69 was answered correctly by only 18 percent.

  It is important to remember that these percentages are based on only one particular group of students; had this edition of the test been given to other groups of students at that time, the percentages would probably have been different.

  If you find that you missed several questions that would be considered easy, you may want to review those questions carefully. They may cover some aspect of the subject that you need to review. Perhaps you misunderstood the directions for one part of the test or you thought the questions were so easy that you did not spend as much time on them as you might have.

The SAT II: Physics Subject Test

The SAT II: Physics Subject Test consists of 75 multiple-choice questions. The test assumes that you have had a one-year introductory course in physics and that the course content was at a level suitable for college preparation. Questions appearing in the test have been tried out on college students who are taking an introductory physics course. The questions have also been approved by a committee of high school and college physics teachers appointed by the College Board.

The approximate percentages of the questions on each major topic in the Physics Subject Test are listed in the chart titled "Content of the Test." The test emphasizes the topics that are covered in most high school courses. However, because high school courses differ, both in the percentage of time devoted to each major topic and in the specific subtopics covered, you may encounter questions on topics with which you are not familiar.

In any high school physics course, more material is usually covered and in more detail than can be covered in any single SAT II: Physics Subject Test. So, even if high school physics curriculums were alike, the questions in any particular test edition could be only a sample of all the questions that might be asked. The questions in every edition of the test, however, test knowledge and abilities that might reasonably be expected of high school physics students intending to go to college.

The test is not based on any one textbook or instructional approach but concentrates on the common core of material found in most texts. You should be able to recall and understand the major concepts of physics and to apply physical principles to solve specific problems. You also should be able to organize and interpret results obtained by observation and experimentation and to draw conclusions or make inferences from experimental data. Laboratory experience is a significant factor in developing reasoning and problem-solving skills. Although laboratory skills can be tested only in a limited way in a standardized test, there are occasional questions that ask you to interpret laboratory data. Reasonable laboratory experience is an asset in helping you prepare for the SAT II: Physics Subject Test.

The Physics Subject Test assumes that you understand simple algebraic, trigonometric, and graphical relationships and the concepts of ratio and proportion, and that you can apply these concepts to word problems.

You will *not* be allowed to use an electronic calculator during the test. Numerical calculations are not emphasized and are limited to simple arithmetic. In this test, metric units predominate.

Content of the Test

Topics Covered	Approximate Percentage of Test
I. Mechanics	35-40
A. Kinematics (such as velocity, acceleration, motion in one dimension, and motion of projectiles)	
B. Dynamics (such as force, Newton's laws, and statics)	
C. Energy and Momentum (such as potential and kinetic energy, work, power, impulse, and conservation laws)	
D. Circular Motion and Rotation (such as uniform circular motion, centripetal force, torque, and angular momentum)	
E. Vibrations (such as simple harmonic motion, mass on a spring, and the simple pendulum)	
F. Gravity (such as the law of gravitation and orbits)	
II. Electricity and Magnetism	20-25
A. Electric Fields, Forces, and Potentials (such as Coulomb's law, induced charge, field and potential of groups of point charges, and charged particles in electric fields)	
B. Magnetic Fields and Forces (such as permanent magnets, fields caused by currents, and particles in magnetic fields)	
C. Electromagnetic Induction (such as induced currents and fields)	
D. Circuits and Circuit Elements (such as capacitance, resistance, Ohm's law, Joule's law, and direct-current circuits with resistors and capacitors)	

Topics Covered *(continued)*	Approximate Percentage of Test
III. Waves	19-22
A. General Wave Properties (such as wave speed, frequency, wavelength, and Doppler effect)	
B. Reflection and Refraction (such as Snell's law and changes in wavelength and speed)	
C. Interference, Diffraction, and Polarization (such as single-slit diffraction, double-slit interference, and standing wave patterns)	
D. Ray Optics (such as image formation in mirrors and lenses)	
IV. Heat, Kinetic Theory, and Thermodynamics	7-11
A. Thermal Properties (such as mechanical equivalent of heat, temperature, specific and latent heats, thermal expansion, and heat transfer)	
B. Gases and Kinetic Theory (such as ideal gas law from molecular properties)	
C. Laws of Thermodynamics (such as first and second laws, internal energy, and heat engine efficiency)	
V. Modern Physics	7-11
A. Quantum Phenomena (such as photons, photoelectric effect, and the uncertainty principle)	
B. Atomic (such as the Rutherford and Bohr models, atomic energy levels, and atomic spectra)	
C. Nuclear and Particle Physics (such as radioactivity and nuclear or particle reactions)	
D. Relativity (such as mass-energy equivalence and limiting velocity)	
E. Contemporary Physics (such as astrophysics, biophysics, and superconductivity)	
VI. Miscellaneous (such as measurement, math skills, laboratory skills, history of physics, and questions of a general nature that overlap several major topics)	2-4

Level of Concept Application	Approximate Percentage of Test
Recall (generally involves remembering and understanding concepts or information)	20-33
Single-concept problem (recall and use of a single physical relationship)	40-53
Multiple-concept problem (recall and use of two or more physical relationships that must be combined)	20-33

75 Questions: Time — 60 minutes

Questions Used in the Test

Classification Questions

Each set of classification questions begins with five lettered choices that you will use to answer all of the numbered questions in the set (see sample questions 1-4). In addition, there may be descriptive material that is relevant in answering the questions in the set. The choices may be words, phrases, sentences, graphs, pictures, equations, or data. The numbered questions themselves may also be any of these, or they may be given in the question format directly. To answer each numbered question, select the lettered choice that provides the most appropriate response. You should consider all of the lettered choices before answering a question. The directions for this type of question state specifically that a choice cannot be eliminated just because it is the correct answer to a previous question.

Because the same five choices are applicable to several questions, the classification questions usually require less reading than other types of multiple-choice questions. Therefore, classification questions provide a quick means, in terms of testing time, of determining how well you have mastered the topics represented. The set of questions may ask you to recall appropriate information, or the set may ask you to apply information to a specific situation or to translate information between different forms (descriptive, graphical, mathematical). Thus, different types of abilities can be tested by this type of question.

Directions: Each set of lettered choices below refers to the numbered questions or statements immediately following it. Select the one lettered choice that best answers each question or best fits each statement and then fill in the corresponding oval on the answer sheet. A choice may be used once, more than once, or not at all in each set.

Questions 1-2

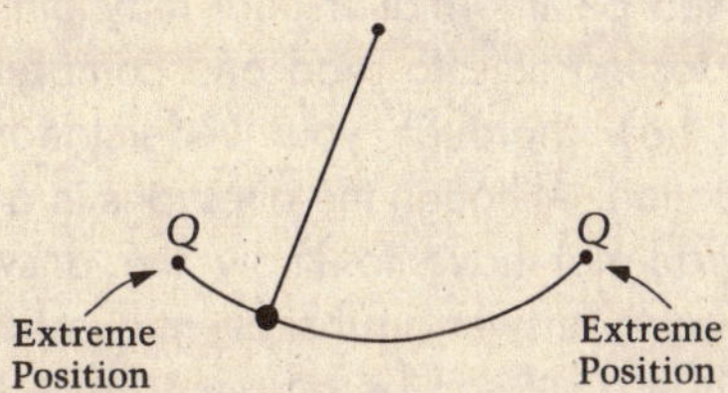

A small sphere attached to the end of a string swings as a simple pendulum. The sphere moves along the arc shown above. Consider the following properties of the sphere.

(A) Acceleration
(B) Kinetic energy
(C) Mass
(D) Potential energy
(E) Velocity

1. **Which property remains constant throughout the motion of the sphere?**
2. **Which property goes to zero and changes direction at each extreme position Q?**

To answer question 1, you may know that in classical mechanics mass is a fundamental property of an object that does not depend on the position or velocity of the object. Thus the answer is (C). Alternately, you may realize that, since a pendulum during its motion repeatedly speeds up, slows down, and changes direction, the sphere's velocity, kinetic energy, and acceleration must also change. Also, since the height of the sphere varies, so must its potential energy. Thus you can also obtain the answer by the process of elimination.

To answer question 2, you must know some specific details about the motion of the pendulum. At each extreme position Q, the velocity and the kinetic energy (which is proportional to the square of the speed) are both zero, but kinetic energy has magnitude only and thus no direction to change. Velocity does have direction, and in this case the velocity of the sphere is directed away from the center, or equilibrium position, just before the sphere reaches Q, but directed toward the center just after leaving Q. The velocity changes direction at each point Q, so the answer is (E). The only other choice that has direction is acceleration, but acceleration has its maximum magnitude at each point Q and is directed toward the center, both shortly before and shortly after the sphere is at Q.

Questions 3-4 relate to the following graphs of the net force *F* on a body *versus* time *t*, for the body in straight-line motion in different situations.

(A)

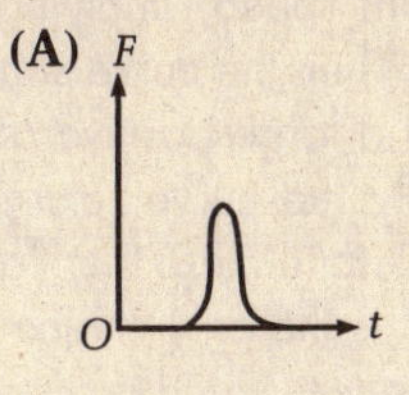

(B)

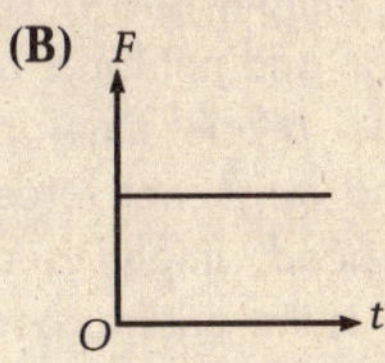

(C)

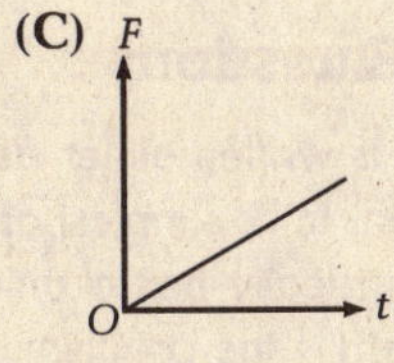

(D)

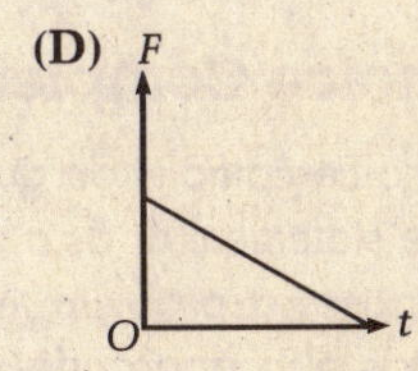

(E)

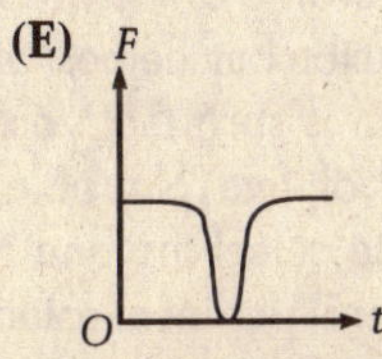

For each of the following speed *v versus* time *t* graphs for the body, choose the graph above with which it is consistent.

3.

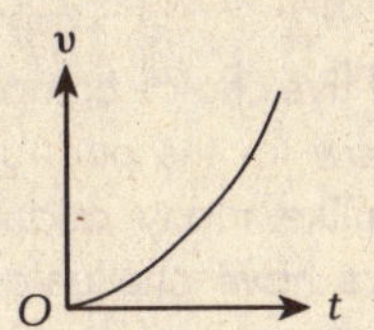

4.

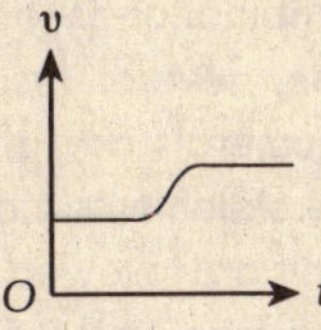

Questions 3 and 4 test the application of physical principles to information presented in graphical form. In each of these questions two concepts are involved. From Newton's second law we know that the net force on a body is equal to the body's acceleration multiplied by the body's mass, a constant. Thus graphs of acceleration *versus* time must have the same shape as the graphs of force *versus* time that are given in the options. We must also know that at a particular time the acceleration of a body in its direction of motion is equal to the rate of change of its speed, as determined by the slope of the speed v *versus* time t graph at that particular time. In question 3, the slope of the graph continually increases with increasing t; therefore, the body's acceleration and consequently the net force on the body must also increase continually. The only graph among the choices that shows this relationship is graph (C), the answer. In question 4, the graph initially shows a constant speed, implying an acceleration and net force of zero. Then the curve sharply increases for a brief time, implying a large positive acceleration and large net force. Finally the curve returns to constant speed, implying a return to a zero net force. Graph (A) is the answer because it is the only choice that shows a force that varies in this manner.

Five-Choice Completion Questions

The five-choice completion question is written either as an incomplete statement or as a question. In its simplest application, it poses a problem that intrinsically has a unique solution. It is also appropriate when: (1) the problem presented is clearly delineated by the wording of the question so that you choose not a universal solution but the best of the five offered solutions; (2) the problem is such that you are required to evaluate the relevance of five plausible, or scientifically accurate, choices and to select the one most pertinent; or (3) the problem has several pertinent solutions and you are required to select the one that is *inappropriate* or *not* correct from among the five choices presented. Questions of this latter type (see sample question 6) will normally contain a word in capital letters such as NOT, EXCEPT, or LEAST.

A special type of five-choice completion question is used in some tests to allow for the possibility of more than one correct answer. Unlike many quantitative problems that must by their nature have one unique solution, situations do arise in which there may be more than one correct response. In such situations, you should evaluate each response independently of the others in order to select the most appropriate combination (see sample question 7). In questions of this type, several (usually three) statements labeled by Roman numerals are given with the question. One or more of these statements may correctly answer the question. The statements are followed by five lettered choices, with each choice consisting of some combination of the Roman numerals that label the statements. You must select from among the five lettered choices the one that gives the combination of statements that best answers the question. In the test, questions of this type are intermixed among the more standard five-choice completion questions.

The five-choice completion question also tests problem-solving skills. With this type of question, you may be asked to convert the information given in a word problem into graphical forms or to select and apply the mathematical relationship necessary to solve the scientific problem. Alternatively, you may be asked to interpret experimental data, graphs, or mathematical expressions. Thus, the five-choice completion question can be adapted to test several kinds of abilities.

When the experimental data or other scientific problems to be analyzed are comparatively long, it is often convenient to organize several five-choice completion questions into sets, with each question in the set relating to the same common material that precedes the set (see sample questions 8-9). This practice allows you to respond to several questions based on information that may otherwise take considerable testing time to read and comprehend. Such sets also test how thorough your understanding is of a particular situation. Although the questions in a set may be related, you do not have to know the answer to one question in a set to answer a subsequent question correctly. Each question in a set can be answered directly from the common material given for the entire set.

Directions: Each of the questions or incomplete statements below is followed by five suggested answers or completions. Select the one that is best in each case and then fill in the corresponding oval on the answer sheet.

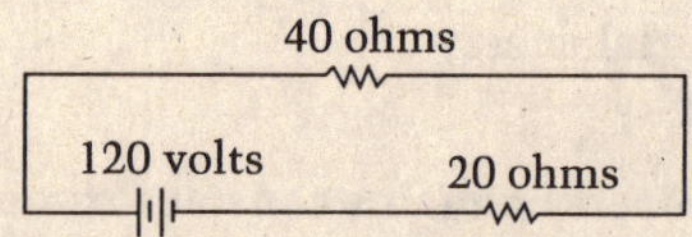

5. If the internal resistance of the 120-volt battery in the circuit shown above is negligible, the current in the wire is

(A) 0 A
(B) 2 A
(C) 3 A
(D) 6 A
(E) 9 A

In question 5, you must apply two concepts to solve the problem. First, you must recognize that the two resistors are connected in series and thus are equivalent to a single resistor whose resistance is 60 ohms, the sum of the two component resistances. Next, applying Ohm's law, you will find that the current is given by the potential difference divided by this equivalent resistance. Thus, the answer is $\frac{120 \text{ volts}}{60 \text{ ohms}}$, which equals 2 amperes. Therefore, (B) is the answer.

6. **All of the following are vector quantities EXCEPT**

   (A) **force**
   (B) **velocity**
   (C) **acceleration**
   (D) **power**
   (E) **momentum**

Question 6 is a straightforward question that tests your knowledge of vector and scalar quantities. A vector quantity is one that has both magnitude and direction. All five quantities have a magnitude associated with them, but only quantities (A), (B), (C), and (E) also have a direction. Power, a rate of change of energy, is not a vector quantity, so the answer is (D).

7. **A ball is thrown vertically upward. Air resistance is negligible. After leaving the hand, the acceleration of the ball is downward under which of the following conditions?**

   I. **On the way up**
   II. **On the way down**
   III. **At the top of its rise**

   (A) **I only**
   (B) **III only**
   (C) **I and II only**
   (D) **II and III only**
   (E) **I, II, and III**

In question 7, one or several of the phrases represented by the Roman numerals may be correct answers to the question. One must evaluate each in turn. When the ball is on the way up, its speed is decreasing so the acceleration of the ball must be directed in the direction opposite to the ball's velocity. Since the velocity is upward, the acceleration must be downward, making I correct. When the ball is on the way down, its speed is increasing, so its acceleration must be directed in the same direction as its velocity, which is downward. So II is also correct. Finally, at the top of the rise, the ball has an instantaneous speed of zero, but its velocity is changing from upward to downward, implying a downward acceleration and making III correct also. A simpler analysis would be to realize that in all three cases, the ball is acted on by the downward force of gravity and no other forces. By Newton's second law, the acceleration must be in the direction of the net force, so it must be downward in all three cases. Since the phrases in I, II, and III are each correct answers to the question, the correct response is (E).

Questions 8-9

In the following graph, the speed of a small object as it moves along a horizontal straight line is plotted against time.

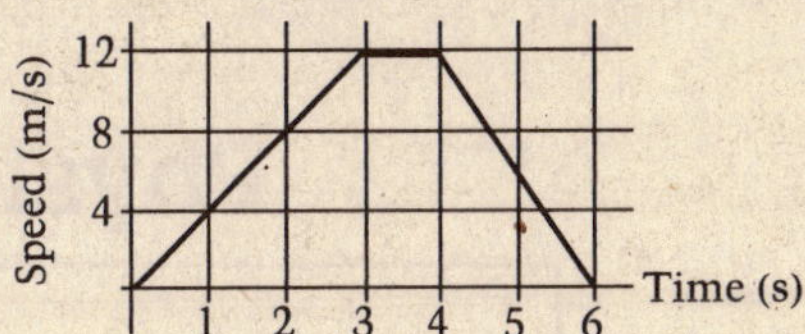

8. **The magnitude of the acceleration of the object during the first 3 seconds is**

   (A) **3 m/s^2**
   (B) **4 m/s^2**
   (C) **6 m/s^2**
   (D) **12 m/s^2**
   (E) **36 m/s^2**

9. **The average speed of the object during the first 4 seconds is**

   (A) **1.9 m/s**
   (B) **3.0 m/s**
   (C) **4.0 m/s**
   (D) **6.0 m/s**
   (E) **7.5 m/s**

Questions 8 and 9 are a set of questions, both based on the graph provided. To answer question 8, you need to know that the magnitude of the acceleration is equal to the magnitude of the slope of a graph of speed *versus* time. In this situation, from time = 0 to time = 3 seconds, the graph has a constant slope of $\frac{12 \text{ m/s}}{3 \text{ s}} = 4 \text{ m/s}^2$, which is the magnitude of the acceleration. So the answer is (B).

The average speed of an object during a certain time is equal to the total distance traveled by the object during that time divided by the time. In question 9, the total distance traveled by the object during the first 4 seconds is equal to the area under the graph from time = 0 to time = 4 seconds. This area is $\frac{1}{2}(3 \text{ s})(12 \text{ m/s}) + (1 \text{ s})(12 \text{ m/s}) = 18 \text{ m} + 12 \text{ m} = 30 \text{ m}$. The average speed is therefore $\frac{30 \text{ m}}{4 \text{ s}} = 7.5 \text{ m/s}$, which is choice (E).

SAT II:

Physics Subject Test

The test that follows is representative of a typical SAT II: Physics Subject Test. It has already been administered. So that you may have an idea of what the national test administration will be like, try to take the test in this book under conditions as close as possible to those of the nationally administered test. It will probably help if you do the following.

- Set aside an hour for the test when you will not be interrupted, so that you can complete all of it in one sitting.
- Sit at a desk with no other papers or books. You can't take a calculator, books, or notes into the test room.
- Have a kitchen timer or clock in front of you for timing yourself.
- Tear out an answer sheet from the back of this book and fill it in just as you would on the day of the test. You can use one answer sheet for as many as three Subject Tests.
- Read the instructions that precede the test. When you take the test, you will be asked to read them before you begin answering questions.
- After you finish the test, read the sections on "How to Score the SAT II: Physics Subject Test" and "Reviewing Your Test Performance," which follow the test.

FORM 3OAC

PHYSICS TEST

The top portion of the section of the answer sheet that you will use in taking the Physics test must be filled in exactly as shown in the illustration below. Note carefully that you have to do all of the following on your answer sheet.

1. Print PHYSICS on the line under the words "Subject (print)."
2. In the shaded box labeled "Test Code" fill in four ovals:

   —Fill in oval 2 in the row labeled V.

   —Fill in oval 3 in the row labeled W.

   —Fill in oval 3 in the row labeled X.

   —Fill in oval C in the row labeled Y.

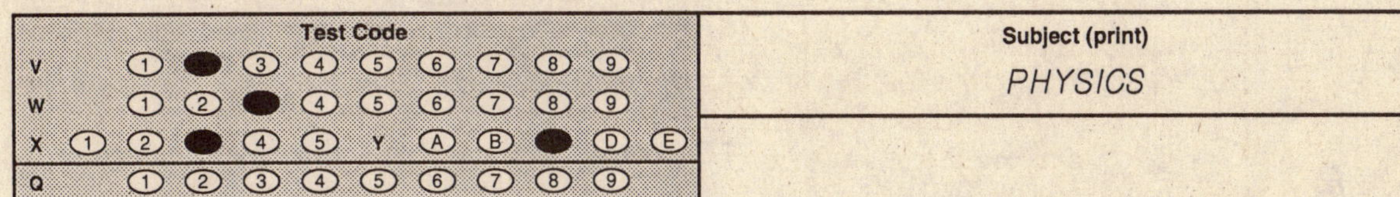

3. Please answer the three questions below by filling in the appropriate ovals in the row labeled Q on the answer sheet. <u>The information you provide is for statistical purposes only and will not affect your score on the test.</u>

<u>Question I</u>

How many semesters of physics have you taken in high school? (If you are taking physics this semester, count it as a full semester.) Fill in only <u>one</u> oval of ovals 1-3.

- One semester or less —Fill in oval 1.
- Two semesters —Fill in oval 2.
- Three semesters or more —Fill in oval 3.

<u>Question II</u>

Which of the following describe courses you have taken or are taking now? (Fill in <u>all</u> ovals that apply.)

- Algebra I or Elementary Algebra —Fill in oval 4.
- Geometry —Fill in oval 5.
- Algebra II or Intermediate Algebra —Fill in oval 6.
- Algebra III or Trigonometry or Precalculus —Fill in oval 7.

<u>Question III</u>

Are you currently taking Advanced Placement Physics? If you are, fill in oval 8.

Leave oval 9 blank.

When the supervisor gives the signal, turn the page and begin the Physics test. There are 100 numbered ovals on the answer sheet and 75 questions in the Physics test. Therefore, use only ovals 1 to 75 for recording your answers.

PHYSICS TEST

Part A

Directions: Each set of lettered choices below refers to the numbered questions immediately following it. Select the one lettered choice that best answers each question and then fill in the corresponding oval on the answer sheet. A choice may be used once, more than once, or not at all in each set.

Questions 1-2 relate to a point charge $+Q$ fixed in position, as shown below. Five points near the charge and in the plane of the page are shown.

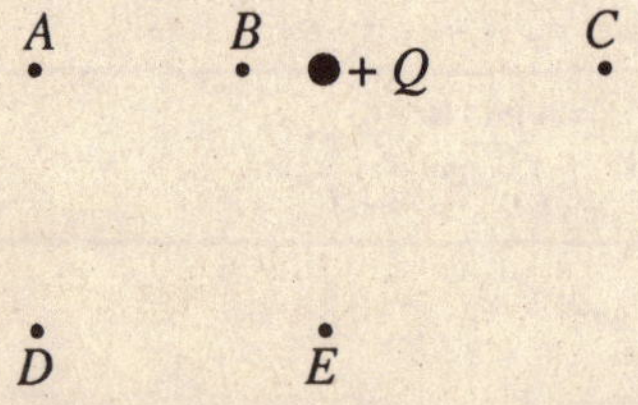

A • B • ●$+Q$ C •

D • E •

1. At which point will the magnitude of the electric field be least?

2. At which point will an electron experience a force directed toward the top of the page?

Questions 3-4 refer to the following particles.

(A) Alpha particle
(B) Beta particle
(C) Neutrino
(D) Muon
(E) Photon

3. Which particle is the nucleus of a helium atom?

4. Which particle has a rest mass between that of an electron and a proton?

GO ON TO THE NEXT PAGE

Questions 5-7

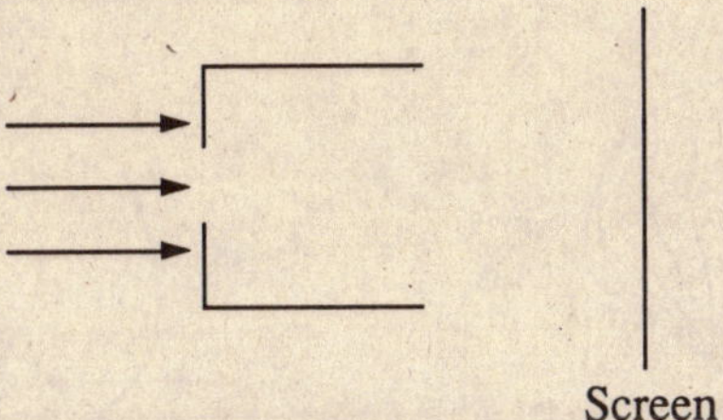

A beam of light is incident on a rectangular opening in the front of a box, as shown in the side view above. The back of the box is open. After passing through the box, the light is incident on a screen. The following devices may be in the box, positioned as shown.

(A) A convex lens

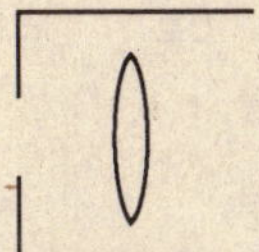

(B) A concave lens

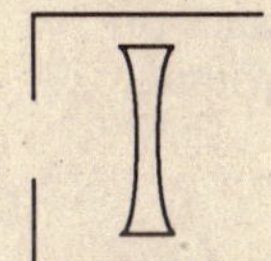

(C) A thick sheet of glass

(D) An opaque card with a very narrow slit

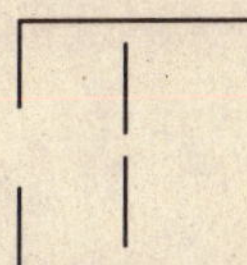

(E) A prism with vertex pointing downward

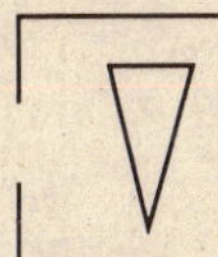

5. Which device could produce a tiny spot of light on the screen?

6. Which device could produce on the screen a rectangular area of light displaced downward from the position at which the light would be if the device were not there?

7. Which device could produce a diffraction pattern consisting of a central bright fringe with parallel secondary fringes that decrease in intensity with increasing distance from the center of the screen?

GO ON TO THE NEXT PAGE

Questions 8-9

Al and Betty are wearing identical massless parachutes, as shown above. Al has 3 times the mass of Betty. They descend to the ground, each with constant velocity.

(A) It is the same.
(B) It is 3 times greater.
(C) It is $\frac{1}{3}$ as great.
(D) It is greater, but the ratio cannot be calculated unless their velocities are known.
(E) It is less, but the ratio cannot be calculated unless their velocities are known.

8. How does the net force on Al compare to the net force on Betty?

9. How does the force of air resistance on Al and his parachute compare to the force of air resistance on Betty and her parachute?

Questions 10-11

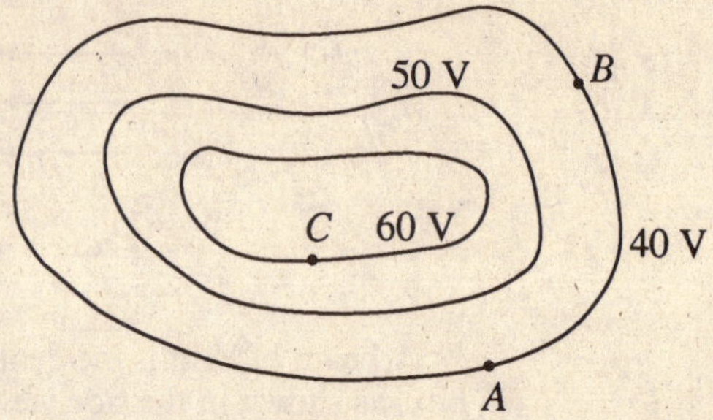

The diagram above shows lines of electrical equipotential in a region of space.

(A) Zero
(B) 20 J
(C) 40 J
(D) 60 J
(E) 80 J

10. What is the work done by an external force in moving a charge of +2 coulombs from *A* to *B*?

11. What is the work done by an external force in moving a charge of +2 coulombs from *A* to *C*?

GO ON TO THE NEXT PAGE

Questions 12-13 relate to various physical quantities that are functions of time.

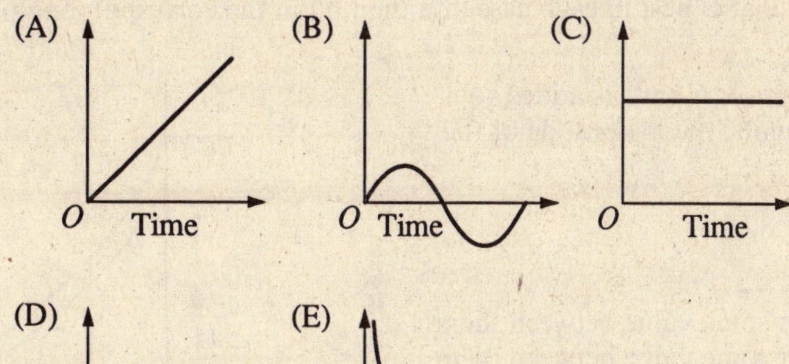

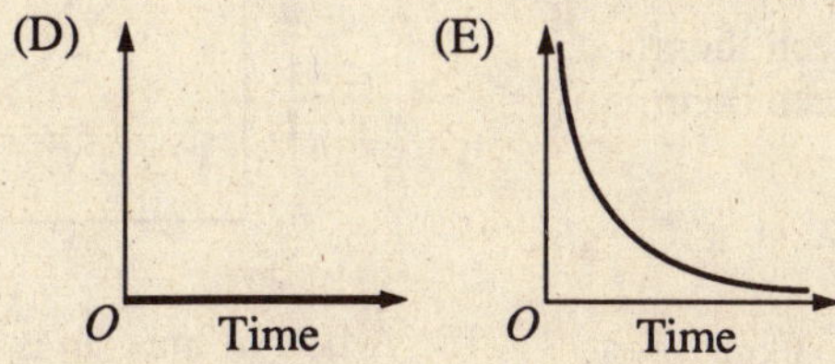

12. Which graph best represents the magnetic field established at the center of a coil by a steady current in the coil?

13. Which graph represents the total heat developed from time $t = 0$ by a resistor carrying a steady current?

GO ON TO THE NEXT PAGE

Part B

<u>Directions:</u> Each of the questions or incomplete statements below is followed by five suggested answers or completions. Select the one that is best in each case and then fill in the corresponding oval on the answer sheet.

14. When a vector of magnitude 6 units is added to a vector of magnitude 8 units, the magnitude of the resultant vector will be

(A) exactly 2 units
(B) exactly 10 units
(C) exactly 14 units
(D) 0 units, 10 units, or some value between them
(E) 2 units, 14 units, or some value between them

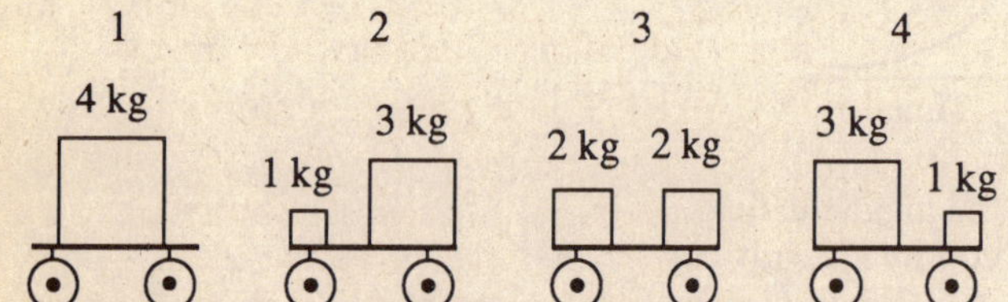

15. Each of the four identical carts shown above is loaded with a total mass of 4 kilograms. All of the carts are initially at rest on the same level surface. Forces of the same magnitude directed to the right act on each of the carts for the same length of time. If friction and air resistance are negligible, which cart will have the greatest velocity when the forces cease to act?

(A) Cart 1
(B) Cart 2
(C) Cart 3
(D) Cart 4
(E) All four carts will have the same velocity.

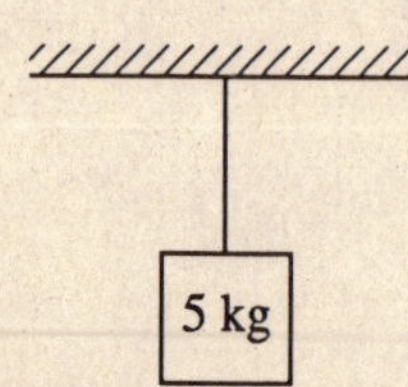

16. A 5-kilogram block is suspended by a cord from the ceiling, as shown above. The force exerted on the block by the cord is most nearly

(A) zero
(B) 25 N
(C) 50 N
(D) 100 N
(E) 200 N

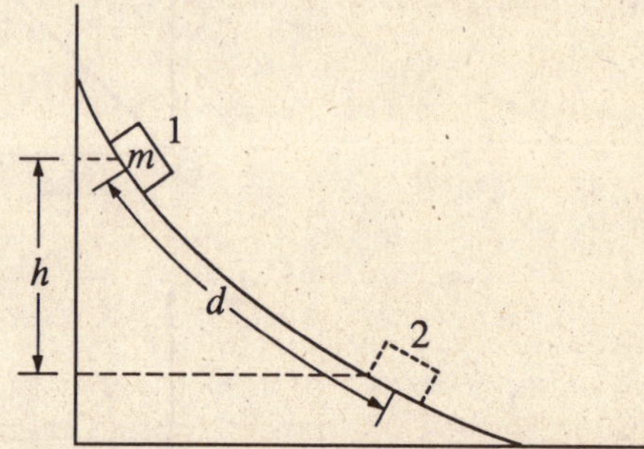

17. A box of mass m is released from rest at position 1 on the frictionless curved track shown above. It slides a distance d along the track in time t to reach position 2, dropping a vertical distance h. Let v and a be the instantaneous speed and instantaneous acceleration, respectively, of the box at position 2. Which of the following equations is valid for this situation?

(A) $h = vt$

(B) $h = \frac{1}{2}gt^2$

(C) $d = \frac{1}{2}at^2$

(D) $v^2 = 2ad$

(E) $mgh = \frac{1}{2}mv^2$

18. An object initially at rest "explodes" into two fragments of equal mass. Assume that no other forces affect the motion of the fragments during the explosion. Immediately after the explosion, all of the following statements are true EXCEPT:

(A) The fragments have equal speeds.
(B) The fragments have equal kinetic energies.
(C) The fragments move in opposite directions.
(D) The total momentum of the two fragments is zero.
(E) The total kinetic energy of the two fragments is zero.

GO ON TO THE NEXT PAGE

Questions 19-20

Ocean waves moving toward a beach have a speed of 10 meters per second and a frequency of 2 per second.

19. The wavelength of the waves is most nearly

(A) 0.2 m
(B) 0.5 m
(C) 5 m
(D) 10 m
(E) 20 m

20. The waves are observed by a child sitting in a rowboat offshore. Which of the following properties of the waves seen by the child would be greater when the boat is moving away from the beach than when the boat is stationary with respect to the beach?

I. Speed of the waves with respect to the boat
II. Frequency at which the boat encounters successive wave crests
III. Distance between adjacent wave crests

(A) I only
(B) III only
(C) I and II only
(D) II and III only
(E) I, II, and III

---

21. Appropriate magnetic field lines between two magnetic poles are shown in which of the following diagrams?

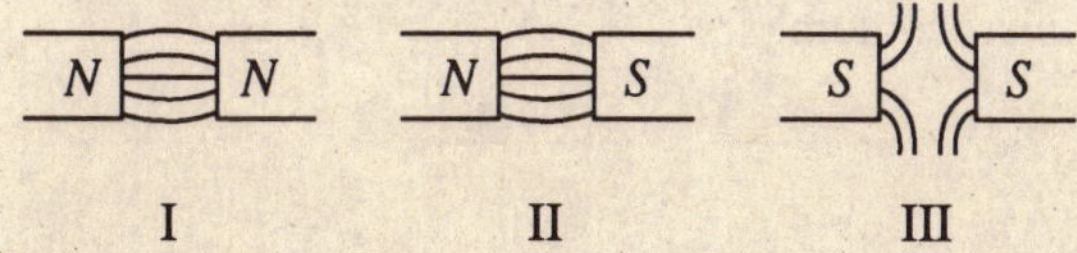

(A) I only
(B) II only
(C) III only
(D) I and II only
(E) II and III only

Q_1 P Q_2

22. A known positive charge is located at point P, as shown above, between two unknown charges, Q_1 and Q_2. P is closer to Q_2 than to Q_1. If the net electric force acting on the charge at P is zero, it may correctly be concluded that

(A) both Q_1 and Q_2 are positive
(B) both Q_1 and Q_2 are negative
(C) Q_1 and Q_2 have opposite signs
(D) Q_1 and Q_2 have the same sign, but the magnitude of Q_1 is greater than the magnitude of Q_2
(E) Q_1 and Q_2 have the same sign, but the magnitude of Q_1 is less than the magnitude of Q_2

23. A person can become sunburned outdoors on a cloudy day, but will not burn indoors behind a plate-glass window on a bright day for which of the following reasons?

(A) The glass absorbs ultraviolet light, but the clouds do not.
(B) The clouds absorb infrared light, but the glass does not.
(C) The clouds scatter light, but the glass does not.
(D) The speed of the light coming through the clouds is greater than that of the light coming through the glass.
(E) The wavelength of the light coming through the clouds is greater than that of the light coming through the glass.

24. Which of the following would be LEAST likely to result in the separation of white light into spectral colors?

(A) Diffraction
(B) Dispersion
(C) Reflection
(D) Interference
(E) Refraction

GO ON TO THE NEXT PAGE

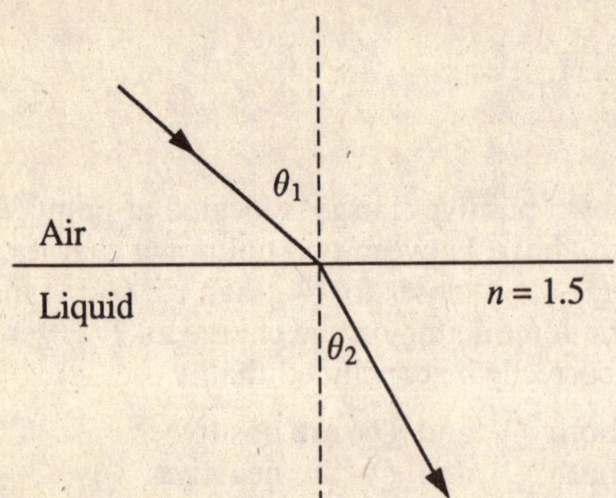

25. A ray of light passes from air into a liquid that has an index of refraction of 1.5, as shown above. If the sine of the angle of incidence θ_1 is 0.75, then the sine of the angle of refraction θ_2 is

    (A) 0.11
    (B) 0.25
    (C) 0.50
    (D) 0.67
    (E) 1.1

26. Which of the following electromagnetic waves may have a wavelength of 20 meters?

    (A) X-ray
    (B) Microwave
    (C) Radio wave
    (D) Gamma ray
    (E) Infrared ray

27. An experiment is performed to measure the specific heat of copper. A lump of copper is heated in an oven, then dropped into a beaker of water. To calculate the specific heat of copper, the experimenter must know or measure the value of all of the quantities below EXCEPT the

    (A) mass of the water
    (B) original temperatures of the copper and the water
    (C) final (equilibrium) temperature of the copper and the water
    (D) time taken to achieve equilibrium after the copper is dropped into the water
    (E) specific heat of the water

28. In a given process, 12 joules of heat is added to an ideal gas and the gas does 8 joules of work. Which of the following is true about the internal energy of the gas during this process?

    (A) It has increased by 20 joules.
    (B) It has increased by 4 joules.
    (C) It has not changed.
    (D) It has decreased by 4 joules.
    (E) It has decreased by 20 joules.

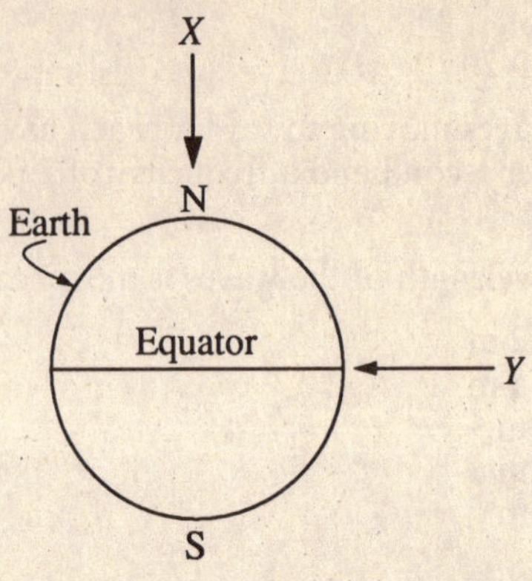

29. Cosmic ray protons in space headed toward one of the Earth's poles (direction *X* shown above) are only slightly deflected, whereas those headed toward the equator (direction *Y* shown above) are strongly deflected. The difference can be attributed to the

    (A) electrical storms that occur mainly in tropical regions
    (B) positive charge of the Earth
    (C) maximum strength of the Earth's magnetic field near the equator
    (D) greater intensity of the solar wind near the equator than near the poles
    (E) greater deflection of charged particles crossing magnetic field lines than of those moving along magnetic field lines

30. Two small conducting spheres are identical except that sphere *X* has a charge of −10 microcoulombs and sphere *Y* has a charge of +6 microcoulombs. After the spheres are brought in contact and then separated, what is the charge on each sphere, in microcoulombs?

	Sphere *X*	Sphere *Y*
(A)	−4	0
(B)	−2	−2
(C)	+2	−2
(D)	+4	0
(E)	+6	10

GO ON TO THE NEXT PAGE

31. Which of the following graphs best represents the kinetic energy K of an elementary particle as a function of its speed v, where c is the speed of light?

(A)

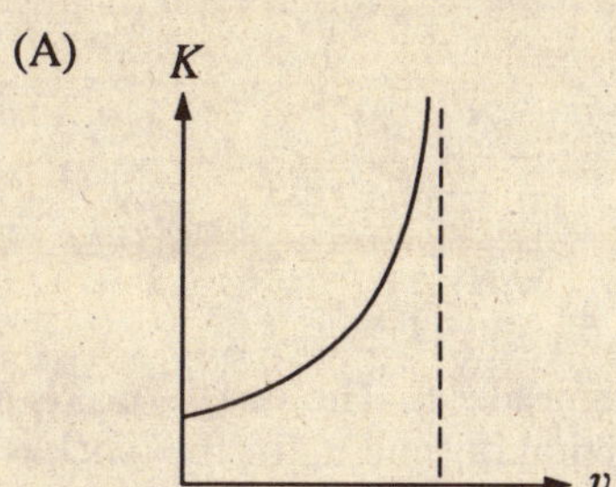

(B)

K O c v

(C)

K O c v

(D)

K O c v

(E)

K O c v

32. When acted on by a net force F, an object of mass M experiences an acceleration a. If the net force is increased to $3F$ and the mass is increased to $6M$, then the new acceleration is

(A) $a/6$
(B) $a/3$
(C) $a/2$
(D) $2a$
(E) $3a$

GO ON TO THE NEXT PAGE

Questions 33-35

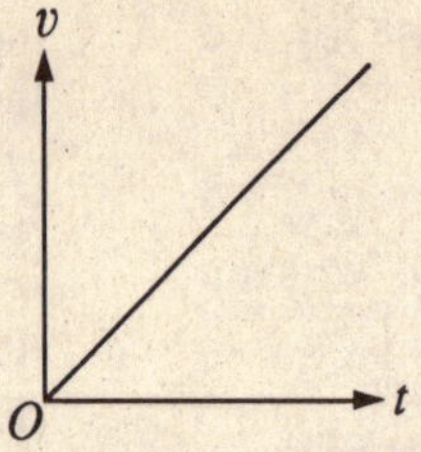

A block is pulled along a horizontal surface with a constant horizontal force of magnitude F. The surface exerts a frictional force of constant magnitude f on the block. The graph of speed v as a function of time t for the block is shown above.

33. Which of the following relationships between F and f is correct?

    (A) $F < f$
    (B) $F = f$
    (C) $F > f$
    (D) It cannot be determined without knowing the mass of the block.
    (E) It cannot be determined without knowing the value of g at this location.

34. Which of the following shows the graph of acceleration a as a function of time t for the block?

(A) 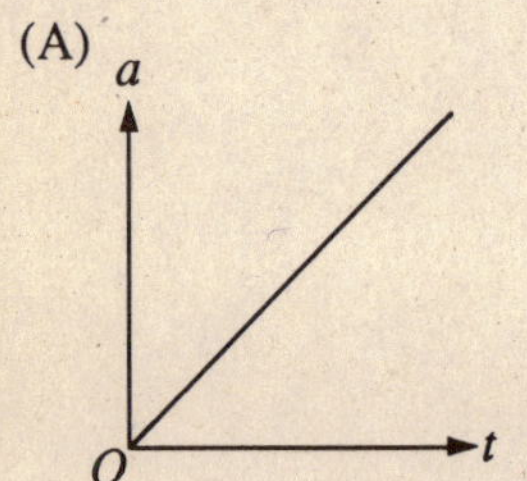

(B) 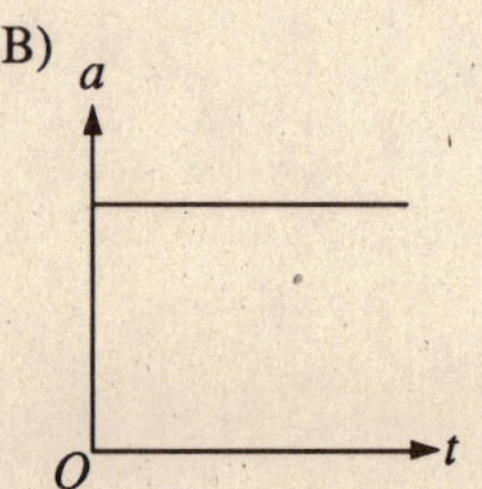

(C) 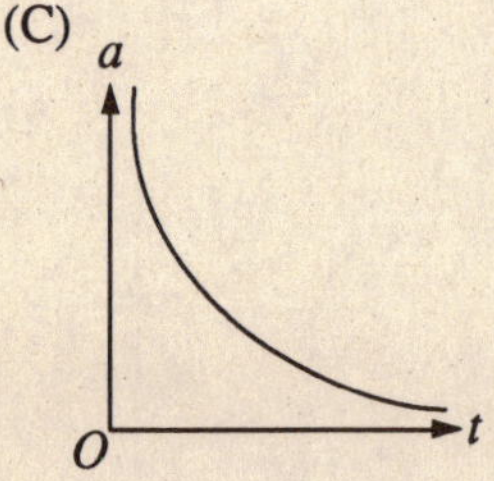

(D) 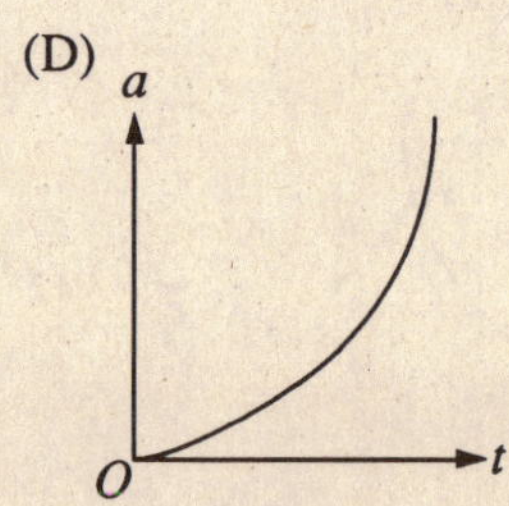

(E) 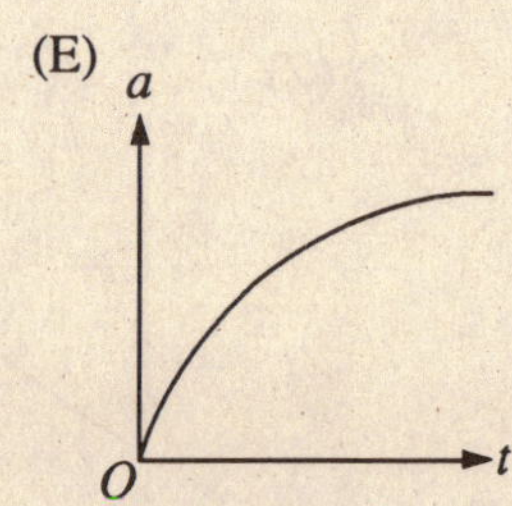

35. If, instead, the block slides without friction but is pulled with the same horizontal force of magnitude F, which of the following would be a possible new graph of speed v as a function of time t? (The dashed line represents the old graph.)

(A) 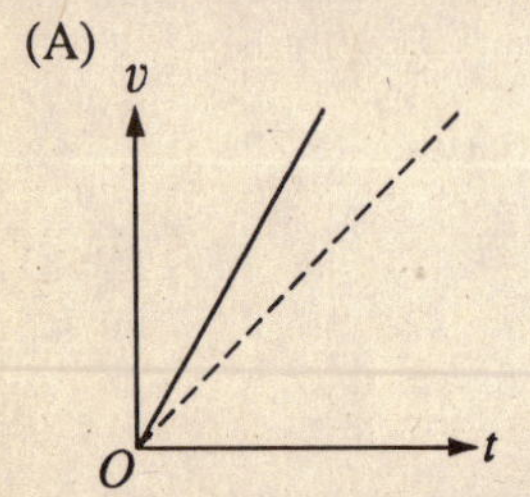

(B) 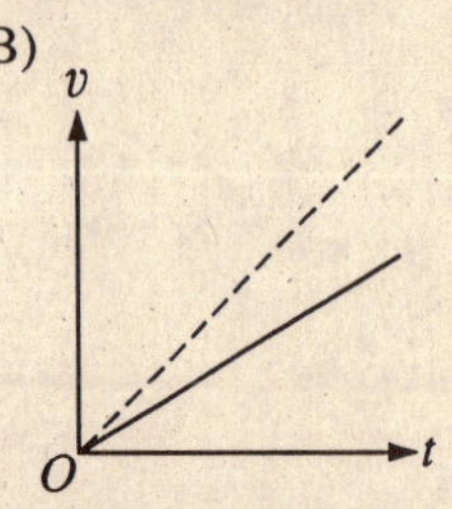

(C) 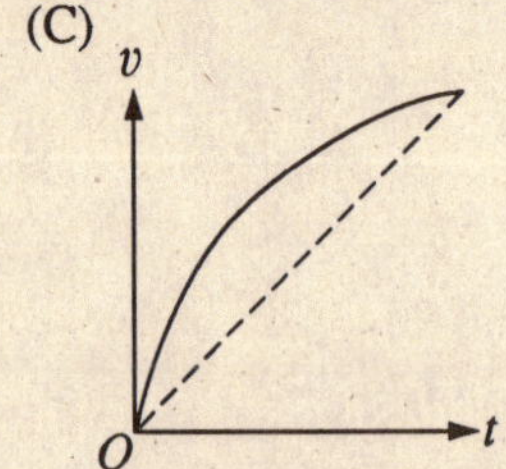

(D) 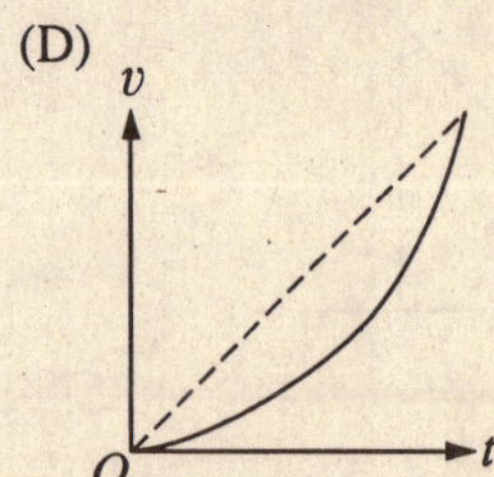

(E) 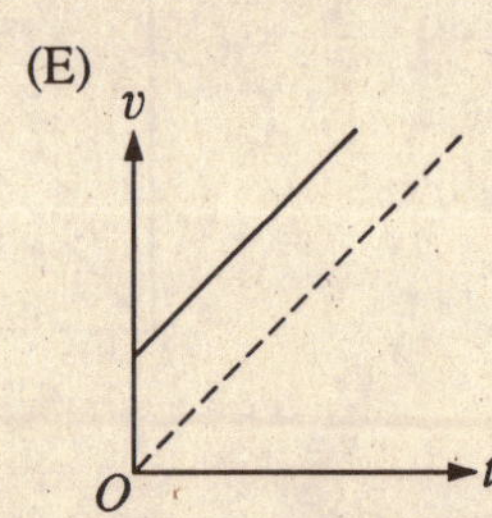

GO ON TO THE NEXT PAGE

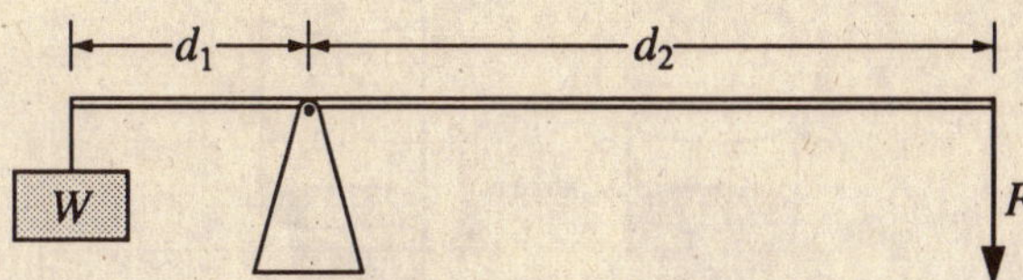

36. A block of weight 30 newtons is hung at one end of a bar of negligible mass, as shown in the diagram above. If d_2 is equal to $3d_1$, what is the magnitude of the vertical force F needed to balance the bar?

(A) 10 N
(B) 15 N
(C) 30 N
(D) 60 N
(E) 90 N

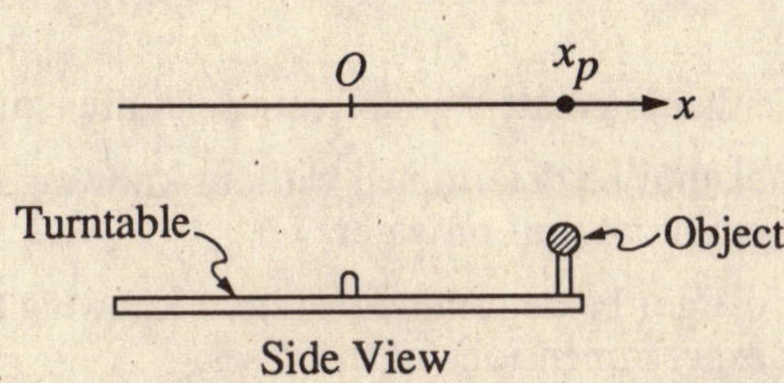

Side View

37. When an object on a rotating turntable is viewed from the side, it appears to oscillate back and forth. If its horizontal position x_p is observed as a function of time and the turntable rotates once in 1.5 seconds, the frequency of oscillation is most nearly

(A) 0.11 Hz
(B) 0.33 Hz
(C) 0.67 Hz
(D) 1.33 Hz
(E) 4.19 Hz

Position

O

Time

38. The graph of position *versus* time for an object moving along a straight line is given above. During the time shown on the graph, the speed and acceleration of the object will have which of the following characteristics?

	Speed	Acceleration
(A)	Increasing	Increasing
(B)	Increasing	Constant but not zero
(C)	Constant but not zero	Increasing
(D)	Constant but not zero	Zero
(E)	Zero	Constant but not zero

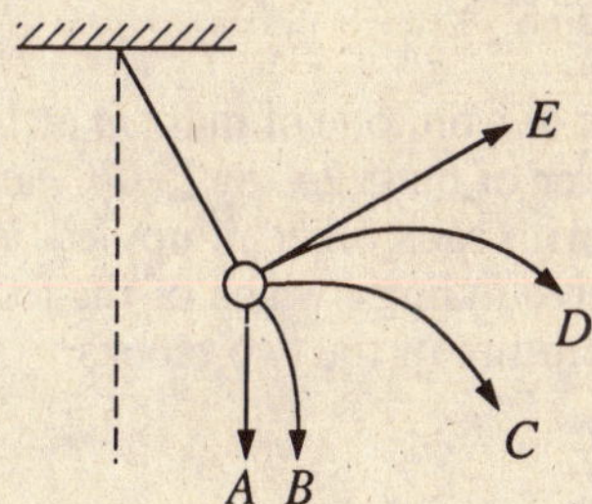

39. A pendulum is swinging upward and is halfway toward its highest position, as shown above, when the string breaks. Which of the paths shown best represents the one that the ball would take after the string breaks?

(A) *A*
(B) *B*
(C) *C*
(D) *D*
(E) *E*

GO ON TO THE NEXT PAGE

40. After landing on a planet that has no atmosphere, an astronaut drops a 4-kilogram object from a height of 1 meter above the surface. The speed of the object just before it hits the surface is 2 meters per second. The acceleration due to gravity near the surface of the planet is

(A) 1 m/s^2
(B) 2 m/s^2
(C) 4 m/s^2
(D) 8 m/s^2
(E) 16 m/s^2

41. If the addition of 20 calories of heat to 100 grams of a substance raises its temperature 2° C, the specific heat of the substance is

(A) 0.02 cal/g · ° C
(B) 0.1 cal/g · ° C
(C) 0.2 cal/g · ° C
(D) 10 cal/g · ° C
(E) 20 cal/g · ° C

42. Two blocks of iron, one of mass m at 10.0°C and the other of mass $2m$ at 25.0°C, are placed in contact with each other. If no heat is exchanged with the surroundings, which of the following is the final temperature of the two blocks?

(A) 10.0 °C
(B) 15.0 °C
(C) 17.5 °C
(D) 20.0 °C
(E) 25.0 °C

43. A constant net force F_1 acts for 10 seconds on an object of mass m and accelerates it from rest to velocity v. The object is then brought to rest in 2 seconds by a constant net force F_2. The magnitude of F_2 is equal to

(A) $5F_1$
(B) $2F_1$
(C) F_1
(D) $\frac{F_1}{m}$
(E) mv

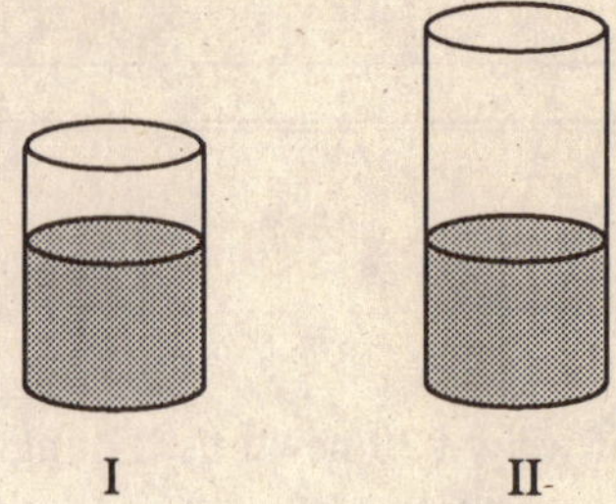

44. Two cylindrical vases, I and II, are open at the top and have equal cross sections, but vase II is taller than vase I, as shown above. Both vases are filled to equal heights with water. The frequencies of the fundamental standing waves in the air columns are f_I and f_{II}, respectively. Which of these is greater?

(A) f_I
(B) f_{II}
(C) Neither is greater: the frequencies are equal.
(D) It cannot be determined without knowing the exact amount of water.
(E) It cannot be determined without knowing the exact dimensions of the vases.

45. Light is reflected from a plane mirror. Statements that are always true about the incident ray, the reflected ray, and the normal to the surface at the point of incidence include which of the following?

I. They lie in the same plane.
II. They lie along the same straight line.
III. They are perpendicular to the surface of the mirror.

(A) I only
(B) II only
(C) I and III only
(D) II and III only
(E) I, II, and III

46. Both transverse waves and longitudinal waves may exhibit all of the following properties EXCEPT

(A) interference
(B) polarization
(C) dispersion
(D) reflection
(E) refraction

GO ON TO THE NEXT PAGE

47. The following diagrams show the path of a light ray from an object O passing through a thin lens having focal points F. In which diagram is the ray correct for both a diverging lens and a converging lens?

(A)

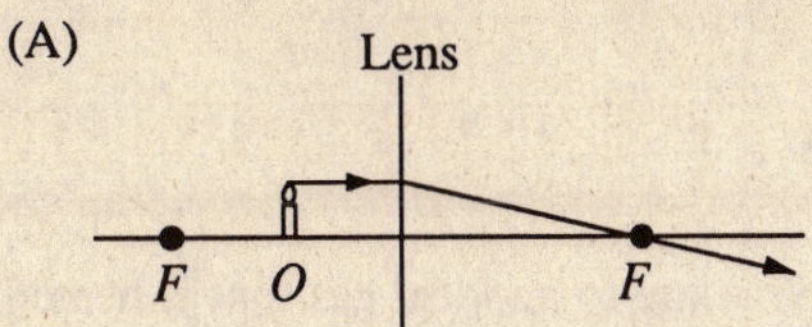

(B)

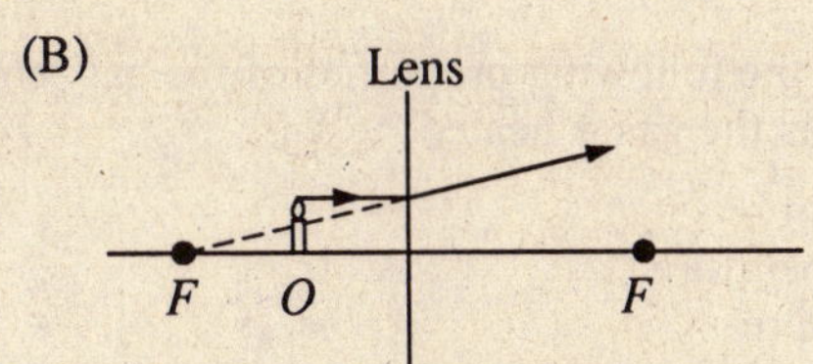

(C)

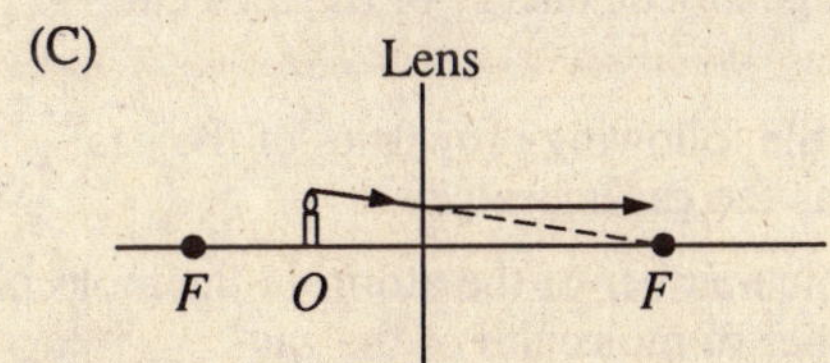

(D)

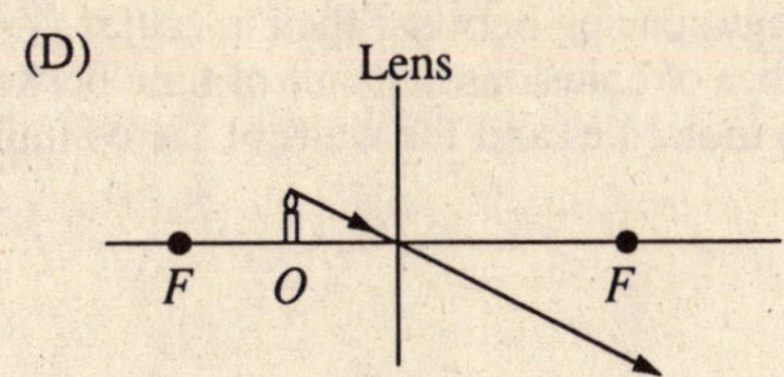

(E)

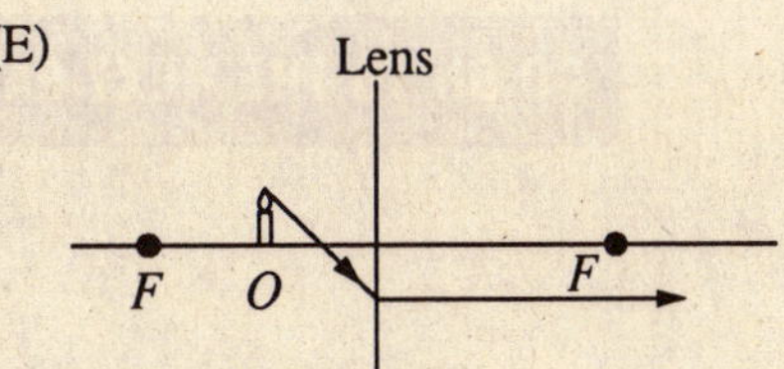

48. Which of the following is true of the magnetic field produced by a current in a long, straight wire?

(A) The field is uniform.
(B) The field increases in strength as the distance from the wire increases.
(C) The field lines are directed parallel to the wire, but opposite to the direction of the current.
(D) The field lines are directed radially outward from the wire.
(E) The field lines form circles about the wire.

GO ON TO THE NEXT PAGE

49. Which of the following graphs best represents the force that one point charge exerts on another as a function of the distance between them?

(A)

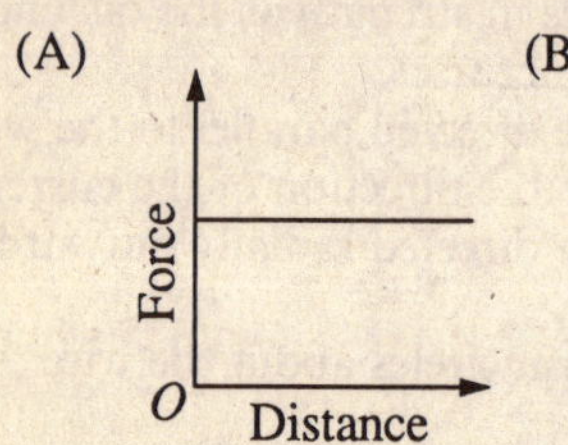

(B)

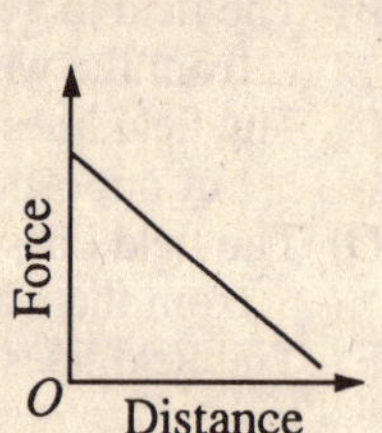

(C)

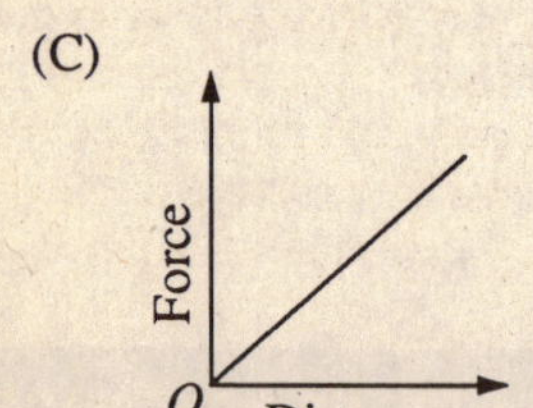

(D)

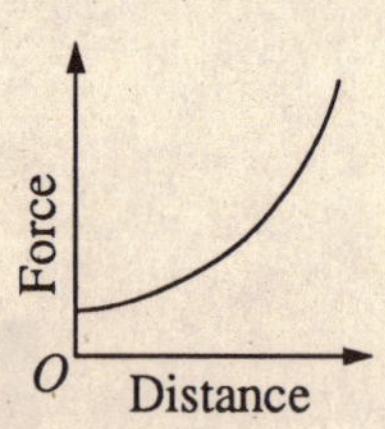

(E)

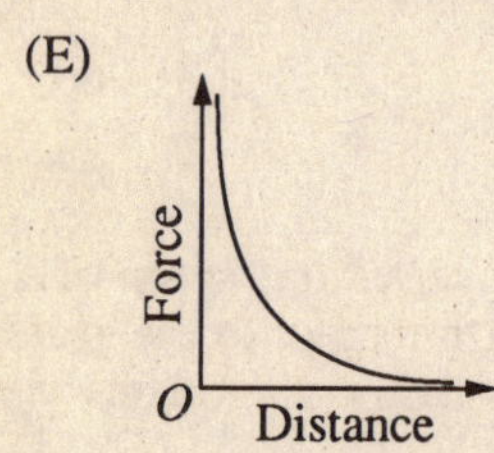

50. The impossibility of making simultaneous precise measurements of both the position and the momentum of a particle is a consequence of

(A) the exclusion principle
(B) relativity
(C) strangeness
(D) the uncertainty principle
(E) complementarity

51. A source emits light of frequency 5.0×10^{14} hertz. Planck's constant h is 6.6×10^{-34} joule-second. The energy of one photon of this light is most nearly

(A) 10^{-19} J
(B) 10^{-6} J
(C) 1 J
(D) 10^{6} J
(E) 10^{19} J

Questions 52-53 relate to an ideal gas that is heated in a closed container at constant volume.

52. Which of the following properties of the gas remains constant as the gas is heated?

(A) Density
(B) Temperature
(C) Pressure
(D) Internal energy
(E) Average kinetic energy of the molecules

53. Which of the following properties of the gas increases as the gas is heated?

(A) Atomic number of the atoms in the molecules
(B) Number of molecules of the gas
(C) Molecular weight of the gas
(D) Average spacing between the molecules
(E) Number of collisions per unit of time between the molecules and the walls of the container

GO ON TO THE NEXT PAGE

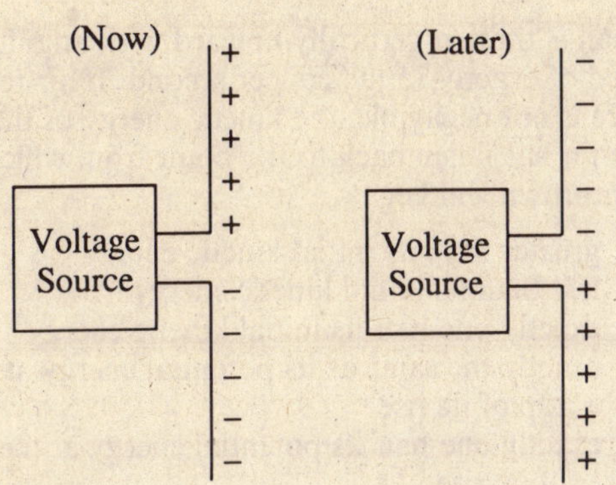

54. Two rods are connected to a source of voltage as shown above. The polarity of the source of voltage is changing periodically so that the rods are charged alternately as shown. True statements about this phenomenon include which of the following?

    I. A constant electric field is established throughout all space.
    II. A changing electric field is produced near the rods.
    III. Electromagnetic radiation is produced.

(A) I only
(B) III only
(C) I and II only
(D) II and III only
(E) I, II, and III

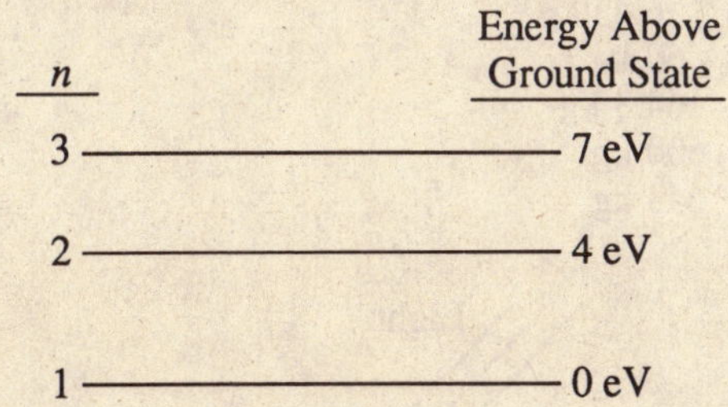

55. Three energy levels of an atom are shown above. Atoms in the $n = 2$ state can spontaneously emit photons having which of the following energies?

(A) 4 eV only
(B) 7 eV only
(C) 3 eV and 4 eV only
(D) 3 eV and 7 eV only
(E) 3 eV, 4 eV, and 7 eV

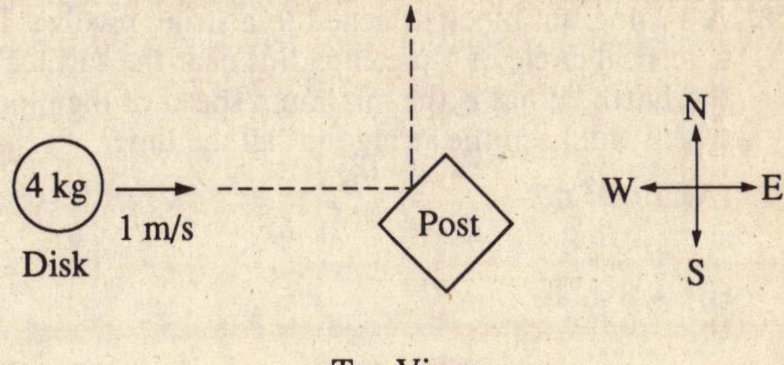

Top View

56. A 4-kilogram disk slides over level ice toward the east at a velocity of 1 meter per second, as shown above. The disk strikes a post and rebounds toward the north at the same speed. The change in the magnitude of the eastward component of the momentum of the disk is

(A) -4 kg · m/s
(B) -1 kg · m/s
(C) 0 kg · m/s
(D) 1 kg · m/s
(E) 4 kg · m/s

57. A 10-kilogram steel ball is raised to the top of a tower 100 meters high. With respect to the ground, the potential energy of the ball when it is at the top of the tower is most nearly

(A) 10 J
(B) 10^2 J
(C) 10^3 J
(D) 10^4 J
(E) 10^5 J

GO ON TO THE NEXT PAGE

58. A 1-kilogram block attached to a string revolves in a vertical circle of 1-meter radius near the surface of the Earth. What is the minimum speed of the block which will keep the string taut all the time?

(A) $(9.8)^2$ m/s

(B) 9.8 m/s

(C) $(9.8)^{\frac{1}{2}}$ m/s

(D) $\frac{1}{9.8}$ m/s

(E) $\frac{1}{(9.8)^2}$ m/s

59. A projectile of mass m traveling horizontally with velocity v strikes a stationary block of equal mass resting on a horizontal frictionless plane. If the projectile remains embedded in the block, which of the following is the velocity of the projectile-block system immediately after the collision?

(A) $\frac{v}{4}$

(B) $\frac{v}{2}$

(C) v

(D) $2v$

(E) $4v$

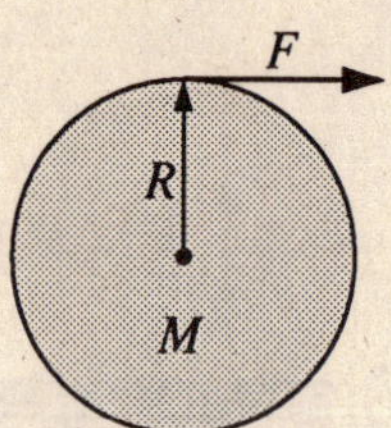

60. A uniform cylindrical disk of mass M and radius R is free to turn about an axle through its center, which is fixed in space. A tangential force of magnitude F is exerted on the disk, as shown above. The angular acceleration can be maximized by making

(A) F, M, and R as large as possible
(B) F and M as large as possible and R as small as possible
(C) F as large as possible and M and R as small as possible
(D) M as large as possible and F and R as small as possible
(E) R as large as possible and F and M as small as possible

61. A ball is thrown vertically upward with an initial speed of exactly 15 meters per second. If air resistance is not negligible, the kinetic energy of the ball when it has fallen back to the point from which it was thrown will be

(A) greater than its initial kinetic energy
(B) less than its initial kinetic energy
(C) exactly one-half its initial kinetic energy
(D) exactly the same as its potential energy at the top of its rise
(E) exactly one-half its potential energy at the top of its rise

62. Which of the following may transmit energy from one point to another?

I. Electromagnetic radiation
II. Sound waves
III. Convection currents

(A) I only
(B) III only
(C) I and II only
(D) II and III only
(E) I, II, and III

63. A teacher measures and records her own mass to an accuracy of better than $\frac{1}{2}$ percent. Which of the following is most likely the mass that she recorded?

(A) 6.43 kg
(B) 60 kg
(C) 64.3 kg
(D) 600 kg
(E) 643 kg

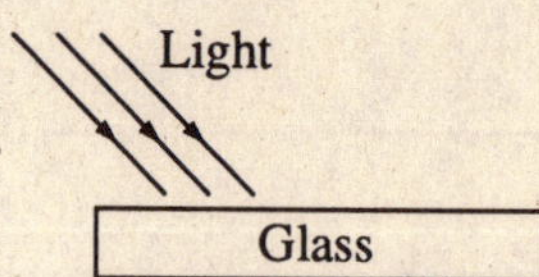

64. Parallel light rays are incident on a rectangular block of clear glass, as shown above. Which of the following phenomena does NOT occur?

(A) Reflection
(B) Transmission
(C) Refraction
(D) Focusing
(E) Absorption

GO ON TO THE NEXT PAGE

65. A pendulum of length ℓ with a bob of mass m is oscillating with small amplitude. Which of the following changes in the pendulum would double its period?

(A) Doubling the mass m of the bob
(B) Doubling the initial force used to set the pendulum in motion
(C) Doubling the amplitude of the pendulum's swing
(D) Quadrupling the mass m of the bob
(E) Quadrupling the length ℓ of the pendulum

66. The Earth has a radius of 6,400 kilometers. A satellite orbits the Earth at a distance of 12,800 kilometers from the center of the Earth. If the weight of the satellite on Earth is 100 kilonewtons, the gravitational force on the satellite in orbit is

(A) 11 kilonewtons
(B) 25 kilonewtons
(C) 50 kilonewtons
(D) 100 kilonewtons
(E) 200 kilonewtons

Questions 67-68 relate to the following circuit.

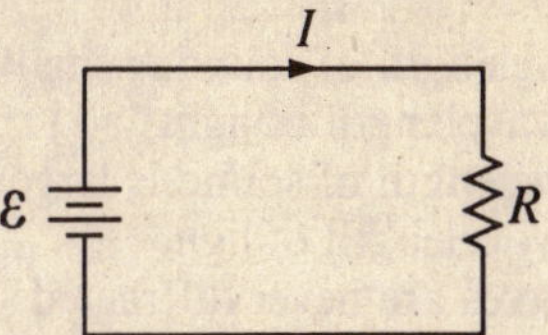

A single resistor R is connected to a battery as shown above. The current is I and the power dissipated as heat is P. The circuit is changed by doubling the emf $\mathcal{E}$ of the battery while R is kept constant.

67. After the change, the current is

(A) $\frac{I}{4}$

(B) $\frac{I}{2}$

(C) I

(D) $2I$

(E) $4I$

68. After the change, the power dissipated in R is

(A) $\frac{P}{4}$

(B) $\frac{P}{2}$

(C) P

(D) $2P$

(E) $4P$

GO ON TO THE NEXT PAGE

69. The diffraction of sound waves is more evident than that of light waves in ordinary experience because

    (A) the wavelength of sound is small compared with the wavelength of light
    (B) the wavelength of sound is large compared with the wavelength of light
    (C) light waves are never diffracted
    (D) sound is a longitudinal wave whereas light is a transverse wave
    (E) sound waves are mechanical whereas light waves are electromagnetic

70. A ball, initially at rest at $t = 0$ seconds, rolls with constant acceleration down an inclined plane 10 meters long. If the ball rolls 1 meter in the first 2 seconds, how far will it have rolled at $t = 4$ seconds?

    (A) 2 m
    (B) 3 m
    (C) 4 m
    (D) 5 m
    (E) 8 m

Questions 71-72

A piece of chalk is thrown vertically upward and caught during its descent at the same height from which it was thrown. Position is measured from the location of the chalk when it left the hand. The positive direction for position, velocity, and acceleration is upward.

71. What are the signs of the position, velocity, and acceleration during the ascending part of the trajectory?

	Position	Velocity	Acceleration
(A)	Positive	Positive	Positive
(B)	Positive	Positive	Negative
(C)	Positive	Negative	Negative
(D)	Negative	Positive	Negative
(E)	Negative	Negative	Negative

72. What are the signs of the position, velocity, and acceleration during the descending part of the trajectory?

	Position	Velocity	Acceleration
(A)	Positive	Positive	Positive
(B)	Positive	Positive	Negative
(C)	Positive	Negative	Negative
(D)	Negative	Positive	Negative
(E)	Negative	Negative	Negative

GO ON TO THE NEXT PAGE

73. Part of the energy of a wave traveling in a material medium is dissipated in the form of heat. This is sure to cause a decrease in which of the following properties of the wave?

    (A) Amplitude
    (B) Frequency
    (C) Period
    (D) Speed
    (E) Wavelength

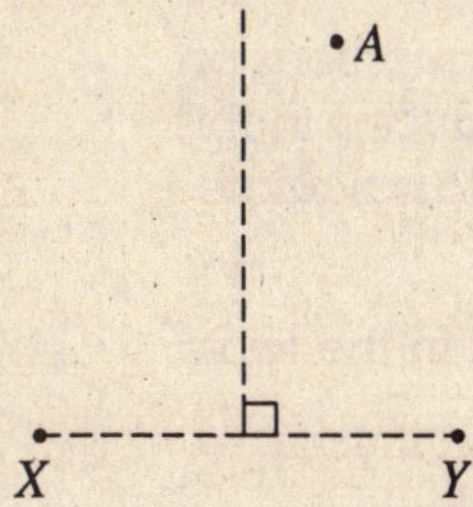

74. Two wave generators of the same frequency and phase operate at points X and Y shown above. If point A is a distance of seven wavelengths from Y and eight wavelengths from X, then A is

    (A) on the central antinodal line
    (B) at a point where there is always destructive interference
    (C) at a point where there is always constructive interference
    (D) at a point where there is alternate constructive and destructive interference during one period
    (E) at a point where the two waves originating at X and Y are superimposed to produce a standing wave

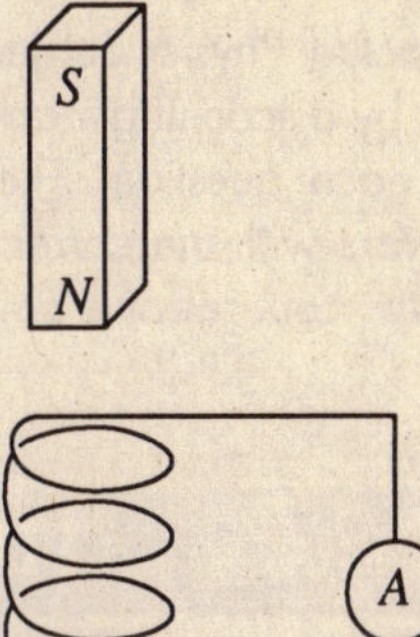

75. A bar magnet is located next to a coil of wire that is fixed in position and connected to an ammeter A, as shown above. There will be an induced electric current through the ammeter if the magnet is moving in which of the following ways?

    I. Toward the coil with constant speed
    II. Toward the coil with increasing speed
    III. Away from the coil with constant speed
    IV. Away from the coil with increasing speed

    (A) I or II only
    (B) I or III only
    (C) II or IV only
    (D) III or IV only
    (E) I or II or III or IV

STOP

IF YOU FINISH BEFORE TIME IS CALLED, YOU MAY CHECK YOUR WORK ON THIS TEST ONLY.
DO NOT TURN TO ANY OTHER TEST IN THIS BOOK.

How to Score the SAT II: Physics Subject Test

When you take an actual Physics Subject Test, your answer sheet will be "read" by a scanning machine that will record your responses to each question. Then a computer will compare your answers with the correct answers and produce your raw score. You get one point for each correct answer. For each wrong answer, you lose one-fourth of a point. Questions you omit (and any for which you mark more than one answer) are not counted. This raw score is converted to a College Board scaled score that is reported to you and to the colleges you specify. After you have taken the practice test, you can get an idea of what your score might be by following the instructions in the next two sections.

FINDING YOUR RAW TEST SCORE

Step 1: Table A lists the correct answers for all the questions on the SAT II: Physics Subject Test that is reproduced in this book. It also serves as a worksheet for you to calculate your raw score.

- Compare your answers with those given in the table.
- Put a check in the column marked "Right" if your answer is correct.
- Put a check in the column marked "Wrong" if your answer is incorrect.
- Leave both columns blank if you omitted the question.

Step 2: Count the number of right answers and enter the total here: .... ________

Step 3: Count the number of wrong answers and enter the total here: .... ________

Step 4: Divide the number of wrong answers by 4 and enter the result here: .... ________

Step 5: Subtract the result obtained in Step 4 from the total you obtained in Step 2. Enter the result here: .... ________

Step 6: Round the number obtained in Step 5 to the nearest whole number. Enter the result here: .... ________

The number you obtained in Step 6 is your raw test score.

TABLE A

Answers to the SAT II: Physics Subject Test, Form 3OAC, and Percentage of Students Answering Each Question Correctly

Question Number	Correct Answer	Right	Wrong	Percentage of Students Answering the Question Correctly*	Question Number	Correct Answer	Right	Wrong	Percentage of Students Answering the Question Correctly*
1	D			89	41	B			60
2	E			77	42	D			51
3	A			59	43	A			78
4	D			14	44	A			34
5	A			65	45	A			66
6	C			55	46	B			65
7	D			68	47	D			51
8	A			30	48	E			61
9	B			30	49	E			62
10	A			49	50	D			46
11	C			40	51	A			61
12	C			64	52	A			60
13	A			76	53	E			81
14	E			73	54	D			47
15	E			90	55	A			52
16	C			90	56	A			47
17	E			53	57	D			63
18	E			57	58	C			28
19	C			82	59	B			70
20	C			59	60	C			52
21	E			92	61	B			44
22	D			63	62	E			52
23	A			69	63	C			57
24	C			56	64	D			64
25	C			70	65	E			42
26	C			57	66	B			26
27	D			61	67	D			64
28	B			64	68	E			33
29	E			66	69	B			40
30	B			70	70	C			30
31	B			72	71	B			45
32	C			81	72	C			31
33	C			77	73	A			33
34	B			75	74	C			24
35	A			76	75	E			28
36	A			75					
37	C			62					
38	D			71					
39	D			64					
40	B			59					

*These percentages are based on an analysis of the answer sheets for a random sample of 6,255 students who took this form of the test in June 1992 and whose mean score was 618. They may be used as an indication of the relative difficulty of a particular question. Each percentage may also be used to predict the likelihood that a typical SAT II: Physics Subject Test candidate will answer correctly that question on this edition of this test.

Finding Your College Board Scaled Score

When you take SAT II: Subject Tests, the scores sent to the colleges you specify are reported on the College Board scale, which ranges from 200 to 800. You can convert your practice test score to a scaled score by using Table B. To find your scaled score, locate your raw score in the left-hand column of Table B; the corresponding score in the right-hand column is your College Board scaled score. For example, a raw score of 60 on this particular edition of the SAT II: Physics Subject Test corresponds to a College Board scaled score of 760.

Raw scores are converted to scaled scores to ensure that a score earned on any one edition of a particular Subject Test is comparable to the same scaled score earned on any other edition of the same Subject Test. Because some editions of tests may be slightly easier or more difficult than others, College Board scaled scores are adjusted so that they indicate the same level of performance regardless of the edition of the test taken and the ability of the group that takes it. Thus, for example, a score of 400 on one edition of a test taken at a particular administration indicates the same level of achievement as a score of 400 on a different edition of the test taken at a different administration.

When you take the SAT II: Subject Tests during a national administration, your scores are likely to differ somewhat from the scores you obtain on the tests in this book. People perform at different levels at different times for reasons unrelated to the tests themselves. The precision of any test is also limited because it represents only a sample of all the possible questions that could be asked.

TABLE B

Score Conversion Table
SAT II: Physics Subject Test, Form 3OAC

Raw Score	College Board Scaled Score	Raw Score	College Board Scaled Score
75	800	25	530
74	800	24	530
73	800	23	520
72	800	22	510
71	800	21	510
70	800	20	500
69	800	19	500
68	800	18	490
67	800	17	480
66	800	16	480
65	800	15	470
64	790	14	460
63	780	13	460
62	770	12	450
61	770	11	450
60	760	10	440
59	750	9	430
58	750	8	430
57	740	7	420
56	730	6	420
55	730	5	410
54	720	4	400
53	710	3	400
52	710	2	390
51	700	1	380
50	690	0	380
49	690	−1	370
48	680	−2	370
47	670	−3	360
46	670	−4	350
45	660	−5	350
44	650	−6	340
43	650	−7	340
42	640	−8	330
41	630	−9	320
40	630	−10	320
39	620	−11	310
38	610	−12	300
37	610	−13	300
36	600	−14	290
35	590	−15	290
34	590	−16	280
33	580	−17	270
32	580	−18	270
31	570	−19	260
30	560		
29	560		
28	550		
27	540		
26	540		

Reviewing Your Test Performance

After you have scored your test, you should take some time to consider the following points in relation to your performance on the test.

- *Did you run out of time before you reached the end of the test?*

  If you did, you may want to consider pacing yourself better. For example, you may have spent too much time working on one or two difficult questions. A better approach might have been to continue the test and return to those questions after you had attempted to answer the remaining questions on the test.

- *Did you take a long time reading the directions for the test?*

  The directions in this test are the same as those in the Physics Subject Tests now being administered. You will save time when you take the test if you become thoroughly familiar with them in advance.

- *How did you handle questions you were unsure of?*

  If you were able to eliminate one or more of the answer choices and you guessed from the remaining choices, then your approach probably worked to your advantage. On the other hand, omitting questions about which you have some knowledge or guessing answers haphazardly would probably be a mistake.

- *How difficult were the questions for you compared with other students who took the test?*

  By referring to Table A, you can find out how difficult each question was for the group of students who took this test. The right-hand column in the table tells you what percentage of this group answered the question correctly. A question that was answered correctly by almost everyone in the group is obviously an easy question. Question 21, for example, was answered correctly by 92 percent of the students in the sample. On the other hand, question 58 was answered correctly by only 28 percent.

  It is important to remember that these percentages are based on only one particular group of students; had this edition of the test been given to other groups of students at that time, the percentages would probably have been different.

  If you find that you missed several questions that would be considered easy, you may want to review those questions carefully. They may cover some aspect of the subject that you need to review. Perhaps you misunderstood the directions for one part of the test or you thought the questions were so easy that you did not spend as much time on them as you might have.

The SAT II: Chinese Subject Test with Listening

The Chinese Subject Test with Listening is a one-hour test that consists of 85 multiple-choice questions. It is offered in participating secondary schools in November.

A major goal of the test is to measure the ability of students to engage in meaningful communication about the Chinese culture in contemporary Chinese. Therefore, some test materials are taken from real life. The test is designed for students who have studied Chinese as a second or foreign language in high school for two, three, or four years.

There are three parts to the test:

The listening comprehension questions test the student's ability to understand the spoken language. They are based on short spoken dialogues and narratives primarily about everyday topics. In this section there are two different kinds of questions:

(1) brief utterances or exchanges, after which students choose the most appropriate response;

(2) short dialogues or monologues in Mandarin Chinese followed by questions about what was said. The questions and answers options in this part are in English.

The usage questions require students to complete Chinese sentences so that they are structurally and logically correct. In this part, students are to select an appropriate syntactic structure or lexical term. Knowledge of vocabulary is tested implicitly throughout the test; some usage questions specifically test word meaning in the context of a sentence that reflects spoken or written language. Usage questions (Section II) are printed in four writing systems. From left to right, the Chinese is transcribed in traditional characters, simplified characters, Pinyin romanization, and Chinese phonetic alphabet (Bo Po Mo Fo).

The reading comprehension questions test the understanding of such points as main and supporting ideas, themes, and the setting of passages. All passages are written in both traditional and simplified Chinese characters. Most questions deal with understanding of literal meaning although some inference questions may be included. Some of the Chinese selections on which the questions are based are drawn from authentic materials, such as timetables, forms, advertisements, notes, letters, diaries, and newspaper articles. All reading comprehension questions are in English.

Skills Measured	Approximate Percentage of Test
Listening Comprehension	33
Usage	33
Reading Comprehension	33

Sample Questions

Following are some samples for each section of the SAT II: Chinese Subject Test with Listening. All questions are multiple choice. You must choose the best response from the three or four choices offered for each question.

In an actual test administration, all spoken Chinese will be presented by tape playback. Text that appears in this book in brackets ([ ]) will be recorded in an actual test and it will *not* be printed in your test booklet. Spoken text appears in printed form here because a taped version is not available.

Section I: Listening

Part A

Directions: In this part of the test, you will hear short questions, statements, or commands in Mandarin Chinese followed by *three* responses in Mandarin Chinese designated (A), (B), and (C). You will hear the statements or questions, as well as the responses, just *one* time, and they will not be printed in your test booklet. Therefore, you must listen very carefully. Select the best choice and fill in the corresponding oval on your answer sheet. Now listen to the following examples.

(Narrator) [Number 1.]

(Woman) [請問圖書館在哪兒?]

(Man) [(A) 圖書館九點開門。
(B) 圖書館裡書很多。
(C) 圖書館就在前面。] (5 seconds)

(Narrator) [Number 2.]

(Man) [我想請你幫個忙。]

(Woman) [(A) 沒問題。
(B) 謝謝你。
(C) 差不多。] (5 seconds)

(Narrator) [Number 3.]

(Man) [你想什麼時候到中國去看朋友?]

(Woman) [(A) 我的朋友是去年來的。
(B) 我打算下個月去。
(C) 我想坐船去中國。] (5 seconds)

Part B

Directions: You will now hear a series of short selections. You will hear them *only once*, and they are not printed in your test booklet. After each selection, you will be asked one or more questions about what you have just heard. These questions, with four possible answers, are printed in your test booklet. Select the best answer to each question from among the four choices printed, and fill in the corresponding oval on your answer sheet. You will have fifteen seconds to answer each question.

Now listen to the following examples.

Questions 4 and 5

(Narrator) [Questions 4 and 5. Listen to find out what the couple's plans are.]

(Woman) [這個房子真不錯。夠大，地點也好。

(Man) 可惜，裡頭沒什麼家具。

(Woman) 這有什麼關係? 你看，床和櫃子都還可以用。電話也裝好了。我們只要買張桌子，兩把椅子，就行了。

(Man) 好吧! 既然房租不貴，我們就先住幾個月再說吧!]

(Narrator) [Now answer questions number 4 and 5.] (30 seconds)

4. What are the people doing?

(A) Looking for a house.
(B) Buying furniture.
(C) Renovating their home.
(D) Cleaning their house.

5. What does the woman think they need to buy?

(A) A telephone.
(B) A bed and dresser.
(C) A desk and chairs.
(D) Cleaning materials.

Question 6

(Narrator) [Question 6. Listen to what the woman says.]

(Woman) [我的球鞋穿了兩年了，已經破了。
可是這些新鞋又太貴。我怎麼買得起呢?]

(Narrator) [Now answer question 6.] (15 seconds)

6. The woman's comment about the new shoes concerns their

(A) size
(B) style
(C) color
(D) price

Section II: Usage

Directions: This section consists of a number of incomplete statements, each of which has four suggested completions. Select the word or phrase that best completes the sentence structurally and logically and fill in the corresponding oval on the answer sheet.

THIS PART OF THE TEST IS PRESENTED IN FOUR COLUMNS ACROSS TWO PAGES TO ALLOW EACH ITEM TO BE SHOWN IN FOUR WRITING SYSTEMS: TRADITIONAL CHARACTERS, SIMPLIFIED CHARACTERS, PINYIN ROMANIZATION, AND CHINESE PHONETIC ALPHABET (BO PO MO FO). TO SAVE TIME, IT IS RECOMMENDED THAT YOU CHOOSE THE WRITING SYSTEM WITH WHICH YOU ARE MOST FAMILIAR AND READ ONLY FROM THAT COLUMN.

[THIS PAGE INTENTIONALLY LEFT BLANK]

7. 我很喜歡這部電影。

你 _____?

(A) 啊

(B) 嗎

(C) 吧

(D) 呢

8. 我從來沒吃 _____ 這麼好吃的菜。

(A) 得

(B) 過

(C) 給

(D) 成

9. 他在中國 _____ 住了三年了。

(A) 經過

(B) 曾經

(C) 已經

(D) 經常

10. _____ 我哥哥比我大五歲，_____ 我比哥哥高得多。

(A) 雖然 ..... 可是

(B) 因爲 ..... 所以

(C) 既然 ..... 就

(D) 就是 ..... 也

11. 星期天我要在家休息，_____。

(A) 不去都哪兒

(B) 都哪兒不去

(C) 不去哪兒都

(D) 哪兒都不去

7. 我很喜欢这部电影。

你 _____?

(A) 啊

(B) 吗

(C) 吧

(D) 呢

8. 我从来没吃 _____ 这么好吃的菜。

(A) 得

(B) 过

(C) 给

(D) 成

9. 他在中国 _____ 住了三年了。

(A) 经过

(B) 曾经

(C) 已经

(D) 经常

10. _____ 我哥哥比我大五岁，_____ 我比哥哥高得多。

(A) 虽然 ..... 可是

(B) 因为 ..... 所以

(C) 既然 ..... 就

(D) 就是 ..... 也

11. 星期天我要在家休息，_____。

(A) 不去都哪儿

(B) 都哪儿不去

(C) 不去哪儿都

(D) 哪儿都不去

7. Wǒ hěn xǐhuan zhèi bù diànyǐng.

Nǐ ____ ?

(A) a

(B) ma

(C) ba

(D) ne

7. ㄨㄛˇ ㄏㄣˇ ㄒㄧˇ ㄏㄨㄢ ㄓㄟˋ ㄅㄨˋ ㄉㄧㄢˋ ㄧㄥˇ。

ㄋㄧˇ ______?

(A) ˙ㄚ

(B) ˙ㄇㄚ

(C) ˙ㄅㄚ

(D) ˙ㄋㄜ

8. Wǒ cónglái méi chī ____

zhème hǎochī de cài.

(A) de

(B) guo

(C) gěi

(D) chéng

8. ㄨㄛˇ ㄘㄨㄥˊ ㄌㄞˊ ㄇㄟˊ ㄔ ______

ㄓㄜˋ ˙ㄇㄜ ㄏㄠˇ ㄔ ˙ㄉㄜ ㄘㄞˋ。

(A) ˙ㄉㄜ

(B) ㄍㄨㄛˋ

(C) ㄍㄟˇ

(D) ㄔㄥˊ

9. Tā zài Zhōngguó ____ zhù le

sān nián le.

(A) jīngguò

(B) céngjīng

(C) yǐjīng

(D) jīngcháng

9. ㄊㄚ ㄗㄞˋ ㄓㄨㄥ ㄍㄨㄛˊ ______ ㄓㄨˋ ˙ㄌㄜ

ㄙㄢ ㄋㄧㄢˊ ˙ㄌㄜ。

(A) ㄐㄧㄥ ㄍㄨㄛˋ

(B) ㄘㄥˊ ㄐㄧㄥ

(C) ㄧˇ ㄐㄧㄥ

(D) ㄐㄧㄥ ㄔㄤˊ

10. ____ wǒ gēge bǐ wǒ dà wǔ suì,

____ wǒ bǐ gēge gāo de duō.

(A) Suīrán ..... kěshì

(B) Yīnwei ..... suǒyǐ

(C) Jìrán ..... jiù

(D) Jiùshì ..... yě

10. ______ㄨㄛˇ ㄍㄜ ˙ㄍㄜ ㄅㄧˇ ㄨㄛˇ ㄉㄚˋ ㄨˇ ㄙㄨㄟˋ，

______ㄨㄛˇ ㄅㄧˇ ㄍㄜ ˙ㄍㄜ ㄍㄠ ˙ㄉㄜ ㄉㄨㄛ。

(A) ㄙㄨㄟ ㄖㄢˊ ..... ㄎㄜˇ ㄕˋ

(B) ㄧㄣ ㄨㄟˋ ..... ㄙㄨㄛˇ ㄧˇ

(C) ㄐㄧˋ ㄖㄢˊ ..... ㄐㄧㄡˋ

(D) ㄐㄧㄡˋ ㄕˋ ..... ㄧㄝˇ

11. Xīngqītiān wǒ yào zài jiā xiūxi,

____.

(A) bú qù dōu nǎr

(B) dōu nǎr bú qù

(C) bú qù nǎr dōu

(D) nǎr dōu bú qù

11. ㄒㄧㄥ ㄑㄧ ㄊㄧㄢ ㄨㄛˇ ㄧㄠˋ ㄗㄞˋ ㄐㄧㄚ ㄒㄧㄡ ㄒㄧ，

______。

(A) ㄅㄨˊ ㄑㄩˋ ㄉㄡ ㄋㄚˇㄦ

(B) ㄉㄡ ㄋㄚˇㄦ ㄅㄨˊ ㄑㄩˋ

(C) ㄅㄨˊ ㄑㄩˋ ㄋㄚˇㄦ ㄉㄡ

(D) ㄋㄚˇㄦ ㄉㄡ ㄅㄨˊ ㄑㄩˋ

Section III: Reading

<u>Directions:</u> **Read the following texts carefully for comprehension. Each is followed by one or more questions or incomplete statements. Select the answer or completion that is best according to the text and fill in the corresponding oval on the answer sheet. There is no example for this part.**

THIS SECTION OF THE TEST IS PRESENTED IN TWO WRITING SYSTEMS: TRADITIONAL CHARACTERS AND SIMPLIFIED CHARACTERS. IT IS RECOMMENDED THAT YOU CHOOSE ONLY THAT WRITING SYSTEM WITH WHICH YOU ARE MOST FAMILIAR AS YOU WORK THROUGH THIS SECTION OF THE TEST.

<u>Questions 12 – 13</u>

老王: 李平林打電話來説他今天病了，不能來上課。請你幫他代課。 小 陳	老王: 李平林打电话来说他今天病了，不能来上课。请你帮他代课。 小 陈

12. This note tells us that

(A) Wang is a teacher and Li is a student
(B) Wang is a teacher and Chen is a student
(C) Wang and Li are both teachers
(D) Li and Chen are both students

13. Who called in sick?

(A) Wang
(B) Chen
(C) Lin
(D) Li

Questions 14 – 15

去年夏天，我從紐約回國了一趟。這是我從一九七五年到美國以後，第一次回國。這次我回去還特地到我上過的小學去看看。我很高興地發現二十多年前我念書的教室還在。

去年夏天，我从纽约回国了一趟。这是我从一九七五年到美国以后，第一次回国。这次我回去还特地到我上过的小学去看看。我很高兴地发现二十多年前我念书的教室还在。

14. When did the writer come to the United States?

(A) In 1920
(B) In 1975
(C) Last year
(D) This summer

15. The writer was most delighted to

(A) see his parents
(B) return to New York
(C) attend a class reunion
(D) visit his elementary school

Answers to the SAT II: Chinese Subject Test with Listening

Question Number	Correct Answer
1	C
2	A
3	B
4	A
5	C
6	D
7	D
8	B
9	C
10	A
11	D
12	C
13	D
14	B
15	D

The SAT II: French and French with Listening

The College Board offers two types of one-hour SAT II: French Subject Tests. The traditional reading-only test (offered on four national test dates) consists of 85 multiple-choice questions. The French Subject Test with Listening (offered only in November at participating high schools) consists of 85-90 multiple-choice listening and reading questions. This test has a 20-minute listening section and a 40-minute reading section and requires a special registration form (see your counselor).

The tests are not based on a particular textbook or teaching method, but are designed to allow for variation in language preparation. The French Tests are appropriate for students who have studied the language for three or four years in secondary school, or the equivalent; however, students with two years of strong preparation in French are also encouraged to take the tests. The best preparation for the tests is the gradual development of competence in French over a period of years.

Content Outline for the French Subject Test with Listening

Kinds of Questions		Approximate Percentage of Test
Listening Section		
Pictures:	8-12 questions	40
Short Dialogues:	10-12 questions	
Long Dialogues:	10-15 questions	
Reading Section		
Vocabulary:	16-20 questions	60
Structure:	16-20 questions	
Reading Comprehension:	20-25 questions	

The SAT II: French Subject Test with Listening tests your ability to understand the spoken language by three types of *listening* questions. The first type asks you to identify the sentence that most accurately describes what is presented in a picture or a photograph. The second type tests your ability to answer general content questions based on short dialogues or monologues. The third type requires that you answer more specific questions based on longer dialogues or monologues.

All questions in this section of the test are multiple-choice questions in which you must choose the best response from *three* or *four* choices offered. Text in brackets ([ ]) is *only* recorded; it is not printed in your test booklet.

Sample Questions for the Listening Section

PLEASE NOTE THAT YOUR ANSWER SHEET HAS FIVE ANSWER POSITIONS MARKED A, B, C, D, AND E, WHILE THE QUESTIONS THROUGHOUT THIS PART CONTAIN ONLY FOUR CHOICES. BE SURE* NOT *TO MAKE ANY MARKS IN COLUMN E.

Part A

Directions: For each item in this part, you will hear four sentences designated (A), (B), (C), and (D). They will not be printed in your test booklet. As you listen, look at the picture in your test booklet and select the choice that best reflects what you see in the picture or what someone in the picture might say. Then fill in the corresponding oval on the answer sheet. You will hear the choices only once. Now look at the following example.

You see:

You hear:

(A) Quelle joie d'être seul!
(B) Que c'est agréable de faire du vélo!
(C) Le moteur fait trop de bruit!
(D) Nous adorons la course à pied.

Statement (B), "Que c'est agréable de faire du vélo!" best reflects what you see in the picture or what someone in the picture might say. Therefore, you should choose answer (B).

1. You see:

You hear:

[Numéro 1

(Man) (A) Allons faire le marché en ville.
(B) Promenons-nous dans le jardin.
(C) Regardons les tableaux dans le musée.
(D) Cueillons ces beaux légumes.]

(7 seconds)

2. You see:

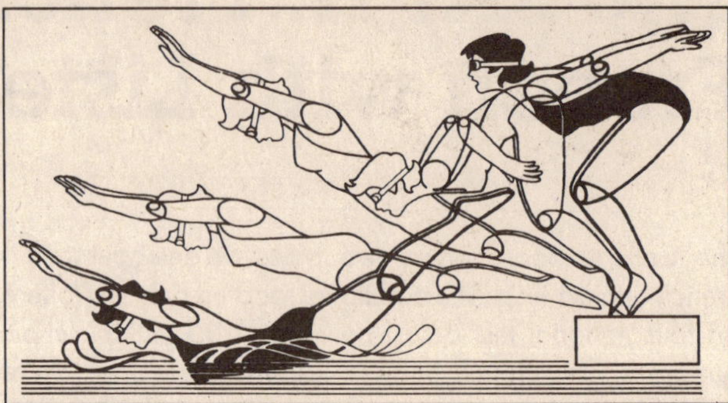

You hear:

[Numéro 2

(Woman) (A) Elle porte toujours un bonnet de bain.
(B) Elle a toujours peur de l'eau.
(C) Le ski nautique lui plaît beaucoup.
(D) Elle s'entraîne pour les Jeux Olympiques.]

(7 seconds)

PLEASE NOTE THAT YOUR ANSWER SHEET HAS FIVE ANSWER POSITIONS MARKED A, B, C, D, AND E, WHILE THE QUESTIONS THROUGHOUT PART B CONTAIN ONLY THREE CHOICES. BE SURE* NOT *TO MAKE ANY MARKS IN COLUMNS D AND/OR E.

Part B

Directions: In this part of the test you will hear several short selections. A tone will announce each new selection. The selections will not be printed in your test booklet, but each will be repeated. At the end of each selection, you will be asked one or two questions about what was said, each followed by three possible answers, (A), (B), and (C). The answers are not printed in your test booklet. You will hear them only once. Select the best answer and fill in the corresponding oval on the answer sheet. Now listen to the following example, but do not mark the answer on your answer sheet.

You hear:

[(Tone)
(Man B) Papa, ta voiture est chez le garagiste.
(Man A) Mais pourquoi? Elle a toujours bien marché.
(Man B) Euh, en réalité, j'ai eu un accident.
(Man A) Quoi? Tu plaisantes, n'est-ce pas?

(Repeat)

(Woman) Qu'est-ce qu'on peut dire de la voiture en question?

(A) Elle est en réparation.
(B) Elle est sur la route.
(C) Elle est chez un ami.]

The best answer to the question, "Qu'est-ce qu'on peut dire de la voiture en question?" is (A), "Elle est en réparation." Therefore, you should choose answer (A).

Questions 3-4.

[(Tone)
(Man) Au fait, Louise, connais-tu de bons endroits pour aller manger?
(Woman) Oh, oui, il y en a beaucoup. Qu'est-ce que tu aimes?
(Man) J'aime beaucoup les fruits de mer. Tout ce qui est poisson, crevettes, etc.
(Woman) Pour ce genre de choses, le "Bec fin" est le meilleur, je crois.]

(5 seconds)

(Repeat)

3. [Numéro 3

(Man) De quoi parlent les deux amis?

(A) De fruits.
(B) De la pêche.
(C) D'un restaurant.]

(7 seconds)

4. [Numéro 4

(Man) Qu'est-ce qu'on trouve surtout au "Bec fin"?

(A) Du poisson.
(B) De la charcuterie.
(C) Du poulet.]

(7 seconds)

Questions 5-6.

[(Tone)
(Man) Votre passeport, madame.
(Woman) Voilà.
(Man) Et qu'est-ce que vous ferez au Canada?
(Woman) Je vais passer les vacances avec ma famille.
(Man) Très bien, madame. Je vous souhaite un bon séjour.]

(5 seconds)

(Repeat)

5. [Numéro 5

(Man) Qui parle à cette femme?

(A) Un professeur.
(B) Un douanier.
(C) Un chauffeur.]

(7 seconds)

6. [Numéro 6

(Man) Qu'est-ce que la femme va faire?

(A) Obtenir un passeport.
(B) Chercher sa famille.
(C) Entrer au Canada.]

(7 seconds)

PLEASE NOTE THAT YOUR ANSWER SHEET HAS FIVE ANSWER POSITIONS MARKED A, B, C, D, AND E, WHILE THE QUESTIONS THROUGHOUT THIS PART CONTAIN ONLY FOUR CHOICES. BE SURE* NOT *TO MAKE ANY MARKS IN COLUMN E.

Part C

Directions: You will now hear some extended dialogues. You will hear each only once. After each dialogue, you will be asked several questions about what you have just heard. These questions are also printed in your test booklet. Select the best answer to each question from among the four choices printed in your test booklet and fill in the corresponding oval on the answer sheet. There is no sample question for this part.

Questions 7-10.

(Man) [Dialogue numéro 3. Marie-Hélène et son amie Maude parlent de cinéma et de littérature.

(Woman A) Tiens, Marie-Hélène, tu as acheté *Danse avec les loups* en anglais?

(Woman B) Oui, j'ai acheté ce livre à Boston. Je me suis dit que c'était, euh, d'abord je n'avais pas vu le film et avant de voir le film j'avais vraiment envie de lire le livre; c'est tout. Et finalement je n'ai pas pu le lire, je n'ai pas eu le temps.

(Woman A) Il faudra te dépêcher de le lire parce que le film est encore sur les écrans mais je ne sais pas combien de temps il va y rester. Il a beaucoup de succès, le film; le livre, je ne le connais pas. Il paraît qu'il est très très bien, le film, mais un peu long; moi, je compte aller le voir la semaine prochaine.]

7. (Man) [Qu'est-ce que Marie-Hélène déclare?]
(12 seconds)
Qu'est-ce que Marie-Hélène déclare?

(A) Avoir vu un film.
(B) Avoir l'intention de lire un livre.
(C) Avoir lu un livre.
(D) Avoir loué un film.

8. (Man) [A propos du livre, qu'est-ce que Maude conseille à Marie-Hélène de faire?]
(12 seconds)
A propos du livre, qu'est-ce que Maude conseille à Marie-Hélène de faire?

(A) De se dépêcher de le lire.
(B) De l'acheter en solde.
(C) De l'emprunter à la bibliothèque.
(D) De le lire en français.

9. (Man) [Qu'est-ce que Maude avoue à son amie?]
(12 seconds)
Qu'est-ce que Maude avoue à son amie?

(A) Elle a lu le livre.
(B) Elle n'a pas encore vu le film.
(C) Elle n'a pas compris la critique.
(D) Elle a écouté la cassette.

10. (Man) [Dans cette discussion, qu'est-ce qu'on peut dire des deux amies?]
(12 seconds)
Dans cette discussion, qu'est-ce qu'on peut dire des deux amies?

(A) Elles se font des compliments.
(B) Elles s'ignorent.
(C) Elles s'inquiètent.
(D) Elles partagent les mêmes goûts.

Answers for the Sample Listening Questions			
Question Number	**Correct Answer**	**Question Number**	**Correct Answer**
1	B	6	C
2	D	7	B
3	C	8	A
4	A	9	B
5	B	10	D

The SAT II: French Subject Test (Reading Only)

In addition to the Sat II: French Subject Test with Listening, there is a Reading Test that does *not* have a listening section. The test evaluates your reading ability in three areas: precision of vocabulary, structure, and reading comprehension (see the chart below) through a variety of questions requiring a wide-ranging knowledge of the language. Vocabulary-in-context questions test lexical items representing different parts of speech and some basic idioms within culturally authentic contexts. Structure questions measure your ability to select an appropriate word or expression that is grammatically correct within a sentence. One part of the test contains vocabulary and structure questions embedded in longer paragraphs. Reading comprehension questions test your understanding of such points as main and supporting ideas, themes, and setting of a passage. Selections are drawn from fiction, essays, historical works, and newspaper and magazine articles. They may also be taken from such sources as advertisements, timetables, forms, and tickets.

Skills Measured	Approximate Percentage of Test
Vocabulary in Context	30
Structure	30-40
Reading Comprehension	30-40

SAT II:

French Subject Mini Test

The test that follows is a shortened version of a typical SAT II: French Subject Test. So that you may have an idea of what the national test administration will be like, try to take the test in this book under conditions as close as possible to those of the nationally administered test. It will probably help if you do the following.

- Set aside 30 minutes for the test when you will not be interrupted, so that you can complete all of it in one sitting.
- Sit at a desk with no other papers or books. You can't take a dictionary, other books, or notes into the test room.
- Have a kitchen timer or clock in front of you for timing yourself.
- Tear out an answer sheet from the back of this book and fill it in just as you would on the day of the test. You can use one answer sheet for as many as three Subject Tests.
- Read the instructions that precede the test. When you take the test, you will be asked to read them before you begin answering questions.

FRENCH TEST

The top portion of the section of the answer sheet that you will use in taking the French test must be filled in exactly as shown in the illustration below. Note carefully that you have to do all of the following on your answer sheet.

1. Print FRENCH on the line under the words "Subject (print)."

2. In the shaded box labeled "Test Code" fill in four ovals:

   —Fill in oval 3 in the row labeled V.

   —Fill in oval 3 in the row labeled W.

   —Fill in oval 1 in the row labeled X.

   —Fill in oval B in the row labeled Y.

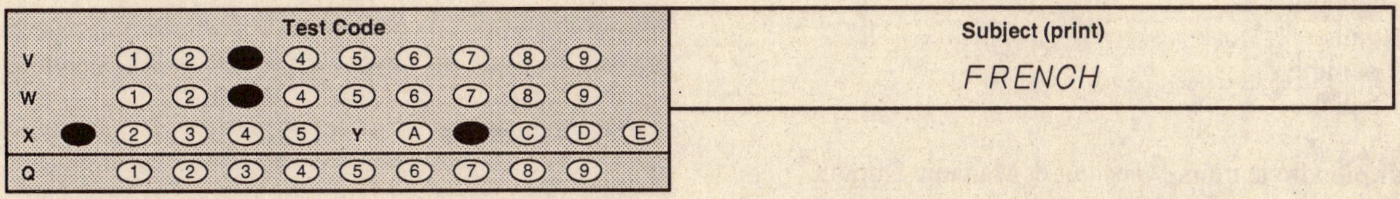

Test Code											Subject (print)
V	1	2	●	4	5	6	7	8	9		FRENCH
W	1	2	●	4	5	6	7	8	9		
X ●	2	3	4	5	Y	A	●	C	D	E	
Q	1	2	3	4	5	6	7	8	9		

Please answer either Part I or Part II by filling in the specific oval in row Q. You are to fill in ONE and ONLY ONE oval as described below, to indicate how you obtained your knowledge of French. The information you provide is for statistical purposes only and will not influence your score on the test.

Part I — If your knowledge of French does not come primarily from courses taken in grades 9 through 12, fill in oval 9 and leave the remaining ovals blank, regardless of how long you studied the subject in school. For example, you are to fill in oval 9 if your knowledge of French comes primarily from any of the following sources: study prior to the ninth grade, courses taken at a college, or special study, extensive residence abroad, or living in a home in which French is the principal language spoken, or extensive residence abroad that includes significant experience in the French language.

Part II — If your knowledge of French does come primarily from courses taken in secondary school, fill in the oval that indicates the level of the French course in which you are currently enrolled. If you are not now enrolled in a French course, fill in the oval that indicates the level of the most advanced course in French that you have completed.

First year:	first or second half	—fill in oval 1
Second year:	first half	—fill in oval 2
	second half	—fill in oval 3
Third year:	first half	—fill in oval 4
	second half	—fill in oval 5
Fourth year:	first half	—fill in oval 6
	second half	—fill in oval 7
Advanced Placement course or a course at a level higher than fourth year, second half or high school course work plus a minimum of four weeks of study abroad		—fill in oval 8

When the supervisor gives the signal, turn the page and begin the French test. There are 100 numbered ovals on the answer sheet and 42 questions in the French test. Therefore, use only ovals 1 to 42 for recording your answers.

FRENCH TEST

PLEASE NOTE THAT YOUR ANSWER SHEET HAS FIVE ANSWER POSITIONS MARKED A, B, C, D, E, WHILE THE QUESTIONS THROUGHOUT THIS TEST CONTAIN ONLY FOUR CHOICES. BE SURE NOT TO MAKE ANY MARKS IN COLUMN E.

Part A

Directions: This part consists of a number of incomplete statements, each having four suggested completions. Select the most appropriate completion and fill in the corresponding oval on the answer sheet.

1. Si vous avez trop chaud, ouvrez la . . .

   (A) fenêtre
   (B) valise
   (C) pomme
   (D) bouche

2. Pour prendre le train, Monsieur et Madame Dupont vont à . . .

   (A) la station-service
   (B) la guerre
   (C) la gare
   (D) l'atelier

3. J'ai perdu mon argent parce qu'il y avait un trou dans la . . . de mon pantalon.

   (A) manche
   (B) jambe
   (C) poche
   (D) ceinture

4. Pour aller en Espagne, les Français doivent . . . une frontière.

   (A) transformer
   (B) traverser
   (C) transférer
   (D) transporter

5. Ouvre la boîte, et . . . tu trouveras du fil et une aiguille.

   (A) désormais
   (B) d'ailleurs
   (C) déjà
   (D) dedans

6. Charles avait tant mangé qu'il ne pouvait plus . . . une bouchée.

   (A) soutenir
   (B) emporter
   (C) avaler
   (D) évaluer

7. J'étais bloqué dans la file de voitures. Pas moyen d'avancer ni de . . .

   (A) repasser
   (B) retarder
   (C) repousser
   (D) reculer

8. Les banques sont fermées parce que c'est un jour . . .

   (A) férié
   (B) sacré
   (C) saint
   (D) libre

GO ON TO THE NEXT PAGE

Part B

Directions: Each of the following sentences contains a blank. From the four choices given, select the one that can be inserted in the blank to form a grammatically correct sentence and fill in the corresponding oval on the answer sheet. Choice (A) may consist of dashes that indicate that no insertion is required to form a grammatically correct sentence.

9. ------- est le meilleur joueur de cette équipe?

(A) Qu'
(B) Quelle
(C) Qu'est-ce qu'
(D) Qui

10. C'est ------- hiver qu'il fait le plus froid?

(A) avec l'
(B) dans l'
(C) sans l'
(D) pendant l'

11. Ce sont ------- que je vois tous les weekends.

(A) eux
(B) vous
(C) nous
(D) leur

12. Il ------- beau quand le match a commencé.

(A) avait fait
(B) faisait
(C) ait fait
(D) ferait

13. Tu connais le Café Métropole? Nous nous ------- retrouvons tous les jours après les cours.

(A) le
(B) en
(C) y
(D) là

14. Si tu leur avais téléphoné plus tôt, ils ------- des billets pour le concert.

(A) auraient pris
(B) prendraient
(C) ont pris
(D) prennent

15. ------- -vous! Nous sommes déjà en retard pour le concert.

(A) Partez
(B) Dépêchez
(C) Courez
(D) Venez

16. Dans sa cuisine, il fallait toujours que tout ------- impeccable et reluisant.

(A) est
(B) soit
(C) était
(D) serait

17. C'est par ------- que nous avons été prévenus du danger.

(A) soi
(B) elle
(C) leur
(D) il

GO ON TO THE NEXT PAGE

Part C

Directions: The paragraphs below contain blank spaces indicating omissions in the text. For some blanks it is necessary to choose the completion that is most appropriate to the meaning of the passage; for other blanks, to choose the one completion that forms a grammatically correct sentence. In some instances, choice (A) may consist of dashes that indicate that no insertion is required to form a grammatically correct sentence. In each case, indicate your answer by filling in the corresponding oval on the answer sheet. Be sure to read each paragraph completely before answering the questions related to it.

L'hôtelier, ------- à un journaliste, justifiait l'augmentation des prix -------

18. (A) parlera
(B) parle
(C) parlant
(D) parlé

19. (A) à cause
(B) avant que
(C) pour que
(D) depuis

la guerre. Il citait, parmi ------- raisons, ------- du tourisme et le fait que

20. (A) d'autres
(B) tant
(C) beaucoup
(D) de

21. (A) la croisière
(B) l'addition
(C) l'accroissement
(D) la poussière

les touristes ------- les chambres de luxe. Il trouvait que ------- de nouvelle construction

22. (A) préférer
(B) préférant
(C) préférait
(D) préfèrent

23. (A) la faute
(B) le dégât
(C) la peine
(D) le manque

hôtelière contribuait ------- rendre la situation encore plus ------- .

24. (A) -------
(B) de
(C) pour
(D) à

25. (A) méchante
(B) grave
(C) savante
(D) profonde

Dès que vous ------- le temps ------- prendre contact avec elle, donnez- ------- un

26. (A) auriez
(B) ayez
(C) aurez
(D) aviez

27. (A) -------
(B) à
(C) de
(D) pour

28. (A) lui
(B) elle
(C) vous
(D) la

coup de téléphone. Il faut l'avertir que tout ------- arrangé et que j'arriverai ------- vingt.

29. (A) a
(B) est
(C) ait
(D) soit

30. (A) le
(B) au
(C) sur le
(D) dans le

GO ON TO THE NEXT PAGE

Part D

Directions: Read the following texts carefully for comprehension. Each is followed by a number of questions or incomplete statements. Select the completion or answer that is best according to the text and fill in the corresponding oval on the answer sheet.

«Image Center» est l'histoire d'une passion. Hésitant entre l'art et la science, Sylvie Magnus, 24 ans, passe deux ans à l'Ecole des Beaux Arts et complète sa formation à Londres, où elle apprend les applications de l'informatique sur l'image. Et c'est le déclic, peindre avec la lumière, créer des décors magiques pour des défilés de mode, ou des effets spéciaux pour le cinéma, tout la fascine. Une étude de marché lui apprend qu'il n'existe pas d'agence spécialisée dans la conception de ces images. Sylvie décide donc de combler l'espace: elle crée en 1986, grâce à un prêt de famille et à des subventions, la première agence européenne conseil en image de synthèse : «Image Center».

— L'image de synthèse, explique Sylvie, c'est la révolution graphique des années 80. Chaque fois que l'on a besoin d'une image impossible à visualiser, l'ordinateur la crée. Ce sont des images nouvelles qui surprennent l'oeil, la conscience et font naître du beau, de l'art sous d'autres formes. Cela peut être la représentation d'objets, de personnes, et d'environnements réels, ou bien la concrétisation de l'imagination. En médecine, ce peut être l'intérieur du corps humain, en art c'est un plus sur l'image existante. Mon domaine d'application est donc illimité.

— Ma spécialité c'est de détourner des images scientifiques à des fins artistiques. Je considère qu'en toute chose l'esthétisme est une valeur ajoutée. Mon souci est davantage de susciter l'émotion que de parvenir à la perfection.

31. Avec les services d' «Image Center» on peut

(A) peindre des chefs-d'oeuvre
(B) écrire des histoires
(C) appliquer un diagnostic
(D) faire des graphiques

32. Qu'est-ce que Sylvie Magnus a étudié après ses deux ans à l'Ecole des Beaux Arts?

(A) Les arts décoratifs
(B) La cinématographie
(C) Les nouvelles technologies
(D) La médicine

33. A la ligne 10, «combler l'espace» veut dire

(A) répondre à un besoin
(B) louer un bureau
(C) faire des recherches scientifiques
(D) faire des subventions

34. Comment est-ce que Sylvie Magnus a trouvé l'argent pour lancer «Image Center»?

(A) Elle a travaillé dans un hôpital.
(B) Elle en a gagné pendant la révolution.
(C) Elle a organisé des défilés de mode.
(D) Elle en a emprunté à ses parents.

35. Selon le texte, qui pourrait se trouver parmi les clients d'«Image Center»?

(A) Des mannequins cherchant à perfectionner leur maquillage
(B) Des restaurateurs de monuments historiques
(C) Des chirurgiens qui veulent une image des organes humains
(D) Des candidats politiques cherchant à améliorer leur image

36. Quel est le rôle de l'art dans l'image produite par «Image Center»?

(A) Il est toujours secondaire au but scientifique.
(B) Il est important dans toutes ses créations.
(C) Il est impossible à visualiser.
(D) Il est souvent subordonné aux effets spéciaux.

GO ON TO THE NEXT PAGE

Sondage

Vous, amateurs de télé—

Question 1
Utilisez-vous personnellement une télécommande?

Question 2
Vous-même, quand vous utilisez cette télécommande, vous vous en servez pour: couper le son et faire autre chose? changer de chaîne dès que le programme ne vous plaît pas? suivre plusieurs émissions en même temps? chercher une émission particulière? éviter la publicité? rechercher la publicité?

en %

Proportion des Français âgés de 15 ans et plus qui utilisent personnellement une télécommande	**46**
qui s'en servent pour	
— couper le son pour faire autre chose	26
— changer de chaîne dès que le programme ne leur plaît pas	43
— suivre plusieurs émissions en même temps	12
— chercher une émission particulière	31
— éviter la publicité	23
— rechercher la publicité	2

37. Qu'est-ce qu'une télécommande?

(A) Une sorte de téléviseur
(B) Une émission de télévision
(C) Une sorte de publicité
(D) Un appareil électronique

38. Selon ce sondage, on se sert le plus souvent d'une télécommande pour

(A) acheter quelque chose
(B) trouver une émission plus intéressante
(C) pouvoir regarder deux émissions à la fois
(D) vérifier le bon fonctionnement de son téléviseur

GO ON TO THE NEXT PAGE

Le choc fut tel que je ne pus rester en selle et je tombai de cheval. C'est tout ce dont je me souviens. Quand je revins à moi, j'étais dans mon lit. De violents maux de tête et des douleurs dans tous les membres signalèrent mon retour à la vie. Bientôt je regrettai ma défaillance pendant laquelle j'avais été maintenu dans un état cotonneux d'où la souffrance était exclue.

39. L'auteur a été victime

(A) d'une maladie
(B) d'un accident
(C) d'un oubli
(D) d'une hallucination

40. On comprend que l'auteur s'est

(A) évadé
(B) évanoui
(C) tué
(D) endormi

41. L'auteur est conscient d'avoir

(A) enfin raison
(B) peur de la mort
(C) honte de sa sottise
(D) mal partout

42. A la fin du passage l'auteur regrette

(A) d'avoir trop dormi
(B) d'avoir abandonné son cheval
(C) de ne pas pouvoir sortir
(D) d'être revenu à lui

S T O P

IF YOU FINISH BEFORE TIME IS CALLED, YOU MAY CHECK YOUR WORK ON THIS TEST ONLY.
DO NOT WORK ON ANY OTHER TEST IN THIS BOOK.

Answers to the French Achievment Mini Test

Question Number	Correct Answer	Question Number	Correct Answer
1	A	22	D
2	C	23	D
3	C	24	D
4	B	25	B
5	D	26	C
6	C	27	C
7	D	28	A
8	A	29	B
9	D	30	A
10	D	31	D
11	A	32	C
12	B	33	A
13	C	34	D
14	A	35	C
15	B	36	B
16	B	37	D
17	B	38	B
18	C	39	B
19	D	40	B
20	A	41	D
21	C	42	D

The SAT II: German and German with Listening

The College Board offers two types of one-hour German Subject Tests. The traditional reading-only test consists of 80–85 multiple-choice questions. The new German Subject Test with Listening consists of 85–90 multiple-choice listening and reading questions.

The German Subject Test (reading only) assumes differences in language preparation; you are neither favored nor penalized for having followed a specific method of instruction. The test is designed for students who have studied the language for three or four years in secondary school (or the equivalent). However, students with two years of strong preparation in German are also encouraged to take the test. The best preparation for the test is the gradual development of competence in German over a period of years. Reading comprehension, knowledge of vocabulary, and mastery of structure (grammar) are tested (see chart below); listening, writing, and speaking are not tested.

In addition to reading questions, the German Subject Test with Listening measures your ability to understand spoken language by means of three types of listening questions. The first type (rejoinders) tests your ability to identify a plausible response to a short question or statement. The second and third types require that you answer questions based on short and longer listening selections.

The SAT II: German Subject Test with Listening

Sections of Test		Approximate Percentage of Test
Listening Section Short Stimuli Short Dialogues/Monologues Long Dialogues/Monologues	(20 minutes)	35
Reading Section Vocabulary in Context Structure in Context (grammar) Reading Comprehension — (authentic stimulus materials and passages)	(40 minutes)	65

The German Subject Test with Listening tests your ability to understand the spoken language by means of three types of listening questions. The first type asks you to respond to a very brief oral stimulus. The second and third types test your ability to answer questions based on dialogues or monologues. All questions in this section of the test are multiple-choice questions in which you must choose the best response from *three* or *four* choices offered. Text in brackets [ ] is *only* recorded; it is not printed in your test booklet.

Sample Questions for the Listening Section

Part A

Directions: In this part of the test you will hear statements or questions spoken in German, each followed by three responses also spoken in German. You will hear the statements or questions twice, but the responses will be spoken just one time. The sentences and responses you hear will *not* be written in your test booklet. Therefore, you must listen very carefully. Select the best answer and fill in the corresponding oval on the answer sheet. Please note that your answer sheet has four answer positions, marked A, B, C, and D. Because the questions throughout this part contain only three choices, do not make any marks in column D.

1. (Man) **[Wann fährt der nächste Zug nach Köln? . . . Wann fährt der nächste Zug nach Köln?]**

(Woman) **[(A) Um wieviel Uhr?**
(B) Um elf Uhr acht.
(C) Um die Stadt.]

(5 seconds)

2. (Woman) **[Hast du schon deinen Studentenausweis? . . . Hast du schon deinen Studentenausweis?]**

(Man) **[(A) Ja, ich trampe gern.**
(B) Nein, den muß ich mir noch besorgen.
(C) Nein, man kann nicht studieren.]

(5 seconds)

3. (Man) [Bring mir bitte eine Tasse Kaffee mit. . . . Bring mir bitte eine Tasse Kaffee mit.]

(Woman) [(A) Gern. Mit Milch?
(B) Hat es geschmeckt?
(C) Ich mahle den Kaffee selbst.]
(5 seconds)

Part B

Directions: In this part of the test you will hear several selections. They will not be printed in your test booklet. You will hear them *only once*. Therefore, you must listen very carefully. In your test booklet you will read one or two short questions about what was said. Another speaker will read the questions for you. Each question will be followed by *four* choices marked (A), (B), (C), and (D). The choices are *not* printed in your test booklet. You will hear them *once*. Select the best answer and fill in the corresponding oval on your answer sheet.

(Narrator) [Question 4 refers to the following short dialogue.]

(Woman) [Ich möchte gern meinem Freund in Amerika ein Fax schicken.

(Man) Füllen Sie dieses Formular aus mit Namen und Nummer.

(Woman) Wieviel wird das kosten?

(Man) Das hängt ganz davon ab, wieviele Seiten Sie schicken.]

4. (Man) [Was möchte die Frau?] Was möchte die Frau?

(Woman) [(A) Fahrkarten kaufen.
(B) Briefe aufgeben.
(C) Ein Fax schicken.
(D) Einen Freund abholen.]
(5 seconds)

(Narrator) [Questions 5 and 6 refer to the following exchange.]

(Woman) [Könnten Sie mir bitte dieses Kleid heute noch reinigen.

(Man) Das ist leider unmöglich. Wir machen in einer Stunde, um neunzehn Uhr, Feierabend.

(Woman) Aber bitte, ich muß dieses Kleid unbedingt heute zum Konzert tragen!]

5. (Man) [Wo findet dieser Dialog wohl statt?] Wo findet dieser Dialog wohl statt?

(Woman) [(A) In einer Reinigung.
(B) In einer Konzerthalle.
(C) In einer Boutique.
(D) Auf einem Ball.]
(5 seconds)

6. (Man) [Welche Tageszeit ist es?] Welche Tageszeit ist es?

(Woman) [(A) Morgen.
(B) Mittag.
(C) Abend.
(D) Nachtmittag.]
(5 seconds)

Part C

<u>Directions:</u> You will now listen to some extended dialogues or monologues. You will hear each *only once*. After each dialogue or monologue, you will be asked several questions about what you have just heard. These questions are not printed in your test booklet. From the four printed choices, select the best answer to each question and fill in the corresponding oval on the answer sheet.

Questions 7-10.

(Narrator) [Two students talk about Chris's year abroad.]

(Woman) [Du, Chris, stimmt es? Du wirst das nächste Schuljahr in Amerika verbringen?

(Man) Ja, und vorgestern habe ich schon alle nötigen Papiere bekommen. Ich soll bei einer Familie Lazarro in Los Angeles wohnen und mit ihrem Sohn Miguel zur Schule gehen.

(Woman) Welche Fächer wirst du denn da haben?

(Man) Weiß ich noch nicht, aber ich werde mit Miguel die 11. Klasse besuchen.

(Woman) In amerikanischen Highschools wird auch viel Sport getrieben, nicht?

(Man) Ja, Miguel soll sogar ein recht guter Schwimmer sein. Ich glaube, er hat schon einige Medaillen gewonnen.

(Woman) Das ist ja was für dich! Du schwimmst doch auch so gern!

(Man) Ja, aber jetzt muß ich zuerst noch fleißig Englisch üben. Ich will doch so viel wie möglich im Unterricht verstehen und mich natürlich auch mit meiner neuen Familie unterhalten können.]

7. (Man) [Wann hat Chris seine Reisepapiere erhalten?]
(12 seconds)

(A) Vor einer Woche.
(B) Vor einer Stunde.
(C) Vormittags.
(D) Vorgestern.

8. (Man) [Was für eine Schule wird Chris in Amerika besuchen?]
(12 seconds)

(A) Eine Kunstakademie.
(B) Eine Universität.
(C) Eine Oberschule.
(D) Eine Sportschule.

9. (Man) [Warum glaubt Chris, daß Miguel ein guter Schwimmer ist?]
(12 seconds)

(A) Er besucht die Highschool.
(B) Er hat Auszeichnungen gewonnen.
(C) Er wohnt in Kalifornien.
(D) Er ist im Fernsehen erschienen.

10. (Man) [Was will Chris noch vor seiner Reise tun?]
(12 seconds)

(A) Studienfächer auswählen.
(B) Medaillen gewinnen.
(C) Englisch lernen.
(D) Viel schwimmen

Answers for the Sample Listening Questions			
Question Number	Correct Answer	Question Number	Correct Answer
1	B	6	C
2	B	7	D
3	A	8	C
4	C	9	B
5	A	10	C

The SAT II: German Subject Test (Reading Only)

In addition to the German Subject Test with Listening there is a Reading Test that does *not* have a listening section. This test includes a variety of questions requiring wide-ranging knowledge of the language. Sentence completion questions that test vocabulary require you to know the meaning of words and idiomatic expressions in context. Sentence completion questions that test grammar require you to identify usage that is structurally correct and appropriate. Paragraph completion questions that test both vocabulary and grammar present you with sentences from which words have been omitted. You must select the choice that best fits each sentence. Reading comprehension questions test your understanding of the content of various materials taken from sources such as advertisements, timetables, street signs, forms, and tickets. They also examine your ability to read passages representative of various styles and levels of difficulty. Each edition of the German Subject Test contains several prose passages followed by questions that test your understanding of the passage. The passages are generally one or two paragraphs in length, and most of them are adapted from literary sources and newspapers or magazines. The questions test whether you comprehend the main idea and facts or details contained in the text.

Skills Measured	Approximate Percentage of Test
Vocabulary in Context	30
Structure in Context (grammar)	30-40
Reading Comprehension — authentic stimulus materials and passages	30-40

SAT II:

German Subject Mini Test

The test that follows is a shortened version of a typical SAT II: German Subject Test. So that you may have an idea of what the national test administration will be like, try to take the test in this book under conditions as close as possible to those of the nationally administered test. It will probably help if you do the following.

- Set aside 35 minutes for the test when you will not be interrupted, so that you can complete all of it in one sitting.
- Sit at a desk with no other papers or books. You can't take a dictionary, other books, or notes into the test room.
- Have a kitchen timer or clock in front of you for timing yourself.
- Tear out an answer sheet from the back of this book and fill it in just as you would on the day of the test. You can use one answer sheet for as many as three Subject Tests.
- Read the instructions that precede the test. When you take the test, you will be asked to read them before you begin answering questions.

GERMAN TEST

The top portion of the section of the answer sheet that you will use in taking the German test must be filled in exactly as shown in the illustration below. Note carefully that you have to do all of the following on your answer sheet.

1. Print GERMAN on the line under the words "Subject (print)."

2. In the shaded box labeled "Test Code" fill in four ovals:

   —Fill in oval 3 in the row labeled V.

   —Fill in oval 4 in the row labeled W.

   —Fill in oval 2 in the row labeled X.

   —Fill in oval D in the row labeled Y.

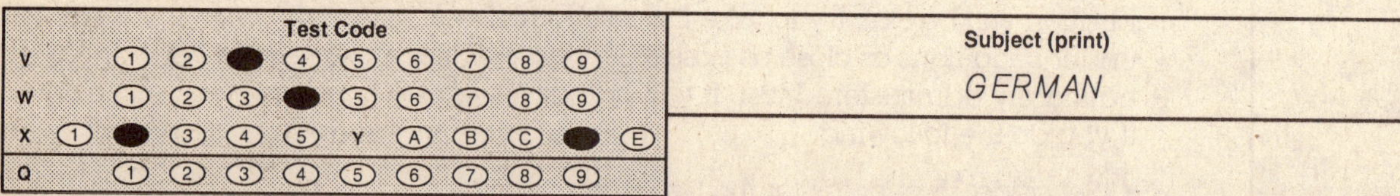

Please answer either Part I or Part II by filling in the specific oval in row Q. You are to fill in ONE and ONLY ONE oval as described below, to indicate how you obtained your knowledge of German. The information you provide is for statistical purposes only and will not influence your score on the test.

Part I If your knowledge of German does not come primarily from courses taken in grades 9 through 12, fill in oval 9 and leave the remaining ovals blank, regardless of how long you studied the subject in school. For example, you are to fill in oval 9 if your knowledge of German comes primarily from any of the following sources: study prior to the ninth grade, courses taken at a college, special study, living in a home in which German is the principal language spoken, or extensive residence abroad that includes significant experience in the German language.

Part II If your knowledge of German does come primarily from courses taken in secondary school, fill in the oval that indicates the level of the German course in which you are currently enrolled. If you are not now enrolled in a German course, fill in the oval that indicates the level of the most advanced course in German that you have completed.

First year:	first or second half	—fill in oval 1
Second year:	first half	—fill in oval 2
	second half	—fill in oval 3
Third year:	first half	—fill in oval 4
	second half	—fill in oval 5
Fourth year:	first half	—fill in oval 6
	second half	—fill in oval 7
Advanced Placement course or a course at a level higher than fourth year, second half or high school course work plus a minimum of four weeks of study abroad		—fill in oval 8

When the supervisor gives the signal, turn the page and begin the German test. There are 100 numbered ovals on the answer sheet and 44 questions in the German test. Therefore, use only ovals 1 to 44 for recording your answers.

GERMAN TEST

PLEASE NOTE THAT YOUR ANSWER SHEET HAS FIVE ANSWER POSITIONS MARKED A, B, C, D, E, WHILE THE QUESTIONS THROUGHOUT THIS TEST CONTAIN ONLY FOUR CHOICES. BE SURE NOT TO MAKE ANY MARKS IN COLUMN E.

Part A

Directions: This part consists of a number of incomplete statements, each having four suggested completions. Select the most appropriate completion and fill in the corresponding oval on the answer sheet.

1. Unsere Gäste sind gestern . . .

(A) kommend
(B) zu kommen
(C) kommen
(D) gekommen

2. Wir sind gestern nicht schwimmen gegangen, . . . es regnete.

(A) weil
(B) seit
(C) für
(D) darum

3. Das Haus dort drüben ist . . .

(A) schönes
(B) schön
(C) schönste
(D) schöne

4. Das ging viel . . . als vorher.

(A) mehr
(B) lieber
(C) besser
(D) größer

5. Ich habe noch Durst. Bringen Sie mir . . . Glas Bier!

(A) anderes
(B) etwas
(C) noch ein
(D) ein Paar

6. Ich habe ihn kennengelernt, . . . ich in Köln war.

(A) wann
(B) wenn
(C) denn
(D) als

7. Er stellt viele Fragen, denn er ist sehr . . .

(A) schweigsam
(B) behaglich
(C) fraglich
(D) neugierig

8. Der Milchmann kommt . . . Tag um sechs Uhr.

(A) jeder
(B) jedes
(C) jedem
(D) jeden

9. Sie kommt erst am 21. Dezember zurück, also kurz . . . Weihnachten.

(A) zu
(B) für
(C) bei
(D) vor

10. Kennen Sie die Mutter des . . . ?

(A) Student
(B) Studentin
(C) Studenten
(D) Studentinnen

11. Er . . . , weil er einen roten Hut trägt.

(A) wacht auf
(B) fällt auf
(C) nimmt an
(D) sieht aus

12. Weder Hunde . . . Katzen können fliegen.

(A) anderseits
(B) oder
(C) als auch
(D) noch

GO ON TO THE NEXT PAGE

GERMAN TEST — *Continued*

13. Kommt der Zug aus München auf . . . sieben an?

 (A) Gleis
 (B) Bürgersteig
 (C) Bank
 (D) Haltestelle

14. Stell dir vor, . . . Bücher sind ins Wasser gefallen!

 (A) allen meinen
 (B) aller meiner
 (C) alle meine
 (D) alle meinen

15. Wenn Monika zu uns gekommen . . . , hätten wir uns gefreut.

 (A) hätte
 (B) würde
 (C) wäre
 (D) seid

16. Was für . . . Dichter ist er?

 (A) ein
 (B) einen
 (C) einer
 (D) eines

17. Meiner Meinung . . . kostet das zuviel.

 (A) nach
 (B) wegen
 (C) trotz
 (D) auf

18. Auch gesunde Zähne soll man regelmäßig . . .

 (A) schlucken
 (B) essen
 (C) putzen
 (D) beißen

19. Wissen Sie darüber . . . ?

 (A) Bedauern
 (B) Entscheidung
 (C) Bescheid
 (D) Rücksicht

GO ON TO THE NEXT PAGE

Part B

Directions: In each of the following paragraphs, there are numbered blanks indicating that words or phrases have been omitted. For each numbered blank, four completions are provided. First read through the entire paragraph. Then, for each numbered blank, choose the completion that is most appropriate and fill in the corresponding oval on the answer sheet.

Da es schon spät ist, ------- ich mich verabschieden. Ich muß morgen sehr -------

20. (A) möchte
    (B) möge
    (C) mochte
    (D) machte

21. (A) abend
    (B) früh
    (C) schon
    (D) langsam

aufstehen und ------- Berlin zu einer wichtigen Konferenz -------.

22. (A) auf
    (B) an
    (C) nach
    (D) zu

23. (A) bleiben
    (B) anrufen
    (C) ankommen
    (D) fahren

Mein Nachbar ist ein Mensch, ------- immer zuviel ißt, ------- er zu dick ist

24. (A) wo
    (B) wer
    (C) was
    (D) der

25. (A) obwohl
    (B) wenn auch
    (C) ungleich
    (D) ebenso

und seine Ärztin ------- schon lange streng -------.

26. (A) es ihm
    (B) ihn es
    (C) ihr ihn
    (D) er es

27. (A) verboten wurde
    (B) verboten hat
    (C) ist verboten
    (D) verboten worden

------- Sie mir bitte, ------- Mann. Ich kenne diesen Stadtteil nicht und habe mich -------.

28. (A) Helfen
    (B) Hilft
    (C) Hilfst
    (D) Helft

29. (A) jung
    (B) junger
    (C) jünger
    (D) jungen

30. (A) verstanden
    (B) versprochen
    (C) vergangen
    (D) verlaufen

GO ON TO THE NEXT PAGE

Part C

Directions: Read the following texts carefully for comprehension. Each is followed by a number of questions or incomplete statements. Select the answer or completion that is best according to the text and fill in the corresponding oval on the answer sheet.

Betreten der Baustelle verboten

Eltern haften für ihre Kinder!

31. Wo findet man dieses Schild?

    (A) Auf einem Kinderspielplatz
    (B) An einem Gefängnis
    (C) Vor einer Baumschule
    (D) Auf einem Bauplatz

GO ON TO THE NEXT PAGE

Questions 32-34

Ihre Urlaubs–Checkliste

1. Personalausweis/Paß/Kinderausweis sind vorhanden und gültig? ○
2. Führerschein/Internationaler Führerschein/Grüne Versicherungskarte? ○
3. Krankenscheinheft bzw. Internationale Anspruchsbescheinigung bzw. private Urlaubskrankenversicherung? Reiseapotheke komplett? ○
4. Reise-, Unfall-, Haftpflicht-, Gepäckversicherung? ○
5. Ihre Reiseunterlagen sind komplett? Fahrkarten/Flugscheine/Benzingutscheine/Platzkarten Bahn/Buchungsbestätigung? ○
6. Ihr Haus ist gesichert? Brötchen/Zeitung abbestellt bzw. Regelungen mit Ihrem Nachbarn getroffen? Sieht jemand während Ihrer Abwesenheit nach dem Rechten? ○
7. Sie haben sich mit Bargeld/Devisen/Reiseschecks/Eurocheques versorgt? Das Postsparbuch und die Ausweiskarte sind mit dabei? ○
8. Von Paß/Personalausweis und Führerschein haben Sie einen Satz Fotokopien eingepackt? ○
9. Satz neuer Straßenkarten? ○
10. Sprachführer/Taschenwörterbuch/Reiseführer? ○

32. Für wen ist diese Liste wohl geschrieben? Für Leute,

(A) die im Ausland arbeiten
(B) die verreisen wollen
(C) die ein Haus kaufen
(D) die nach einer Apotheke suchen

33. Was bedeutet in Punkt 1 wohl das Wort gültig?

(A) Der Ausweis ist schon abgelaufen.
(B) Der Ausweis muß bezahlt werden.
(C) Der Ausweis gilt immer noch.
(D) Der Ausweis muß abgeholt werden.

34. Wovon wird in Punkt 6 der Urlaubscheckliste gesprochen?

(A) Hinterlassen der Ferienadresse
(B) Reiseunterlagen
(C) Versicherungen
(D) Absicherung des Hauses

GO ON TO THE NEXT PAGE

Fernsehen

MI. 8. DEZEMBER

1. PROGRAMM

16.15 Tagesschau
16.20 Klassenbild einer Hauptschule. Bericht
17.05 Kann 'ne Kanne Kunst sein? Kinderprogramm
17.55 Tagesschau
München: 18.05 Wartet nur, bis Vater kommt. 19.03 Notarztwagen 7. **Frankfurt:** 18.10 DerFuchs mit dem goldenen Ohrring. 18.40 Im Werknotiert. **Hamburg/Bremen:** 18.00 Journal. 19.26 Lokalseite unten links. **Saarbrücken:** 18.25 DerFuchs mit dem goldenen Ohrring. 19.01 Im Werknotiert. **Berlin:** 18.20 Das Geheimnis der blauen Tropfen. 18.40 Zwischenlandung. **Stuttgart/ Baden-Baden:** 18.30 Der Fuchs mit dem goldenen Ohrring. 19.10 Im Werk notiert. **Köln:** 18.05 Schaurige Geschichten. 18.40 Die Vögel im Park von Meiji Jingu.
20.00 Tagesschau, Wetter
20.15 Maschinen statt Menschen
Kann die Vernichtung von Arbeitsplätzen aufgehalten werden?
21.00 Bei Westwing hört man keinen Schuß
Eine Insel-Ballade

35. Um wievel Uhr beginnen die ersten Nachrichten?

(A) Um neun Uhr
(B) Um viertel nach vier
(C) Um halb sieben
(D) Um viertel vor neun

GO ON TO THE NEXT PAGE

Die vielen Jugendlichen, die abends in den Frankfurter Sinkkasten kommen, fühlen sich sehr wohl: Langeweile kennt man hier überhaupt nicht. Die Abende bei Pop, Jazz, Folk, Theater und Filmen vergehen für sie wie im Fluge.

Der Sinkkasten ist ein Verein, der 1971 von drei jungen Leuten — Aina, Wolfgang und Werner — in einem Kellergewölbe am Main gegründet wurde, nachdem sie sich eines Tages entschlossen hatten, ihren Feierabend nicht weiter in Kneipen zu verbringen.

Der Sinkkasten verlangt einen Mitgliedsbeitrag von fünf Mark monatlich, obgleich es ihm gar nicht um Gewinne geht. Hier können aber endlich jeden Abend Jugendliche zusammenkommen und fröhlich sein. Im Sinkkasten treten außerdem viele prominente Musiker und Gruppen auf. Dazu kommen dann noch interessante Theateraufführungen. Oft werden den Gästen auch sehr gute Filme gezeigt. Junge Maler können hier ihre ersten Werke ausstellen, und regelmäßig dürfen die jungen Gäste selbst auch mal Künstler spielen: sie können beim freien Malen ihre bisher verborgenen Talente entdecken. Die schönsten Werke werden anschließend ausgestellt.

Das Programm ersetzt den Jugendlichen Theater, Kino und Kneipe zugleich. Deshalb kommen sie auch in Scharen! Längst hat es sich herumgesprochen, daß man im Sinkkasten ganz nette Leute kennenlernen kann. Die Stadtverwaltung von Frankfurt am Main hat inzwischen den Sinkkasten schätzen gelernt: seit Anfang 1975 wird der Klub vom Kulturamt mit Geld unterstützt.

36. Die Abende im Sinkkasten vergehen den Jugendlichen im allgemeinen

    (A) aus lauter Langeweile viel zu schnell
    (B) wegen der vielen Unterhaltungsmöglichkeiten sehr rasch
    (C) ziemlich langsam, weil das Programm zu lange dauert
    (D) sehr angenehm, denn sie machen große Gewinne

37. Wo ist der Sinkkasten untergebracht?

    (A) In einem alten Theater
    (B) Gleich neben der Konzerthalle
    (C) In der Kneipe eines Kinos
    (D) Ganz unten in einem Gebäude

38. Was können die Gäste in diesem Klub tun?

    (A) Ihre eigenen Schöpfungen ausstellen
    (B) Endlich ihre Kochkunst zeigen
    (C) Ohne monatlichen Beitrag alles mitmachen
    (D) Die täglichen Hausaufgaben erledigen

39. Was kann man im allgemeinen über den Klub sagen?

    (A) Er ist das Kulturzentrum der Stadt Frankfurt.
    (B) Er ist finanzieller Mittelpunkt für die Stadtväter
    (C) Er ist Anziehungspunkt für viele junge Leute.
    (D) Er ist als kutureller Treffpunkt nicht erfolgreich.

GO ON TO THE NEXT PAGE

Wer schwimmt, um abzunehmen, müht sich vergebens. Der Wassersport, so fanden Mediziner, ist als Schlankheitskur nutzlos. — Schwimmen macht zuviel Appetit.

Um die Auswirkung verschiedener Sportarten auf das Körpergewicht zu testen, mußten drei Gruppen „mäßig übergewichtiger" Personen täglich eine Stunde lang entweder schnell gehen, auf dem Standfahrrad fahren oder schwimmen. Die Patienten durften nach Lust und Laune essen, mußten aber ihr Trainingsprogramm genau einhalten. Nach sechs Monaten wurden sie gewogen. Wer nur gegangen war, hatte zehn Prozent des Gewichts verloren; die Radfahrer hatten zwölf Prozent abgenommen; wer jedoch geschwommen war, hatte drei Prozent zugenommen. Obwohl die aufgewandte Energie bei allen etwa gleich gewesen war, war das Resultat für die Schwimmer das Gegenteil von dem für die anderen zwei Vergleichsgruppen.

Aus diesen Resultaten haben die Forscher den Schluß gezogen, daß die Bewegung im kalten Wasser und der damit verbundene Wärmeverlust den Appetit stimulierten.

40. Was wollten die Mediziner herausfinden?

(A) Welche Sportarten für Patienten besonders ungesund sind
(B) Ob Radfahrer oder Schwimmer mehr essen
(C) Warum übergewichtige Personen so selten schwimmen
(D) Wie sportliche Übung das Körpergewicht beeinflußt

41. Wie wurden die Teilnehmer für dieses Experiment ausgewählt?

(A) Sie wogen mehr als sie sollten.
(B) Sie wollten Ärzte werden.
(C) Sie hatten wenig Zeit für Sport.
(D) Sie hofften, athletischer zu werden.

42. Was mußten die Patienten während des Experiments jeden Tag machen?

(A) Sich nach dem Mittagessen wiegen
(B) Eine Stunde lang eine gewisse Sportart treiben
(C) Genau aufschreiben, wie oft sie hungrig waren
(D) Vor dem Frühstück einen einstündigen Spaziergang machen

43. Die Forscher haben am Ende des Experiments entdeckt; die Personen, die

(A) am meisten gewogen hatten, haben das meiste Gewicht verloren
(B) geschwommen waren, haben nach sechs Monaten mehr gewogen
(C) die meiste Energie verbraucht hatten, haben zu viel gegessen
(D) Radfahrer waren, haben das geringste Gewicht abgenommen

44. Wie haben die Forscher das Resultat des Experiments erklärt?

(A) Man erkältet sich leicht beim Schwimmen.
(B) Die Schwimmgruppe war immer zu faul.
(C) Sechs Monate waren eine zu kurze Zeit für das Experiment.
(D) Verlust von Körperwärme verursacht einen größeren Appetit.

S T O P

IF YOU FINISH BEFORE TIME IS CALLED, YOU MAY CHECK YOUR WORK ON THIS TEST ONLY. DO NOT WORK ON ANY OTHER TEST IN THIS BOOK.

Answers to the SAT II: German Subject Mini Test			
Question Number	**Correct Answer**	**Question Number**	**Correct Answer**
1	D	23	D
2	A	24	D
3	B	25	A
4	C	26	A
5	C	27	B
6	D	28	A
7	D	29	B
8	D	30	D
9	D	31	D
10	C	32	B
11	B	33	C
12	D	34	D
13	A	35	B
14	C	36	B
15	C	37	D
16	A	38	A
17	A	39	C
18	C	40	D
19	C	41	A
20	A	42	B
21	B	43	B
22	C	44	D

The SAT II: Modern Hebrew Subject Test

The SAT II: Modern Hebrew Subject Test consists of 85 multiple-choice questions. It is designed to measure competence in Modern Hebrew and to allow for variation in language preparation. The test is independent of particular textbooks or methods of instruction. It is intended primarily for students who have studied Hebrew in high school for two to four years. The best preparation for the test is the gradual development of competence in Hebrew over a period of years.

The Modern Hebrew Subject Test evaluates your mastery of vocabulary, structure, and reading comprehension through a variety of questions that require a wide-ranging knowledge of the language. The questions on vocabulary and structure test your familiarity with definitions and parts of speech, as well as your ability to recognize appropriate language patterns. Reading comprehension questions test your understanding of passages of varying levels of difficulty. These passages, most of which are vocalized, are generally adapted from literary sources and newspaper or magazine articles. While some passages have Biblical references, no material in the test is written in Biblical Hebrew.

Skills Measured	Approximate Percentage of Test
Vocabulary in Context	35
Structure in Context (grammar)	35
Reading Comprehension	30

85 Questions; Time — 60 minutes

Except for the directions, the entire test is in Hebrew; there are no questions that require you to translate from English to Hebrew or from Hebrew to English.

Each question is followed by four choices from which you must choose the best answer.

The questions are numbered on the RIGHT side of each column and begin on the RIGHT side of the page.

Questions Used in the Test

The three types of questions used in the Modern Hebrew Subject Test are sentence completion questions, paragraph completion questions, and questions based on a series of passages that test your understanding of those passages.

Sample Test

The test that follows is a representative sample of the Modern Hebrew Subject Test, so that you may familiarize yourself with the kinds of questions included in the test. These 60 questions should be completed in 45 minutes, which is approximately three-quarters of the regular test (80-85 items in 60 minutes). The purpose is to allow teachers to practice with their students during a regular class period. The directions, the background questionnaire, and the different sections and types of questions in this mini test are similar to those on the actual test. The principal differences are the number of questions and the amount of time allotted for the test.

SAT II:

Modern Hebrew Subject Mini Test

The test that follows is a shortened version of a typical SAT II: Modern Hebrew Subject Test. So that you may have an idea of what the national test administration will be like, try to take the test in this book under conditions as close as possible to those of the nationally administered test. It will probably help if you do the following.

- Set aside 45 minutes for the test when you will not be interrupted, so that you can complete all of it in one sitting.
- Sit at a desk with no other papers or books. You can't take a dictionary, other books, or notes into the test room.
- Have a kitchen timer or clock in front of you for timing yourself.
- Tear out an answer sheet from the back of this book and fill it in just as you would on the day of the test. You can use one answer sheet for as many as three Subject Tests.
- Read the instructions that precede the test. When you take the test, you will be asked to read them before you begin answering questions.

MODERN HEBREW TEST

The top portion of the section of the answer sheet that you will use in taking the Modern Hebrew test must be filled in exactly as shown in the illustration below. Note carefully that you have to do all of the following on your answer sheet.

1. Print MODERN HEBREW on the line under the words "Subject (print)."

2. In the shaded box labeled "Test Code" fill in four ovals:

—Fill in oval 1 in the row labeled V.

—Fill in oval 3 in the row labeled W.

—Fill in oval 4 in the row labeled X.

—Fill in oval C in the row labeled Y.

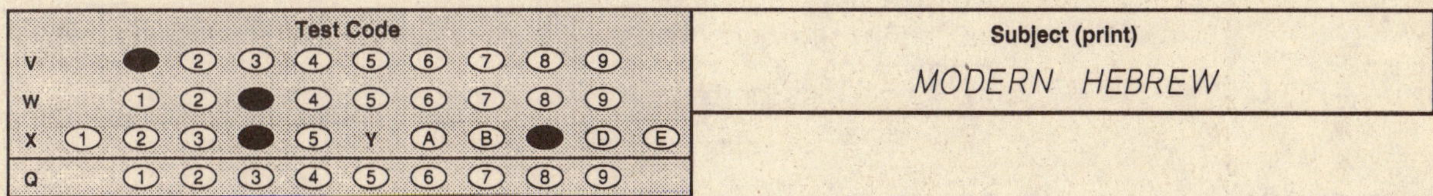

Please answer either Part I or Part II by filling in the specific oval in row Q. The information you provide is for statistical purposes only and will not influence your score on the test.

Part I — If your knowledge of Hebrew comes primarily from extensive residence in Israel after age 10, courses taken in college, or from living in a home where Hebrew is the principal language spoken, fill in OVAL 9 and skip the remaining questions on this page.

Part II — If your knowledge of Hebrew comes primarily from courses taken in grades 9 through 12, fill in the oval that represents the total number of years you have studied Hebrew. Fill in only one of ovals 1-7. (Leave oval 8 blank).

Less than 2 years	fill in oval 4
2 - 2 1/2 years	fill in oval 5
3 - 3 1/2 years	fill in oval 6
4 years	fill in oval 7
If you have studied Hebrew in a Jewish/Hebrew Day School up to the 8th grade only	fill in oval 1
If you have studied Hebrew in a Jewish/Hebrew Day School and less than 2 years in High School	fill in oval 2
If you have studied Hebrew in a Jewish/Hebrew Day School and 2 or more years of study beyond 8th grade	fill in oval 3

When the supervisor gives the signal, turn the page and begin the Modern Hebrew test. There are 100 numbered ovals on the answer sheet and 60 questions in the Modern Hebrew test. Therefore, use only ovals 1 to 60 for recording your answers.

MODERN HEBREW TEST

Part A

Directions: This part consists of a number of incomplete statements, each having four suggested completions. Select the most appropriate completion and fill in the corresponding oval on the answer sheet.

1. הוּא אוֹמֵר שֶׁאֵין חָדָשׁ תַּחַת הַשֶּׁמֶשׁ, וְהוּא ______.

(A) צוֹדֵק

(B) נָכוֹן

(C) אֱמֶת

(D) טָעוּת

2. הַשִּׂמְלָה שֶׁלִּי ______ מְאֹד; קָנִיתִי אוֹתָהּ לִפְנֵי עֶשֶׂר שָׁנִים.

(A) עֲיֵפָה

(B) זְקֵנָה

(C) וָתִיקָה

(D) יְשָׁנָה

3. הַפְּגִישָׁה בֵּין מֹשֶׁה וְרָחֵל ______ לְשָׁעָה תֵּשַׁע.

(A) נִגְמְרָה

(B) נִזְכְּרָה

(C) נִקְבְּעָה

(D) נִשְׁמְעָה

4. אַרְבַּע ______ הַשָּׁנָה הֵן: סְתָו, חֹרֶף, אָבִיב וְקַיִץ.

(A) קוֹמוֹת

(B) כּוֹחוֹת

(C) עוֹנוֹת

(D) רוּחוֹת

5. הוּא נוֹעֵל אֶת הַדֶּלֶת, וְשָׂם בַּכִּיס אֶת ______ שֶׁל הַבַּיִת.

(A) הַשָּׁטִיחַ

(B) הַחַלּוֹן

(C) הַמִּזְוָדָה

(D) הַמַּפְתֵּחַ

6. אִם הָרַכֶּבֶת לֹא ______, נִצְטָרֵךְ לָלֶכֶת בָּרֶגֶל.

(A) תָּעוּף

(B) תַּגִּיעַ

(C) תָּשׁוּט

(D) תַּפְלִיג

7. לֹא הָיִיתִי בִּירוּשָׁלַיִם זְמַן רַב, וְלָכֵן ______ לִנְסֹעַ לְשָׁם הַשָּׁבוּעַ.

(A) הֶחְבֵּאתִי

(B) הֶחְלַטְתִּי

(C) הִשְׁלַמְתִּי

(D) הֶרְאֵיתִי

GO ON TO THE NEXT PAGE

8. הֵם בָּאוּ מִן הָעִיר כְּדֵי ______ אֶת פְּנֵי הָעוֹלִים הַחֲדָשִׁים.

(A) לְבַקֵּשׁ

(B) לִשְׁמֹעַ

(C) לְבַקֵּר

(D) לְקַבֵּל

9. קַמְתִּי הַבֹּקֶר עָיֵף לַעֲבוֹדָה, כִּי הָלַכְתִּי אֶתְמוֹל לִישׁוֹן בְּשָׁעָה ______ .

(A) אֲחוֹרִית

(B) אַחֶרֶת

(C) מְאֻחֶרֶת

(D) מְאַחֶרֶת

10. אָבִי מַסְכִּים שֶׁאֵצֵא לְטִיּוּל, אֲבָל אִמִּי ______ לְכָךְ.

(A) מִתְקַבֶּלֶת

(B) מַדְאִיגָה

(C) מַפְסִיקָה

(D) מִתְנַגֶּדֶת

11. אֲחוֹתִי בִּקְּרָה בְּיִשְׂרָאֵל ______: הַבִּקּוּר הָרִאשׁוֹן הָיָה בִּשְׁנַת 1970, וְהַבִּקּוּר הַשֵּׁנִי בִּשְׁנַת 1989.

(A) מָאתַיִם

(B) פַּעֲמַיִם

(C) שְׁתַּיִם

(D) מָחֳרָתַיִם

12. הַמְּסִבָּה תִּתְקַיֵּם בְּבֵית הַהוֹרִים, מִפְּנֵי שֶׁכֻּלָּם מַכִּירִים אֶת הַדֶּרֶךְ ______ .

(A) לְבֵיתָם

(B) לְבָתֵּיהֶם

(C) לְבָתֶּיהָ

(D) לְבָתָּיו

13. אֲנִי רוֹצָה, שֶׁבֶּעָתִיד ______ לִי הַרְבֵּה יְלָדִים.

(A) אֶהְיֶה

(B) נִהְיֶה

(C) יִהְיוּ

(D) לִהְיוֹת

14. לֹא הֵבַנְתִּי אֶת הָעִבְרִית בַּסִּפּוּר ______ .

(A) הַזֶּה

(B) הַזֹּאת

(C) הַהִיא

(D) הָהֵם

15. הָאוֹרְחִים ______ אֶת הַמִּזְוָדוֹת הַבַּיְתָה.

(A) הִכְנִיסוּ

(B) נִכְנְסוּ

(C) הִכְנַסְתֶּם

(D) נִכְנַסְתֶּם

GO ON TO THE NEXT PAGE

MODERN HEBREW TEST — *Continued*

16. "רוּת, לָמָּה לֹא ______ עֲדַיִן אֶת הַפְּרָחִים?"
(A) סִדַּרְתְּ
(B) מְסַדְּרִים
(C) תְּסַדֵּר
(D) מְסַדֶּרֶת

17. אִמָּא אָמְרָה לְיָאִיר: "______ תֵּצֵא הַחוּצָה, כִּי קַר בַּחוּץ".
(A) בִּלְתִּי
(B) אִם
(C) רַק
(D) אַל

18. הוּא נוֹהֵג ______ מְכוֹנִית שֶׁל אָבִיו.
(A) עִם
(B) אֶת
(C) מִ
(D) בַּ

19. "בְּבַקָּשָׁה ______ אֵלַי הָעֶרֶב בֵּין שֶׁבַע לִשְׁמוֹנֶה".
(A) מִתְקַשֵּׁר
(B) הִתְקַשֵּׁר
(C) הִתְקַשַּׁרְתָּ
(D) אֶתְקַשֵּׁר

20. אַבְרָהָם, יִצְחָק וְיַעֲקֹב הֵם ______ הָאָבוֹת.
(A) שְׁלִישׁ
(B) שְׁלִישִׁי
(C) שְׁלֹשֶׁת
(D) שְׁלָשְׁתְּכֶם

21. כִּבַּסְתִּי אֶת בְּגָדַי בִּמְכוֹנַת ______ שֶׁלִּי.
(A) כּוֹבֶסֶת
(B) כְּבִיסַת
(C) הַכְּבִיסָה
(D) הַכְּבִיסוֹת

22. תָּמִיד כְּשֶׁבָּאוּ אֵלֵינוּ אוֹרְחִים אִמָּא טִפְּלָה ______ כְּאִלּוּ הָיוּ מְלָכִים.
(A) אוֹתָם
(B) אִתָּם
(C) בָּהֶם
(D) לָהֶם

GO ON TO THE NEXT PAGE

Part B

Directions: In each of the following passages, there are numbered blanks indicating that words or phrases have been omitted. For each numbered blank, four completions are provided, of which only one is correct. First read through the entire passage. Then for each numbered blank, choose the completion that is most appropriate and fill in the corresponding oval on the answer sheet.

שְׁמוּאֵל הוּא מְנַהֵל מַחְלָקָה בְּבֵית חֲרֹשֶׁת. הוּא אַחֲרַאי עַל ______ עוֹבְדִים. חֵלֶק

23. (A) אַרְבַּע
(B) רְבִיעִי
(C) אַרְבָּעָה
(D) רֶבַע

מֵהָעוֹבְדִים ______ הֵם יְדִידָיו, וּשְׁמוּאֵל רוֹצֶה לִשְׁמֹר עַל ______, מִבְּלִי שֶׁהַדָּבָר

24. (A) הַהוּא
(B) הָאֵלֶּה
(C) הָהֵן
(D) הַזּוֹ

25. (A) יְדִידוּתְךָ
(B) יְדִידוּתִי
(C) יְדִידוּתֵנוּ
(D) יְדִידוּתָם

יַפְרִיעַ לַעֲבוֹדָתוֹ כִּמְנַהֵל הַמַּחְלָקָה. הוּא אָמְנָם ______ שֶׁ"עֲסָקִים וִידִידוּת ______

26. (A) נַאֲמִין
(B) מַאֲמִין
(C) תַּאֲמִין
(D) לְהַאֲמִין

27. (A) אֵינָהּ
(B) אֵינוֹ
(C) אֵינָם
(D) אֵינָן

GO ON TO THE NEXT PAGE

מִשְׁתַּלְּבִים יַחַד", אֲבָל הוּא ______ שֶׁמְּנַהֵל ______ יָכוֹל גַּם לִהְיוֹת מְיֻדָּד עִם הָעוֹבְדִים.

28. (A) יוֹשֵׁב
(B) חוֹשֵׁב
(C) עוֹזֵב
(D) שׁוֹמֵר

29. (A) מַסְפִּיק
(B) מַרְגִּישׁ
(C) מַצְלִיחַ
(D) מַרְגִּיז

GO ON TO THE NEXT PAGE

"הַבִּימָה" הַתֵּיאַטְרוֹן הַלְּאוּמִי שֶׁל יִשְׂרָאֵל, הוּא גַּם הַתֵּיאַטְרוֹן הָרִאשׁוֹן וְהֶחָשׁוּב ______ .

30. (A) הַרְבֵּה
(B) בְּיוֹתֵר
(C) הָעִקָּר
(D) בְּעִקָּר

לִפְנֵי חֲמִשִּׁים שָׁנָה בָּאוּ לְאֶרֶץ יִשְׂרָאֵל הַשַּׂחְקָנִים ______ שֶׁל "הַבִּימָה" מֵרוּסְיָה. תֵּיאַטְרוֹן

31. (A) רִאשׁוֹנִים
(B) לָרִאשׁוֹנָה
(C) הָרִאשׁוֹנִים
(D) הָרִאשׁוֹנוֹת

"הַבִּימָה" הָיָה ______ שָׁנִים רַבּוֹת הַתֵּיאַטְרוֹן הַיְחִידִי בְּאֶרֶץ יִשְׂרָאֵל. הַיּוֹם יֵשׁ הַרְבֵּה

32. (A) בִּשְׁבִיל
(B) אֵצֶל
(C) לַמְרוֹת
(D) בְּמֶשֶׁךְ

תֵּיאַטְרוֹנִים ______ . "הַדִּבּוּק" הִיא הַהַצָּגָה ______ בְּיוֹתֵר שֶׁל "הַבִּימָה". אֶת "הַדִּבּוּק"

33. (A) אַחֲרוֹנִים
(B) אֲחֵרִים
(C) אֲחֵרוֹת
(D) הָאֲחֵרִים

34. (A) הַיְּדוּעָה
(B) הַיְּחִידָה
(C) הַמְּקֻיֶּמֶת
(D) הַקַּיֶּמֶת

GO ON TO THE NEXT PAGE

הִצִיגוּ ______ רַבּוֹת מְאֹד בְּיִשְׂרָאֵל וּבְאַרְצוֹת הַבְּרִית. הַשַּׂחְקָנִים הַוָּתִיקִים כְּבָר אֵינָם

35. (A) פַּעַם
(B) פְּעָמִים
(C) פַּעֲמֵי
(D) הַפַּעַם

מְשַׂחֲקִים יוֹתֵר, אֲבָל ______ שֶׁלָּהֶם עַל הַתֵּיאַטְרוֹן בְּיִשְׂרָאֵל מֻרְגֶּשֶׁת עַד הַיּוֹם.

36. (A) הַהַגְדָּלָה
(B) הַהַתְחָלָה
(C) הַהַשְׁפָּעָה
(D) הַהַרְגָּשָׁה

GO ON TO THE NEXT PAGE

MODERN HEBREW TEST — *Continued*

Part C

Directions: Read the following passages carefully for comprehension. Each passage is followed by a number of questions or incomplete statements. Select the answer or completion that is best according to the passage and fill in the corresponding oval on the answer sheet.

אַנְשֵׁי מַדָּע עָרְכוּ מֶחְקָר כְּדֵי לִבְדֹּק אִם לְגִיל הַנֶּהָג יֵשׁ הַשְׁפָּעָה עַל מִסְפַּר תְּאוּנוֹת הַדְּרָכִים שֶׁבָּהֶן הָיָה מְעֹרָב. הַחוֹקְרִים מָצְאוּ כִּי נֶהָגִים צְעִירִים מִתַּחַת לְגִיל שְׁלוֹשִׁים גָּרְמוּ פָּחוֹת תְּאוּנוֹת מֵאֲשֶׁר נֶהָגִים בִּקְבוּצַת הַגִּיל שְׁלוֹשִׁים עַד חֲמִשִּׁים. כְּמוֹ-כֵן לֹא מָצְאוּ הֶבְדֵּל בֵּין נֶהָגִים מֵעַל גִּיל שִׁשִּׁים לְבֵין נֶהָגִים מִתַּחַת לְגִיל שְׁלוֹשִׁים.

37. בְּכַמָּה קְבוּצוֹת גִּיל נִבְדְּקוּ לְפִי הַקֶּטַע?

(A) שְׁתַּיִם

(B) שָׁלֹשׁ

(C) אַרְבַּע

(D) חָמֵשׁ

38. לְפִי הַמֶּחְקָר, נֶהָג בְּגִיל שִׁשִּׁים וְחָמֵשׁ הוּא

(A) יוֹתֵר טוֹב מִנֶּהָג צָעִיר

(B) טוֹב כְּמוֹ נֶהָג צָעִיר

(C) נֶהָג מְסֻכָּן יוֹתֵר

(D) נֶהָג מְבֻגָּר מִדַּי

39. לָמָּה עָרְכוּ אֶת הַמֶּחְקָר?

(A) כְּדֵי לְבָרֵר אִם יֵשׁ קֶשֶׁר בֵּין הַגִּיל וּמִסְפַּר הַתְּאוּנוֹת

(B) כְּדֵי לִבְדֹּק מַה מִּסְפַּר הַנֶּהָגִים מִתַּחַת לְגִיל שְׁלוֹשִׁים

(C) כְּדֵי לָתֵת עֲבוֹדָה לְאַנְשֵׁי הַמַּדָּע בָּאוּנִיבֶרְסִיטָה

(D) כְּדֵי לִמְצֹא אֶת הַקֶּשֶׁר בֵּין שְׁתִיָּה לִתְאוּנוֹת דְּרָכִים

GO ON TO THE NEXT PAGE

חָבֵר סִפֵּר לִי, שֶׁפַּעַם אַחַת הוּא הִסִּיעַ בַּמְּכוֹנִית שֶׁלּוֹ לְבֵית-הַחוֹלִים אִשָּׁה שֶׁעָמְדָה לָלֶדֶת. הוּא נָסַע מַהֵר, וּכְשֶׁרָאָה שֶׁהַכְּבִישׁ רֵיק, לֹא עָצַר בְּאוֹר אָדֹם. שׁוֹטֵר עָצַר אוֹתוֹ, הֵבִיא אוֹתוֹ לְבֵית מִשְׁפָּט, וְהַשּׁוֹפֵט הֶחְלִיט שֶׁאָסוּר לַחֲבֵרִי לִנְהֹג בִּמֶשֶׁךְ שְׁנָתַיִם. כְּתוֹצָאָה מִכָּךְ לֹא הָיְתָה לוֹ עֲבוֹדָה וּפַרְנָסָה.

לְדַעְתִּי, צְרִיכִים הָיוּ הַשּׁוֹטֵר וְגַם הַשּׁוֹפֵט לְהִתְחַשֵּׁב בַּמַּצָּב הַמְיֻחָד, וְלֹא לְהַעֲנִישׁ אֶת הָאִישׁ.

40. מִי כָּתַב אֶת הַקֶּטַע?

(A) הָאִשָּׁה הַיּוֹלֶדֶת

(B) הַשּׁוֹטֵר

(C) הַנֶּהָג

(D) חֲבֵרוֹ שֶׁל הַנֶּהָג

41. הַשּׁוֹטֵר עָצַר אֶת הָאִישׁ כִּי הוּא

(A) עָבַר בְּאוֹר אָדֹם

(B) צָעַק עַל הַשּׁוֹטֵר

(C) עָצַר בְּאוֹר יָרֹק

(D) הִסִּיעַ אִשָּׁה יוֹלֶדֶת

42. מַה חוֹשֵׁב הַמְּסַפֵּר?

(A) שֶׁהַנֶּהָג נָסַע מַהֵר מִדַּי

(B) שֶׁפַּרְנָסַת הַשּׁוֹטֵר נִפְגְּעָה

(C) שֶׁהַשּׁוֹפֵט לֹא הָיָה צָרִיךְ לִנְהֹג

(D) שֶׁהַנֶּהָג לֹא הָיָה צָרִיךְ לְהֵעָנֵשׁ

GO ON TO THE NEXT PAGE

תִּשְׁעָה בְּאָב הוּא יוֹם צוֹם לַגְּדוֹלִים וְיוֹם חֹפֶשׁ מִלִּמּוּדִים לְתַלְמִידֵי בָּתֵּי-הַסֵּפֶר. בְּעֶרֶב תִּשְׁעָה בְּאָב, כַּאֲשֶׁר גָּמַרְנוּ אֶת הַלִּמּוּדִים, אָמְרָה לָנוּ הַמּוֹרָה לֹא לָרוּץ בַּחוּץ וְלֹא לְהִשְׁתּוֹבֵב, מִפְּנֵי שֶׁתִּשְׁעָה בְּאָב אֵינוֹ יוֹם שִׂמְחָה, אֶלָּא יוֹם אֵבֶל, יוֹם שֶׁבּוֹ נִשְׂרַף בֵּית הַמִּקְדָּשׁ.

תַּלְמִידֵי בֵּית-הַסֵּפֶר כְּבָר הִכִּירוּ אוֹתִי כְּיֶלֶד שֶׁשּׁוֹאֵל שְׁאֵלוֹת וּמְבַקֵּשׁ מֵהַמּוֹרָה תְּשׁוּבָה לְכָל דָּבָר. שָׁאַלְתִּי: "מַה זֶּה בֵּית הַמִּקְדָּשׁ?" אָמְרָה הַמּוֹרָה: "בֵּית הַמִּקְדָּשׁ הוּא בֵּית-כְּנֶסֶת שֶׁכָּל הַיְּהוּדִים מִתְפַּלְּלִים בּוֹ." אָמַרְתִּי לָהּ: "הֲלֹא יֵשׁ לָנוּ בֵּית כְּנֶסֶת שֶׁמִּתְפַּלְּלִים בּוֹ, וְהוּא עֲדַיִן לֹא נִשְׂרַף." אָמְרָה הַמּוֹרָה: "בְּבֵית הַמִּקְדָּשׁ הָיוּ מַקְרִיבִים גַּם קָרְבָּנוֹת." "מַה זֶּה קָרְבָּנוֹת?" אָמְרָה הַמּוֹרָה: "כְּשֶׁתִּגְדַּל תֵּדַע". עַל כָּל דָּבָר שֶׁאֲנִי שׁוֹאֵל אֶת הַמּוֹרָה תְּשׁוּבָה אַחַת בְּפִיהָ: "כְּשֶׁתִּגְדַּל תֵּדַע". וְאוּלָם אֲנִי רוֹצֶה לָדַעַת הַיּוֹם, תֵּכֶף וּמִיָּד, כִּי מִי יוֹדֵעַ מָתַי אֶגְדַּל? הִנֵּה אֲנִי לוֹמֵד כָּל הַקַּיִץ, וַעֲדַיִן לֹא גָּדַלְתִּי.

43.מָה אָמְרָה הַמּוֹרָה לַיְּלָדִים בְּעֶרֶב תִּשְׁעָה בְּאָב?

(A) לֹא לֶאֱכֹל

(B) לֹא לָצוּם

(C) לֹא לְשַׂחֵק כַּדּוּרֶגֶל

(D) לֹא לָצֵאת מִן הַחֶדֶר

44.הַמְּסַפֵּר הָיָה יָדוּעַ כִּמְבַקֵּשׁ

(A) דְּבָרִים מֵהַמּוֹרָה

(B) הֶסְבֵּרִים מֵהַמּוֹרָה

(C) עֵצוֹת מֵהַמּוֹרָה

(D) טוֹבוֹת מֵהַמּוֹרָה

45.מֶה עָנְתָה הַמּוֹרָה לַתַּלְמִיד?

(A) תָּבִין בְּעוֹד כַּמָּה שָׁנִים.

(B) לְמַד כָּל הַקַּיִץ.

(C) אֵין פִּתְרוֹן לְכָל דָּבָר.

(D) עוֹד מְעַט אַסְבִּיר לְךָ.

46.הַיֶּלֶד רוֹצֶה לָדַעַת הַכֹּל הַיּוֹם, מִפְּנֵי שֶׁהוּא

(A) אֵינֶנּוּ יוֹדֵעַ אִם מָחָר יִחְיֶה

(B) אֵינֶנּוּ רוֹצֶה לְחַכּוֹת עַד שֶׁיִּגְדַּל

(C) רוֹצֶה לְהַצְלִיחַ בַּבְּחִינָה

(D) רוֹצֶה לִהְיוֹת הֶחָכָם בְּיוֹתֵר בַּכִּתָּה

47.הָרַעְיוֹן הָעִקָּרִי בַּסִּפּוּר הוּא

(A) תִּשְׁעָה בְּאָב הוּא יוֹם שֶׁל מִשְׂחָקִים

(B) הַיֶּלֶד רוֹצֶה לָדַעַת דְּבָרִים שֶׁהוּא אֵינֶנּוּ מֵבִין

(C) הַיְּהוּדִים מִתְפַּלְּלִים בְּבֵית-הַכְּנֶסֶת

(D) הַיְּהוּדִים מִתְפַּלְּלִים בְּבֵית-הַמִּקְדָּשׁ

GO ON TO THE NEXT PAGE

כְּשֶׁהָיִיתִי יַלְדָּה קְטַנָּה, הַמִּשְׁפָּחָה שֶׁלִּי גָּרָה בְּדִירָה בִּרְחוֹב הֶרְצֶל בְּתֵל-אָבִיב.

הָיוּ בַּדִּירָה אַרְבָּעָה חֲדָרִים. בִּשְׁנֵי חֲדָרִים גָּרָה הַמִּשְׁפָּחָה שֶׁלִּי וּבִשְׁנֵי הַחֲדָרִים הָאֲחֵרִים גָּרָה מִשְׁפָּחָה אַחֶרֶת. הָיָה לָנוּ וְלַשְּׁכֵנִים שֶׁלָּנוּ רַק מִטְבָּח אֶחָד, וַחֲדַר אַמְבַּטְיָה אֶחָד. אֲנִי חוֹשֶׁבֶת שֶׁהַהוֹרִים שֶׁל שְׁתֵּי הַמִּשְׁפָּחוֹת לֹא אָהֲבוּ לָגוּר בְּיַחַד, אֲבָל לֹא הָיָה לָהֶם מַסְפִּיק כֶּסֶף לְדִירָה אַחֶרֶת, יוֹתֵר גְּדוֹלָה.

לַשְּׁכֵנִים שֶׁלָּנוּ הָיוּ שְׁנֵי בָּנִים וּבַמִּשְׁפָּחָה שֶׁלָּנוּ הָיוּ שְׁתֵּי בָּנוֹת. אֲנַחְנוּ, הַיְלָדִים אָהַבְנוּ מְאֹד לִהְיוֹת בְּיַחַד. תָּמִיד הָיָה לָנוּ עִם מִי לְשַׂחֵק וְעִם מִי לְדַבֵּר.

הָיוּ בַּבַּיִת שָׁלֹשׁ קוֹמוֹת וּבְכָל קוֹמָה הָיְתָה דִּירָה אַחַת. אֲנַחְנוּ גַּרְנוּ בַּקּוֹמָה הַשְּׁנִיָּה. גַּם בַּקּוֹמָה הָרִאשׁוֹנָה גָּרוּ שְׁתֵּי מִשְׁפָּחוֹת, וְגַם שָׁם הָיוּ הַרְבֵּה יְלָדִים. בַּקּוֹמָה הַשְּׁלִישִׁית, לְעֻמַּת זֹאת, גָּרָה מִשְׁפָּחָה עֲשִׁירָה. כָּל הַדִּירָה הָיְתָה שֶׁלָּהֶם, בְּלִי שְׁכֵנִים. הָיָה לָהֶם רַק יֶלֶד אֶחָד. אֲנַחְנוּ לֹא אָהַבְנוּ אוֹתוֹ. הוּא לָבַשׁ תָּמִיד בְּגָדִים יָפִים וְלֹא אָהַב לְשַׂחֵק בַּחוּץ. הָיָה לוֹ חֶדֶר מְיֻחָד, רַק בִּשְׁבִילוֹ, עִם שֻׁלְחָן קָטָן וְנֶחְמָד וּמִטָּה גְּדוֹלָה וּמְנוֹרָה עַל יַד הַמִּטָּה. לָנוּ לֹא הָיוּ דְּבָרִים כָּאֵלֶּה. לִפְעָמִים, כְּשֶׁהַהוֹרִים שֶׁלָּנוּ וְשֶׁל הַיֶּלֶד הֶעָשִׁיר לֹא הָיוּ בַּבַּיִת, הָיִינוּ מַרְגִּיזִים אוֹתוֹ מְאֹד. אֲנַחְנוּ הָיִינוּ אַרְבָּעָה וְהוּא רַק אֶחָד.

כַּעֲבֹר כַּמָּה שָׁנִים, כְּשֶׁהָיָה לַהוֹרִים שֶׁלִּי יוֹתֵר כֶּסֶף, קָנִינוּ דִּירָה גְּדוֹלָה בִּרְחוֹב אַחֵר. עַכְשָׁו הָיָה לִי חֶדֶר מִשֶּׁלִּי וְנִזְכַּרְתִּי בַּיֶּלֶד הֶעָשִׁיר. רַק אָז הֵבַנְתִּי אֵיזֶה צַעַר גָּרַמְנוּ לוֹ.

48.גַּרְנוּ עִם עוֹד מִשְׁפָּחָה כִּי

(A) הַדִּירָה הָיְתָה גְּדוֹלָה מִדַּי

(B) זֶה הָיָה טוֹב בִּשְׁבִיל הַהוֹרִים

(C) כָּל הָאֲנָשִׁים גָּרוּ כָּכָה

(D) הָיִינוּ עֲנִיִּים

49.הַמְסַפֶּרֶת חוֹשֶׁבֶת שֶׁבִּגְלַל הַמְּגוּרִים הַמְּשֻׁתָּפִים

(A) הַהוֹרִים לֹא סָבְלוּ

(B) הַיְלָדִים נֶהֱנוּ מְאֹד

(C) הַשְּׁכֵנִים בַּקּוֹמָה הַשְּׁלִישִׁית נֶהֱנוּ

(D) הַשְּׁכֵנִים בַּקּוֹמָה הָרִאשׁוֹנָה נֶהֱנוּ

50.כְּשֶׁהַיְלָדִים נִשְׁאֲרוּ לְבַד הֵם הָיוּ

(A) מְשַׂחֲקִים עִם הַיֶּלֶד הֶעָשִׁיר בָּרְחוֹב

(B) מַכְעִיסִים אֶת הַיֶּלֶד מִן הַקּוֹמָה הַשְּׁלִישִׁית

(C) מַכִּים אֶת הַיֶּלֶד הֶעָשִׁיר

(D) יוֹרְדִים לַקּוֹמָה הַשְּׁנִיָּה

51. מַדּוּעַ הַיְלָדִים הִרְגִּיזוּ אֶת הַיֶּלֶד הֶעָשִׁיר?

(A) כִּי הוּא לֹא יָכוֹל הָיָה לָרוּץ מַהֵר

(B) כִּי לֹא הָיוּ לוֹ אַחִים וַאֲחָיוֹת

(C) כִּי יְלָדִים אֵינָם אוֹהֲבִים מִי שֶׁשּׁוֹנֶה מֵהֶם

(D) כִּי הוּא גָּר בַּקּוֹמָה הַשְּׁלִישִׁית

GO ON TO THE NEXT PAGE

52. מַדּוּעַ עָבְרָה הַמְסַפֶּרֶת לְדִירָה גְּדוֹלָה?

(A) כִּי גָּרָה שָׁם הַמִּשְׁפָּחָה הָעֲשִׁירָה

(B) כִּי הַהוֹרִים נַעֲשׂוּ עֲשִׁירִים יוֹתֵר

(C) כִּי גֵּרְשׁוּ אוֹתָם מֵהַדִּירָה

(D) כִּי הָיוּ יוֹתֵר מִדַּי מַדְרֵגוֹת בַּבִּנְיָן

53. רַעְיוֹן חָשׁוּב בַּסִּפּוּר הוּא:

(A) הָאֹשֶׁר אֵינוֹ תָּלוּי תָּמִיד בָּעֹשֶׁר

(B) תְּנָאֵי הַמְּגוּרִים אֵינָם חֲשׁוּבִים

(C) מַרְבֶּה יְלָדִים מַרְבֶּה דְּאָגָה

(D) גַּם יְלָדִים צְרִיכִים פִּנָּה מִשֶּׁלָּהֶם

54. מֵהַסִּפּוּר אֶפְשָׁר לִלְמֹד שֶׁהַמְסַפֶּרֶת

(A) מִצְטַעֶרֶת עַל מָה שֶׁעָשְׂתָה לַיֶּלֶד

(B) רָצְתָה תָּמִיד לִהְיוֹת עֲשִׁירָה

(C) לֹא אָהֲבָה לָגוּר בְּבַיִת עִם יְלָדִים אֲחֵרִים

(D) לֹא אָהֲבָה לָגוּר בְּבִנְיָן גָּבוֹהַּ

GO ON TO THE NEXT PAGE

פעם אחת חזר השור מן העבודה בשדה. הוא פגש את החמור שהיה חולה באותו יום ולא עבד. שניהם אכלו. פתאום שאל החמור את השור, "מה שלומך, אחי?" "לא טוב", ענה השור, "כל היום אני עובד עבודה קשה בשדה ואין לי כוח לחיות". "יש לי עצה בשבילך", אמר החמור, "עשה את עצמך חולה ואל תאכל הלילה. כך עשיתי גם אני בלילה שעבר, ולכן לא יצאתי לעבודה היום." העצה מצאה חן בעיני השור והוא לא אכל באותו לילה. בלילה קם החמור ואכל את כל מה שנתנו לו וגם מה שנתנו לשור.

המלך שלמה שמע את השיחה ביניהם וצחק צחוק גדול. בבוקר, אמר המלך לאחד מאנשיו: "השור חולה ואין לו כוח. לכן, קח את החמור שיעבוד היום פי שניים.

בערב חזר החמור מן השדה והוא עייף מאוד. שאל אותו השור: "מה שלומך, אחי?" "לא טוב", אמר החמור. אומרים שאם השור לא יהיה בריא מהר, ישחטו אותו, יבשלו ויאכלו אותו."

השור פחד מאוד. קם ממקומו ואכל את כל מה שהיה לפניו ולא השאיר דבר.

55. השור לא רצה לחיות יותר, מפני שהוא

(A) אכל יותר מידי

(B) שתה יותר מידי

(C) עבד יותר מידי

(D) דיבר יותר מידי

56. העצה שהחמור נתן לשור היא שיתנהג כאילו הוא

(A) שבע

(B) רעב

(C) צמא

(D) חולה

57. העצה מצאה חן בעיני השור, כי הוא היה

(A) חכם

(B) עצל

(C) זקן

(D) חולה

58. מדוע אכל החמור את האוכל של השור?

(A) כי לא רצה שהשור יהיה חולה

(B) כי רצה לאכול יותר

(C) כי שמע את מה שאמר שלמה המלך

(D) כי רצה שיהיה לו כוח לעבוד

59. כששמע המלך את דברי החמור, הוא

(A) שלח את השור לעבודה

(B) כעס על השור החכם

(C) שלח את החמור לעשות עבודה כפולה

(D) נתן לשור מנה גדולה של אוכל

60. השור אכל את האוכל שלפניו, כי הוא

(A) שמע שהחמור חולה

(B) רצה שהחמור יעבוד קשה

(C) פחד שיהרגו אותו

(D) רצה שלחמור יהיה פחות אוכל

S T O P

IF YOU FINISH BEFORE TIME IS CALLED, YOU MAY CHECK YOUR WORK ON THIS TEST ONLY.
DO NOT WORK ON ANY OTHER TEST IN THIS BOOK.

Answers to the SAT II: Modern Hebrew Subject Mini Test

Question Number	Correct Answer	Question Number	Correct Answer
1	A	31	C
2	D	32	D
3	C	33	B
4	C	34	A
5	D	35	B
6	B	36	C
7	B	37	B
8	D	38	B
9	C	39	A
10	D	40	D
11	B	41	A
12	A	42	D
13	C	43	C
14	A	44	B
15	A	45	A
16	A	46	B
17	D	47	B
18	D	48	D
19	B	49	B
20	C	50	B
21	C	51	C
22	C	52	B
23	C	53	A
24	B	54	A
25	D	55	C
26	B	56	D
27	C	57	B
28	B	58	B
29	C	59	C
30	B	60	C

The SAT II: Italian Subject Test

The SAT II: Italian Subject Test consists of 80-85 multiple-choice questions. It is written to reflect current trends in secondary school curricula, although it tests only reading skills and familiarity with the structure of the language. It is designed to allow for variation in language preparation and is independent of particular textbooks or methods of instruction. The test measures reading proficiency based on communicative materials authentic to the Italian culture. The Italian Subject Test is appropriate for students who have studied the language for two to four years in high school or the equivalent. The difficulty levels of the questions range from elementary through advanced, with the majority of the questions at the intermediate level. The best preparation for the test is the gradual development of competence in Italian over a period of years.

The test includes a variety of questions that require a wide-ranging knowledge of the language. Reading is tested in various ways. First, in the context of passages, sentence completion questions test your knowledge of high-frequency vocabulary and appropriate idiomatic expressions. Second, comprehension questions test your understanding of the content of various authentic stimulus materials. The materials are taken from sources such as advertisements, timetables, street signs, forms, and tickets. Third, comprehension questions relating to short and longer passages test your understanding of the content of the passages, which are taken from newspaper and magazine articles, prose fiction, and historical works. In addition to these three types of questions that measure your ability to read texts, individual questions that are arranged in sets of cultural themes test your familiarity with the structure of the Italian language. Only commonly taught grammatical constructions are tested, and all questions represent natural language.

The sample test reproduced in this book has the content outline described by the following chart. Italian Subject Tests currently being administered have been modified so that the approximate percentage of the first two categories is 30 instead of 25, and the last two categories are replaced by an Authentic Stimulus and Reading Comprehension category representing about 40 percent of the test.

Skills Measured	Approximate Percentage of Test
Vocabulary in Context	25
Structure in Blank	25
Reading Comprehension — authentic stimulus materials	25
Reading Comprehension — passages	25

Sample Questions

Four types of questions are used in the Italian Subject Test. All questions in the test are multiple-choice questions in which you must choose the best response from the four choices offered.

SAT II:

Italian Subject Mini Test

The test that follows is a shortened version of an SAT II: Italian Subject Test. So that you may have an idea of what the national test administration will be like, try to take the test in this book under conditions as close as possible to those of the nationally administered test. It will probably help if you do the following.

- Set aside 45 minutes for the test when you will not be interrupted, so that you can complete all of it in one sitting.
- Sit at a desk with no other papers or books. You can't take a dictionary, other books, or notes into the test room.
- Have a kitchen timer or clock in front of you for timing yourself.
- Tear out an answer sheet from the back of this book and fill it in just as you would on the day of the test. You can use one answer sheet for as many as three Subject Tests.
- Read the instructions that precede the test. When you take the test, you will be asked to read them before you begin answering questions.

ITALIAN TEST

The top portion of the section of the answer sheet that you will use in taking the Italian test must be filled in exactly as shown in the illustration below. Note carefully that you have to do all of the following on your answer sheet.

1. Print ITALIAN on the line under the words "Subject (print)."

2. In the shaded box labeled "Test Code" fill in four ovals:

   —Fill in oval 1 in the row labeled V.

   —Fill in oval 4 in the row labeled W.

   —Fill in oval 2 in the row labeled X.

   —Fill in oval B in the row labeled Y.

Test Code		Subject (print)
V	● ② ③ ④ ⑤ ⑥ ⑦ ⑧ ⑨	ITALIAN
W	① ② ③ ● ⑤ ⑥ ⑦ ⑧ ⑨	
X	① ● ③ ④ ⑤ Y Ⓐ ● Ⓒ Ⓓ Ⓔ	
Q	① ② ③ ④ ⑤ ⑥ ⑦ ⑧ ⑨	

Please answer either Part I or Part II by filling in the specific oval in row Q. You are to fill in ONE and ONLY ONE oval as described below, to indicate how you obtained your knowledge of Italian. The information you provide is for statistical purposes only and will not influence your score on the test.

Part I If your knowledge of Italian does not come primarily from courses taken in grades 9 through 12, fill in oval 9 and leave the remaining ovals blank, regardless of how long you studied the subject in school. For example, you are to fill in oval 9 if your knowledge of Italian comes primarily from any of the following sources: study prior to the ninth grade, courses taken at a college, special study, extensive residence abroad, or living in a home in which Italian is the principal language spoken.

Part II If your knowledge of Italian does come primarily from courses taken in secondary school, fill in the oval that indicates the level of the Italian course in which you are currently enrolled. If you are not now enrolled in a Italian course, fill in the oval that indicates the level of the most advanced course in Italian that you have completed.

First year:	first or second half	—fill in oval 1
Second year:	first half	—fill in oval 2
	second half	—fill in oval 3
Third year:	first half	—fill in oval 4
	second half	—fill in oval 5
Fourth year:	first half	—fill in oval 6
	second half	—fill in oval 7
Course at a level higher than fourth year, second half or high school course work plus a minimum of four weeks of study abroad		—fill in oval 8

When the supervisor gives the signal, turn the page and begin the Italian test. There are 100 numbered ovals on the answer sheet and 60 questions in the Italian test. Therefore, use only ovals 1 to 60 for recording your answers.

ITALIAN TEST

PLEASE NOTE THAT YOUR ANSWER SHEET HAS FIVE ANSWER POSITIONS MARKED A, B, C, D, E, WHILE THE QUESTIONS THROUGHOUT THIS TEST CONTAIN ONLY FOUR CHOICES. BE SURE NOT TO MAKE ANY MARKS IN COLUMN E.

Directions: Each of the following passages contains numbered blanks indicating that words or phrases have been omitted from the text. For each numbered blank, four completions are provided. In each case, select the best completion and indicate your answer by filling in the corresponding oval on the answer sheet. Be sure to read each passage completely before answering the questions related to it.

Un piccolo villaggio siciliano

Baia Dorica è il nome di un piccolo villaggio estivo situato sulla costa siciliana. Tutte le __(1)__ del villaggio danno sulla piazzetta, dove si trova l'unico locale pubblico: il bar, che fa anche da panineria, pizzeria e panetteria. Di fronte al bar è situato l'unico telefono pubblico del __(2)__.

La piazzetta è un luogo __(3)__ riservato solamente ai pedoni e i bambini vi possono correre e giocare liberamente.

Di pomeriggio __(4)__ l'immancabile partita di calcio fra ragazzini, e non mancano mai gli spettatori. La sera, i bambini formano dei gruppetti sparsi qua e là e __(5)__ animatamente degli eventi della giornata.

I genitori passeggiano tranquillamente, chiacchierano e tengono per __(6)__ i più piccini. Fino a tarda sera tutto è animato e risuona di voci come se fosse ancora mezzogiorno.

1. (A) macchine
   (B) strade
   (C) luci
   (D) corriere

2. (A) paesetto
   (B) sindacato
   (C) continente
   (D) regno

3. (A) silenzioso
   (B) solitario
   (C) sicuro
   (D) privato

4. (A) si svolge
   (B) si compra
   (C) si proibisce
   (D) si mangia

5. (A) cantano
   (B) leggono
   (C) parlano
   (D) pensano

6. (A) braccio
   (B) dito
   (C) polso
   (D) mano

GO ON TO THE NEXT PAGE

Al Gran Sole

È stato inaugurato a Milano l'ipermercato "Al Gran Sole". Pubblico e autorità hanno partecipato numerosi all'avvenimento.

Gironzolando per i ___(7)___ reparti si può vedere e acquistare di tutto, a prezzi davvero convenienti. Al fornitissimo banco del pesce, la freschezza salta subito all' ___(8)___. Chi decide di rinnovare il guardaroba scoprirà che il reparto ___(9)___ propone uno stile di vita casual. I prodotti sono codificati per facilitare il passaggio alla cassa, affinchè la coda non superi i cinque ___(10)___.

7. (A) sforniti
   (B) nuovi
   (C) cari
   (D) capo

8. (A) occhio
   (B) aspetto
   (C) orecchio
   (D) assalto

9. (A) calzature
   (B) giocattoli
   (C) abbigliamento
   (D) strumenti musicali

10. (A) codici
    (B) carrelli
    (C) impiegati
    (D) cassieri

GO ON TO THE NEXT PAGE

"La Molisana"

Non dimenticherò mai Nonno Nicola, che ci ha ___(11)___ la più forte caratteristica di famiglia. La passione per la pasta.

È stato proprio mio nonno ad insegnarmi a riconoscere il grano duro ___(12)___, come quello del Tavoliere. E il capo pastaio?

Oggi dovrebbe essere in pensione. E invece eccolo lì che sorveglia con occhio ___(13)___ le macchine, chè la pasta è viva, naturale, e può ribellarsi alla macchina.

Per i buongustai abbiamo creato 124 ___(14)___ di pasta ricreati dalle più antiche tradizioni regionali.

Ma non fatemi più ___(15)___: sarei parziale. Giudicate voi "La Molisana". Assaggiatela. E se non sapete ascoltare il cuore, date retta al ___(16)___.

11. (A) spedito
    (B) portato
    (C) rimandato
    (D) trasmesso

12. (A) minimo
    (B) migliore
    (C) peggiore
    (D) massimo

13. (A) severo
    (B) facile
    (C) malato
    (D) triste

14. (A) scatole
    (B) tipi
    (C) usi
    (D) passioni

15. (A) cantare
    (B) parlare
    (C) telefonare
    (D) giudicare

16. (A) naso
    (B) fegato
    (C) palato
    (D) volto

GO ON TO THE NEXT PAGE

Directions: Each of the sentences below contains a blank space indicating that a word or phrase has been omitted. Following each sentence are four words or phrases. Select the word or phrase that best completes the sentence structurally and logically and fill in the corresponding oval on the answer sheet. The questions within a group do not depend on each other although they are on the same topic.

Direzioni

17. — Scusi, signore, c'è un bar qui vicino?
— Sì, ------- uno a due passi.

(A) ce n' è
(B) ne ho
(C) gliene
(D) ci è

18. Signora, posso ------- un caffè?

(A) offrirlo
(B) offrirci
(C) offrirsi
(D) offrirle

19. — Per arrivare alla stazione, dove vado esattamente?
— Signorina, ------- questa strada e poi a sinistra.

(A) prendi
(B) prendiamo
(C) prenda
(D) prendo

20. — Vuole che la -------?
— Sì, grazie.

(A) accompagnasse
(B) accompagnassi
(C) accompagni
(D) accompagna

La spesa

21. Molte turiste preferiscono comprare ------- regali nei negozi del centro.

(A) il loro
(B) il suo
(C) i loro
(D) i suoi

22. Il negoziante ------- vende sempre tanta merce.

(A) fiorentine
(B) fiorentino
(C) fiorentini
(D) fiorentina

23. ------- tovaglioli sono di puro lino.

(A) Questi
(B) Queste
(C) Questa
(D) Questo

24. — Dove hai comprato quella borsa?
— ------- al mercato della paglia.

(A) La compro
(B) L'hai comprata
(C) L'ho comprato
(D) L'ho comprata

25. — Ci sono molti mercati all'aperto a Firenze?
— Sì, ------- sono molti.

(A) ce li
(B) glieli
(C) ce ne
(D) te ne

GO ON TO THE NEXT PAGE

<u>In un negozio di abbigliamento</u>

26. Il commesso domanda al cliente:
    — Signor Rossi, ------- piacciono queste camicie?

    (A) vi
    (B) le
    (C) gli
    (D) ti

27. Sì, sono molto belle. Me ne ------- tre.

    (A) dà
    (B) dia
    (C) date
    (D) diano

28. La cliente domanda:
    — Quanto costano ------- calzoni?

    (A) quegli
    (B) quelle
    (C) quei
    (D) quel

29. Questi pantaloni costano 200.000 lire, ma sono ------- eleganti!

    (A) molto
    (B) molta
    (C) molti
    (D) molte

30. Dopo ------- le camicie e i calzoni, il cliente saluta e esce.

    (A) aver comprato
    (B) comprava
    (C) abbia comprato
    (D) comprerà

GO ON TO THE NEXT PAGE

Directions: Each selection below is followed by one or more incomplete statements or questions based on its content. Examine the advertisement, table, chart, or other material, then select the completion or answer that is most appropriate according to the information given and fill in the corresponding oval on the answer sheet.

Questions 31-32

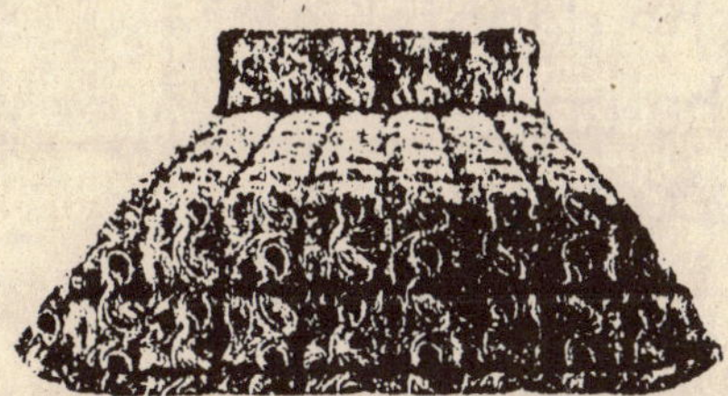

I piumini e le trapunte Daunenstep migliorano la qualità del sonno e sono fatte ancora artigianalmente, con vero piumino d'oca, secondo una tradizione che si tramanda, di padre in figlio, da 80 anni.

Chi prova un piumino o una trapunta Daunenstep farà certamente una piacevolissima scoperta.

Piumini e trapunte dell'Alto Adige.

31. I piumini e le trapunte vengono ancora manifatturati con
    (A) oche vecchie
    (B) appunti personali
    (C) macchine automatizzate
    (D) attenzione individuale

32. Secondo questo annuncio chi usa il piumino Daunenstep dorme
    (A) scoperto
    (B) meglio
    (C) in alto
    (D) sicuro

GO ON TO THE NEXT PAGE

Question 33

Oggi il regalo che denota stile e buon gusto ha un nome preciso: Cioccolatini Perugina.

È da sempre la firma più prestigiosa e più imitata del "made in Italy". Per questo regalare Cioccolatini Perugina significa assaporare ogni volta il piacere di fare un regalo di classe.

33. Chi regala Perugina dimostra di avere

    (A) un nome di classe
    (B) un sapore preciso
    (C) una firma prestigiosa
    (D) un certo stile

GO ON TO THE NEXT PAGE

Questions 34-35

Il tempo

PREVISIONI

TEMPO PREVISTO: al Sud della penisola e sulle isole maggiori molto nuvoloso o coperto con piogge intermittenti e temporali sparsi; nevicate sull'Appennino meridionale. Sul resto del Paese da poco nuvoloso a nuvoloso con brevi precipitazioni in prossimità dei rilievi. — **MARI:** mossi.

34. Secondo le previsioni, che tempo farà domani al sud?

(A) Farà molto freddo
(B) Farà brutto tempo
(C) Sarà molto caldo.
(D) Sarà soleggiato.

35. Per quanto riguarda i mari, saranno

(A) limpidi
(B) lisci
(C) agitati
(D) torbidi

GO ON TO THE NEXT PAGE

Question 36

36. Brite è usato per

    (A) lucidare pavimenti e pareti
    (B) lavare bene i vestiti
    (C) pulire piatti e bicchieri
    (D) fare il bagno

GO ON TO THE NEXT PAGE

Questions 37-38

Olio Cuore
ti aiuta a stare in forma
con tutto il sapore del mais.

37. Olio Cuore è

    (A) una lozione
    (B) un detersivo
    (C) un condimento
    (D) una vitamina

38. Secondo l'annuncio, chi dovrebbe far uso di questo prodotto?

    (A) Chi è a dieta
    (B) Malati di cuore
    (C) Chi si prepara a un esame
    (D) Le persone anziane

GO ON TO THE NEXT PAGE

Questions 39-40

QUEL FANTASTICO VENERDI' DI REPUBBLICA.

"Il Venerdì", tutte le settimane con Repubblica, vi porta attualità, grandi reportages, viaggi, inchieste e interviste: centotrentadue pagine a colori tutte per voi. "Il Venerdì" è in edicola ogni venerdì insieme a Repubblica e Affari& Finanza. Il tutto, per sole lire mille.

la Repubblica

39. In quest' annuncio, che cos' è "Il Venerdì"?

    (A) Un libro
    (B) Un settimanale
    (C) Un notiziario
    (D) Un' inchiesta

40. Come si ottiene "Il Venerdì"?

    (A) Si deve andare in un negozio.
    (B) Si deve comprare la *Repubblica.*
    (C) Si devono spendere due mila lire.
    (D) Si deve aspettare la fine del mese.

GO ON TO THE NEXT PAGE

Question 41

ARRIVA IL NUOVO ATLANTE STRADALE DEL TOURING.

Dal Touring Club, ecco la nuovissima edizione dell' Atlante Stradale d'Italia, scala 1:200.000, indispensabile per viaggiare al passo con i tempi con un elenco completo di tutti i comuni con le distanze chilometriche dai relativi capoluoghi.

Lo trovate in 3 bellissimi volumi (Nord-Centro-Sud), nelle Sedi T.C.I., nelle Librerie e Agenzie Succursali, nelle cartolibrerie e in autostrada in tutti i grandi locali di Autogrill.

PRATICO, PRECISO E AGGIORNATISSIMO. **Touring Club Italiano**

41. Dove si possono comprare questi atlanti?

(A) Solamente presso il Touring Club
(B) Solo lungo le autostrade
(C) In tutti i comuni
(D) In posti diversi

GO ON TO THE NEXT PAGE

Questions 42-43

L'amore per le tagliatelle è qualcosa che tutti portano da sempre nel cuore. Barilla le fa ancora impastando la semola con 6 uova per ogni chilo. Perchè per la festa, qualunque giorno sia, nessuno vuole lesinare sulla bontà. E per chi ama cambiare il sapore della festa ci sono le tagliatelle verdi, le pappardelle e la paglia e fieno.

BARILLA. UN MONDO DI IDEE
PER OGNI TUA VOGLIA.

42. Che cosa offre questa ditta ai lettori?
    (A) Parecchi tipi di pasta
    (B) L'amore per la bontà
    (C) Un chilo di semola e sei uova
    (D) La paglia per le feste

43. Quale delle seguenti qualità distingue questo prodotto?
    (A) È sempre a fette.
    (B) È fatto con il fieno.
    (C) È sempre verde.
    (D) È fatto con la semola.

GO ON TO THE NEXT PAGE

Question 44

44. Secondo "Oggi", le persone nate sotto il segno del Sagittario amano la vita

(A) tranquilla
(B) modesta
(C) intellettuale
(D) movimentata

GO ON TO THE NEXT PAGE

Question 45

La tua prima colazione aspettava uno spicchio di sole per diventare più sana e nutriente. Ed ecco i frollini nuovi pieni di sole. Dorati come il sole e come il sole ricchi e genuini.

45. Questo annuncio pubblicitario concerne

(A) un alimento
(B) uno spicchio di sole
(C) un fiore
(D) un mulino a vento

GO ON TO THE NEXT PAGE

Question 46

46. Che cosa si offre gratuitamente al pubblico in quest'annuncio pubblicitario?

(A) Una busta di caffè
(B) Una tazzina
(C) Un bicchiere di latte
(D) Una collana d'oro

GO ON TO THE NEXT PAGE

Directions: Read the following passages carefully for comprehension. Each passage is followed by a number of questions or incomplete statements based on its content. Select the answer or completion that is best according to the passage and fill in the corresponding oval on the answer sheet.

Regalo, dono, presente, omaggio. Quant'è piacevole riceverlo e quant'è bello farlo. Ma quant'è difficile, qualche volta, farlo o non farlo, al momento giusto, scegliendo la cosa giusta. Due signore torinesi danno una mano a chi si dibatte in queste difficoltà.

Hanno raccolto in FAR REGALI, in questi giorni in libreria, un certo numero di consigli divisi in brevi capitoli.

Divertente è l'elenco delle occasioni classiche nelle quali è meglio non fare regali. Ci sono spunti e idee per tutti e per tutte le circostanze e cento modi per dire "ti amo" (esempi: un videotape con un camino acceso per venti ardenti minuti, due calamite. . .). E poi c'è la confezione del regalo alla quale è giusto dare un certo rilievo.

47. FAR REGALI è stato concepito per

(A) le persone indecise
(B) le persone ricche
(C) proprietari di librerie
(D) due signore torinesi

48. L'elenco delle occasioni in cui non si richiedono regali è

(A) giusto
(B) strano
(C) lungo
(D) spiritoso

49. Cosa offre FAR REGALI?

(A) sconti
(B) consigli
(C) rimborsi
(D) doni

Sto per entrare in classe: sebbene sia preparato, oggi ho un batticuore che non riesco a dominare . . . . È giovedì: il giorno del compito in classe di matematica.

Sulla classe incombe un'atmosfera di ansia e di paura. Ecco la professoressa! Tutti ci alziamo in piedi per salutarla; poi tutti si siedono, lasciando sfuggire un profondo sospiro.

E così, in quest'atmosfera non certo allegra, la professoressa detta il problema. La sua voce è chiara e calma, il suo sguardo, dietro gli occhiali, sereno ed incoraggiante.

Quando la dettatura è finita si sentono vari commenti, ma presto tutti si mettono al lavoro. La classe è diventata silenziosa: le teste sono chinate sui fogli: si sente solo il leggero rumore delle penne.

50. Il protagonista è apprensivo perchè

(A) non sta bene
(B) non è preparato
(C) deve fare un esame
(D) deve fare un discorso

51. Che cosa fa la professoressa?

(A) Scrive il compito sulla lavagna.
(B) Legge il compito ad alta voce.
(C) Corregge il compito in classe.
(D) Distribuisce il compito da fare.

52. La professoressa descritta in questo brano sembra

(A) aggressiva
(B) nervosa
(C) distratta
(D) gentile

53. In questa classe c'è un senso di

(A) allegria
(B) tranquillità
(C) preoccupazione
(D) leggerezza

GO ON TO THE NEXT PAGE

È "Ferragosto", festa nazionale, e se ne sono andati tutti. Finalmente riesco a passeggiare senza dover fare lo slalom tra le scatole di sardine posteggiate sul marciapiede. Restano solo alcune auto, abbandonate lo scorso inverno, ancora più solitarie sotto il sole d'agosto. Dove saranno i loro proprietari? . . .

È incredibile, poter attraversare Milano in un quarto d'ora, da un capo all'altro, come riusciva a fare un automobilista nel primo dopoguerra. E poi fermarsi e parcheggiare dove si vuole. Bellissimo, ma per fare che cosa, se è tutto chiuso da una settimana? . . .

Vado all'edicola e la trovo sprangata. Il tabaccaio più vicino adesso si trova a un chilometro di distanza, e non ha più francobolli. Se in questo momento si fulmina una lampadina di casa sono perduto, non saprei dove comprarne una. Milano sembra in svendita, in liquidazione. Fortuna che per cibi e bevande mi ero fatto una scorta. L'assedio durerà fino al giorno 20, e occorre resistere.

Del resto non mi è mai piaciuto lo spettacolo di questo fuggi fuggi, di questo esodo di massa, come se a Milano fosse scoppiata un'epidemia di peste.

54. Tutti sono fuori Milano perchè

(A) è vacanza
(B) c'è uno sciopero
(C) è una giornata invernale
(D) è scoppiata la guerra

55. Secondo il brano durante il "Ferragosto" è probabile che chi ha una macchina possa

(A) comprare la benzina a buon mercato
(B) avere difficoltà nel parcheggiare
(C) muoversi facilmente in auto per la città
(D) stare in coda per un'ora per arrivare in centro

56. Che orario hanno i negozi durante il "Ferragosto"?

(A) Hanno tutti lo stesso orario.
(B) Sono quasi tutti chiusi.
(C) Aprono solo la mattina.
(D) Sono chiusi il sabato.

57. L'autore del brano si lamenta perchè

(A) la città è affollata
(B) è difficile attraversare la città
(C) gli abitanti se ne vanno
(D) c'è la peste

58. L'autore non morirà di fame perchè

(A) sua moglie gli ha lasciato cibi e bevande
(B) suo cognato ha un ristorante
(C) ha deciso di non fare più la dieta
(D) ha già comprato provviste sufficienti

59. Che cosa ricorda all'autore Milano in questo periodo?

(A) La città nel dopoguerra
(B) Milano negli anni '20
(C) La Milano notturna dopo la chiusura dei locali
(D) Il marciapiede d'inverno

60. Dove si comprano di solito i francobolli a Milano?

(A) Nel negozio di sali e tabacchi
(B) All'edicola
(C) Nel negozio di elettrodomestici
(D) Dal farmacista

S T O P

IF YOU FINISH BEFORE TIME IS CALLED, YOU MAY CHECK YOUR WORK ON THIS TEST ONLY.
DO NOT WORK ON ANY OTHER TEST IN THIS BOOK.

Answers to the SAT II: Italian Subject Mini Test

Question Number	Correct Answer	Question Number	Correct Answer
1	B	31	D
2	A	32	B
3	C	33	D
4	A	34	B
5	C	35	C
6	D	36	C
7	B	37	C
8	A	38	A
9	C	39	B
10	B	40	B
11	D	41	D
12	B	42	A
13	A	43	D
14	B	44	D
15	B	45	A
16	C	46	B
17	A	47	A
18	D	48	D
19	C	49	B
20	C	50	C
21	C	51	B
22	B	52	D
23	A	53	C
24	D	54	A
25	C	55	C
26	B	56	B
27	B	57	C
28	C	58	D
29	A	59	A
30	A	60	A

The SAT II: Japanese Subject Test with Listening

The SAT II: Japanese Subject Test with Listening is a one-hour test that consists of 80-85 multiple-choice questions and is written to reflect evolving trends in secondary school curriculums. It is offered annually in November only and only in participating secondary schools.

The development of the test was supported by funding from the National Endowment for the Humanities to the College Board and the National Foreign Language Center. A major goal of the test is to measure the ability of students to engage in purposeful communication in Japanese in the context of contemporary Japanese culture. Therefore, the test materials are taken from real life. The test is designed for students who have studied the language for two, three, or four years in secondary school or the equivalent. The difficulty levels of the questions range from elementary through advanced, with the majority at the intermediate level.

The test includes a variety of questions requiring a wide-ranging knowledge of the language (see the chart at the right). The listening comprehension questions are based on short, spoken dialogues and narratives primarily about everyday topics. The questions in that part are in English.

The usage questions require you to complete Japanese sentences so that they are structurally and logically correct. In that part, you are to select an appropriate syntactic structure or lexical term. Knowledge of vocabulary is tested implicitly throughout the test; some usage questions specifically test word meaning in the context of a sentence that reflects spoken or written language. Usage questions are printed in three versions of orthography so as not to make the testing of the features orthography-dependent. In the left column, the Japanese is transcribed in modified Hepburn romanization; in the middle column in standard Japanese orthography with *furigana;* and in the third column in modified *kunrei-shiki* romanization. Modified *kunrei-shiki* uses vowel letters to indicate long vowels (e.g., *tooi*) rather than a macron (e.g., *tōi*).

The reading comprehension questions test your understanding of such points as main and supporting ideas and the setting of passages, all of which are written in appropriate standard Japanese orthography. Most questions deal with the understanding of literal meaning although some inference questions may be included. The Japanese selections on which they are based are drawn from authentic materials, such as diaries, notes, menus, newspaper articles, advertisements, and letters. Students are expected to be able to read *katakana* as well as *hiragana* and to be able to deal with *kanji* without the help of *furigana.* All reading comprehension questions are in English.

Skills Measured	Approximate Percentage of Test
Listening Comprehension	33
Usage	33
Reading Comprehension	33

Sample Questions

Three types of questions are used in the Japanese with Listening Subject Test. All questions in the test are multiple-choice. You must choose the best response from the four choices offered for each question.

When the test is administered, all spoken Japanese will be presented by tape playback. Each dialogue or narrative will have the English lead-in line printed in the test booklet.

In an actual test administration, the text that appears in brackets ([ ]) in this book would be recorded and not printed in your test booklet. It appears in printed form here because a taped version is not available.

General Directions: In this test you will have an opportunity to demonstrate your ability to understand spoken Japanese. There are three sections to this test, each with special directions. Listen carefully since all recorded material will be spoken only once.

SECTION I

Listening

Approximate time - 20 minutes

Directions: In this section of the test you will hear short dialogues and monologues. You will hear them only once, and they are not printed in your test book. At the end of each selection, you will be asked questions about what was said.

(Narrator) [This is a conversation in a restaurant.]

(Man) [すみません。まだ注文していないんですが. . .]

(Woman) [あ、失礼しました。何になさいますか。]

(Man) [すき焼定食を三人前。]

(Woman) [はい。]

(Narrator) [Question 1. What is the customer's problem?] (16 seconds)

1. (A) He wants to change his order.
   (B) The waitress has not yet taken his order.
   (C) His original order is no longer available.
   (D) His order came without the soup.

(Narrator) [Listen to the following conversation in an office.]

(Man) [明日（あした）家に電話してくださいませんか。]

(Woman) [ええ、いいですよ。　電話番号は？]

(Man) [あ、書きましょう。]

(Narrator) [Question 2. What does the man ask the woman to do?] (16 seconds)

2. (A) Tell him her phone number.
   (B) Call him at home.
   (C) Check with him tomorrow at work.
   (D) Write down her phone number.

SECTION II

Usage

Suggested time - 10 minutes

Directions: This section consists of a number of incomplete statements, each of which has four suggested completions. In some instances, choice (A) may consist of dashes that indicate that no insertion is required to form a correct sentence. Select the word or phrase that best completes the sentence structurally and logically and fill in the corresponding oval on the answer sheet.

THIS SECTION OF THE TEST IS PRESENTED IN THREE COLUMNS THAT PROVIDE IDENTICAL INFORMATION. LOOK AT THE EXAMPLE BELOW AND CHOOSE THE ONE COLUMN OF WRITING WITH WHICH YOU ARE MOST FAMILIAR IN ORDER TO ANSWER THE QUESTION. DO NOT WASTE TIME BY SWITCHING FROM COLUMN TO COLUMN IN THIS SECTION.

Example:

Tōkyō wa ----- ni arimasu.

(A) Amerika
(B) Kanada
(C) Furansu
(D) Nihon

東京(とうきょう)は-----にあります。

(A) アメリカ
(B) カナダ
(C) フランス
(D) 日本(にほん)

Tookyoo wa ----- ni arimasu.

(A) Amerika
(B) Kanada
(C) Hurañsu
(D) Nihoñ

The best completion is choice (D). Therefore, you would select choice (D) and fill in the corresponding oval on the answer sheet. Remember to work with one column only.

3. Sore wa totemo kirei ----- hana desu nē.

(A) -----
(B) no
(C) ni
(D) na

3. それはとてもきれい-----花(はな)ですねえ。

(A) -----
(B) の
(C) に
(D) な

3. Sore wa totemo kiree ----- hana desu nee.

(A) -----
(B) no
(C) ni
(D) na

4. Boku wa terebi o ----- gohan o tabeta.

(A) mitara
(B) miru toki
(C) miru aida
(D) minagara

4. ぼくはテレビを -----御飯(ごはん)を食(た)べた。

(A) 見(み)たら
(B) 見(み)る時(とき)
(C) 見(み)る間(あいだ)
(D) 見(み)ながら

4. Boku wa terebi o ----- gohañ o tabeta.

(A) mitara
(B) miru toki
(C) miru aida
(D) minagara

SECTION III

Reading

Suggested time - 15 minutes

Directions: Read the following texts carefully for comprehension. Each text is followed by one or more questions or incomplete statements based on its content. Select the answer or completion that is best according to the text and fill in the corresponding oval on the answer sheet.

This is an advertisement for a hotel.

上野駅３分
ファミリーホテル　田中屋

シングル	¥ 5,500
デラックスシングル	¥ 7,600
ツイン	¥ 12,000
トリプル	¥ 15,000

全室カラーテレビ、バストイレ付
和室もございます。
(03) 3771-3211

5. The hotel advertises
   - (A) a Japanese restaurant
   - (B) cable television in all rooms
   - (C) bus service from the train station
   - (D) a private bath with each room

6. The hotel's nightly charge for two persons in one room is
   - (A) 5,500 yen
   - (B) 7,600 yen
   - (C) 12,000 yen
   - (D) 15,000 yen

This is a note to Akio from his mother.

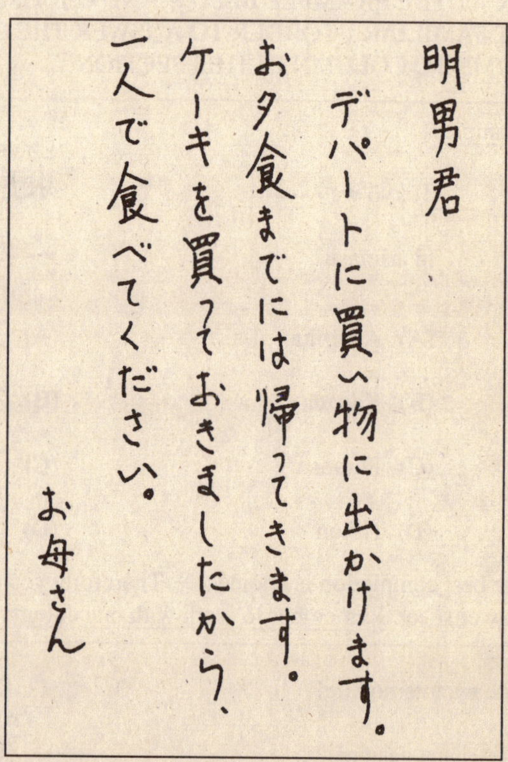

明男君
デパートに買い物に出かけます。
お夕食までには帰ってきます。
ケーキを買っておきましたから、
一人で食べてください。
お母さん

7. What does Akio's mother tell him to do?
   - (A) Come home by dinnertime
   - (B) Eat the cake she bought
   - (C) Buy some cake
   - (D) Have dinner by himself

Answers to the SAT II: Japanese with Listening Subject Test

Question Number	Correct Answer
1	B
2	A
3	D
4	D
5	D
6	C
7	B

The SAT II: Latin Subject Test

The SAT II: Latin Subject Test is written to reflect general trends in high school curricula and is independent of particular textbooks or methods of instruction. Most students taking the Latin Subject Test have studied two to four years of Latin in high school (the equivalent of two to four semesters in college). The best preparation for the test is the gradual development of competence in sight-reading Latin over a period of years, but you may also prepare for the Latin Subject Test as you would for any comprehensive examination that requires knowledge of facts and concepts and the ability to apply them. Reading the explanations and descriptions in this book should give you an indication of what to expect.

Since the SAT II: Latin Subject Test is intended to measure the Latin reading and grammatical skills of secondary school students between the second and fourth year of language study, the difficulty level of the questions varies. Some questions are directed toward students who have had only two years of Latin study and some to students who have had three or four years. The questions range from very easy ones that can be answered correctly by almost all of the students to difficult ones that only 15 percent to 20 percent can answer.

Colleges that require their applicants to take the Latin Subject Test may use the scores for course placement. Because scores are not adjusted on the basis of years of study, colleges should consider the preparation of students when evaluating their scores.

Content of the Test

The SAT II: Latin Subject Test measures knowledge and ability in the following areas of reading skill: grammar and syntax, derivatives, and translation and reading comprehension. These skills are tested in certain percentages (see the chart below) by six different types of questions.

Skills Measured	Approximate Percentage of Test
Grammar and Syntax	30
Derivatives	5
Translation and Reading Comprehension	65

70-75 Questions; Time — 60 minutes

Questions Used in the Test

Forms

This type of question asks you to select a specific grammatical form of a Latin word. Any form of a noun, pronoun, adjective, adverb, or verb can be asked for.

Directions: In the statement below, you are asked to give a specific form of the underlined word. Select the correct form from the choices given. Then fill in the corresponding oval on the answer sheet.

1. The dative singular of senātus is

(A) senātū

(B) senātum

(C) senātūs

(D) senātuī

In this question, you are asked to identify the dative singular of a fourth-declension noun. The answer is (D). (A) is ablative singular, (B) accusative singular, and (C) genitive singular, nominative plural, or accusative plural.

Derivatives

In this type of question, you are given an English sentence with one word underlined. You must choose the Latin word from which the underlined English word is derived.

Directions: The English sentence below contains a word that is underlined. Select from among the choices the Latin word to which the underlined word is related by derivation. Then fill in the corresponding oval on the answer sheet.

2. The event ruptured the relationship.

(A) reperiō

(B) rapiō

(C) reficiō

(D) rumpō

The English word *ruptured* is derived from Latin *ruptus,* the past participle of *rumpō.* So, (D) is the answer. Note that you will need to know the various forms of different Latin words to answer these questions.

Translation

You must choose the correct translation of the underlined Latin word or words. This type of question is more complex than the previous types, as it is based on the syntax of a complete Latin sentence.

Directions: In this part, part or all of the sentence is underlined. Select from among the choices the best translation for the underlined words. Then fill in the corresponding oval on the answer sheet.

3. Si vocāvissēs, laetī fuissēmus.

(A) If you were calling
(B) If you had called
(C) If you are calling
(D) If you should call

To answer this question correctly, you must know that *vocāvissēs* and *fuissēmus* are pluperfect subjunctives, appearing in a contrary-to-fact condition in the past. Only (B) expresses a past contrary-to-fact condition, and is therefore the correct choice.

Sentence Completion

This type of question contains a Latin sentence in which a word or phrase has been omitted. You must select the Latin word or phrase that best fits grammatically into the sentence.

Directions: The sentence below contains a blank space indicating that a word or phrase has been omitted. For each blank, four completions are provided. Choose the one that best completes the sentence and fill in the corresponding oval on the answer sheet.

4. Servus . . . vulnerātur.

(A) ā saxō
(B) saxum
(C) cum saxō
(D) saxō

In order to answer this question correctly, you must be able to translate the two words *servus vulnerātur* ("the slave is wounded") and then select the only choice that can be added to these two words to make a complete, grammatical Latin sentence. Here the correct choice is (D) *saxō*, which expresses the means or instrument by which the slave is wounded.

Substitution

This type of question contains a complete Latin sentence, part of which is underlined. You are asked to select the substitution that is closest in meaning to the underlined words.

Directions: In the sentence below, part of the sentence is underlined. Select from the choices the expression that, when substituted for the underlined portion of the sentence, changes the meaning of the sentence LEAST. Then fill in the corresponding oval on the answer sheet.

5. Cum haec dīxisset, discēdere nōn potuit.

(A) Haec dīcens
(B) Hīs dictīs
(C) Haec ab eō dicta
(D) Ut haec dīcerentur

In this example, the underlined clause is translated: "When he had said these things." You must select the answer choice whose translation is closest in meaning to this underlined clause. The correct choice is (B), the ablative absolute. None of the other choices is an appropriate substitution.

Reading Comprehension

This type of question presents you with a series of short passages of prose or poetry followed by several questions. These questions test either grammatical points (9 and 11 below), translation of a phrase or clause (7) or of a word (10), grammatical reference (12), or summary/comprehension (6 and 8). In addition, poetry passages always have one question on the scansion of the first four feet of a line of dactylic hexameter verse. Note that uncommon words that appear in the passages are defined and that the passages are adapted from Latin authors. There are approximately four or five passages with a total of 32 to 37 questions on the test. At least one (and no more than two) poetry passage appears on the test.

Directions: Read the following text carefully for comprehension. The text is followed by a number of questions or incomplete statements. Select the answer or completion that is best according to the text and fill in the corresponding oval on the answer sheet.

A wicked governor

Metellus[1], quī in Africā prōpraetor[2] erat, in oppidum vēnit, inflammātus furōre. Mīrābantur omnēs quid actūrus esset. Tum subitō hominem veterem in medium forum trahī iussit (jussit). Clāmābat ille miser sē cīvem esse Rōmānum, mīlitem fortem et fidēlem. Cum haec audīvisset, Metellus tamen servō suō imperāvit ut illum interficeret.

[1]Metellus, Metellī, m.: proper name
[2]prōpraetor, prōpraetōris, m.: governor

6. The words inflammātus furōre (line 2) indicate that

(A) the town was on fire
(B) Metellus came to set a fire
(C) Metellus was angry
(D) the people in town were angry

The word *inflammātus* modifies Metellus and *furōre* is an ablative dependent on *inflammātus*. While Metellus is the subject in both (B) and (C), only (C), the correct choice, expresses the idea that he is inflamed with rage.

7. The expression quid actūrus esset (line 3) is translated

(A) what must be done
(B) what he was about to do
(C) what he was doing
(D) what had been done

The clause *quid actūrus esset* expresses an indirect question; *actūrus* is the future active participle and *esset* the imperfect subjunctive. (A) is incorrect because it expresses obligation; neither (C) nor (D) conveys the notion of future time found in *actūrus*. (B) is the answer.

8. The sentence "Tum . . . iussit (jussit)" (lines 3-4) tells us that

(A) Metellus ordered an old man to leave the forum
(B) an old man offered to surrender in the forum
(C) an old man ordered the forum to be cleared
(D) Metellus ordered an old man to be brought into the forum

To answer this question correctly, you must know that *iussit (jussit)* takes an accusative with the infinitive (*hominem veterem . . . trahī*) (lines 3-4). You must also know that Metellus is the subject of *iussit (jussit)* and that *trahī* is a passive infinitive. The answer is (D).

9. In line 5, the case and number of sē are

(A) accusative singular
(B) ablative singular
(C) accusative plural
(D) ablative plural

In line 5, *sē* is the subject of an infinitive in indirect discourse and refers to the subject of the main clause, *"ille miser."* (A) is the answer.

10. Cum (line 6) is translated as

(A) With
(B) Since
(C) Although
(D) If

Cum is used here to introduce a clause; (A), a preposition, is therefore incorrect. The presence of *tamen* (nevertheless) in the main clause indicates that the dependent clause is concessive. The answer is (C).

11. The case of servō (line 7) is

(A) nominative
(B) dative
(C) accusative
(D) ablative

In line 7, *servō* is the indirect object of the verb *imperāvit*, and is therefore in the dative case. (B) is the answer.

12. In line 7, illum refers to

(A) hominem (line 3)
(B) forum (line 4)
(C) Metellus (line 7)
(D) servō (line 7)

In line 7, *illum* is the direct object of *interficeret;* the one to be killed is the old man brought into the forum. The answer is (A).

SAT II:

Latin Subject Test

The test that follows is a shortened edition of a typical SAT II: Latin Subject Test that has been administered. So that you will have an idea of what the actual test administration will be like, try to take this test under conditions as close as possible to those of the actual test. It will probably help if you do the following.

- Set aside an hour for the test when you will not be interrupted, so that you can complete all of it in one sitting.
- Sit at a desk with no other papers or books. You can't take a dictionary, other books, or notes into the test room.
- Have a kitchen timer or clock in front of you for timing yourself.
- Tear out an answer sheet from the back of this book and fill it in just as you would on the day of the test. You can use one answer sheet for as many as three Subject Tests.
- Read the instructions that precede the test. When you take the test, you will be asked to read them before you begin answering questions.
- After you finish the test, read the sections on "How to Score the SAT II: Latin Subject Test" and "Reviewing Your Test Performance," which follow the test.

FORM 3MAC

LATIN TEST

The top portion of the section of the answer sheet that you will use in taking the Latin test must be filled in exactly as shown in the illustration below. Note carefully that you have to do all of the following on your answer sheet.

1. Print LATIN on the line under the words "Subject (print)."

2. In the shaded box labeled "Test Code" fill in four ovals:

   —Fill in oval 4 in the row labeled V.

   —Fill in oval 2 in the row labeled W.

   —Fill in oval 2 in the row labeled X.

   —Fill in oval C in the row labeled Y.

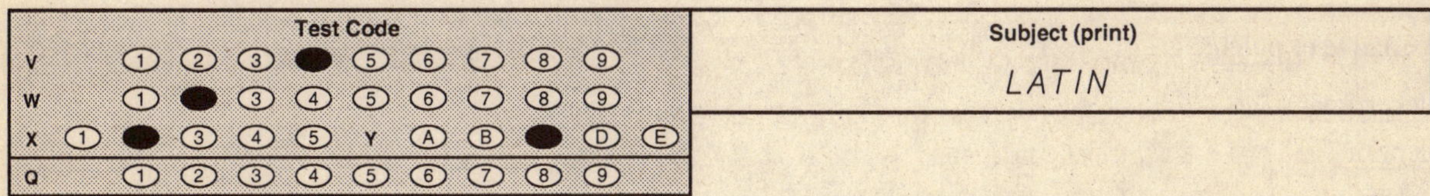

In the group of nine ovals labeled Q, you are to fill in ONE and ONLY ONE oval, as described below, to indicate how you obtained your knowledge of Latin. The information you provide is for statistical purposes only and will not influence your score on the test.

Part I If your knowledge of Latin does not come primarily from courses taken in grades 9 through 12, fill in oval 9 and leave the remaining ovals blank, regardless of how long you studied the subject in school. For example, you are to fill in oval 9 if your knowledge of Latin comes primarily from any of the following sources: study prior to the ninth grade, courses taken at a college, or special study.

Part II If your knowledge of Latin does come primarily from courses taken in grades 9 through 12, fill in the oval that indicates the level of the Latin course in which you are currently enrolled. If you are not now enrolled in a Latin course, fill in the oval that indicates the level of the most advanced course in Latin that you have completed.

First year:	first or second half	—fill in oval 1
Second year:	first half	—fill in oval 2
	second half	—fill in oval 3
Third year:	first half	—fill in oval 4
	second half	—fill in oval 5
Fourth year:	first half	—fill in oval 6
	second half	—fill in oval 7
Advanced Placement course or a course at a level higher than fourth year, second half		—fill in oval 8

When the supervisor gives the signal, turn the page and begin the Latin test. There are 100 numbered ovals on the answer sheet and 54 questions in the Latin test. Therefore, use only ovals 1 to 54 for recording your answers.

LATIN TEST

PLEASE NOTE THAT YOUR ANSWER SHEET HAS FIVE ANSWER POSITIONS MARKED A, B, C, D, E, WHILE THE QUESTIONS THROUGHOUT THIS TEST CONTAIN ONLY FOUR CHOICES. BE SURE NOT TO MAKE ANY MARKS IN COLUMN E.

Note: In some questions in this test, variations of Latin terms will appear in parentheses.

Part A

Directions: In each statement below, you are asked to give a specific form of the underlined word. Select the correct form from the choices given. Then fill in the corresponding oval on the answer sheet.

1. The superlative of pulchrē is

(A) pulcherrimē
(B) pulchrior
(C) pulchrō
(D) pulchrius

2. The dative plural of mare is

(A) maribus
(B) marium
(C) maris
(D) marī

3. The genitive plural of similis is

(A) similem
(B) similis
(C) similium
(D) similī

4. The present participle of amō is

(A) amāre
(B) amāns
(C) amandus
(D) amātūrus

5. The future indicative of potest is

(A) posuerat
(B) poterat
(C) posuerit
(D) poterit

6. The perfect active indicative of dēfendimus is

(A) dēfendēbāmus
(B) dēfendēbāmur
(C) dēfendimus
(D) dēfēnsī sumus

7. The accusative singular neuter of quis is

(A) quod
(B) quae
(C) quem
(D) quid

GO ON TO THE NEXT PAGE

Part B

Directions: Each of the following English sentences contains a word that is underlined. Select from among the choices the Latin word to which the underlined word is related by derivation. Then fill in the corresponding oval on the answer sheet.

8. The suppression of the evidence was considered a very serious matter.

   (A) premō
   (B) pretium
   (C) prehendō
   (D) prex

9. The accident caused the boy to lose his auditory sense.

   (A) audeō
   (B) auctor
   (C) audiō
   (D) audāx

10. The goalkeeper was out of position.

    (A) populus
    (B) pons
    (C) possum
    (D) pōnō

GO ON TO THE NEXT PAGE

LATIN TEST—*Continued*

Part C

Directions: In each of the sentences below, part or all of the sentence is underlined. Select from among the choices the best translation for the underlined word or words. Then fill in the corresponding oval on the answer sheet.

11. Fūrem fūr et pauperem pauper cognoscit.

    (A) A thief is a thief, and a poor man recognizes a poor man.
    (B) There is a thief and the poor man recognizes the thief and the poor man.
    (C) A poor man is poor, and a thief recognizes a thief.
    (D) A thief recognizes a thief and a poor man recognizes a poor man.

12. Rēgēs laudāvimus quōrum rēgna sunt magna.

    (A) whose
    (B) for whom
    (C) whom
    (D) who

13. Cum in scholam venīs, magister tē docet.

    (A) Since you come to school
    (B) When you come to school
    (C) When you came to school
    (D) Although you came to school

14. Dux dīxit sē mīlitēs laudātūrum esse.

    (A) that they would praise the soldiers
    (B) that the soldiers had praised him
    (C) that he would praise the soldiers
    (D) that the soldiers should be praised

15. Haec mihi nōlīte dīcere.

    (A) This woman does not want to speak to me.
    (B) You do not want to tell me these things.
    (C) She does not know how to speak for me.
    (D) Do not tell me these things.

16. Nōnne hoc crēdis?

    (A) Do you believe this?
    (B) Would you not believe this?
    (C) You don't believe this, do you?
    (D) You believe this, don't you?

17. Inter amīcōs vīvere omnibus iūcundum (jūcundum) est.

    (A) He pleases everybody by living among friends.
    (B) Living among friends is pleasant for all.
    (C) He is pleased by all who live among friends.
    (D) It is pleasing to live with all one's friends.

18. Castra nōbīs occupanda sunt.

    (A) Let us seize the camp.
    (B) We must seize the camp.
    (C) We have seized the camp.
    (D) The camp is being seized by us.

19. Quīnque hōrīs amīcōs vidēbimus.

    (A) At five o'clock
    (B) In the fifth hour
    (C) Within five hours
    (D) For five hours

20. Dux auxiliō cōpiīs lēgātōs mīsit.

    (A) by means of the help of the troops
    (B) as a help to the troops
    (C) with a supply of help
    (D) with the helpful troops

GO ON TO THE NEXT PAGE

Part D

Directions: Each of the sentences below contains a blank space indicating that a word or phrase has been omitted. For each blank, four completions are provided. Choose the one that best completes the sentence and fill in the corresponding oval on the answer sheet.

21. Tē . . . appellō.

    (A) dictātōrem
    (B) dictātōris
    (C) dictātōre
    (D) dictātōrum

22. . . . semper audiunt?

    (A) Quem
    (B) Quōrum
    (C) Quis
    (D) Cui

23. Ē castrīs . . . nōluit.

    (A) ēgressus est
    (B) ēgredere
    (C) ut ēgrediātur
    (D) ēgredī

24. Nēmo dubitāvit . . . īret.

    (A) nōn
    (B) quīn
    (C) tam
    (D) sē

25. Imperātōrem . . . praefēcit.

    (A) castra
    (B) castrōrum
    (C) castrīs
    (D) ā castrīs

GO ON TO THE NEXT PAGE

Part E

Directions: In each of the sentences below, part or all of the sentence is underlined. Select from the choices the expression that, when substituted for the underlined portion of the sentence, changes the meaning of the sentence LEAST. Then fill in the corresponding oval on the answer sheet.

26. Hī cīvēs urbem cōnservābunt.

(A) Urbs hōs cīvēs cōnservābit.

(B) Urbs ab hīs cīvibus cōnservābitur.

(C) Hae urbēs cīvēs cōnservābunt.

(D) Hī cīvēs in urbe cōnservābuntur.

27. Vēnit Rōmam ad mātrem videndam.

(A) cum mātrem vīdisset

(B) mātre vīsā

(C) quī mātrem vīdit

(D) mātris videndae causā

28. Quod hostēs vīsī sunt, equitēs ad castra revertērunt.

(A) Hostēs videns

(B) Hostēs vīsī

(C) Hostibus vīsīs

(D) Hostibus videntibus

29. Mīlitem quī fortiter pugnāret vulnerātum esse audīvimus.

(A) fortiter pugnantēs

(B) fortiter pugnātum

(C) fortiter pugnans

(D) fortiter pugnantem

GO ON TO THE NEXT PAGE

Part F

Directions: Read each of the following texts carefully for comprehension. Each is followed by a number of questions or incomplete statements. Select the answer or completion that is best according to the text, and fill in the corresponding oval on the answer sheet.

An enemy attack

Sabīnī multī, ut ad moenia Rōmae venīrent, illōs in agrīs vīventēs oppugnābant. Agrī dēlēbantur; terror urbī iniectus (injectus) est. Tum plēbs benignē arma cēpit ad Sabīnōs repellendōs. Recūsantibus[1] frūstrā senātōribus duo tamen exercitūs magnī cōnscrīptī sunt.

[1]recūsō, recūsāre: oppose

30. The word vīventēs (line 2) refers to

(A) Sabīnī (line 1)
(B) moenia (line 1)
(C) illōs (line 1)
(D) agrīs (line 2)

31. The sentence Sabīnī . . . oppugnābant (lines 1-2) tells us that the

(A) Sabines wanted to get to the city walls
(B) Sabines were the people living in the fields
(C) Romans wanted to go nearer to the city walls
(D) Romans wanted to attack the people living in the fields

32. The sentence Agrī . . . iniectus (injectus) est (lines 2-3) tells us that the

(A) Sabines were destroyed in the fields
(B) Sabines were frightened of the city
(C) fearful city was destroyed
(D) city was filled with fear

33. The subject of cēpit (line 3) is

(A) terror (line 2)
(B) plēbs (line 3)
(C) arma (line 3)
(D) he (understood)

34. The sentence Recūsantibus . . . cōnscrīptī sunt (lines 4-5) tells us that

(A) armies were raised for the senators
(B) armies were raised in vain
(C) the senators prevented the raising of armies
(D) the senators did not want armies to be raised

GO ON TO THE NEXT PAGE

Balbinus and Maximus become joint emperors, only to be replaced by Gordian, a rival.

Imperātōres factī sunt Maximus atque Balbīnus. Ēgressī igitur ē senātū, sacrificiō factō, in forum populum convocāvērunt. Cum ōrātiōnem dē senātūs sententiā et dē suā ēlectiōne habuissent, populus Rōmānus cum mīlitibus, quī forte convēnerant, acclāmāvit: "Gordiānum esse imperātōrem volumus." Quī statim raptus est et, inductus in senātum, imperātor appellātus est. Novō genere senātūs cōnsultī[1] hoc est actum.

[1]senātūs cōnsultum, senātūs cōnsultī: a decree of the senate

35. The phrase Ēgressī . . . ē senātū (line 2) is translated

(A) While they were going out of the senate
(B) I went out of the senate
(C) After the senate had gone out
(D) After they had gone out of the senate

36. From the words sacrificiō factō (line 2), we learn that

(A) this event had been prophesied
(B) Maximus and Balbinus made a sacrifice
(C) Gordian made a sacrifice
(D) the gods were pleased with the deed

37. The case and number of senātūs (line 3) are

(A) genitive singular
(B) ablative singular
(C) nominative plural
(D) accusative plural

38. Quī (line 7) refers to

(A) populus (line 4)
(B) Gordiānum (line 6)
(C) senātum (line 7)
(D) Balbīnus (understood)

39. In lines 8-9, hoc est actum refers to

(A) the naming of Gordian as emperor
(B) an entrance into the senate
(C) the decree of the senate
(D) a new kind of senate

40. The passage suggests that

(A) the senate did not accept the people's preferences when choosing an emperor
(B) the office of emperor was viewed as a hereditary right at this time
(C) divine signs indicated that Gordian would have the title "emperor"
(D) the people and the military ultimately had control over who was chosen as emperor

GO ON TO THE NEXT PAGE

A challenge from a Gaul

Gallus quīdam nūdus praeter scūtum et gladiōs duōs prōcessit, quī et vīribus et magnitūdine et virtūte cēterīs praestābat. Is, maximē proeliō commōtō, manū sīgnificāre coepit utrīsque ut quiēscerent. Pugnae pausa facta est. Silentiō factō, cum vōce maximā conclāmāvit sī quis sēcum pugnāre vellet, ut prōdīret. Nēmō audēbat propter magnitūdinem atque saevam faciem. Deinde Gallus rīdēre coepit.

41. The first sentence tells us that the Gaul

    (A) wore battle armor and carried two swords
    (B) relied only on his size, not on weapons
    (C) had surrendered his shield and swords
    (D) surpassed all others in strength and courage

42. In line 3, maximē modifies

    (A) Is (line 3)
    (B) proeliō (line 3)
    (C) commōtō (line 3)
    (D) manū (line 3)

43. The words manū . . . quiēscerent (lines 3-4) tell us that the

    (A) signal to begin the battle had been given
    (B) Gaul signaled for each side to stop fighting
    (C) ominous silence indicated that the battle would be fierce
    (D) armies were waiting quietly for the battle signal

44. The case of Pugnae (line 4) is

    (A) genitive
    (B) locative
    (C) nominative
    (D) ablative

45. The words Silentiō factō (line 5) are translated

    (A) When silence had been secured
    (B) With a silent deed
    (C) In the silence of the act
    (D) Although it was a silent action

46. The word quis (line 6) is translated

    (A) who
    (B) anyone
    (C) a certain one
    (D) each one

47. In the last two sentences (lines 6-8), we learn that

    (A) no one listened when the Gaul boasted
    (B) the Gaul laughed when no one dared to fight him
    (C) everyone began to laugh at the Gaul's appearance
    (D) the challenge was quickly accepted in spite of the Gaul's great size

GO ON TO THE NEXT PAGE

Learning a foreign language

Hīc nihil addidicī[1], modicumque quod ante sciēbam
hīc ego mē tōtum dēdidicisse[2] sciō.
Gallica verba duo tantum[3] retinēre loquīque
sī possem, certē grātia magna foret[4].

[1]addiscō, addiscere, addidicī: learn further

[2]dēdiscō, dēdiscere, dēdidicī: forget

[3]tantum: only

[4]foret = esset

48. The case, number, and gender of modicum (line 1) are

(A) accusative singular masculine
(B) dative plural masculine
(C) nominative singular neuter
(D) accusative singular neuter

49. In line 1, -que connects

(A) Hīc (line 1) and hīc (line 2)
(B) nihil (line 1) and modicum (line 1)
(C) nihil (line 1) and tōtum (line 2)
(D) addidicī (line 1) and sciō (line 2)

50. In line 1, quod is translated

(A) because
(B) why
(C) which
(D) the fact that

51. The metrical pattern of the first four feet of line 1 is

(A) –⏑⏑|–⏑⏑|––|––
(B) ––|–⏑⏑|–⏑⏑|––
(C) ––|–⏑⏑|–⏑⏑|–⏑⏑
(D) –⏑⏑|–⏑⏑|–⏑⏑|–⏑⏑

52. The case of duo (line 3) is

(A) nominative
(B) accusative
(C) dative
(D) ablative

53. In line 4, sī possem is translated

(A) if I were able
(B) if I will be able
(C) if I am able
(D) if I had been able

54. The passage as a whole tells us that the author finds that learning a foreign language is

(A) difficult
(B) time-consuming
(C) rewarding
(D) necessary

STOP

IF YOU FINISH BEFORE TIME IS CALLED, YOU MAY CHECK YOUR WORK ON THIS TEST ONLY.
DO NOT TURN TO ANY OTHER TEST IN THIS BOOK.

How to Score the SAT II: Latin Subject Test

When you take the Latin Subject Test, your answer sheet will be "read" by a scanning machine that will record your responses to each question. Then a computer will compare your answers with the correct answers and produce your raw score. You get one point for each correct answer. For each wrong answer, you lose one-third of a point. Questions you omit (and any for which you mark more than one answer) are not counted. This raw score is converted to a College Board scaled score that is reported to you and to the colleges you specify. After you have taken this test, you can get an idea of what your raw score might be by following the instructions in the next section.

FINDING YOUR RAW TEST SCORE	
Step 1:	Table A lists the correct answers for all the questions on the SAT II: Latin Subject Test that is reproduced in this book. It also serves as a worksheet for you to calculate your raw score. • Compare your answers with those given in the table. • Put a check in the column marked "Right" if your answer is correct. • Put a check in the column marked "Wrong" if your answer is incorrect. • Leave both columns blank if you omitted the question.
Step 2:	Count the number of right answers and enter the total here: .... ________
Step 3:	Count the number of wrong answers and enter the total here: .... ________
Step 4:	Divide the number of wrong answers by 3 and enter the result here: .... ________
Step 5:	Subtract the result obtained in Step 4 from the total you obtained in Step 2. Enter the result here: .... ________
Step 6:	Round the number obtained in Step 5 to the nearest whole number. Enter the result here: .... ________
The number you obtained in Step 6 is your raw test score.	

TABLE A

Answers to the SAT II: Latin Subject Test, Form 3MAC, and Percentage of Students Answering Each Question Correctly

Question Number	Correct Answer	Right	Wrong	Percentage of Students Answering the Question Correctly*	Question Number	Correct Answer	Right	Wrong	Percentage of Students Answering the Question Correctly*
1	A			93	31	A			74
2	A			85	32	D			82
3	C			88	33	B			84
4	B			90	34	D			52
5	D			82	35	D			60
6	C			83	36	B			79
7	D			51	37	A			47
8	A			65	38	B			66
9	C			88	39	A			53
10	D			90	40	D			70
11	D			85	41	D			40
12	A			89	42	C			35
13	B			79	43	B			46
14	C			67	44	A			64
15	D			69	45	A			78
16	D			51	46	B			75
17	B			53	47	B			75
18	B			54	48	D			45
19	C			45	49	D			25
20	B			60	50	C			43
21	A			64	51	D			54
22	A			42	52	B			35
23	D			35	53	A			44
24	B			33	54	A			34
25	C			40					
26	B			77					
27	D			72					
28	C			47					
29	D			44					
30	C			67					

*These percentages are based on an analysis of the answer sheets for a random sample of 1,100 students who took this form of the test in June 1990 and whose mean score was 562. They may be used as an indication of the relative difficulty of a particular question. Each percentage may also be used to predict the likelihood that a typical SAT II: Latin Subject Test candidate will answer correctly that question on this edition of this test.

Reviewing Your Test Performance

After you have scored your test, you should take some time to consider the following points in relation to your performance on the test.

- *Did you run out of time before you reached the end of the test?*

  If you did, you may want to consider pacing yourself better. For example, you may have spent too much time working on one or two difficult questions. A better approach might have been to continue the test and return to those questions after you had attempted to answer the remaining questions on the test.

- *Did you take a long time reading the directions for the test?*

  The directions in the test are the same as those in the Latin Subject Tests now being administered. You will save time when you read the directions on the test day if you become thoroughly familiar with them in advance.

- *How did you handle questions you were unsure of?*

  If you were able to eliminate one or more of the answer choices and you guessed from the remaining choices, then your approach probably worked to your advantage. On the other hand, omitting questions about which you have some knowledge or guessing answers haphazardly would probably be a mistake.

- *How difficult were the questions for you compared with other students who took the test?*

  By referring to Table A, you can find out how difficult each question was for the group of students who took this test. The right-hand column in the table tells you what percentage of this group answered the question correctly. A question that was answered correctly by almost everyone in the group is obviously an easy question. Question 1, for example, was answered correctly by 93 percent of the students in the sample. On the other hand, question 24 was answered correctly by only 33 percent.

  It is important to remember that these percentages are based on only one particular group of students; had this edition of the test been given to other groups of students at the time, the percentages would probably have been different.

  If you find that you missed several questions that would be considered easy, you may want to review those questions carefully. They may cover some aspect of the subject that you need to review. Perhaps you misunderstood the directions for one part of the test or you thought the questions were so easy that you did not spend as much time on them as you might have.

The SAT II: Spanish and Spanish with Listening

The College Board offers two types of one-hour Spanish Subject Tests. The traditional reading test consists of 85 multiple-choice reading questions and is offered on four national test dates. The new Spanish Subject Test with Listening (offered only in November at participating high schools) consists of 85 multiple-choice listening and reading questions.

The tests are written to reflect general trends in secondary school curricula and are independent of particular textbooks or methods of instruction. They are designed to test the ability of students who have completed three to four years of language study. Outstanding students with just two years of study are also encouraged to take the tests. You should prepare for the tests as you would for any comprehensive examination that requires knowledge of facts and concepts, and that tests your level of reading and listening comprehension. However, the best preparation for the tests is the gradual development of competence in Spanish over a period of years.

In addition to reading questions, the Spanish Subject Test with Listening measures your ability to understand spoken language by means of three types of *listening* questions. The first type (pictures) asks you to identify the sentence that most accurately describes what is presented in a photograph or drawing. The second type (rejoinders) tests your ability to identify a plausible continuation of a short conversation. The third type requires that you answer questions based on more extensive listening selections.

Content Outline for the Spanish Subject Test with Listening

Kinds of Questions	Approximate Percentage of Test
Listening Section (approximately 35 questions)	
Pictures	
Rejoinders	
Selections	40
Reading Section (approximately 50 questions)	
Vocabulary and Structure	
Paragraph Completion	
Reading Comprehension	60

Questions for the listening section follow. Note that text in brackets ([ ]) is recorded; it is not printed in your test booklet.

Section I — Listening

Part A

Directions: For each item in this part, you will hear four sentences designated (A), (B), (C), and (D). They will not be printed in your test booklet. As you listen, look at the picture in your test booklet and select the choice that best reflects what you see in the picture or what someone in the picture might say. Then fill in the corresponding oval on the answer sheet. You will hear the choices only once. Now look at the following example.

You see:

You hear:

(Woman) **[(A) Siento darles tan mala noticia.**
(B) Tiene quince días para pagar la multa.
(C) Y aquí les mando la foto más reciente.
(D) Es preciso que se presente ante el juez.]

(7 seconds)

Statement (C), "Y aquí les mando la foto más reciente," best reflects what you see in the picture or what someone in the picture might say. Therefore, you would choose answer (C). Now we will begin. Look at the first picture and listen to the four choices.

J. Wachter Photo Researchers, Inc.

UPI/Bettmann

(Narrator) [Número 1]

(Woman) [(A) ¡Te dije que el agua estaría fría!
(B) Con tanta nieve no podremos ir muy lejos.
(C) ¡Qué día tan fantástico para correr!
(D) ¿Qué es eso que estás leyendo?]
(7 seconds)

(Narrator) [Número 2]

(Man) [(A) ¡Otro micrófono, por favor!
(B) La guitarra no tiene cuerdas.
(C) ¡Cantemos todos juntos!
(D) Adiós, ya estoy aburrido.]
(7 seconds)

Part B

Directions: In this part of the test you will hear several short conversations, or parts of conversations, followed by four choices designated (A), (B), (C), and (D). After you hear the four choices, choose the one that most logically continues or completes the conversation and mark your answer on your answer sheet. Neither the conversations nor the choices will be printed in your test booklet. Now listen to the following example.

You will hear:

(Man) [Yo creo que leer es muy importante.]

You will also hear:

(Woman) [(A) Pues no leas tanto.
(B) Estoy totalmente de acuerdo.
(C) No te acuerdas de nada.
(D) No me importan esas leyes.]
(7 seconds)

The choice that most logically continues the conversation is (B), "Estoy totalmente de acuerdo." Therefore, you should choose answer (B). Now listen to the first conversation.

(Narrator) [Número 3]

(Woman A) [¿Crees que vamos a ganar el campeonato?

(Woman B) Seguro, tenemos el mejor equipo.]

(Woman A) [(A) Todas llevan camisetas azules.
(B) Perdió casi todos los partidos.
(C) Las jugadoras consiguieron llegar a tiempo.
(D) Y también la mejor entrenadora.]
(7 seconds)

(Narrator) [Número 4]

(Woman) [Llegaste tarde; ¡ya no quedan entradas para esa obra!]

(Man) [(A) ¡Qué entradas tan caras!
(B) Hay otra puerta por aquí.
(C) Perdona, se atrasó el autobús.
(D) A la izquierda está la entrada.]
(7 seconds)

Part C

Directions: You will now hear a series of selections. For each selection, you will see printed in your test booklet one or more questions with four possible answers. They will not be spoken. Select the best answer to each question from among the four choices printed and fill in the corresponding oval on your answer sheet. You will have 12 seconds to answer each question. There will be no example for this part. Now listen to the first selection.

(Narrator) [Selección Número 1. Escuchen esta conversación en la recepción del Hotel California.]

(Man) [Hola, buenas tardes, señorita. ¿Tiene Ud. una reservación a nombre de Escalante?

(Woman) Déjeme ver. Mmm. . . No la veo, señor. ¿La hizo directamente con nostros?

(Man) Sí, con ustedes. Aquí tengo la confirmación.

(Woman) Pues, señor, el problema es que el hotel está lleno y no quedan habitaciones.

(Man) Pero, ¿qué hago yo? He pagado un depósito.

(Woman) Un momento, por favor. Llamaré al gerente para solucionar el problema.]

(Narrator) [Ahora contesten las preguntas 5 y 6.]
(24 seconds)

Selección Número 1.

5. ¿Qué problema tiene el Sr. Escalante?

(A) Perdió su confirmación.
(B) No quiere alojarse en el Hotel California.
(C) El hotel no tiene su reservación.
(D) Olvidó pagar el depósito.

6. ¿Cómo trata la recepcionista al Sr. Escalante?

(A) Bruscamente.
(B) Respetuosamente.
(C) Insolentemente.
(D) Alegremente.

(Narrator) **[Selección Número 2. Escuchen a este presentador.]**

(Man) **[¡Pasen, señores, pasen! Vean a los mejores acróbatas del mundo desafiar la muerte en la cuerda floja. Deléitense con los payasos más divertidos que jamás hayan visto. Compren sus boletos aquí. ¡No se pierdan esta gran función!]**

(Narrator) **[Ahora contesten la pregunta 7.]**
(12 seconds)

Selección Número 2.

7. **¿Qué tipo de función es ésta?**

   (A) Un circo.
   (B) Un evento deportivo.
   (C) Una reunión.
   (D) Un concierto.

Answers to the Listening Questions

Question Number	Correct Answer	Question Number	Correct Answer
1	C	5	C
2	C	6	B
3	D	7	A
4	C		

Section II — Reading

In addition to the Spanish Subject Test with Listening, there is a reading test that does not include a listening section. The Spanish Subject Tests evaluate your reading skills through precision of vocabulary and structure use, and comprehension of a variety of texts (see the chart below). Knowledge of vocabulary is tested implicitly throughout the test, but some questions specifically test word meaning in the context of a sentence that reflects spoken or written language. Understanding of various parts of speech (nouns, verbs, adjectives, adverbs, etc.) and idiomatic expressions is tested. "Structure" questions test your ability to identify usage that is both correct structurally and appropriate in context. Another part of the test has vocabulary and grammatical usage embedded in longer paragraphs. "Reading comprehension" questions test points such as main and supporting ideas, themes, and spatial and temporal setting of a passage. Prose fiction, historical works, and newspaper and magazine articles are used as the varied selections on which these questions are based. Beginning in June 1994, they may also be taken from such sources as advertisements, tickets, and schedules.

Reading Skills Measured by Both Spanish Subject Tests

	Approximate Percentage of Test
Vocabulary and Structure	40
Paragraph Completion	30
Reading Comprehension	30

SAT II:

Spanish Subject Mini Test

The test that follows is a shortened version of a typical SAT II: Spanish Subject Test. So that you may have an idea of what the national test administration will be like, try to take the test in this book under conditions as similar as possible to those of the nationally administered test. It will probably help if you do the following.

- Set aside 35 minutes for the test when you will not be interrupted, so that you can complete all of it in one sitting.
- Sit at a desk with no other papers or books. You can't take a dictionary, other books, or notes into the test room.
- Have a kitchen timer or clock in front of you to time yourself.
- Tear out an answer sheet from the back of this book and fill it in just as you would on the day of the test. You can use one answer sheet for as many as three Subject Tests.
- Read the instructions that precede the test. When you take the test, you will be asked to read them before you begin answering questions.

SPANISH TEST

The top portion of the section of the answer sheet that you will use in taking the Spanish test must be filled in exactly as shown in the illustration below. Note carefully that you have to do all of the following on your answer sheet.

1. Print SPANISH on the line under the words "Subject (print)."

2. In the shaded box labeled "Test Code" fill in four ovals:

—Fill in oval 4 in the row labeled V.

—Fill in oval 1 in the row labeled W.

—Fill in oval 3 in the row labeled X.

—Fill in oval B in the row labeled Y.

Test Code											
V		1	2	3	●	5	6	7	8	9	
W		●	2	3	4	5	6	7	8	9	
X	1	2	●	4	5	Y	A	●	C	D	E
Q		1	2	3	4	5	6	7	8	9	

Subject (print)
SPANISH

Please answer either Part I or Part II by filling in the specific oval in row Q. You are to fill in ONE and ONLY ONE oval as described below, to indicate how you obtained your knowledge of Spanish. The information you provide is for statistical purposes only and will not influence your score on the test.

Part I If your knowledge of Spanish does not come primarily from courses taken in grades 9 through 12, fill in oval 9 and leave the remaining ovals blank, regardless of how long you studied the subject in school. For example, you are to fill in oval 9 if your knowledge of Spanish comes primarily from any of the following sources: study prior to the ninth grade, courses taken at a college, special study, living in a home in which Spanish is the principal language spoken, or extensive residence abroad that includes significant experience in the Spanish language.

Part II If your knowledge of Spanish does come primarily from courses taken in secondary school, fill in the oval that indicates the level of the Spanish course in which you are currently enrolled. If you are not now enrolled in a Spanish course, fill in the oval that indicates the level of the most advanced course in Spanish that you have completed.

First year:	first or second half	—fill in oval 1
Second year:	first half	—fill in oval 2
	second half	—fill in oval 3
Third year:	first half	—fill in oval 4
	second half	—fill in oval 5
Fourth year:	first half	—fill in oval 6
	second half	—fill in oval 7
Advanced Placement course or a course at a level higher than fourth year, second half or high school course work plus a minimum of four weeks of study abroad		—fill in oval 8

When the supervisor gives the signal, turn the page and begin the Spanish test. There are 100 numbered ovals on the answer sheet and 47 questions in the Spanish test. Therefore, use only ovals 1 to 47 for recording your answers.

SPANISH TEST

PLEASE NOTE THAT YOUR ANSWER SHEET HAS FIVE ANSWER POSITIONS MARKED A, B, C, D, E, WHILE THE QUESTIONS THROUGHOUT THIS TEST CONTAIN ONLY FOUR CHOICES. BE SURE NOT TO MAKE ANY MARKS IN COLUMN E.

Part A

Directions: This part consists of a number of incomplete statements, each having four suggested completions. Select the most appropriate completion and fill in the corresponding oval on the answer sheet.

1. Vaya por este ------- para ir a la ciudad.

(A) camino
(B) piso
(C) viaje
(D) caso

2. Juan Pablo tuvo que esperar unos minutos antes de tomar la sopa porque estaba demasiado -------.

(A) caliente
(B) calurosa
(C) mojada
(D) perfumada

3. Recientemente, un arqueólogo ha ------- nuevas ruinas mayas en Guatemala.

(A) hecho
(B) construido
(C) desterrado
(D) descubierto

4. Mientras bailaba el grupo de danza, Manuel ------- fotografías.

(A) saca
(B) sacaría
(C) sacaba
(D) sacara

5. Paquito, si quieres comer en casa con nosotros, vuelve -------.

(A) a tiempo
(B) a fondo
(C) con profundidad
(D) por regla general

6. García Lorca, el gran poeta español, escribió ------- teatral, *Yerma*.

(A) la playa
(B) la obra
(C) el acta
(D) el verso

7. La Sra. Solís decidió viajar a Buenos Aires en barco. ¿------- van Uds.?

(A) Cuánto
(B) Cómo
(C) Qué
(D) Cuál

8. Si quieren echar las cartas al correo, ------- un buzón en la esquina.

(A) haya
(B) es
(C) hay
(D) son

9. Creo que viajaré a Colombia ------- ir a México.

(A) en vez de
(B) acerca de
(C) a mediados de
(D) alrededor de

10. ¡Qué música tan estupenda! Esta orquesta ------- muy bien.

(A) juega
(B) sabe
(C) maneja
(D) toca

11. ¿No te dieron helado, Cristina? ¿Quieres -------?

(A) el mío
(B) mía
(C) la mía
(D) mío

12. Habla ------- bien el francés.

(A) bastante
(B) mucho
(C) tanto
(D) tal

GO ON TO THE NEXT PAGE

13. Para mi clase de geografía, tuve que comprar ------- mapa del Caribe.

(A) una
(B) un
(C) alguna
(D) alguno

14. Marta fue a ver al médico porque estaba -------.

(A) enferma
(B) dormida
(C) sentada
(D) oscura

15. Elena ha cambiado mucho desde la última vez que nosotros la -------.

(A) veamos
(B) veríamos
(C) veíamos
(D) vimos

16. Dicen que el español es el ------- más estudiado en el Japón después del inglés.

(A) trabajo
(B) negocio
(C) estudio
(D) idioma

17. La dominación romana de la población de la Península Ibérica duró más de seis -------.

(A) cinturas
(B) centenarios
(C) sillones
(D) siglos

18. Me parece que no querían terminar el proyecto porque lo hicieron -------.

(A) bien hecho
(B) sin falta
(C) de mala gana
(D) con cariño

19. Si ------- en el Brasil, hablaríamos portugués y no español.

(A) vivamos
(B) vivimos
(C) vivíamos
(D) viviéramos

20. Cuando Lupita oyó la mala noticia, ------- muy pálida.

(A) se volvió
(B) llegó a ser
(C) se puso
(D) se hizo

21. Me gustó tanto la novela de Isabel Allende que ------- voy a recomendar a mis amigos.

(A) le
(B) lo
(C) se la
(D) me la

22. Ellos saben mucho más ------- creen.

(A) que
(B) como
(C) de lo que
(D) de que

23. Alguien está tocando a la puerta; ¿quién ------- a estas horas?

(A) será
(B) sería
(C) era
(D) fue

24. He gastado tanto dinero que ahora sólo me ------- cincuenta pesos.

(A) quedo
(B) quedan
(C) queda
(D) queden

GO ON TO THE NEXT PAGE

Part B

Directions: In each of the following paragraphs, there are numbered blanks indicating that words or phrases have been omitted. For each numbered blank, four completions are provided. First read through the entire paragraph. Then, for each numbered blank, choose the completion that is most appropriate given the context of the entire paragraph and fill in the corresponding oval on the answer sheet.

El mural más polémico del siempre volcánico Diego Rivera, *Sueño de una tarde dominical en la Alameda Central*, ya está por fin ___(25)___ de todos. Considerada una de las ___(26)___ más logradas de la corriente nacionalista mexicana, este mural ___(27)___ encendidas controversias desde su creación en 1948. Primero Rivera incluyó una frase de un conocido escritor mexicano que dice: "Dios no existe", y esto provocó una ___(28)___ reacción de grupos ultraderechistas y de la propia Iglesia Católica. Situado en el Hotel del Prado, el mural ___(29)___ ser trasladado del restaurante al sótano del establecimiento, donde se ocultó durante ocho años por la insistencia de los católicos ortodoxos que, en una ocasión, obligaron a un albañil ___(30)___ cubrir la frase controvertida. ___(31)___, el propio Rivera se vio obligado a cambiar las palabras y puso "Conferencia de la Academia de Letras", para apagar las críticas y que el mural ___(32)___ exhibido.

25. (A) en vez
    (B) al lado
    (C) a la vista
    (D) a mediados

26. (A) manifestaciones
    (B) cuadras
    (C) artes
    (D) paredes

27. (A) despertó
    (B) apagó
    (C) cerró
    (D) sorprendió

28. (A) tardía
    (B) furiosa
    (C) agradable
    (D) cordial

29. (A) debió
    (B) debiera
    (C) deberá
    (D) debería

30. (A) de
    (B) en
    (C) por
    (D) a

31. (A) Positivamente
    (B) Posteriormente
    (C) De ninguna manera
    (D) De vez en cuando

32. (A) sea
    (B) será
    (C) fuera
    (D) fue

GO ON TO THE NEXT PAGE

Part C

Directions: Read the following texts carefully for comprehension. Each is followed by a number of questions or incomplete statements. Select the answer or completion that is best according to the text and fill in the corresponding oval on the answer sheet.

En la Residencia del Seguro de Enfermedad de Oviedo acaba de ser practicada una operación quirúrgica rara: la extracción de 132 pesetas en monedas del estómago de Manuel Soages, fogonero de un barco de pesca. El enfermo, de cincuenta y cinco años, venía quejándose de dolores de estómago y le fue falsamente diagnosticada una úlcera. Lo que no ha sido aclarado aún es si las comía como postre riquísimo o si se trataba de una manía ahorrativa.

33. La condición de Manuel Soages se debió a

    (A) una úlcera
    (B) un exceso de postres
    (C) unas monedas
    (D) pescado podrido

34. El remedio consistió en

    (A) una comida ligera
    (B) una operación estomacal
    (C) unas pastillas contra la acidez
    (D) un tratamiento médico

35. La noticia da a entender que el paciente estaba motivado por

    (A) exhibicionismo
    (B) una dieta insuficiente
    (C) una manía de ahorrar
    (D) causas desconocidas

GO ON TO THE NEXT PAGE

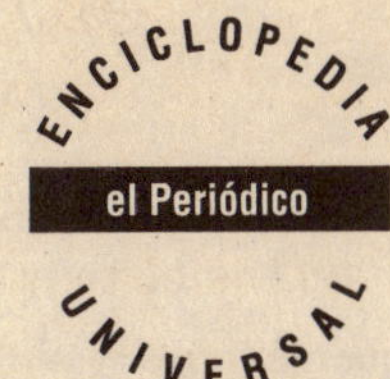

Complete su Enciclopedia Universal El Periódico

*Para conseguir los tomos que le falten de la **Enciclopedia Universal El Periódico,** sólo tiene que rellenar el cupón de pedido — adjuntando 125.-Ptas. en sellos por cada tomo que solicite, más 75.-Ptas. en sellos por gastos de envío — y remitirlo a la siguiente dirección:*

El Periódico de Catalunya
Departamento de Distribución
C/. Comte d'Urgell, n.º 100
08011 Barcelona

36. ¿Para qué hay que mandar 75 pesetas?

(A) Para pagar el costo de correos
(B) Para recibir cupones de pedido
(C) Para comprar un periódico catalán
(D) Para pagar un anuncio ilustrado

GO ON TO THE NEXT PAGE

El emperador Salus quería que un pintor imaginara el rostro femenino más hermoso del mundo. Buscaron a un pintor que se encargara del cuadro y al fin lo encontraron en una aldea remota.

— ¡Difícil, difícil! — dijo el pintor, al oír de qué se trataba —. Pero lo intentaré. Eso sí, que reúnan en el palacio a las mujeres más hermosas del imperio para que yo pueda verlas cuando vaya.

Así se hizo. El pintor fue al palacio, eligió de las cincuenta mujeres invitadas las diez que más le impresionaron y, haciendo como que copiaba los ojos de una, la boca de otra, y así, compuso un retrato que fue la suma de todas las perfecciones imaginables.

El emperador, satisfecho, le pagó generosamente al pintor y colgó el cuadro en su palacio.

El pintor volvió a su casa y le dijo a su mujer:

—Tendremos que mudarnos aun más lejos a otro reino. No sea que un día de estos el emperador te vea y te lleve con él: en su palacio ya tiene el retrato tuyo.

37. ¿Cuál es el deseo especial del emperador?

    (A) Vivir en un palacio en otro reino
    (B) Ser dueño de un retrato extraordinario
    (C) Aprender a pintar bien el cuerpo humano
    (D) Tener la mejor fiesta del mundo

38. Cuando el pintor se enteró de lo que el emperador quería, reaccionó de una manera

    (A) crítica y vengativa
    (B) egoísta y codiciosa
    (C) burlona y cómica
    (D) cuidadosa y astuta

39. ¿Qué pidió el pintor antes de ir al palacio?

    (A) Que se le diera una nueva casa
    (B) Que se llevara a la corte a un grupo de mujeres
    (C) Que le dieran a su esposa permiso de acompañarlo
    (D) Que el emperador le pagara cierta suma de dinero

40. ¿Qué hizo el pintor cuando llegó al palacio?

    (A) Escogió a las cincuenta mujeres más atractivas para pintarlas.
    (B) Pintó a la mujer más hermosa de las diez finalistas.
    (C) Fingió que estaba pintando un compuesto de ciertas modelos.
    (D) Permitió que el emperador lo observara mientras pintaba.

41. ¿Cuál fue la reacción del emperador al ver el producto final?

    (A) Le dijo al pintor que se mudara inmediatamente.
    (B) Se sintió contento y complacido.
    (C) Creyó que el pintor era una persona engañosa.
    (D) Quiso conocer a la esposa del pintor.

42. ¿Por qué estaba preocupado el pintor al volver a casa?

    (A) Temía que su mujer lo abandonara.
    (B) Creía que a su esposa ya no le gustaba su casa.
    (C) Había pintado la cara de su mujer en el retrato.
    (D) Temía que alguien le robara el dinero.

GO ON TO THE NEXT PAGE

El olor especial, el gran rumor de la gente, las luces siempre tristes de la estación de tren, tenían para mí un gran encanto, ya que envolvían todas mis impresiones en la maravilla de haber llegado por fin a una ciudad grande, adorada en mis ensueños por desconocida.

Empecé a seguir el rumbo de la masa humana que, cargada de maletas, se volcaba en la salida. Mi equipaje era un maletón muy pesado — porque estaba casi lleno de libros — y lo llevaba yo misma con toda la fuerza de mi juventud y de mi ansiosa expectación.

Un aire marino, pesado y fresco, entró en mis pulmones con la primera sensación confusa de la ciudad: una masa de casas dormidas, de establecimientos cerrados, de faroles como centinelas borrachos de soledad. Una respiración grande, dificultosa, venía con el cuchicheo de la madrugada. Muy cerca, a mi espalda, enfrente de las callejuelas misteriosas que conducen al Borne, sobre mi corazón excitado, estaba el mar.

Debía parecer una figura extraña con mi aspecto risueño y mi viejo abrigo que, a impulsos de la brisa, me azotaba las piernas. Recuerdo que, en pocos minutos, me quedé sola en la gran acera, porque la gente corría a coger los escasos taxis o luchaba por arracimarse en el tranvía.

Uno de esos viejos coches de caballos que han vuelto a surgir después de la guerra se detuvo delante de mí y lo tomé sin titubear, causando la envidia de un señor que se lanzaba detrás de él desesperado, agitando el sombrero.

Corrí en el desvencijado vehículo, por anchas calles vacías y atravesé el corazón de la ciudad lleno de luz a toda hora, como yo quería que estuviera, en un viaje que me pareció corto y para mí se cargaba de belleza.

43. ¿Cómo se siente la narradora al llegar a la ciudad?

(A) Perdida
(B) Encantada
(C) Cansada
(D) Tranquila

44. ¿Qué efecto producen en la narradora las luces de la estación?

(A) Le agradan mucho.
(B) Le dan vergüenza.
(C) La desorientan.
(D) La adormecen.

45. ¿Dónde está la ciudad a la que llega la narradora?

(A) En la costa
(B) En una cordillera
(C) Al lado de un río
(D) Cerca de un lago

46. El vehículo que la narradora toma es

(A) anticuado
(B) reluciente
(C) misterioso
(D) incómodo

47. ¿Quién narra este pasaje?

(A) Una joven que vuelve de sus vacaciones
(B) Una muchacha que viene de un lugar pequeño
(C) Una persona que regresa del extranjero
(D) Una mujer que va a vivir al Borne

S T O P

IF YOU FINISH BEFORE TIME IS CALLED, YOU MAY CHECK YOUR WORK ON THIS TEST ONLY. DO NOT WORK ON ANY OTHER TEST IN THIS BOOK.

Answers to the SAT II: Spanish Subject Mini Test

Question Number	Correct Answer	Question Number	Correct Answer
1	A	25	C
2	A	26	A
3	D	27	A
4	C	28	B
5	A	29	A
6	B	30	D
7	B	31	B
8	C	32	C
9	A	33	C
10	D	34	B
11	A	35	D
12	A	36	A
13	B	37	B
14	A	38	D
15	D	39	B
16	D	40	C
17	D	41	B
18	C	42	C
19	D	43	B
20	C	44	A
21	C	45	A
22	C	46	A
23	A	47	B
24	B		

Use a No. 2 pencil only. Be sure each mark is dark and completely fills the intended oval. Completely erase any errors or stray marks.

1.
Your Name: ______ Last ______ First ______ M.I.
(Print)
Signature: ______ Date: ___/___/___
Home Address: ______ Number and Street
(Print)
______ City ______ State ______ Zip Code
Center: ______ City ______ State ______ Center Number
(Print)

Test Code

V	1	2	3	4	5	6	7	8	9	
W	1	2	3	4	5	6	7	8	9	
X	1	2	3	4	5	Y	A	B	C	D	E
Q	1	2	3	4	5	6	7	8	9	

Subject (print)

FOR ETS USE ONLY	R/C	W/S1	FS/S2	CS/S3	ES

2. Your Name

First 4 letters of last name				First Initial	M.I.
A	A	A	A	A	A
B	B	B	B	B	B
C	C	C	C	C	C
D	D	D	D	D	D
E	E	E	E	E	E
F	F	F	F	F	F
G	G	G	G	G	G
H	H	H	H	H	H
I	I	I	I	I	I
J	J	J	J	J	J
K	K	K	K	K	K
L	L	L	L	L	L
M	M	M	M	M	M
N	N	N	N	N	N
O	O	O	O	O	O
P	P	P	P	P	P
Q	Q	Q	Q	Q	Q
R	R	R	R	R	R
S	S	S	S	S	S
T	T	T	T	T	T
U	U	U	U	U	U
V	V	V	V	V	V
W	W	W	W	W	W
X	X	X	X	X	X
Y	Y	Y	Y	Y	Y
Z	Z	Z	Z	Z	Z

IMPORTANT: Please fill in items 6 and 7 exactly as shown on the back cover of your test book.

4. Date Of Birth

Month	Day		Year	
Jan.				
Feb.				
Mar.	0	0	0	0
Apr.	1	1	1	1
May	2	2	2	2
June	3	3	3	3
July		4	4	4
Aug.		5	5	5
Sept.		6	6	6
Oct.		7	7	7
Nov.		8	8	8
Dec.		9		9

6. Form Code

(Copy and grid as on back of test book.)

0	A	0
1	B	1
2	C	2
3	D	3
4	E	4
5	F	5
6	G	6
7	H	7
8	I	8
9	J	9
	K	
	L	
	M	
	N	
	O	
	P	
	Q	
	R	
	S	
	T	
	U	
	V	
	W	
	X	
	Y	
	Z	

5. Registration Number

(Copy from your Admission Ticket.)

0	0	0	0	0	0	0
1	1	1	1	1	1	1
2	2	2	2	2	2	2
3	3	3	3	3	3	3
4	4	4	4	4	4	4
5	5	5	5	5	5	5
6	6	6	6	6	6	6
7	7	7	7	7	7	7
8	8	8	8	8	8	8
9	9	9	9	9	9	9

3. Social Security Number

0	0	0	0	0	0	0	0	0
1	1	1	1	1	1	1	1	1
2	2	2	2	2	2	2	2	2
3	3	3	3	3	3	3	3	3
4	4	4	4	4	4	4	4	4
5	5	5	5	5	5	5	5	5
6	6	6	6	6	6	6	6	6
7	7	7	7	7	7	7	7	7
8	8	8	8	8	8	8	8	8
9	9	9	9	9	9	9	9	9

7. Test Form

(Copy from back cover of your test book.)

8. Test Book Serial Number

(Copy from front cover of your test book.)

9. Sex

Female ◯ Male ◯

FOR ETS USE ONLY

DO NOT WRITE IN THIS AREA.

0

You may find more answer spaces than you need. If so, please leave them blank.

1	A	B	C	D	E	51	A	B	C	D	E
2	A	B	C	D	E	52	A	B	C	D	E
3	A	B	C	D	E	53	A	B	C	D	E
4	A	B	C	D	E	54	A	B	C	D	E
5	A	B	C	D	E	55	A	B	C	D	E
6	A	B	C	D	E	56	A	B	C	D	E
7	A	B	C	D	E	57	A	B	C	D	E
8	A	B	C	D	E	58	A	B	C	D	E
9	A	B	C	D	E	59	A	B	C	D	E
10	A	B	C	D	E	60	A	B	C	D	E
11	A	B	C	D	E	61	A	B	C	D	E
12	A	B	C	D	E	62	A	B	C	D	E
13	A	B	C	D	E	63	A	B	C	D	E
14	A	B	C	D	E	64	A	B	C	D	E
15	A	B	C	D	E	65	A	B	C	D	E
16	A	B	C	D	E	66	A	B	C	D	E
17	A	B	C	D	E	67	A	B	C	D	E
18	A	B	C	D	E	68	A	B	C	D	E
19	A	B	C	D	E	69	A	B	C	D	E
20	A	B	C	D	E	70	A	B	C	D	E
21	A	B	C	D	E	71	A	B	C	D	E
22	A	B	C	D	E	72	A	B	C	D	E
23	A	B	C	D	E	73	A	B	C	D	E
24	A	B	C	D	E	74	A	B	C	D	E
25	A	B	C	D	E	75	A	B	C	D	E
26	A	B	C	D	E	76	A	B	C	D	E
27	A	B	C	D	E	77	A	B	C	D	E
28	A	B	C	D	E	78	A	B	C	D	E
29	A	B	C	D	E	79	A	B	C	D	E
30	A	B	C	D	E	80	A	B	C	D	E
31	A	B	C	D	E	81	A	B	C	D	E
32	A	B	C	D	E	82	A	B	C	D	E
33	A	B	C	D	E	83	A	B	C	D	E
34	A	B	C	D	E	84	A	B	C	D	E
35	A	B	C	D	E	85	A	B	C	D	E
36	A	B	C	D	E	86	A	B	C	D	E
37	A	B	C	D	E	87	A	B	C	D	E
38	A	B	C	D	E	88	A	B	C	D	E
39	A	B	C	D	E	89	A	B	C	D	E
40	A	B	C	D	E	90	A	B	C	D	E
41	A	B	C	D	E	91	A	B	C	D	E
42	A	B	C	D	E	92	A	B	C	D	E
43	A	B	C	D	E	93	A	B	C	D	E
44	A	B	C	D	E	94	A	B	C	D	E
45	A	B	C	D	E	95	A	B	C	D	E
46	A	B	C	D	E	96	A	B	C	D	E
47	A	B	C	D	E	97	A	B	C	D	E
48	A	B	C	D	E	98	A	B	C	D	E
49	A	B	C	D	E	99	A	B	C	D	E
50	A	B	C	D	E	100	A	B	C	D	E

Q2618-06/1 CHW93067 11012 • 09225 • TF33P172.5e 1 I.N.207098

COLLEGE BOARD — SAT II **Page 2**

Use a No. 2 pencil only. Be sure each mark is dark and completely fills the intended oval. Completely erase any errors or stray marks.

You may find more answer spaces than you need. If so, please leave them blank.

Test Code

V	(1) (2) (3) (4) (5) (6) (7) (8) (9)
W	(1) (2) (3) (4) (5) (6) (7) (8) (9)
X	(1) (2) (3) (4) (5) Y (A) (B) (C) (D) (E)
Q	(1) (2) (3) (4) (5) (6) (7) (8) (9)

Subject (print)

FOR ETS USE ONLY	R/C	W/S1	FS/S2	CS/S3	ES

1 (A) (B) (C) (D) (E)	21 (A) (B) (C) (D) (E)	41 (A) (B) (C) (D) (E)	61 (A) (B) (C) (D) (E)	81 (A) (B) (C) (D) (E)
2 (A) (B) (C) (D) (E)	22 (A) (B) (C) (D) (E)	42 (A) (B) (C) (D) (E)	62 (A) (B) (C) (D) (E)	82 (A) (B) (C) (D) (E)
3 (A) (B) (C) (D) (E)	23 (A) (B) (C) (D) (E)	43 (A) (B) (C) (D) (E)	63 (A) (B) (C) (D) (E)	83 (A) (B) (C) (D) (E)
4 (A) (B) (C) (D) (E)	24 (A) (B) (C) (D) (E)	44 (A) (B) (C) (D) (E)	64 (A) (B) (C) (D) (E)	84 (A) (B) (C) (D) (E)
5 (A) (B) (C) (D) (E)	25 (A) (B) (C) (D) (E)	45 (A) (B) (C) (D) (E)	65 (A) (B) (C) (D) (E)	85 (A) (B) (C) (D) (E)
6 (A) (B) (C) (D) (E)	26 (A) (B) (C) (D) (E)	46 (A) (B) (C) (D) (E)	66 (A) (B) (C) (D) (E)	86 (A) (B) (C) (D) (E)
7 (A) (B) (C) (D) (E)	27 (A) (B) (C) (D) (E)	47 (A) (B) (C) (D) (E)	67 (A) (B) (C) (D) (E)	87 (A) (B) (C) (D) (E)
8 (A) (B) (C) (D) (E)	28 (A) (B) (C) (D) (E)	48 (A) (B) (C) (D) (E)	68 (A) (B) (C) (D) (E)	88 (A) (B) (C) (D) (E)
9 (A) (B) (C) (D) (E)	29 (A) (B) (C) (D) (E)	49 (A) (B) (C) (D) (E)	69 (A) (B) (C) (D) (E)	89 (A) (B) (C) (D) (E)
10 (A) (B) (C) (D) (E)	30 (A) (B) (C) (D) (E)	50 (A) (B) (C) (D) (E)	70 (A) (B) (C) (D) (E)	90 (A) (B) (C) (D) (E)
11 (A) (B) (C) (D) (E)	31 (A) (B) (C) (D) (E)	51 (A) (B) (C) (D) (E)	71 (A) (B) (C) (D) (E)	91 (A) (B) (C) (D) (E)
12 (A) (B) (C) (D) (E)	32 (A) (B) (C) (D) (E)	52 (A) (B) (C) (D) (E)	72 (A) (B) (C) (D) (E)	92 (A) (B) (C) (D) (E)
13 (A) (B) (C) (D) (E)	33 (A) (B) (C) (D) (E)	53 (A) (B) (C) (D) (E)	73 (A) (B) (C) (D) (E)	93 (A) (B) (C) (D) (E)
14 (A) (B) (C) (D) (E)	34 (A) (B) (C) (D) (E)	54 (A) (B) (C) (D) (E)	74 (A) (B) (C) (D) (E)	94 (A) (B) (C) (D) (E)
15 (A) (B) (C) (D) (E)	35 (A) (B) (C) (D) (E)	55 (A) (B) (C) (D) (E)	75 (A) (B) (C) (D) (E)	95 (A) (B) (C) (D) (E)
16 (A) (B) (C) (D) (E)	36 (A) (B) (C) (D) (E)	56 (A) (B) (C) (D) (E)	76 (A) (B) (C) (D) (E)	96 (A) (B) (C) (D) (E)
17 (A) (B) (C) (D) (E)	37 (A) (B) (C) (D) (E)	57 (A) (B) (C) (D) (E)	77 (A) (B) (C) (D) (E)	97 (A) (B) (C) (D) (E)
18 (A) (B) (C) (D) (E)	38 (A) (B) (C) (D) (E)	58 (A) (B) (C) (D) (E)	78 (A) (B) (C) (D) (E)	98 (A) (B) (C) (D) (E)
19 (A) (B) (C) (D) (E)	39 (A) (B) (C) (D) (E)	59 (A) (B) (C) (D) (E)	79 (A) (B) (C) (D) (E)	99 (A) (B) (C) (D) (E)
20 (A) (B) (C) (D) (E)	40 (A) (B) (C) (D) (E)	60 (A) (B) (C) (D) (E)	80 (A) (B) (C) (D) (E)	100 (A) (B) (C) (D) (E)

You may find more answer spaces than you need. If so, please leave them blank.

Test Code

V	(1) (2) (3) (4) (5) (6) (7) (8) (9)
W	(1) (2) (3) (4) (5) (6) (7) (8) (9)
X	(1) (2) (3) (4) (5) Y (A) (B) (C) (D) (E)
Q	(1) (2) (3) (4) (5) (6) (7) (8) (9)

Subject (print)

FOR ETS USE ONLY	R/C	W/S1	FS/S2	CS/S3	ES

1 (A) (B) (C) (D) (E)	21 (A) (B) (C) (D) (E)	41 (A) (B) (C) (D) (E)	61 (A) (B) (C) (D) (E)	81 (A) (B) (C) (D) (E)
2 (A) (B) (C) (D) (E)	22 (A) (B) (C) (D) (E)	42 (A) (B) (C) (D) (E)	62 (A) (B) (C) (D) (E)	82 (A) (B) (C) (D) (E)
3 (A) (B) (C) (D) (E)	23 (A) (B) (C) (D) (E)	43 (A) (B) (C) (D) (E)	63 (A) (B) (C) (D) (E)	83 (A) (B) (C) (D) (E)
4 (A) (B) (C) (D) (E)	24 (A) (B) (C) (D) (E)	44 (A) (B) (C) (D) (E)	64 (A) (B) (C) (D) (E)	84 (A) (B) (C) (D) (E)
5 (A) (B) (C) (D) (E)	25 (A) (B) (C) (D) (E)	45 (A) (B) (C) (D) (E)	65 (A) (B) (C) (D) (E)	85 (A) (B) (C) (D) (E)
6 (A) (B) (C) (D) (E)	26 (A) (B) (C) (D) (E)	46 (A) (B) (C) (D) (E)	66 (A) (B) (C) (D) (E)	86 (A) (B) (C) (D) (E)
7 (A) (B) (C) (D) (E)	27 (A) (B) (C) (D) (E)	47 (A) (B) (C) (D) (E)	67 (A) (B) (C) (D) (E)	87 (A) (B) (C) (D) (E)
8 (A) (B) (C) (D) (E)	28 (A) (B) (C) (D) (E)	48 (A) (B) (C) (D) (E)	68 (A) (B) (C) (D) (E)	88 (A) (B) (C) (D) (E)
9 (A) (B) (C) (D) (E)	29 (A) (B) (C) (D) (E)	49 (A) (B) (C) (D) (E)	69 (A) (B) (C) (D) (E)	89 (A) (B) (C) (D) (E)
10 (A) (B) (C) (D) (E)	30 (A) (B) (C) (D) (E)	50 (A) (B) (C) (D) (E)	70 (A) (B) (C) (D) (E)	90 (A) (B) (C) (D) (E)
11 (A) (B) (C) (D) (E)	31 (A) (B) (C) (D) (E)	51 (A) (B) (C) (D) (E)	71 (A) (B) (C) (D) (E)	91 (A) (B) (C) (D) (E)
12 (A) (B) (C) (D) (E)	32 (A) (B) (C) (D) (E)	52 (A) (B) (C) (D) (E)	72 (A) (B) (C) (D) (E)	92 (A) (B) (C) (D) (E)
13 (A) (B) (C) (D) (E)	33 (A) (B) (C) (D) (E)	53 (A) (B) (C) (D) (E)	73 (A) (B) (C) (D) (E)	93 (A) (B) (C) (D) (E)
14 (A) (B) (C) (D) (E)	34 (A) (B) (C) (D) (E)	54 (A) (B) (C) (D) (E)	74 (A) (B) (C) (D) (E)	94 (A) (B) (C) (D) (E)
15 (A) (B) (C) (D) (E)	35 (A) (B) (C) (D) (E)	55 (A) (B) (C) (D) (E)	75 (A) (B) (C) (D) (E)	95 (A) (B) (C) (D) (E)
16 (A) (B) (C) (D) (E)	36 (A) (B) (C) (D) (E)	56 (A) (B) (C) (D) (E)	76 (A) (B) (C) (D) (E)	96 (A) (B) (C) (D) (E)
17 (A) (B) (C) (D) (E)	37 (A) (B) (C) (D) (E)	57 (A) (B) (C) (D) (E)	77 (A) (B) (C) (D) (E)	97 (A) (B) (C) (D) (E)
18 (A) (B) (C) (D) (E)	38 (A) (B) (C) (D) (E)	58 (A) (B) (C) (D) (E)	78 (A) (B) (C) (D) (E)	98 (A) (B) (C) (D) (E)
19 (A) (B) (C) (D) (E)	39 (A) (B) (C) (D) (E)	59 (A) (B) (C) (D) (E)	79 (A) (B) (C) (D) (E)	99 (A) (B) (C) (D) (E)
20 (A) (B) (C) (D) (E)	40 (A) (B) (C) (D) (E)	60 (A) (B) (C) (D) (E)	80 (A) (B) (C) (D) (E)	100 (A) (B) (C) (D) (E)

Chemistry *Fill in oval CE only if II is correct explanation of I.

	I	II	CE*		I	II	CE*
101	(T) (F)	(T) (F)	( )	109	(T) (F)	(T) (F)	( )
102	(T) (F)	(T) (F)	( )	110	(T) (F)	(T) (F)	( )
103	(T) (F)	(T) (F)	( )	111	(T) (F)	(T) (F)	( )
104	(T) (F)	(T) (F)	( )	112	(T) (F)	(T) (F)	( )
105	(T) (F)	(T) (F)	( )	113	(T) (F)	(T) (F)	( )
106	(T) (F)	(T) (F)	( )	114	(T) (F)	(T) (F)	( )
107	(T) (F)	(T) (F)	( )	115	(T) (F)	(T) (F)	( )
108	(T) (F)	(T) (F)	( )	116	(T) (F)	(T) (F)	( )

Certification Statement

Please write the following statement in longhand on the lines below, and sign your full name.

"I am the person whose name and address appear on this answer sheet."

____

____

____

Signature:____________________ Date: __________

Continuation of Part A (ESSAY) from reverse side. Write below only if you need more space.

Last Name
First 2 letters

DO NOT WRITE IN THIS AREA. FOR ETS USE ONLY.

R	Reader Number	0 1 2 3 4 5 6 7 8 9 / 0 1 2 3 4 5 6 7 8 9 / 0 1 2 3 4 5 6 7 8 9	A B C D E F G H I J K L M / N O P Q R S T U V W X Y Z / Reading Sequence: 1 2 3
S	Reader Number	0 1 2 3 4 5 6 7 8 9 / 0 1 2 3 4 5 6 7 8 9 / 0 1 2 3 4 5 6 7 8 9	A B C D E F G H I J K L M / N O P Q R S T U V W X Y Z / Reading Sequence: 1 2 3
T	Reader Number	0 1 2 3 4 5 6 7 8 9 / 0 1 2 3 4 5 6 7 8 9 / 0 1 2 3 4 5 6 7 8 9	A B C D E F G H I J K L M / N O P Q R S T U V W X Y Z / Reading Sequence: 1 2 3

Date Of Birth		
Day		0 1 2 3 4 5 6 7 8 9
		0 1 2 3
Month		0 1 2 3 4 5 6 7 8 9
		0 1

DO NOT WRITE IN THIS AREA.

0

Last Name First 2 letters		
		A B C D E F G H I J K L M N O P Q R S T U V W X Y Z
		A B C D E F G H I J K L M N O P Q R S T U V W X Y Z

Registration Number						

Test Center Number					
		—			

Test Date		
Month	Day	Year

Form Code		

Topic Code

Part A (ESSAY) ***Begin*** **your composition on this side. If you need more space, you may continue on the reverse side.**

Continue on the reverse side if necessary.

Use a No. 2 pencil only. Be sure each mark is dark and completely fills the intended oval. Completely erase any errors or stray marks.

1.
Your Name: (Print) Last First M.I.
Signature: Date: / /
Home Address: (Print) Number and Street
City State Zip Code
Center: (Print) City State Center Number

Test Code
V 1 2 3 4 5 6 7 8 9
W 1 2 3 4 5 6 7 8 9
X 1 2 3 4 5 Y A B C D E
Q 1 2 3 4 5 6 7 8 9

Subject (print)

FOR ETS USE ONLY	R/C	W/S1	FS/S2	CS/S3	ES

IMPORTANT: Please fill in items 6 and 7 exactly as shown on the back cover of your test book.

2. Your Name

First 4 letters of last name | First Initial | M.I.

4. Date Of Birth

Month | Day | Year

Jan. Feb. Mar. Apr. May June July Aug. Sept. Oct. Nov. Dec.

6. Form Code

(Copy and grid as on back of test book.)

5. Registration Number

(Copy from your Admission Ticket.)

3. Social Security Number

7. Test Form

(Copy from back cover of your test book.)

8. Test Book Serial Number

(Copy from front cover of your test book.)

9. Sex

Female Male

FOR ETS USE ONLY

You may find more answer spaces than you need. If so, please leave them blank.

1–100 A B C D E

DO NOT WRITE IN THIS AREA.

0

Q2618-06/1 CHW93067 11012 • 09225 • TF33P172.5e 1 I.N.207098

Use a No. 2 pencil only. Be sure each mark is dark and completely fills the intended oval. Completely erase any errors or stray marks.

You may find more answer spaces than you need. If so, please leave them blank.

Test Code										
V		1	2	3	4	5	6	7	8	9
W		1	2	3	4	5	6	7	8	9
X	1	2	3	4	5	Y	A	B	C	D	E
Q		1	2	3	4	5	6	7	8	9

Subject (print)

FOR ETS USE ONLY	R/C	W/S1	FS/S2	CS/S3	ES

1	A	B	C	D	E	21	A	B	C	D	E	41	A	B	C	D	E	61	A	B	C	D	E	81	A	B	C	D	E
2	A	B	C	D	E	22	A	B	C	D	E	42	A	B	C	D	E	62	A	B	C	D	E	82	A	B	C	D	E
3	A	B	C	D	E	23	A	B	C	D	E	43	A	B	C	D	E	63	A	B	C	D	E	83	A	B	C	D	E
4	A	B	C	D	E	24	A	B	C	D	E	44	A	B	C	D	E	64	A	B	C	D	E	84	A	B	C	D	E
5	A	B	C	D	E	25	A	B	C	D	E	45	A	B	C	D	E	65	A	B	C	D	E	85	A	B	C	D	E
6	A	B	C	D	E	26	A	B	C	D	E	46	A	B	C	D	E	66	A	B	C	D	E	86	A	B	C	D	E
7	A	B	C	D	E	27	A	B	C	D	E	47	A	B	C	D	E	67	A	B	C	D	E	87	A	B	C	D	E
8	A	B	C	D	E	28	A	B	C	D	E	48	A	B	C	D	E	68	A	B	C	D	E	88	A	B	C	D	E
9	A	B	C	D	E	29	A	B	C	D	E	49	A	B	C	D	E	69	A	B	C	D	E	89	A	B	C	D	E
10	A	B	C	D	E	30	A	B	C	D	E	50	A	B	C	D	E	70	A	B	C	D	E	90	A	B	C	D	E
11	A	B	C	D	E	31	A	B	C	D	E	51	A	B	C	D	E	71	A	B	C	D	E	91	A	B	C	D	E
12	A	B	C	D	E	32	A	B	C	D	E	52	A	B	C	D	E	72	A	B	C	D	E	92	A	B	C	D	E
13	A	B	C	D	E	33	A	B	C	D	E	53	A	B	C	D	E	73	A	B	C	D	E	93	A	B	C	D	E
14	A	B	C	D	E	34	A	B	C	D	E	54	A	B	C	D	E	74	A	B	C	D	E	94	A	B	C	D	E
15	A	B	C	D	E	35	A	B	C	D	E	55	A	B	C	D	E	75	A	B	C	D	E	95	A	B	C	D	E
16	A	B	C	D	E	36	A	B	C	D	E	56	A	B	C	D	E	76	A	B	C	D	E	96	A	B	C	D	E
17	A	B	C	D	E	37	A	B	C	D	E	57	A	B	C	D	E	77	A	B	C	D	E	97	A	B	C	D	E
18	A	B	C	D	E	38	A	B	C	D	E	58	A	B	C	D	E	78	A	B	C	D	E	98	A	B	C	D	E
19	A	B	C	D	E	39	A	B	C	D	E	59	A	B	C	D	E	79	A	B	C	D	E	99	A	B	C	D	E
20	A	B	C	D	E	40	A	B	C	D	E	60	A	B	C	D	E	80	A	B	C	D	E	100	A	B	C	D	E

You may find more answer spaces than you need. If so, please leave them blank.

Test Code										
V		1	2	3	4	5	6	7	8	9
W		1	2	3	4	5	6	7	8	9
X	1	2	3	4	5	Y	A	B	C	D	E
Q		1	2	3	4	5	6	7	8	9

Subject (print)

FOR ETS USE ONLY	R/C	W/S1	FS/S2	CS/S3	ES

1	A	B	C	D	E	21	A	B	C	D	E	41	A	B	C	D	E	61	A	B	C	D	E	81	A	B	C	D	E
2	A	B	C	D	E	22	A	B	C	D	E	42	A	B	C	D	E	62	A	B	C	D	E	82	A	B	C	D	E
3	A	B	C	D	E	23	A	B	C	D	E	43	A	B	C	D	E	63	A	B	C	D	E	83	A	B	C	D	E
4	A	B	C	D	E	24	A	B	C	D	E	44	A	B	C	D	E	64	A	B	C	D	E	84	A	B	C	D	E
5	A	B	C	D	E	25	A	B	C	D	E	45	A	B	C	D	E	65	A	B	C	D	E	85	A	B	C	D	E
6	A	B	C	D	E	26	A	B	C	D	E	46	A	B	C	D	E	66	A	B	C	D	E	86	A	B	C	D	E
7	A	B	C	D	E	27	A	B	C	D	E	47	A	B	C	D	E	67	A	B	C	D	E	87	A	B	C	D	E
8	A	B	C	D	E	28	A	B	C	D	E	48	A	B	C	D	E	68	A	B	C	D	E	88	A	B	C	D	E
9	A	B	C	D	E	29	A	B	C	D	E	49	A	B	C	D	E	69	A	B	C	D	E	89	A	B	C	D	E
10	A	B	C	D	E	30	A	B	C	D	E	50	A	B	C	D	E	70	A	B	C	D	E	90	A	B	C	D	E
11	A	B	C	D	E	31	A	B	C	D	E	51	A	B	C	D	E	71	A	B	C	D	E	91	A	B	C	D	E
12	A	B	C	D	E	32	A	B	C	D	E	52	A	B	C	D	E	72	A	B	C	D	E	92	A	B	C	D	E
13	A	B	C	D	E	33	A	B	C	D	E	53	A	B	C	D	E	73	A	B	C	D	E	93	A	B	C	D	E
14	A	B	C	D	E	34	A	B	C	D	E	54	A	B	C	D	E	74	A	B	C	D	E	94	A	B	C	D	E
15	A	B	C	D	E	35	A	B	C	D	E	55	A	B	C	D	E	75	A	B	C	D	E	95	A	B	C	D	E
16	A	B	C	D	E	36	A	B	C	D	E	56	A	B	C	D	E	76	A	B	C	D	E	96	A	B	C	D	E
17	A	B	C	D	E	37	A	B	C	D	E	57	A	B	C	D	E	77	A	B	C	D	E	97	A	B	C	D	E
18	A	B	C	D	E	38	A	B	C	D	E	58	A	B	C	D	E	78	A	B	C	D	E	98	A	B	C	D	E
19	A	B	C	D	E	39	A	B	C	D	E	59	A	B	C	D	E	79	A	B	C	D	E	99	A	B	C	D	E
20	A	B	C	D	E	40	A	B	C	D	E	60	A	B	C	D	E	80	A	B	C	D	E	100	A	B	C	D	E

Chemistry *Fill in oval CE only if II is correct explanation of I.

	I		II		CE*		I		II		CE*
101	T	F	T	F	◯	109	T	F	T	F	◯
102	T	F	T	F	◯	110	T	F	T	F	◯
103	T	F	T	F	◯	111	T	F	T	F	◯
104	T	F	T	F	◯	112	T	F	T	F	◯
105	T	F	T	F	◯	113	T	F	T	F	◯
106	T	F	T	F	◯	114	T	F	T	F	◯
107	T	F	T	F	◯	115	T	F	T	F	◯
108	T	F	T	F	◯	116	T	F	T	F	◯

Certification Statement Please write the following statement in longhand on the lines below, and sign your full name.

"I am the person whose name and address appear on this answer sheet."

Signature:____________________ Date: __________

Last Name
First 2 letters

DO NOT WRITE IN THIS AREA. FOR ETS USE ONLY.

R Reader Number
0 1 2 3 4 5 6 7 8 9
0 1 2 3 4 5 6 7 8 9
0 1 2 3 4 5 6 7 8 9
A B C D E F G H I J K L M
N O P Q R S T U V W X Y Z
Reading Sequence: 1 2 3

S Reader Number
0 1 2 3 4 5 6 7 8 9
0 1 2 3 4 5 6 7 8 9
0 1 2 3 4 5 6 7 8 9
A B C D E F G H I J K L M
N O P Q R S T U V W X Y Z
Reading Sequence: 1 2 3

T Reader Number
0 1 2 3 4 5 6 7 8 9
0 1 2 3 4 5 6 7 8 9
0 1 2 3 4 5 6 7 8 9
A B C D E F G H I J K L M
N O P Q R S T U V W X Y Z
Reading Sequence: 1 2 3

Date Of Birth	Day		0 1 2 3 4 5 6 7 8 9
			0 1 2 3
	Month		0 1 2 3 4 5 6 7 8 9
			0 1

DO NOT WRITE IN THIS AREA.

0

Last Name First 2 letters		A B C D E F G H I J K L M N O P Q R S T U V W X Y Z
		A B C D E F G H I J K L M N O P Q R S T U V W X Y Z

Registration Number	Test Center Number	Test Date (Month / Day / Year)	Form Code	Topic Code
	—			

Part A (ESSAY) ***Begin*** **your composition on this side. If you need more space, you may continue on the reverse side.**

I have experienced various things that have mad me feel worthwhile, but I have never felt better then when I

Continue on the reverse side if necessary.

Use a No. 2 pencil only. Be sure each mark is dark and completely fills the intended oval. Completely erase any errors or stray marks.

1.
Your Name: (Print) Last First M.I.
Signature: Date:
Home Address: (Print) Number and Street
City State Zip Code
Center: (Print) City State Center Number

Test Code
V 1 2 3 4 5 6 7 8 9
W 1 2 3 4 5 6 7 8 9
X 1 2 3 4 5 Y A B C D E
Q 1 2 3 4 5 6 7 8 9

Subject (print)

FOR ETS USE ONLY	R/C	W/S1	FS/S2	CS/S3	ES

2. Your Name

First 4 letters of last name | First Initial | M.I.

A B C D E F G H I J K L M N O P Q R S T U V W X Y Z

IMPORTANT: Please fill in items 6 and 7 exactly as shown on the back cover of your test book.

4. Date Of Birth

Month: Jan. Feb. Mar. Apr. May June July Aug. Sept. Oct. Nov. Dec.
Day: 0 1 2 3 / 0 1 2 3 4 5 6 7 8 9
Year: 0–9 / 0–9

6. Form Code

(Copy and grid as on back of test book.)

0–9 | A–Z | 0–9

5. Registration Number

(Copy from your Admission Ticket.)

0 1 2 3 4 5 6 7 8 9

3. Social Security Number

0 1 2 3 4 5 6 7 8 9

7. Test Form

(Copy from back cover of your test book.)

8. Test Book Serial Number

(Copy from front cover of your test book.)

9. Sex

Female Male

FOR ETS USE ONLY

You may find more answer spaces than you need. If so, please leave them blank.

1–100 A B C D E

DO NOT WRITE IN THIS AREA.

0

Q2618-06/1 CHW93067 11012 • 09225 • TF33P172.5e 1 I.N.207098

Use a No. 2 pencil only. Be sure each mark is dark and completely fills the intended oval. Completely erase any errors or stray marks.

You may find more answer spaces than you need. If so, please leave them blank.

Test Code

V		1	2	3	4	5	6	7	8	9	
W		1	2	3	4	5	6	7	8	9	
X	1	2	3	4	5	Y	A	B	C	D	E
Q		1	2	3	4	5	6	7	8	9	

Subject (print)

FOR ETS USE ONLY	R/C	W/S1	FS/S2	CS/S3	ES

1	A	B	C	D	E	21	A	B	C	D	E	41	A	B	C	D	E	61	A	B	C	D	E	81	A	B	C	D	E
2	A	B	C	D	E	22	A	B	C	D	E	42	A	B	C	D	E	62	A	B	C	D	E	82	A	B	C	D	E
3	A	B	C	D	E	23	A	B	C	D	E	43	A	B	C	D	E	63	A	B	C	D	E	83	A	B	C	D	E
4	A	B	C	D	E	24	A	B	C	D	E	44	A	B	C	D	E	64	A	B	C	D	E	84	A	B	C	D	E
5	A	B	C	D	E	25	A	B	C	D	E	45	A	B	C	D	E	65	A	B	C	D	E	85	A	B	C	D	E
6	A	B	C	D	E	26	A	B	C	D	E	46	A	B	C	D	E	66	A	B	C	D	E	86	A	B	C	D	E
7	A	B	C	D	E	27	A	B	C	D	E	47	A	B	C	D	E	67	A	B	C	D	E	87	A	B	C	D	E
8	A	B	C	D	E	28	A	B	C	D	E	48	A	B	C	D	E	68	A	B	C	D	E	88	A	B	C	D	E
9	A	B	C	D	E	29	A	B	C	D	E	49	A	B	C	D	E	69	A	B	C	D	E	89	A	B	C	D	E
10	A	B	C	D	E	30	A	B	C	D	E	50	A	B	C	D	E	70	A	B	C	D	E	90	A	B	C	D	E
11	A	B	C	D	E	31	A	B	C	D	E	51	A	B	C	D	E	71	A	B	C	D	E	91	A	B	C	D	E
12	A	B	C	D	E	32	A	B	C	D	E	52	A	B	C	D	E	72	A	B	C	D	E	92	A	B	C	D	E
13	A	B	C	D	E	33	A	B	C	D	E	53	A	B	C	D	E	73	A	B	C	D	E	93	A	B	C	D	E
14	A	B	C	D	E	34	A	B	C	D	E	54	A	B	C	D	E	74	A	B	C	D	E	94	A	B	C	D	E
15	A	B	C	D	E	35	A	B	C	D	E	55	A	B	C	D	E	75	A	B	C	D	E	95	A	B	C	D	E
16	A	B	C	D	E	36	A	B	C	D	E	56	A	B	C	D	E	76	A	B	C	D	E	96	A	B	C	D	E
17	A	B	C	D	E	37	A	B	C	D	E	57	A	B	C	D	E	77	A	B	C	D	E	97	A	B	C	D	E
18	A	B	C	D	E	38	A	B	C	D	E	58	A	B	C	D	E	78	A	B	C	D	E	98	A	B	C	D	E
19	A	B	C	D	E	39	A	B	C	D	E	59	A	B	C	D	E	79	A	B	C	D	E	99	A	B	C	D	E
20	A	B	C	D	E	40	A	B	C	D	E	60	A	B	C	D	E	80	A	B	C	D	E	100	A	B	C	D	E

You may find more answer spaces than you need. If so, please leave them blank.

Test Code

V		1	2	3	4	5	6	7	8	9	
W		1	2	3	4	5	6	7	8	9	
X	1	2	3	4	5	Y	A	B	C	D	E
Q		1	2	3	4	5	6	7	8	9	

Subject (print)

FOR ETS USE ONLY	R/C	W/S1	FS/S2	CS/S3	ES

1	A	B	C	D	E	21	A	B	C	D	E	41	A	B	C	D	E	61	A	B	C	D	E	81	A	B	C	D	E
2	A	B	C	D	E	22	A	B	C	D	E	42	A	B	C	D	E	62	A	B	C	D	E	82	A	B	C	D	E
3	A	B	C	D	E	23	A	B	C	D	E	43	A	B	C	D	E	63	A	B	C	D	E	83	A	B	C	D	E
4	A	B	C	D	E	24	A	B	C	D	E	44	A	B	C	D	E	64	A	B	C	D	E	84	A	B	C	D	E
5	A	B	C	D	E	25	A	B	C	D	E	45	A	B	C	D	E	65	A	B	C	D	E	85	A	B	C	D	E
6	A	B	C	D	E	26	A	B	C	D	E	46	A	B	C	D	E	66	A	B	C	D	E	86	A	B	C	D	E
7	A	B	C	D	E	27	A	B	C	D	E	47	A	B	C	D	E	67	A	B	C	D	E	87	A	B	C	D	E
8	A	B	C	D	E	28	A	B	C	D	E	48	A	B	C	D	E	68	A	B	C	D	E	88	A	B	C	D	E
9	A	B	C	D	E	29	A	B	C	D	E	49	A	B	C	D	E	69	A	B	C	D	E	89	A	B	C	D	E
10	A	B	C	D	E	30	A	B	C	D	E	50	A	B	C	D	E	70	A	B	C	D	E	90	A	B	C	D	E
11	A	B	C	D	E	31	A	B	C	D	E	51	A	B	C	D	E	71	A	B	C	D	E	91	A	B	C	D	E
12	A	B	C	D	E	32	A	B	C	D	E	52	A	B	C	D	E	72	A	B	C	D	E	92	A	B	C	D	E
13	A	B	C	D	E	33	A	B	C	D	E	53	A	B	C	D	E	73	A	B	C	D	E	93	A	B	C	D	E
14	A	B	C	D	E	34	A	B	C	D	E	54	A	B	C	D	E	74	A	B	C	D	E	94	A	B	C	D	E
15	A	B	C	D	E	35	A	B	C	D	E	55	A	B	C	D	E	75	A	B	C	D	E	95	A	B	C	D	E
16	A	B	C	D	E	36	A	B	C	D	E	56	A	B	C	D	E	76	A	B	C	D	E	96	A	B	C	D	E
17	A	B	C	D	E	37	A	B	C	D	E	57	A	B	C	D	E	77	A	B	C	D	E	97	A	B	C	D	E
18	A	B	C	D	E	38	A	B	C	D	E	58	A	B	C	D	E	78	A	B	C	D	E	98	A	B	C	D	E
19	A	B	C	D	E	39	A	B	C	D	E	59	A	B	C	D	E	79	A	B	C	D	E	99	A	B	C	D	E
20	A	B	C	D	E	40	A	B	C	D	E	60	A	B	C	D	E	80	A	B	C	D	E	100	A	B	C	D	E

Chemistry *Fill in oval CE only if II is correct explanation of I.

	I		II		CE*		I		II		CE*
101	T	F	T	F	◯	109	T	F	T	F	◯
102	T	F	T	F	◯	110	T	F	T	F	◯
103	T	F	T	F	◯	111	T	F	T	F	◯
104	T	F	T	F	◯	112	T	F	T	F	◯
105	T	F	T	F	◯	113	T	F	T	F	◯
106	T	F	T	F	◯	114	T	F	T	F	◯
107	T	F	T	F	◯	115	T	F	T	F	◯
108	T	F	T	F	◯	116	T	F	T	F	◯

Certification Statement

Please write the following statement in longhand on the lines below, and sign your full name.

"I am the person whose name and address appear on this answer sheet."

____

____

____

Signature:______________________ Date: ____________

Last Name
First 2 letters

DO NOT WRITE IN THIS AREA. FOR ETS USE ONLY.

R	Reader Number	0 1 2 3 4 5 6 7 8 9 0 1 2 3 4 5 6 7 8 9 0 1 2 3 4 5 6 7 8 9	A B C D E F G H I J K L M N O P Q R S T U V W X Y Z Reading Sequence: 1 2 3
S	Reader Number	0 1 2 3 4 5 6 7 8 9 0 1 2 3 4 5 6 7 8 9 0 1 2 3 4 5 6 7 8 9	A B C D E F G H I J K L M N O P Q R S T U V W X Y Z Reading Sequence: 1 2 3
T	Reader Number	0 1 2 3 4 5 6 7 8 9 0 1 2 3 4 5 6 7 8 9 0 1 2 3 4 5 6 7 8 9	A B C D E F G H I J K L M N O P Q R S T U V W X Y Z Reading Sequence: 1 2 3

Date Of Birth			
Day			0 1 2 3 4 5 6 7 8 9
			0 1 2 3
Month			0 1 2 3 4 5 6 7 8 9
			0 1

DO NOT WRITE IN THIS AREA.

0

Last Name First 2 letters		
		A B C D E F G H I J K L M N O P Q R S T U V W X Y Z
		A B C D E F G H I J K L M N O P Q R S T U V W X Y Z

Registration Number	Test Center Number	Test Date (Month / Day / Year)	Form Code	Topic Code
	—			

Part A (ESSAY) ***Begin*** **your composition on this side. If you need more space, you may continue on the reverse side.**

Continue on the reverse side if necessary.

Use a No. 2 pencil only. Be sure each mark is dark and completely fills the intended oval. Completely erase any errors or stray marks.

1.
Your Name: (Print) Last First M.I.
Signature: Date: / /
Home Address: (Print) Number and Street
City State Zip Code
Center: (Print) City State Center Number

Test Code
V 1 2 3 4 5 6 7 8 9
W 1 2 3 4 5 6 7 8 9
X 1 2 3 4 5 Y A B C D E
Q 1 2 3 4 5 6 7 8 9

Subject (print)

FOR ETS USE ONLY	R/C	W/S1	FS/S2	CS/S3	ES

2. Your Name

First 4 letters of last name | First Initial | M.I.

IMPORTANT: Please fill in items 6 and 7 exactly as shown on the back cover of your test book.

4. Date Of Birth

Month | Day | Year

Jan. Feb. Mar. Apr. May June July Aug. Sept. Oct. Nov. Dec.

6. Form Code

(Copy and grid as on back of test book.)

5. Registration Number

(Copy from your Admission Ticket.)

You may find more answer spaces than you need. If so, please leave them blank.

1–100 A B C D E

3. Social Security Number

7. Test Form

(Copy from back cover of your test book.)

8. Test Book Serial Number

(Copy from front cover of your test book.)

9. Sex

Female Male

FOR ETS USE ONLY

DO NOT WRITE IN THIS AREA.

0

Q2618-06/1 CHW93067 11012 • 09225 • TF33P172.5e 1 I.N.207098

Use a No. 2 pencil only. Be sure each mark is dark and completely fills the intended oval. Completely erase any errors or stray marks.

You may find more answer spaces than you need. If so, please leave them blank.

Test Code											
V		(1)	(2)	(3)	(4)	(5)	(6)	(7)	(8)	(9)	
W		(1)	(2)	(3)	(4)	(5)	(6)	(7)	(8)	(9)	
X	(1)	(2)	(3)	(4)	(5)	Y	(A)	(B)	(C)	(D)	(E)
Q		(1)	(2)	(3)	(4)	(5)	(6)	(7)	(8)	(9)	

Subject (print)

FOR ETS USE ONLY	R/C	W/S1	FS/S2	CS/S3	ES

1 (A) (B) (C) (D) (E)	21 (A) (B) (C) (D) (E)	41 (A) (B) (C) (D) (E)	61 (A) (B) (C) (D) (E)	81 (A) (B) (C) (D) (E)
2 (A) (B) (C) (D) (E)	22 (A) (B) (C) (D) (E)	42 (A) (B) (C) (D) (E)	62 (A) (B) (C) (D) (E)	82 (A) (B) (C) (D) (E)
3 (A) (B) (C) (D) (E)	23 (A) (B) (C) (D) (E)	43 (A) (B) (C) (D) (E)	63 (A) (B) (C) (D) (E)	83 (A) (B) (C) (D) (E)
4 (A) (B) (C) (D) (E)	24 (A) (B) (C) (D) (E)	44 (A) (B) (C) (D) (E)	64 (A) (B) (C) (D) (E)	84 (A) (B) (C) (D) (E)
5 (A) (B) (C) (D) (E)	25 (A) (B) (C) (D) (E)	45 (A) (B) (C) (D) (E)	65 (A) (B) (C) (D) (E)	85 (A) (B) (C) (D) (E)
6 (A) (B) (C) (D) (E)	26 (A) (B) (C) (D) (E)	46 (A) (B) (C) (D) (E)	66 (A) (B) (C) (D) (E)	86 (A) (B) (C) (D) (E)
7 (A) (B) (C) (D) (E)	27 (A) (B) (C) (D) (E)	47 (A) (B) (C) (D) (E)	67 (A) (B) (C) (D) (E)	87 (A) (B) (C) (D) (E)
8 (A) (B) (C) (D) (E)	28 (A) (B) (C) (D) (E)	48 (A) (B) (C) (D) (E)	68 (A) (B) (C) (D) (E)	88 (A) (B) (C) (D) (E)
9 (A) (B) (C) (D) (E)	29 (A) (B) (C) (D) (E)	49 (A) (B) (C) (D) (E)	69 (A) (B) (C) (D) (E)	89 (A) (B) (C) (D) (E)
10 (A) (B) (C) (D) (E)	30 (A) (B) (C) (D) (E)	50 (A) (B) (C) (D) (E)	70 (A) (B) (C) (D) (E)	90 (A) (B) (C) (D) (E)
11 (A) (B) (C) (D) (E)	31 (A) (B) (C) (D) (E)	51 (A) (B) (C) (D) (E)	71 (A) (B) (C) (D) (E)	91 (A) (B) (C) (D) (E)
12 (A) (B) (C) (D) (E)	32 (A) (B) (C) (D) (E)	52 (A) (B) (C) (D) (E)	72 (A) (B) (C) (D) (E)	92 (A) (B) (C) (D) (E)
13 (A) (B) (C) (D) (E)	33 (A) (B) (C) (D) (E)	53 (A) (B) (C) (D) (E)	73 (A) (B) (C) (D) (E)	93 (A) (B) (C) (D) (E)
14 (A) (B) (C) (D) (E)	34 (A) (B) (C) (D) (E)	54 (A) (B) (C) (D) (E)	74 (A) (B) (C) (D) (E)	94 (A) (B) (C) (D) (E)
15 (A) (B) (C) (D) (E)	35 (A) (B) (C) (D) (E)	55 (A) (B) (C) (D) (E)	75 (A) (B) (C) (D) (E)	95 (A) (B) (C) (D) (E)
16 (A) (B) (C) (D) (E)	36 (A) (B) (C) (D) (E)	56 (A) (B) (C) (D) (E)	76 (A) (B) (C) (D) (E)	96 (A) (B) (C) (D) (E)
17 (A) (B) (C) (D) (E)	37 (A) (B) (C) (D) (E)	57 (A) (B) (C) (D) (E)	77 (A) (B) (C) (D) (E)	97 (A) (B) (C) (D) (E)
18 (A) (B) (C) (D) (E)	38 (A) (B) (C) (D) (E)	58 (A) (B) (C) (D) (E)	78 (A) (B) (C) (D) (E)	98 (A) (B) (C) (D) (E)
19 (A) (B) (C) (D) (E)	39 (A) (B) (C) (D) (E)	59 (A) (B) (C) (D) (E)	79 (A) (B) (C) (D) (E)	99 (A) (B) (C) (D) (E)
20 (A) (B) (C) (D) (E)	40 (A) (B) (C) (D) (E)	60 (A) (B) (C) (D) (E)	80 (A) (B) (C) (D) (E)	100 (A) (B) (C) (D) (E)

You may find more answer spaces than you need. If so, please leave them blank.

Test Code											
V		(1)	(2)	(3)	(4)	(5)	(6)	(7)	(8)	(9)	
W		(1)	(2)	(3)	(4)	(5)	(6)	(7)	(8)	(9)	
X	(1)	(2)	(3)	(4)	(5)	Y	(A)	(B)	(C)	(D)	(E)
Q		(1)	(2)	(3)	(4)	(5)	(6)	(7)	(8)	(9)	

Subject (print)

FOR ETS USE ONLY	R/C	W/S1	FS/S2	CS/S3	ES

1 (A) (B) (C) (D) (E)	21 (A) (B) (C) (D) (E)	41 (A) (B) (C) (D) (E)	61 (A) (B) (C) (D) (E)	81 (A) (B) (C) (D) (E)
2 (A) (B) (C) (D) (E)	22 (A) (B) (C) (D) (E)	42 (A) (B) (C) (D) (E)	62 (A) (B) (C) (D) (E)	82 (A) (B) (C) (D) (E)
3 (A) (B) (C) (D) (E)	23 (A) (B) (C) (D) (E)	43 (A) (B) (C) (D) (E)	63 (A) (B) (C) (D) (E)	83 (A) (B) (C) (D) (E)
4 (A) (B) (C) (D) (E)	24 (A) (B) (C) (D) (E)	44 (A) (B) (C) (D) (E)	64 (A) (B) (C) (D) (E)	84 (A) (B) (C) (D) (E)
5 (A) (B) (C) (D) (E)	25 (A) (B) (C) (D) (E)	45 (A) (B) (C) (D) (E)	65 (A) (B) (C) (D) (E)	85 (A) (B) (C) (D) (E)
6 (A) (B) (C) (D) (E)	26 (A) (B) (C) (D) (E)	46 (A) (B) (C) (D) (E)	66 (A) (B) (C) (D) (E)	86 (A) (B) (C) (D) (E)
7 (A) (B) (C) (D) (E)	27 (A) (B) (C) (D) (E)	47 (A) (B) (C) (D) (E)	67 (A) (B) (C) (D) (E)	87 (A) (B) (C) (D) (E)
8 (A) (B) (C) (D) (E)	28 (A) (B) (C) (D) (E)	48 (A) (B) (C) (D) (E)	68 (A) (B) (C) (D) (E)	88 (A) (B) (C) (D) (E)
9 (A) (B) (C) (D) (E)	29 (A) (B) (C) (D) (E)	49 (A) (B) (C) (D) (E)	69 (A) (B) (C) (D) (E)	89 (A) (B) (C) (D) (E)
10 (A) (B) (C) (D) (E)	30 (A) (B) (C) (D) (E)	50 (A) (B) (C) (D) (E)	70 (A) (B) (C) (D) (E)	90 (A) (B) (C) (D) (E)
11 (A) (B) (C) (D) (E)	31 (A) (B) (C) (D) (E)	51 (A) (B) (C) (D) (E)	71 (A) (B) (C) (D) (E)	91 (A) (B) (C) (D) (E)
12 (A) (B) (C) (D) (E)	32 (A) (B) (C) (D) (E)	52 (A) (B) (C) (D) (E)	72 (A) (B) (C) (D) (E)	92 (A) (B) (C) (D) (E)
13 (A) (B) (C) (D) (E)	33 (A) (B) (C) (D) (E)	53 (A) (B) (C) (D) (E)	73 (A) (B) (C) (D) (E)	93 (A) (B) (C) (D) (E)
14 (A) (B) (C) (D) (E)	34 (A) (B) (C) (D) (E)	54 (A) (B) (C) (D) (E)	74 (A) (B) (C) (D) (E)	94 (A) (B) (C) (D) (E)
15 (A) (B) (C) (D) (E)	35 (A) (B) (C) (D) (E)	55 (A) (B) (C) (D) (E)	75 (A) (B) (C) (D) (E)	95 (A) (B) (C) (D) (E)
16 (A) (B) (C) (D) (E)	36 (A) (B) (C) (D) (E)	56 (A) (B) (C) (D) (E)	76 (A) (B) (C) (D) (E)	96 (A) (B) (C) (D) (E)
17 (A) (B) (C) (D) (E)	37 (A) (B) (C) (D) (E)	57 (A) (B) (C) (D) (E)	77 (A) (B) (C) (D) (E)	97 (A) (B) (C) (D) (E)
18 (A) (B) (C) (D) (E)	38 (A) (B) (C) (D) (E)	58 (A) (B) (C) (D) (E)	78 (A) (B) (C) (D) (E)	98 (A) (B) (C) (D) (E)
19 (A) (B) (C) (D) (E)	39 (A) (B) (C) (D) (E)	59 (A) (B) (C) (D) (E)	79 (A) (B) (C) (D) (E)	99 (A) (B) (C) (D) (E)
20 (A) (B) (C) (D) (E)	40 (A) (B) (C) (D) (E)	60 (A) (B) (C) (D) (E)	80 (A) (B) (C) (D) (E)	100 (A) (B) (C) (D) (E)

Chemistry *Fill in oval CE only if II is correct explanation of I.

	I		II		CE*		I		II		CE*
101	(T)	(F)	(T)	(F)	( )	109	(T)	(F)	(T)	(F)	( )
102	(T)	(F)	(T)	(F)	( )	110	(T)	(F)	(T)	(F)	( )
103	(T)	(F)	(T)	(F)	( )	111	(T)	(F)	(T)	(F)	( )
104	(T)	(F)	(T)	(F)	( )	112	(T)	(F)	(T)	(F)	( )
105	(T)	(F)	(T)	(F)	( )	113	(T)	(F)	(T)	(F)	( )
106	(T)	(F)	(T)	(F)	( )	114	(T)	(F)	(T)	(F)	( )
107	(T)	(F)	(T)	(F)	( )	115	(T)	(F)	(T)	(F)	( )
108	(T)	(F)	(T)	(F)	( )	116	(T)	(F)	(T)	(F)	( )

Certification Statement Please write the following statement in longhand on the lines below, and sign your full name.

"I am the person whose name and address appear on this answer sheet."

____

____

____

Signature: ______________________ Date: ____________

Last Name
First 2 letters

DO NOT WRITE IN THIS AREA. FOR ETS USE ONLY.

R	Reader Number	0 1 2 3 4 5 6 7 8 9 0 1 2 3 4 5 6 7 8 9 0 1 2 3 4 5 6 7 8 9	A B C D E F G H I J K L M N O P Q R S T U V W X Y Z	Reading Sequence: 1 2 3
S	Reader Number	0 1 2 3 4 5 6 7 8 9 0 1 2 3 4 5 6 7 8 9 0 1 2 3 4 5 6 7 8 9	A B C D E F G H I J K L M N O P Q R S T U V W X Y Z	Reading Sequence: 1 2 3
T	Reader Number	0 1 2 3 4 5 6 7 8 9 0 1 2 3 4 5 6 7 8 9 0 1 2 3 4 5 6 7 8 9	A B C D E F G H I J K L M N O P Q R S T U V W X Y Z	Reading Sequence: 1 2 3

Date Of Birth											
Day	0	1	2	3	4	5	6	7	8	9
	0	1	2	3						
Month	0	1	2	3	4	5	6	7	8	9
	0	1								

DO NOT WRITE IN THIS AREA.

0

Last Name First 2 letters

A B C D E F G H I J K L M N O P Q R S T U V W X Y Z

A B C D E F G H I J K L M N O P Q R S T U V W X Y Z

Registration Number	Test Center Number	Test Date (Month / Day / Year)	Form Code	Topic Code
	—			

Part A (ESSAY) *Begin* your composition on this side. If you need more space, you may continue on the reverse side.

Continue on the reverse side if necessary.